Contemporary Politics in the Middle East

SECOND EDITION

Beverley Milton-Edwards

polity

First published in 2006 by Polity Press

Reprinted 2007, 2008

Polity Press
65 Bridge Street
Cambridge CB2 1UR, UK

Polity Press
350 Main Street
Malden, MA 02148, USA

ISBN-13: 978-0-7456-3593-4
ISBN-13: 978-0-7456-3594-1 (pb)

A catalogue record for this book is available from the British
Library.

Typeset in 10.5 on 13pt Swift
by Servis Filmsetting Ltd, Manchester
Printed and bound in Great Britain by TJ International Ltd,
Padstow, Cornwall

The publisher has used its best endeavours to ensure that the URLs
for external websites referred to in this book are correct and active
at the time of going to press. However, the publisher has no
responsibility for the websites and can make no guarantee that a
site will remain live or that the content is or will remain
appropriate.

Every effort has been made to trace all copyright holders, but if any
have been inadvertently overlooked, the publisher will be pleased
to include any necessary credits in any subsequent reprint or
edition.

For further information on Polity, visit our website:
www.polity.co.uk

Contents

Preface to Second Edition

The first edition of *Contemporary Politics in the Middle East* was published in 1999 at a time when the region – like the rest of the world – was on the cusp of a new century and great change and development seemed increasingly likely. I have been deeply appreciative of the positive response that the publication of this first edition received from the variety of readers who have engaged with this text because of their own interest and enthusiasm for the Middle East.

There are a number of reasons why a second revised, updated and expanded edition of this book has now been published. First, the forte of *Contemporary Politics in the Middle East* rests with the continuing employment of emerging scholarship, debate and discourse in a variety of fields that alter and deepen understanding of the politics of the region. Discourse about the region is not static but is reflective of the changing environment of power that exists within it. Hence the second edition of *Contemporary Politics in the Middle East* seeks to bring to its readers an indication of current as well as past debates about how and why types of politics, governance and expressions of power are found across this region of the globe. I am grateful in this respect to the many students who have read this book and asked me to offer them more in terms of particular issues, debates or countries. Secondly, *Contemporary Politics in the Middle East* in its first edition provided an overview of the Middle East and contemporary developments up to 1998 and since that time a number of important events have taken place within the region that demand some updating for a book of this type. The war in Iraq and the toppling of the regime of Saddam Hussein, the emergence of al-Qaeda into the consciousness of the West and its impact in the region, the death of Hafiz al-Assad, the President of Syria, and that of Yasser Arafat, the President of the Palestinian National Authority, the assassination of former Lebanese Prime Minister Rafiq Harari, the development of nuclear capacity in Iran, the end of civil conflict in Algeria along with many other changes within the region compel me as an author to bring this work up to date and to reflect these changes in the analysis of the specific and yet fundamental issues that I cover. Finally I have, at the suggestion of the many enthusiastic readers of this book, introduced some new material including a chapter on American foreign policy and the Middle East and additional case studies in some chapters as they relate to globalization, al-Qaeda, the Algerian experience of colonialism and the American-led war in Iraq.

This book aims at providing a general introduction to contemporary politics in the Middle East and in the next nine chapters a number of major issues or themes are identified that have shaped and characterized the variety of political systems and social relations which exist across the region. For the purposes of this book the Middle East specifically refers to eighteen states, from Morocco on the Atlantic seaboard to Iran on the Asian continent. As the Introduction will explain, there are very specific reasons for this decision. In addition, it should be noted that Turkey, which is considered by some as a state of the Middle East region, has not been included for historical as well as contemporary reasons. In the past Turkey has had a long association with the region – through Ottoman rule the Turks governed large provinces of the present-day Middle East. That relationship, however, was irrevocably altered by the defeat of the Ottomans and the collapse of the Ottoman Empire during the First World War. Since 1918 the Ottoman attachment to the Middle East has been all but severed. In the contemporary era Turkey is as much, if not more, a European state as a Middle Eastern one.

This book has been written explicitly with the non-specialist reader in mind. The themes that are examined, therefore, are broad, linked to particular cases or events and interwoven with the other topics under discussion to provide a comprehensive account of the factors which influence and shape the development of politics in the region.

The first chronologically significant theme is the impact of colonialism on the region, particularly during the latter half of the nineteenth and first half of the twentieth century. Chapter 1 outlines the relationship of domination and subordination established by the West (Britain and France in particular) over the Middle East. It looks at the nature of political rule and government and the prevailing economic motive behind this imperial and colonial relationship. It has been argued that the colonial experience has had a lasting impact on the region, and the role that the West played, as part of its colonial ambitions, in carving out the state system of the present-day Middle East has seriously disrupted political life in the region since that time. The colonial experience in the Middle East also raised a number of significant debates about the economic and social impact of such strategies in the region and the extent to which the experience has altered or disrupted pre-existing socio-economic relations and patterns. These debates have, in turn, informed academic analyses of modernization and associated theories of development. These theories and concepts have also led to a growing interest in the processes of state formation initiated by the West during the colonial experience and the legacy of this experiment on Arab attempts at state-building in the twentieth century. One of the first indications of this impact is discussed in chapter 2, which charts the rise and development of Arab nationalism and Arab nationalist ideologies such as Ba'thism and Nasserism which characterized many populist regimes of the region in the 1950s and 1960s. The historical overview of this theme is put in context in relation to current theories of nationalism. The growth and popularization of nationalist ideologies in the Middle East is important in understanding the concomitant secularization of politics in the region and the impact of western-style political traditions such as nationalism and socialism on the patterns of politics with which the region had traditionally been associated. In addition, recent debates about the historiography of Arab nationalism, particularly during the so-called era of independence and personified by figures like the Egyptian leader Nasser, will be addressed.

Ideologies aside, the importance of oil and associated issues of political economy, including the political and strategic competition for other scarce and valuable natural resources such as water, are addressed in chapter 3. The focus on political economy, and more specifically the politics of oil and the wealth this has generated in the area, resonates in relation to the nature of political systems within the region. As I shall argue, it is no coincidence that political life in the wealthy states of the Gulf is governed by the same elites who own the wealth derived from the oil fields of Arabia. This chapter will also examine other issues of political economy vital to any understanding of the region, including the debate about rentier economies, policies of economic liberalization, or *infitah* as they are referred to locally, and the poor economic performance of the region as a whole in the global market. The immense wealth and patterns of distribution have altered relations within as well as outside the region and, as I explain in chapter 4, go some way to explain the nature of conflict which has characterized the Middle East in the contemporary era. While the Arab–Israeli conflict has dominated the region, other conflicts have played their part in undermining the stability of the area as a whole. Thus, sectarian, economic and territorial disputes, as well as the Palestinian–Israeli conflict, are examined along with specific case studies of the limited successes in peacemaking. The perspectives of conflict outlined above are by no means conclusive but they do highlight associated issues such as the role of international actors, the role of the military in politics and issues of internal legitimacy and traditional state-to-state rivalries such as those between Iran and its Arab neighbours.

In many respects the themes addressed in the next four chapters of the book – political Islam, democratization, women and ethnicity and minorities – reflect the concerns of non-state actors and say more about the politics of protest than the ruling regimes of the region. In chapter 5 the impact of political Islam is discussed at length. I argue that the manifestation of political Islam encompasses a far broader political spectrum than we are encouraged to believe in the West – indeed, that one is talking about many political Islams and dimensions of Muslim politics which incorporate debates about women, human rights, democracy, state and politics, liberalism and fundamentalism, violence and preaching. Linked with the apparent resurgence of Islam as a political force, the debate, addressed in chapter 6, on democratization first outlines the initial emergence, fall and partial rebirth of democratic politics in the region. The chapter will then focus on recent debates about democratization which have been promoted from outside the region as a means of combating tyranny within the region, particularly the perceived anti-democratic nature of political Islam. This section will include a review of current analyses of democratization and the argument forwarded by some theorists relating to the culture of receptivity to ideas about democracy which are largely western in inspiration and practice. The next two chapters of the book address issues which hitherto have remained on the margins of the formal politics of the region – women, ethnicity and minorities. For a number of decades, however, the role of these groups in the political life of the state systems of the region has been an increasing focus of attention and has also fuelled the debate about the nature of current state types and associated political systems which, by and large, have ignored, suppressed and attempted to eliminate the politics raised by women, by ethnic groups such as the Kurds, or so-called minorities such as the Shi'a in Lebanon or Iraq. I will therefore examine some recent literature which addresses the interpretation of the role of women and other ethnicities in Middle Eastern society. Such studies have paid more attention to the private than the public political arena: the politics of the family, issues of leadership in households and debates about women's status and reproduction. They reflect new trends in scholarship on women and ethnicity in Third World studies, in general recognizing new methodologies which place greater emphasis on gender politics, ethnic or ethno-nationalist ideologies than on historically limited Marxist explanations which were used in the past. This in turn links back to a debate which currently rages in the Middle East: to what extent can primordial definitions of ethnicity, religion and tribe explain the relative resistance of Middle Eastern societies to the institutions and ideologies of the West? The final chapter on

American foreign policy towards the Middle East explores the deep and intimate relationship between the United States of America and the various states of the region in terms of American national interest and the wider ideological debates of the twentieth and twenty-first century.

This book, then, paints a broad picture, not of a monolithic Middle East populated by the caricature figures of Arabs, Israelis and Iranians that we are familiar with through our own media in the West, but a richer vista which includes significant groups of political actors which, in the past, have either been ignored or severely misunderstood in an attempt at reductive accounts of a fascinating region of the contemporary world.

I hope that readers are as stimulated by the second edition as they have been by the first. I would like to offer my thanks to all those cited in the first edition of the book plus Amalendu Misra, Sandy Marshall and Roisin Smith in helping to augment and prepare the second edition of this book and to Ellen McKinlay and Louise Knight at Polity for encouraging me further in this project.

Beverley Milton-Edwards
Queen's University Belfast

Introduction

THIS book is designed to act as a useful introduction to contemporary politics in the Middle East from the end of the Ottoman Empire at the turn of the twentieth century to the present day. My approach is to look at the region through a number of important issues without which any understanding of politics would be meaningless. Thus, as well as charting a chronologically accurate picture of the area, the book will address such themes as democratization, gender, ethnicity and political economy. The connection between these themes is apparent because they are all interrelated in a series of dynamic and intricate layers. Thus, in order to understand the politics of a state and people such as Lebanon, one can examine specific themes such as ethnicity, colonialism, nationalism and Islam as well as war and conflict. The justification for the themes that I have chosen for analysis is that simply to study the state in isolation from such dynamics or to look at one perspective rather than a series of other viewpoints misleads the reader seeking to look at politics in this region. By politics I mean something broader than the mechanisms of power that relate to and revolve around the modern nation-state. This permits us to look at the politics of other non-state actors and elements such as Islamists, women, ethnic groups such as the Berbers or the Kurds and their attempts to move from the periphery to the centre. The connections that emerge from the study of such themes will become increasingly apparent to the reader and allow them to determine independently which factors or theoretical framework works best in terms of wider regional comparisons. In other words I am offering an emancipation mechanism to the reader to determine their own perspectives and analysis. Traditional studies of the politics of the Middle East have tended to focus overly on the state and its associated actors. This approach has its values but it limits the scope for the study of the political dynamic in a wide geographic region such as the Middle East and ignores key factors as outlined above. Other approaches have centred on a country by country study and this too has its value in terms of specifics of power distribution and analysis but is restricted in terms of a comparative overview of the region. With the themes that I have selected the reader can take a comparative overview or look more specifically at a country through the tool of the case studies and further reading sections. Indeed I hope to avoid overgeneralization by presenting case studies in each chapter to illustrate the case in hand. Each chapter will also highlight useful sources of further reading, so that students of the subject will be able to grasp quickly the important conceptual frameworks constructed around the region which help support patterns of study and research, as well as build up specific knowledge of a particular country and its internal political landscape. In this way we will avoid falling into the trap of assuming that all politics in the Middle East are alike in nature and give ourselves room to see the various political systems that operate.

The contemporary Middle East is portrayed as mysterious, a region of intrigue and war, the cradle of terrorism, religious extremism and barbaric rule. Journalists and newspeople regularly report stories of unending conflict and dispute, the abuse of privilege and power and the desperation of popular calls for reform and political change. In some ways the media present the Middle East as being unique in this respect; however, it is not. The Middle East, like many other areas of the globe, suffers in part from the effects of modernization, lack of political participation, poor economic growth, foreign indebtedness to the West, the competition for arms and increasing urbanization. As authors such as Cammack, Pool and Tordoff (1993) and Bromley (1994) highlight, there are no myths to explode: the Middle East is like other developing regions such as Africa or Latin America. In sum, it is not as unique as many authors would have us believe.

Some generalizations, however, cannot be avoided and are particularly necessary and useful in helping new students to the subject understand the region and make sense of cultures, histories and politics so very different to their own. Most people new to the subject already carry with them a generalized, and often stereotyped, view that has played a part in their decision to find out more. There is nothing wrong with this as long as prejudices are acknowledged and the further acquisition of knowledge is based on sound academic reading. Newcomers to the subject tend to see the region and its politics in the following way: as hot, desert-like, poor, undeveloped, backward, governed by Muslim fanatics and tyrants, characterized by rich Arabs in London and terrorists blowing up planes. It is important to recognize that we do bring preconceptions and images with us when we start to study the Middle East. It is no use pretending that we have no knowledge; our opinions, knowledge and views will have come from sources as diverse as Sunday-school Bible stories, our Judeo-Christian cultural context, films, records, books and television programmes. So we should, from the start, stop for a moment and think about our own vision of the region and the images we have received. The objective of this book is to re-examine these views, see how they differ from the reality and build a new store of knowledge that is balanced and informed around the prejudices that we already hold.

In recent decades the growing interest in the region has been accompanied by an increasing number of academic journals, texts and books devoted to the study of the area. Students of politics in the twenty-first century are able to access material through well-stocked libraries, journal collections and the ever-expanding information superhighway through the Internet. Even by the mid to late 1990s a vast array of subject areas covering the Middle East, from political discussion groups, government and official websites, research centres, libraries and cultural developments, could be accessed through the World Wide Web (www). It is questionable, however, to what extent the proliferation of materials on or from the Middle East has encouraged an expansion of prejudices or new perspectives on the region. Since the events of 9/11, when Arab bombers from al-Qaeda attacked America, views on the Middle East have hardened.

What is the Middle East?

Where is the Middle East?

What we mean by the Middle East and where it starts and other regions end may initially seem a rather inane question. Nevertheless, these very basic terms of reference need to be discussed and examined from a number of perspectives. The political events taking place in the Middle East today are the subject of considerable press attention and interest from Europe and the United States of America. The region is fascinating, providing rich contrasts in political, cultural, social and economic spheres. The contribution of the peoples of this region to history, civilization, art, culture, science, religion, music and politics can no longer be neglected or ignored. Ancient civilizations also have their roots in the Middle East. In addition, the three great monotheistic religions, Judaism, Christianity and Islam, were established by prophets and their followers in these lands. Throughout history, great empire-builders, statesmen, religious leaders, poets and scientists have emerged from the area to influence and inform European cultures. The golden age of Islam witnessed the spread of Islam to Europe in the West and Asia in the East. The rich heritage of literature through poetry and story-telling informs us of great empires under the Umayyads, Abbasids and Ottomans, of just rulers, corrupt tyrants, dynastic power struggles, feats of military daring and scientific endeavour. In more recent times the Middle East has been subject to external colonial competition resulting in widespread processes of modernization and development. These have been neither uniform nor universal. Indeed, varieties of modernization have occurred within the region, many externally influenced and driven, some internally propelled as part of idiosyncratic visions of social, political and economic engineering involving whole societies. An example of this is best illustrated in the case of Libya's development, by the rule of Muammar Qaddafi, which has involved the whole of Libyan society in a grandiose modernization project.

The Middle East is also a source of one of the world's most valuable energy sources: oil. Throughout the twentieth century the discovery and subsequent export of oil in the region has led to unimaginable wealth for some Arab states, the impoverishment of others, problems of import–export substitution, rentier economies which have impacted on the nature of political rule in certain countries, attempts to redistribute oil wealth within the region, a migrant labour phenomenon and military conflict and war over territories driven purely by the desire to control oil sources and the wealth derived from them. In addition, the production of so much oil has shaped the relations the region enjoys with other parts of the world, its role in the international community and on capital markets throughout the globe.

Geographically speaking, the region is vast and its borders and boundaries are still open to debate – meaning different things to different people. Depending on which definition of the Middle East is used, the area stretches from Morocco in the West to Iran in the East, and can include sub-Saharan Africa, Turkey, Afghanistan and the Arab/Persian Gulf. Within this region there are vast deserts, modern cities, snow-capped mountain ranges and important natural resources, including water, oil and natural gas. The definition of the Middle East that I adopt in this book refers to the following eighteen countries: Algeria, Bahrain, Egypt, Jordan, Iran, Iraq, Israel, Kuwait, Lebanon, Libya, Morocco, Oman, Qatar, Saudi Arabia, Syria, Tunisia, United Arab Emirates and Yemen. Some might also include Turkey or Sudan, but I would argue that in the contemporary context Turkey should be regarded as a southern European state and Sudan as an African state with Islamic tendencies. Many states in the contemporary Middle East are relatively recent creations, their boundaries and borders being the product, one way or another, of the era of colonial interference in the region. Iraq, for example, is a twentieth-century invention of British officials who 'united' three provinces of ancient Mesopotamia and imported a new Arab monarch from the Hejaz of Arabia. In addition, the independence of the majority of these states is a phenomenon located in the latter part of the twentieth century and linked to the independence movement throughout the Third World and patterns of international politics and relations which subsequently resulted from these global changes.

The region is host to many religious groups. Among Muslims there are Sunni, Shi'a, Sufi, Alawite, Wahabi and Druze. In the Christian community there are Catholics, Greek Orthodox and Maronites, Armenians, Coptics, Assyrians, Protestants, Anglicans and Melkites, to name but a few. In addition, Jews have populated the region, not just in the Holy Land, but in countries like Egypt, Syria, Morocco and Yemen. The religious importance of the region cannot be underestimated, as billions across the globe turn to it for prayer, pilgrimage and worship and the veneration of religious sites which are thousands of years old. Religious diversity, therefore, actually characterizes the region, though the Muslim faith enjoys primary status in many countries. Within the region the religious tag is still used as a means of identifying and setting boundaries between people (Barth, 1969). Diversity has often led to difference both within a particular faith, leading to breakaway sects or schisms, as well as between faiths, witnessed more recently, for example, by an upsurge in Muslim–Coptic Christian tensions in Egypt or the civil war in Lebanon from 1975 to 1990.

Ethnic identity is an important and increasingly pertinent issue affecting the politics of the Middle East. Until the end of the Cold War, the Gulf crisis and the disintegration of the former Soviet Union and many East European states, the ethnic dimension in politics was relatively neglected and largely suppressed and ignored. The emergence of ethno-national conflicts throughout the globe, and the subsequent resolution of some of them, has impacted on the Middle East in a variety of ways. Ethnic diversity is a feature in the majority of its states and characterizes modern nation-states such as Israel (Jew – Ashkenazi or Sephardic – and Arab), Syria (Arab, Kurd and Jew), Iraq (Arab, Kurd and Marsh Arab), Iran (Persian, Arab, Kurd, Circassian) and Algeria (Arab and Berber). Thus, Arabs, Berbers, Kurds, Marsh Arabs, Jews, Bedouin, Persians and Circassians all come from distinct ethnic backgrounds, embracing unique linguistic, cultural and religious characteristics. In addition, some forms of ethno-national identity are relatively recent constructs created in response to the threat of political or other forms of annihilation or assimilation. Such ethnic differences have played a large part in shaping the identity of the inhabitants of the region, many of whom find themselves residing in a modern nation-state to which they feel little real loyalty, remaining as marginal forces on the fringes of society, opposing rule from an alien centre and agitating for a range of changes from more ethnically sensitive policies on education or the preservation of certain linguistic traditions, to outright secession and self-determination.

The Middle East, as described above, is different from the Arab world, which is composed of all of the aforementioned countries except Iran and Israel. The Arab world is something different again from the Muslim world, which includes all of the aforementioned except Israel, but also encompasses countries such as Turkey, Pakistan, Afghanistan, etc. Other terms applied to the region include the Near East, and the Fertile Crescent, which refers to the area from Lebanon in the North, Syria to the East and Israel to the South. The Levant is also commonly used to describe Lebanon and Syria. Labels such as the Gulf states, the Arab-Afro states, the Islamic states and the Maghreb, which refers to the North African states of Morocco, Algeria, Tunisia and sometimes Libya, are also frequently applied both within and from outside the region. Also within the region we can talk about the existence of other worlds, such as Jewish, Islamic, Christian, Arab, Afro-Arab and southern Mediterranean. The use of these labels has more to do with the diffuse notion of identity that often pervades the region than anything else. They also highlight the way in which the region interacts politically as well as in other spheres with these 'other worlds'. At the heart of this debate about the labelling of the region is a subjective/objective setting of boundaries, and the social and political space between the peoples of the region and the rest of the world (Barth, 1969). Here, the Middle East as a label becomes an exclusive term identifying a particular group of peoples as separate and distinct from others, whether they be African, European or Asian. Within the region, the issue of labelling also becomes one of identities, where the nation-state seeks to create and establish identities which compete with other group identities focused on tribe, family, gender, ethnicity or religion.

Who invented the Middle East?

The term 'the Middle East' is a relatively recent one, a product of contemporary rather than historical interest in the region. Previously, those from outside the region who had an interest in it referred to it, or parts of it, as the Near East, the Orient, the Levant, the Maghreb, Zion or the Holy Land. These terms have encouraged a particular association of ideas or a view of the region which is often simplistic and the product of crude reductionism and stereotyping. The Orient, for example, was a term which grew out of European fascination with the Middle East, particularly in the eighteenth and nineteenth centuries. Oriental society, however, was portrayed in a negative manner and seen as symbolizing everything the West was not. As Turner (1994) argues, 'Oriental society can be defined as a system of absences – absent cities, the missing middle classes, missing autonomous urban institutions and missing property' (p. 40). Other terms and labels, such as Zion and the Holy Land, were used to convey a romanticized and reductive vision of certain parts of the region which had as much to do with a utopian vision of redemption for Jew and Christian alike and resonated with Islamophobic memories of the Crusades.

The Middle East label, then, was invented by those from outside the region who sought to make sense of or understand an order of political, economic, social and cultural relations in a geographic region stretching from the Maghreb to Persia. It was not a term that those indigenous to the region used to describe themselves. Common usage of the label can be located in the Second World War when the British military established a Middle East Command in the area under the authority of the War Office. It was an invention of the war, a military necessity, but it remained long after British, and for that matter French, influence in the region declined and was replaced by the superpower competition between the USA and the former USSR. The term also entered the lexicon of diplomats, academics and the military and increasingly replaced the usage, in Europe, of the 'Near East' which in the USA is still used to describe what I refer to as the Middle East. Use of this label by those who study the region from outside its geographic boundaries has led to a debate about the assumptions and prejudices they bring with them from their Eurocentric, post-Enlightenment perspective. This debate was largely initiated following the publication of a text that challenged prevailing western scholarship and perspectives on the region.

Orientalism – the debate

In 1978 a Palestinian academic living in the USA published a book entitled *Orientalism*. The author, Edward Said, aimed to challenge, criticize and shake the foundations and assumptions at the heart of western-based academic study of the Middle East. He set out to describe the symbiotic relationship which scholars had ascribed to the Orient and Occident in which the Orient stood as the moon, the black, the negative, the backward and the barbaric, and the Occident embodied the sun, the white, the positive, the enlightened and the progressive. As Said stated on the first page of his book,

> The Orient is not only adjacent to Europe; it is also the place of Europe's greatest and richest and oldest colonies, the source of civilizations and languages, its cultural contestant, and one of its deepest and most recurring images of the Other. (1978, p. 1)

Any student with a serious interest in the study of the Middle East should read Said's exposition in *Orientalism* and his later work entitled *Culture and Imperialism* (1993a). While Said may not have been the first scholar to highlight orientalist scholarship (Turner, 1994), in essence he develops a three-pronged line of attack on western scholarship of the Orient. This Orient is geographically located in the Middle East and is primarily Muslim in religious character. First, Said criticizes western scholarship for its essentialist perspective of the region and the way in which it both treats and presents Muslim society as one homogeneous and monolithic mass. Second, he argues that western scholarship of the region is politically motivated, and in particular was and remains associated with the political and economic ambitions associated with colonialism and imperialism. As such, western domination of the Orient is the political motive, according to Said, behind most scholarship on the region. Finally, Said presents an argument that academic tradition on the subject in the West has resulted in and created a body of 'authoritarian truths' which must, he argues, be challenged by new scholarship and new thinking. Ultimately, Said is asking the West to rethink its relationship with the 'Other'. He constructs a critique of occidental assumptions about every aspect of the Middle East, whether cultural, political, religious, social or in the sphere of economic relations. His complaint rests on the patronizing attitude which is extended wholesale by the West to the East. Through the pages of his book he charts the development of three types of meaning which together have shaped the perspective of generations of scholars, researchers, policy-makers, missionaries, military and political figures who have all made the Middle East and Muslims their business, their focus or their career (Said, 1978, pp. 2–3).

Does orientalism persist in the present? Does domination persist in the cultural, political and economic relationship between the Middle East and the West? Many, including scholars such as Edward Said and Hisham Sharabi, would point to limited changes, a new generation which is now aware of these factors but a continuing rigidity within the realms of conventional scholarship which persists in characterizing the Middle East in ways basically unchanged since European domination was first established over the region in the late eighteenth and early nineteenth century. In a 'critique of academic scholarship', Hisham Sharabi (1990) identifies three fields of scholarship on the Middle East: orientalism, area studies and liberal humanism. As Sharabi declares, the point of his argument is not to undermine conventional discourse on the region but to present a meaningful critique of the way in which it is conducted, the hitherto unquestioned assumptions held by western scholars even in the present day. Thus, two principal assumptions are questioned, the first, 'the specifically western experience of transformation and change understood as progress . . . The second . . . from the view that non-western cultures somehow belong to a different order of existence and develop according to a different impulse' (Sharabi, 1990, p. 4).

Orientalism persists, but it is increasingly questioned by a new generation of young scholars and students of the region. For them the term (rather than the associated attitudes) is a thing of the past; they are conscious of their 'westernness' and struggle to dissociate themselves from the old lackeys of orientalism. The debate persists: in 1993 Edward Said and Ernest Gellner engaged in a very public row about the persistence of orientalism and Eurocentric bias in the study of the Middle East. In a review of *Culture and Imperialism* Gellner accused Said of 'inventing a bogy called Orientalism' through which rigid lines of good and bad in the study and characterization of the region could be drawn. Gellner questioned this methodology, pointing out that some figures castigated by Said as orientalists had brought positive benefits to the region through the accompanying forces of industry and technology (Gellner, 1993, p. 4). Said's rebuke was vociferous. At one point he remarks: 'Let him [Gellner] delight in his sophomoric patter by all means, but let him not at the same time fool himself that what he says about Islam, or the formerly colonized world or imperialism or postmodernism, has anything to do with what any of them are really about' (1993b, p. 17).

The academic row, symbolized by these two men, over the way in which the Middle East should be studied is as important today, if not more so, than it ever was. It is important because the primary lens through which the Middle East is still represented in the West is filtered through a variety of media – film, television, radio, newspapers, music and magazines – which has very little that is positive to say about the Arabs or Muslims of the region. Indeed, images of Arab society, from Disney's *Aladdin*, films like Hollywood's *True Lies* to Bradford's Muslims burning copies of Salman Rushdie's *Satanic Verses*, all convey the same myopic vision of the region. As a result, other leading academic figures have come into conflict with Said's approach, among whom Bernard Lewis stands out. In his own work, including *Islam and the West* (1993b), and 'The Question of Orientalism' (1982), Lewis argues that Said's success in writing *Orientalism* lay in its antiwestern, pro-Third World perspective which served a purpose for those leftists and others intent on undermining American foreign policy. In addition, he criticized Said's work for simplifying and reducing complex problems affecting the Middle East and the Muslim world. Fred Halliday, writing in 'Orientalism and its Critics', defines himself as falling into neither one camp nor the other, and instead criticizes both for failing to recognize 'what actually happens in these societies' as opposed to their approach of writing about 'what people say' (1996, p. 201).

Studying the Middle East, then, leads one into a world of opposing and critical scholarship where the student of the subject must always be aware of the passions that motivate its scholars. The Middle East, incorporating as it does the Muslim world, the Arab people, the rich and the poor, ethnic groups such as Kurds, Berbers and Marsh Arabs, women, religious minorities including the Jews, the developed and undeveloped, citizen and refugee, urban and rural, religious and secular, powerful and weak, remains essential to any future configuration of the global system. Indeed, global politics, the balance of power, American hegemony, the fate of world economic markets and trade balances are all significantly affected by the Middle East and its varying political strata. The very future and security of the globe are believed to be threatened by Arab and Muslim terrorists from the region, war has been waged on Iraq by western state powers while at the same time Arab capital and the price of oil in Europe, America and the Far East has had and continues to have a significant impact on global economic trends. As I have shown in the debate above, how we choose to study the region matters very much to our understanding of it.

State types: making sense of multiplicity

Once the difficulty of defining a few basic terms of reference has been overcome it is also useful to present a classification of the state system in our study of politics in the contemporary Middle East. The establishment of nation or sovereign states in the region is a contemporary phenomenon associated with the defeat of the Ottoman Empire in World War I and the rising hegemony of Europe over the region in the post-war period. As Roger Owen (2003) remarks, 'As far as the Middle East was concerned, it was generally the dominant colonial power that first created the essential features of a state, by giving it a capital, a legal system, a flag and internationally recognized boundaries' (p. 13). The model of the state that the European powers sought to export to the region was a direct descendant of the state type which had evolved in their own societies, reflecting old tensions between state and church. The model of the state applied in the region also reflected the prevailing philosophical saliency in post-Enlightenment Europe of concepts of sovereignty, democracy, liberalism and secularism, as well as the change in economic modes of production from agrarian to industrialized societies. These factors all played a part in shaping the particular types of model which were exported to the Middle East and used in the construction of new states, new nations and new capital-driven economies. As Hobsbawm (1997) points out, state-creation in the Middle East has been about processes of 'decolonization, revolution and, of course, the intervention of outside powers'.

The subsequent political independence of such states is also a relatively recent event mostly achieved following the decline of European influence in the region after World War II and before the increasingly powerful ascendancy of the USA and former USSR's competition for influence in the region. Yemen was the first state to achieve independence in 1918 and the most recent was the United Arab Emirates in 1971. Most of the territory of the region has known foreign rule in one form or another under the authority of an outside European or western power. Therefore, independence and the further development of the nation-state and nation-building is a relatively recent manifestation of political life in the region (Lustick, 1993). In some countries the state- and nation-building experiment is still under way, often underpinned by the military or occupation by foreign forces and by limited opportunities for mass-based politics. In Iraq since the fall of Saddam Hussein the Ba'thist state has been entirely dismantled and an Allied-led experiment in new nation-building has taken place. The states and state system of the region are diverse and subject to competing typologies drawn and established by academics on the subject. These are useful in that they help us ascertain political patterns of government and the state and the increasing body of evidence of the artificiality of many state systems in the area. The nation-state in the Middle East has manifested itself in a number of ways and its elite has gone a long way to promote characteristics of national – whether Syrian, Iraqi, Kuwaiti or Egyptian – identity within a distinct territorial entity. On the other hand, the nation-state, or rather nation-building, has also been increasingly recognized as failing many so-called 'citizens', ignoring other stronger identities as the homogenizing of the state is brutally imposed from above. Such is the case in Iraq, where ethnic and other identities have been suppressed, first under the banner of Ba'thist ideology and then under Saddam Hussein's myopic vision of 'nation without difference'.

Before we examine these typologies of the state, it is worth remembering some of the more universal features that are shared in the region which created a sense of cohesion in the Middle East before the advent of the European colonial powers and their accompanying political models of development for the nation-state. Under the Ottoman Empire, which preceded the era of 'grand interference', loyalty and identity in the region was bound together through a unified law, political system and taxation, as well as by religion, clan, tribe, family, class, language and ethnic group. A common language,

Arabic, and common religion, Islam, played an important part in forging a sense of identity, even if it did not always result in unity at a political level. Through language and Islam, Arabs share a common history in the region.

In the present day, however, it has been argued that the modern state system works against these unifying factors, often fracturing homogeneous groups with shared ethnic, religious or linguistic traditions. The state system has created fissures and artificial systems of government based on political traditions and thought which are not indigenous to the region, but instead are the product of the period of foreign domination. As a result, the inhabitants of the region have encountered many problems with their state systems. For the most part the problems are attributed to the synthetic nature of the state and its western-influenced roots. Western academics working on the subject of the state and establishing typologies of the state system in the region are aware of these difficulties, and have incorporated them into their models.

Typologies have been devised by a number of scholars, including Giacomo Luciani and Ilia Harik in Luciani (1990), Roger Owen (2003) and Simon Bromley (1994). Other authors on the subject include Nazih Ayubi, Michael Hudson, Philip Khoury and Joseph Kostiner, Sami Zubaida and Ian Lustick. While all of these writers may differ in the perspective from which they work, or in certain methodological techniques that they engage in, or in the arguments they construct on this subject, they all recognize the state, Arab or otherwise, in the region. Before proceeding further, however, a working definition of what is meant by the state is worth elaborating here. The modern nation-state is usually construed as a territorial political unit. It is not a virtual invention, rather it consists of a claim to authority, sovereignty, institutions of rule and government, means of raising state revenue through taxes or other sources, international recognition, a flag and a capital. As Owen (2003) points out, while there can never be one precise definition of the state, and nor is the nation-state in the Middle East a purely western product, the general features outlined above can be recognized as common to the typologies outlined below.

It is worth looking in some detail at the useful debates outlined by Luciani and Harik (1990), Owen (1992), Bromley (1994) and Ayubi (1995). Owen takes a structuralist approach, focusing on class and economic relations, both internally and externally generated. Through this particular lens he identifies three state types which are common in the region:

1 The colonial state, which existed in the post-World War I period in countries such as Egypt, Syria, Lebanon and Iraq. The colonial state,

according to Owen (1992), was distinguished by the following three features: 'central administration; the policies of the colonial power; and colonialism as a conduit for external influences' (p. 13).

2 The immediate post-independent state, where national liberation movements struggled to consolidate a state system based on western forms of government through supporting socialist or other ideologies.

3 The authoritarian state, where participatory democracy is absent, and one-party rule supported by a strong military and internal security structure dominates.

Under this typology Owen addresses one-party states (e.g. Syria and Iraq), family rule (e.g. the Gulf states) and even the examples of Libya under Jamahiriyyah rule. Owen's approach is concise in execution and allows a variety of political circumstances to be incorporated into the three broad headings that he outlines. Luciani (1990) also identifies important features of the Arab state (rather than the Israeli, Iranian or Turkish state) which echo Owen's typology. Luciani believes the first distinguishing feature of the stable state is 'the position of the central strongman, leader or orchestrator, the Great Patron or Manipulator.' Second, he introduces the idea of 'periodicity', where leaders 'sweep the government'. Third is the 'politics of limited association', where political activity exists but is ultimately limited by the ruling elite. Fourth, a broad middle class rules the state. Fifth, Arab states are weighted down by large bureaucracies and, sixth, the states act as 'an organization of control or regulation'. Finally, Luciani remarks that the 'orientalist tradition' would identify the influence of Islam on the Arab state system (pp. xxvii–xxx).

Harik (1990) establishes a useful typology, which differs from Owen's by arguing that many contemporary Arab states (Harik cites fifteen) are indigenous products of the region rather than colonial creations. Here Harik acknowledges the more informal patterns of politics that have remained in the region, evolving and currently resisting the homogenizing ideologies of socialism and capitalism which have been utilized to serve the nation-state and its elites as it attempts to create new identities and loyalties. Harik (1990, pp. 5–6) identifies five traditional Arab state types:

1 The imam-chief system – 'authority in a sanctified leader' (Yemen, Oman, Hijaz).

2 Alliance system of chief and imams – 'authority is invested in a tribal chief supported and awarded legitimate authority beyond the confines of his tribe by virtue of his identification and/or alliance to prominent religious leaders' (Saudi Arabia).

3 Traditional secular system with 'authority invested in a dynasty free from religious attributes' (Qatar, Bahrain, Kuwait, Lebanon).
4 Bureaucratic-military oligarchy type. Authority originates in urban-based garrison commanders, who in time develop an extensive bureaucratic apparatus. Monopoly of the means of coercion in the hands of an administrative caste is the major feature of this state type (Algeria, Egypt, Tunisia).
5 Colonial-created system. States carved out of the now-defunct Ottoman Empire on the basis of foreign imperial interest in the absence of a credible local base of authority to erect new structures (Iraq, Syria, Jordan, Palestine, Israel).

Harik's typology is useful for the alternative perspective it encourages us to take and the less formal patterns of politics – such as the political power of the tribe, ethnic group or religious leader – that it highlights alongside more formal power bases such as the military.

Ayubi (1995) works from both a political economy and comparative approach, seeking to explain why Arab states are 'fierce and hard' in one respect but ultimately feeble in normal state activities such as tax collection and welfare provision. Using the political economy perspective, Ayubi brings the work of authors like Antonio Gramsci and Guillermo O'Donnell into his analysis of the Arab state in the Middle East. He argues that all Arab states are, to one degree or another, authoritarian, engaging in coercive measures against citizens, while also remaining distant from them. In addition, he identifies two state types: the revolutionary state *thawra* (revolution), based on populist, radical, socialist and nationalist rhetoric, and the *tharwa* (wealth) state type, 'relying for survival on kin-based relations, but above all else on financial capital, or wealth' (1995, p. 447).

Bromley (1994) also attempts to reformulate the study of state-formation in the Middle East, through an economic-driven theoretical framework which marks a distinct departure from earlier cultural and modernization theories on the subject. In addition, in defining his own typology, he places great emphasis on social structures, external relations with outside powers and the issue of oil production or non-production. From this economic standpoint, looking at power in terms of capital, surplus appropriation and the position of new states in the world economy, he encourages the reader to rethink the concept of the state. Bromley himself rejects culturalist and mainstream social theory explanations and typologies of the state and instead suggests that we might better understand state-formation through 'historical materialism . . . enabling us both to avoid essentialist arguments about culture and to move beyond the comparative and descriptive nature of Weberian sociology' (1994, p. 4).

In the chapters that follow, the three basic themes outlined above – what is the Middle East?, the debate on orientalism and the concept of the state in the Middle East – will resonate in the discussions of colonialism, Arab nationalism, war and lack of peace in the region, the impact of political Islam, the debate about political participation and democratization, women and ethnicity. The themes and issues affecting the contemporary politics of the Middle East are inextricably interwoven in a fascinating and rich tapestry in which individual threads may only be unravelled in the context of associated themes. The issue of gender in the Middle East, for example, cannot be fully understood without grasping the nature of the state – state type, the make-up of the elite and other power-holders in society, the pros and cons of the debate about orientalism in representing the 'other': all apply equally to the gender theme and highlight the inextricable links between the essential issues discussed in this book.

Further reading

Albert Hourani (1991) offers the most comprehensive introduction to the history of the Arab people which reflects many of the issues raised here. Choueiri's (2005) edited companion history of the Middle East is very useful. Mansfield (1992) and Sluglett and Farouk-Sluglett (1993) offer concise historical overviews and summaries of individual states and their histories. Choueiri (2003) reflects on historical discourse of the nation-state in the region. Cleveland (2004) and Pappe (2005) offer historical analysis of low as well as high historical politics in the region. Hinnebusch (2003) introduces the international dimension. For the debate on orientalism, Said (1978) offers the platform from which many arguments and debates have been constructed. Other authors such as Turner (1994) must be included in any reading on the subject. This can be contrasted with Lewis (1968 and 1976) and the debate in the *New York Review of Books* between Lewis and Said in 1982. Halliday (1996) offers a discussion of orientalism and its critics which attempts an even-handed approach to the debate. In addition, wider aspects of the orientalism controversy may be found in Butterworth (1980), Kerr (1980) and Hussain, Olson and Qureshi (1984). Further rebuttals can be found in Lewis (1993a) and some of the works of Pipes (for example 1983a). Contemporary perspectives on the state can be found in a variety of texts which examine the Middle East. It may be best to start with a more general discussion of the state in the Third World, which can be found in Cammack, Pool and Tordoff (1993) which includes comparative material on the Middle East, Latin America, Africa and southeast Asia, as well as Haynes (1996) who presents a general discussion of state and society. For specific material on the state in the Middle East Owen (2003) establishes a sophisticated level of analysis, as discussed above. Lustick (1993) gives a highly theoretical account of the state and statebuilding, which he develops in reference to Israel, the West Bank and the Gaza Strip but on a more comparative level with Britain and Ireland as well as France and Algeria. Zubaida (1993) highlights the relationship between Islam and the state through an analysis of the Iranian Revolution and the establishment of an Islamic state led by Ayatollah Khomeini. Bromley (1994) is a good point of departure for many of the current analyses of the state in the Middle East with Hakimian and Moshaver (2001) offering strong insight in their edited text pointing to political economy and the state in the region.

Colonial Rule

Introduction

DIRECT colonial rule in the Middle East in the twentieth century was relatively short-lived, yet its impact on the political systems of the region was immense and persists to the present day. The interest of various European powers, and of the British and the French in particular, can be dated to the end of the eighteenth and beginning of the nineteenth century, but it was in the period between the First and Second World War that the potent force of the West made its lasting mark on almost the entire population of the area, from Morocco in the West to Iran in the East. Foreign interest in the region was nothing new, and when the European powers of the time became involved the shadow of earlier crusades fell over them, arming them with biblical and religious justification for their thinly veiled economic and strategic enterprises in the area. In addition, European interference in the Middle East was always competitive, with the French, Italians and British struggling with each other to secure their own national interests in the area. The more benign explanation for this colonial enterprise was that Europe was helping the Middle East fulfil its potential after centuries of backwardness and stagnation. This experience was not unique to the Middle East; rather it was just one other area of the globe alongside Africa and south-east Asia that was exploited as the Industrial Age created new demands for profit at its European base.

The advent of European political as well as economic control over the region began in earnest in the 1880s with Britain's occupation of Egypt and reached an apex after the First World War when Britain and France were awarded mandates and protectorates and the right to redraw boundaries and create new nation-states in the region. The record of colonialism, however, was poor. From 1918 onwards the Middle East was plunged into political turmoil as the colonial powers struggled to exert their power and influence over their subject Arab and Jewish populations. A way of life that had evolved over four centuries of Ottoman rule was disrupted, fractured and shattered by the colonial powers keen to make their mark and shape the region in the European mould of political, economic and social relations. The process of modernization introduced by the colonial powers resulted in social dislocation, with traditional tribal powers undermined by a new class of urban notables, a decline of the rural in favour of the urban and the creation of new states such as Iraq and Jordan where boundaries took no account of pre-existing ethnic, religious and tribal configurations. Cities did not become more urban but more ruralized (Hudson, 1977, p. 143), and the state failed to meet the demands of the new urban mass leading to political mobilization. The end product of all this was a political landscape which was first imposed on the region and then adapted by local elites, giving the entire area an artificial identity which it has spent more than a century coming to terms with.

The impact of foreign intervention in the economy and social fabric of the Middle East is subject to some considerable debate, led by scholars such as Charles Issawi and Roger Owen. Issawi (1982) outlines the matter in a plain fashion when he declares that 'for every single [colonial] country the direct economic costs of empire [in the Middle East] far outweighed the direct economic benefits' (p. 214). If there were no direct economic benefits to be derived from the colonial exploitation of the Middle East, what then of the legacy the colonizers left behind when they were eventually ousted from the region? Mainstream thinking typically ascribes a colonial legacy which has scarred the region, frustrated political as well as economic development and which supports the continuing hostility, suspicion and distrust that still disfigures relations between this particular East and West. Yet, while authors like Owen (2003) also acknowledge this legacy, they factor in other dimensions such as the new political space which the creation of the colonially inspired nation-state created in the Middle East. The secularizing nature of the state is also brought into the equation when measuring the degree to which colonialism was able to transform the pre-existing social, economic and political structures of the region. Building up a black and white vision of colonizers and colonized in the Middle East, of economic and political winners and losers, as both Issawi and Owen argue, is highly problematic and does not truly represent the reality of the experience in the region.

When Britain, France, Spain and Italy relinquished their claims and authority in the Middle East, other foreign forces attempted to fill their shoes. From 1945, for example, the USA became an increasingly important influence in the region, heralding an era of neo-imperialism or *pax Americana* which persists to the present day. Despite the decline of Cold War politics in the Middle East theatre, the American influence in the area has persisted in the absence of a Soviet foe. In the 1990s the USA was reviled throughout the region by entire populations whose own governments remained dependent and tied to American interests. In this chapter I chart the growth of European, and British in particular, interest and interference in the region.

Merchants and missionaries

European interest in the Middle East was always part of the economic enterprise that started in Europe during the Industrial Revolution. As Europe expanded, its populations grew, industrial techniques were refined, transport and trade routes were developed and it was inevitable that the impact of all this would wash up on the shores of the eastern Mediterranean and extend its influence throughout Arabia and Africa. In addition, the economic expansion was accompanied by the growing political, cultural and social interest in what became known as the Orient. As the historian Albert Hourani (1991) points out, 'Behind the merchants and ship-owners of Europe stood the ambassadors and consuls of the great powers, supported in the last resort by the armed might of their governments' (p. 268). The great powers engaged in eager competition for the markets of the Middle East, and throughout the century the British, Russians, Germans, French and Italians struggled with each other to gain an influence over the Ottoman provinces and their governors. In this respect, as Owen (1981) argues, throughout the nineteenth century, 'the major force or group of forces behind the restructuring of Middle Eastern economic life can be shown to have come from Europe and from the world economy' (p. 292). While local or internally driven reforms undertaken by the Ottoman or Egyptian rulers played their part in the great economic transformation of the century, the European imprint had been rapidly established and its effects would reverberate over the whole region.

The vanguard nature of the capitalist adventure in the Middle East should not be forgotten, as it predates the more formal intervention of European governments in the region. European businessmen, investors and merchants had already established strong economic ties with the region by the middle of the nineteenth century. Their ambition was to turn the markets of the East towards the West, create levels of dependency, establish a local bourgeoisie ready to support the capitalist venture at home and encourage the religious and political rulers of the Ottoman Empire to opt into western-based capital markets. The financial adventure in the region paid off in a number of ways, the most important of which was the increasing dependency of the Arab and Turkish markets on Europe. As Ayubi (1995) remarks, 'The ever-increasing need not only for European expertise but also for

European trade and finance eventually led to serious financial and economic difficulties everywhere as well as Ottoman and Egyptian bankruptcy, while Egypt's indebtedness actually brought British occupation to the country' (p. 87). Thus, when Gladstone ordered British troops into Egypt in 1882 he did so to preserve British imperial strategic, economic and financial interests against French competition and Egyptian nationalism, rather than, as was claimed at the time, promote political independence for the Egyptian people. It would take some seventy years before the so-called temporary occupation could be ended and, perhaps more importantly, Britain's financial hold on the country released. Arab independence would never again be a purely political issue. British colonial policy was designed to encourage economic development in Egypt and the generation of wealth that Europeans, not the native Egyptians, would enjoy. The economic and political system was developed in support of this function. The Suez Canal, for example, was an excellent source of income for the Europeans, as Issawi (1982) points out: 'By 1881 Britain accounted for over 80 per cent of canal traffic and nearly two-thirds of its trade east of Suez passed through the canal, as did half of India's total trade . . . Moreover, as a holder of 44 per cent of the canal stock after purchase, the British government drew a substantial income' (p. 51).

In North Africa the French succeeded in extending their political and economic power over Algeria in particular; by the 1830s they had established themselves in the country and were busy promoting themselves through local leaders such as Abd al-Khadar. By the 1840s the French occupation of Algeria was complete and a policy of settling a community of French rulers and bureaucrats in the country was officially adopted. Throughout the 1870s and 1880s thousands of French settlers arrived in Algeria to colonize land given to them for free by the French state. The end of the century saw the European population of the country rise to 578,000, with settlers living in European style, planning cities and spreading throughout the rural areas in large landholdings. The colonization of the country would last for more than a century and would remain unchallenged until the late 1940s. France was also influential in Morocco, competing with the Spanish for power, and in Tunisia, which became a French protectorate in 1881, although the colonization policy did not succeed to the extent it had done in Algeria, as Lustick (1993) points out: 'As early as 1848, Algeria was officially declared an integral part of France. In 1871 Algeria was divided into metropolitan-style departments, shifting primary administrative control of the territory from the Ministry of Colonial Affairs to the Ministry of the Interior' (p. 81). In addition, Algeria's rulers were not drawn from the indigenous Muslim population but from the French settler community.

In other North African countries during this period it was the British and French competition over Egypt which was most significant. French interests were evident with Napoleon's conquest of the country in the 1870s and the Suez Canal project; however, it was Britain which succeeded in occupying the country in 1882 when it was on the brink of bankruptcy. Of course, Britain was not acting altruistically but occupied Egypt to secure the Suez Canal as a passage to India, a strategic defence to the East, a market for British exports and a ready supply of cotton for the Lancashire mills.

The rest of the region was subject to various attempts at incursion and foreign domination by the Russians, Spanish, Germans, French, British and Italians. To a greater or lesser degree the rulers of the Ottoman Empire were unable to resist the foreign encroachment and were increasingly compelled to relinquish economic and strategic rights in paper agreements with the governments of Russia, France and Britain. By the end of the nineteenth century the imperial forces of Europe were dominating the region, while the leaders of the Ottoman Empire were perceived as nothing more than 'paper tigers', struggling against the European tide. Europe was in the region and the region was subsequently defined by Europe, as Edward Said (1978) remarks: 'For despite their differences, the British and French saw the Orient as a geographical and cultural, political, demographic, socio-logical and historical entity over whose destiny they believed them-selves to have traditional entitlement' (p. 221).

The merchants and, subsequently, the governments who engaged in this great escapade were supported morally and religiously in their 'traditional entitlement' by a growing corps of missionaries, artists, writers, gentlemen and lady travellers who began to venture into the region to (re-)discover its people, its archaeological riches and opulent culture. As empire expanded, so too did orientalism as a legitimating ideology of oppression of the native people of the region. Missionary societies were active in the area from the early nineteenth century, with Protestant, Catholic, Anglican, Quaker, American Protestant, Presbyterian and others establishing missions throughout the region with the express purpose of converting the Muslims and Jews to Christianity. The priests of the West were zealous in their efforts to convert the barbarians of the East and were largely insensitive to the traditions of Islam as a faith and system of government. Many believed that the colonial task could only be achieved if Christianity was resurrected, the humiliations of the Crusader kingdoms forgotten and the biblical obligation fulfilled. This obligation manifested itself in a variety of ways and would result in the revival of evangelical activity, missions, schools, libraries, charities, churches, religious colonies in cities such as Jerusalem, Damascus, Beirut and Cairo, and growing support for the notion of the restoration of Zion as a homeland for the Jewish people. In the Ottoman province of Syria, which at that time included Beirut and Damascus, French religious orders were responsible for establishing hundreds of schools to educate thousands of local students. In Damascus, for example, an Irish Presbyterian school was established as early as the 1860s as part of an ongoing mission programme, which, in the words of its founding minister, would mean that everyone 'will know where to find a Bible, a Protestant minister and Christian worship'.

Writers, artists, travellers, poets, archaeologists and surveyors flocked to the region. By the late 1870s tour companies offered pilgrim trips to the Holy Land. Consulates and diplomatic missions were established, land was purchased and European society flourished in the cities of the Orient. Travellers returned and recorded their impressions in print, in poetry or on canvas, thereby feeding the image that the Middle East was a divine gift with a supine population of lazy natives grateful for Europe's role in their countries. William Blake, Robert Browning, David Roberts, George Eliot, Walter Scott and Byron, along with many others, produced a body of literature, poetry and art which became the reality of the Orient. The contribution of these figures would help shape and support the dominant relationship based on the philosophy of colonial expansion in the Middle East that would endure well into the second half of the twentieth century.

By the end of the nineteenth century, British and French primacy in the Middle East seemed assured. Local elites supported the role of foreign forces in their countries, colonial and imperial development policies continued apace and the notion of empire reached its apex. The social fabric of the region had been constantly refashioned or manipulated to suit, in part, western rather than indigenous political or economic agendas, a trend that continued apace and was evident in the politics, literature, art, political thought, dress, social pastimes and culture of the region. Westernization also meant secularization, and the impact of these forces was most obviously apparent in the urban elites of cities such as Algiers, Tunis, Beirut, Cairo and Damascus, where a receptive audience to the ideas of the West was found. The indigenous bonds of identity in the region, whether based on tribe, ethnic loyalty, religion or other factors, were slowly eroded or re-articulated within a western framework. This transformation of society would have class-based features; indeed, the process created new classes, social groupings and touched the lives of some groups far more deeply than others. In this way the colonial encounter brought benefit and privilege for the peoples of the region, but, as Issawi (1982) reminds us, 'per capita incomes . . . [had] . . . certainly risen; however, since a large part of the increment was absorbed by the privileged sections of society – foreigners, minorities, wealthy Muslims, army and bureaucrats – this does not necessarily imply that the levels of living of the mass rose correspondingly' (p. 103). New forms of identity, in particular the rise of nationalist aspirations, were also a response to the colonial domination of the region and the increasing sense of powerlessness and loss of authority within the Ottoman Empire as it stood on the brink of its final decade.

World War I and the death of the Ottoman Empire

The Ottoman Empire survived for over 400 years but ultimately it was unable to withstand the impact of Europe bolstered by the Industrial Revolution and post-Enlightenment thinking. Little by little the Ottoman rulers of Constantinople first lost control over their eastern European provinces, then over Algeria and Egypt (to France and Britain). In 1908, in the heart of the Empire, the Young Turks took political control and openly promoted a secular Turkish nationalism (Kedourie, 1992, pp. 72–4). By 1911 Italy had succeeded in occupying Tripoli and Benghazi in what is present-day Libya. Ottomanism, as government, culture, politics and religious rule, was dying, and a mad scramble took place within the Middle East to establish an alternative. There was no shortage of alternatives: Arab, pan-Arab, pan-Islamic, Wahabi, Turkish and Kurdish responses began to emanate from the region, many in reaction or response to the cultural impact of colonialism. With the exception of Turkey, no indigenous nationalist movement was able to succeed against European competition for power in the region. The European defeat of the Ottomans, who had sided with Germany in the First World War, assured Britain and France the prize of the Middle East. Since the war had been waged in the Middle East as much as in Europe, the European powers found themselves again in the position of enemies, forming strategic alliances between themselves but at the same time pursuing single-mindedly national rather than allied interests. Thus, while Britain and France were allied against the Germans and their Ottoman supporters, they also competed against each other for territorial control of as much land in the Middle East as possible. Behind closed doors Britain and France operated in an atmosphere of mutual suspicion, conspiracy, competition and control, while maintaining a public face of alliance and benign patronage towards the incipient nationalist movements and their leaders.

Militarily, British successes on the battlefields of the Middle East assumed greater strategic as well as symbolic importance than French victories. In November 1917 the British General Allenby marched into the city of Jerusalem to accept the Turkish surrender, a victory that was important symbolically, as well as important to the morale of the British war effort. Strategic and political interests, however, were better served by British success in securing the port of Haifa, and towns like Nazareth and Nablus. The Europeans, however, did not fight the war in the Middle East alone. Through a web of intrigue and double diplomacy the Arabs and the Zionists were brought in to support the Allied effort. In particular, the Hashemites of Mecca and Hijaz, led by Sharif Hussein, fell under British influence. By 1916 the British had succeeded in persuading Sharif Hussein to raise an Arab army to lead a revolt against their Ottoman rulers. The British, in return for Arab support, had promised that Arab independence would be supported, a promise that was made official in the so-called McMahon–Hussein Correspondence. Yet, the interpretation of so-called promises made in the correspondence was later questioned: 'Whether anything was actually promised, and if so what, and whether the Sharif's revolt played a significant part in the allied victory, are matters in dispute, but what is clear is that for the first time the claim that those who spoke Arabic constituted a nation and should have a state had been to some extent accepted by a great power', remarks Hourani (1991, p. 317). The Arab Revolt of 1916 which resulted in the capture of Damascus also involved the legendary Lawrence of Arabia on the Hashemite side. Believed to be pro-Arab, but ultimately constrained by British national interest, T. E. Lawrence and his Arab colleague Prince Faisal, son of Sharif Hussein, would play an important part in the post-war settlement of the Middle East at the Paris and San Remo peace conferences.

Following the war, Britain and France engaged in an embarrassing squabble for territory in the Middle East. At the Paris and San Remo peace conferences Arab and Wilsonian-inspired hopes for a new world order, where the Arabs' right to self-determination would be honoured, were dashed on the altar of British and French ambition. Secret agreements and double promises made during the desperate times of war were now made public, as the new generation of Arab leaders, who had led the Arab Revolt along with T. E. Lawrence as part of the war effort, realized they had been cruelly deceived by the Europeans. Little regard was paid to promises made in the now infamous McMahon–Hussein Correspondence. Sharif Hussein and three of his sons, Princes Abdullah, Faisal and Ali, were thwarted by the British and the French at the international conferences as they tried to achieve the goal of full independence. Instead, they were appointed as the puppet heads of new nation-states – Iraq, Syria and Transjordan – which were placed under the mandate and control of either Britain or France. Arab independence in these states would not be immediately forthcoming and a further world war would be waged before *de jure* or *de facto* independence was achieved.

The Sykes–Picot Agreement of 1916, in which Britain, France and Russia agreed to partition the Middle East between them, and the Balfour Declaration of 1917, in which the British government gave its tacit support for the establishment of a Jewish homeland in Palestine, did little to bolster Arab confidence in the promises of independence which they believed the allied powers had held out to them during the war. Thus, Britain and France engaged in a 'disgusting scramble for the Middle East', described by Elizabeth Monroe as, 'pieces of unabashed self-interest, suggesting to onlookers that all talk of liberating small nations from oppression was so much cant' (1963, p. 66).

It was not only that Arab hopes of independence were betrayed, but the European powers also succeeded in redrawing the boundaries of the region, creating new nation-states, imposing rulers and monarchs in new states and capitals principally to act as local agents for Britain and France. Before 1918 the inhabitants of the Middle East, the majority of whom were Muslim, had lived as subjects of the Ottoman powers of Constantinople, and the borders and boundaries of the region had encompassed provinces in which peoples of various ethnic and religious backgrounds co-existed in relative harmony. The new map that emerged resulted in the artificial creation of new states to which its citizens felt little or no sense of loyalty or identity and in which European political control appeared assured. As Bromley (1994) notes, 'Britain thus came to favour the dismemberment of the Ottoman empire and the independence of the Arab provinces. Of course, by this British officials meant "independence" from Ottoman suzerainty; since the Arabs were unfit for self-government' (p. 74). Appearances, however, could be deceptive. Europe's role and impact on state-formation in the modern Middle East was as much about perception as reality, something that is currently reflected in the ongoing academic controversy over the extent to which colonialism promoted state-formation in the region and the extent to which the western- or European-inspired model was rooted in the region. Both Zubaida and Owen note that while modern states in the Middle East are born out of the western model, they are 'for the most part . . . not modern Western states' (Zubaida, 1993, p. 145). Indeed, the rootedness of the western model may be challenged from this perspective as it would appear that the success or otherwise of the 'compulsory form of the western model' depends very much on the inclusion of the indigenous political field's pre-existing political institutions, religious influences and socio-economic order. This approach contrasts starkly with the claims of authors like Brown, who believe that the politics and state-formation of the region have not just been 'shaped by intrusive western influences in modern times', but rather that 'the Middle East has become so continuously interlocked politically with the West as to have become almost an appendage of the western power system' (1984, p. 5). Bromley sums up the debate in his criticism of Brown and Fromkin's thesis in which they argue that the Middle East is inherently hostile to the nation-state system, when he declares that after the European dismemberment of the Ottoman Empire the 'politics of tribe, Islam and Arabism were all shaped by this context [the modern nation-state], rather than constituting impregnable barriers to modernity' (1994, p. 84).

1918 and after: mandates, protectorates and continued colonization

Between 1918 and 1922, when the French and British were awarded their protectorates and mandates and maintained their colonies, the indigenous populations of the Middle East struggled to assert their national rights, their identity and desire for independence. All of them – Kurds, Armenians and Arabs – failed, as the Europeans met behind closed doors in Paris and San Remo to decide the fate of the region. The end product, the new Middle East, was almost unrecognizable from the old empire where Ottoman rule was Muslim and land was not occupied and settled by strangers from Europe. The region, before and after, highlights the startling changes that the Europeans had wrought in the area. Under the Ottoman Empire the Arabs had co-existed with their ethnic and religious neighbours without boldly demarcated borders. Under the new order entirely new political entities were created, including new states, and protectorates, mandates and colonies, such as in Algeria, were established and maintained. Straight lines, which took no account of the natural demographic, ethnic, linguistic and religious make-up of a territory, were scored across the map of the Middle East by civil servants sitting in offices in London and Paris.

By 1922 the new Middle East was emerging. New states were created, by the British and the French, in Transjordan (which later became the Hashemite Kingdom of Jordan), Syria, Lebanon and Iraq, regardless of the multitudinous ethnic make-up of the territories. In Lebanon alone six distinct communities – Maronite Christians, Druze, Sunni Muslim, Shi'a Muslim, Armenians and Greek-Orthodox Christians – were now under one territorial entity which France governed as a mandated territory. Syria also became a French-mandated territory, and Prince Faisal, the son of Sharif Hussein the Hashemite leader of Mecca who had occupied Syria during the First World War as part of the Arab Revolt, was forced by the French to flee his new capital only to sit later on the throne of the new state of Iraq when it was created by the British in 1920 and awarded mandate status.

As in other parts of the Third World, rule by the West and from the West took a variety of forms and resulted in a range of state types emerging in the region as a result of the colonial legacy. Foreign political authority over the region varied from direct control to limited control with autonomy for specially selected elites or local agents, including an increasing dependency on the military not just for state coercion but for stability in the modernization process.

It is worth making a distinction, at this point, between the three types of political control undertaken by the British and French in the inter-war period – mandates, protectorates and colonies all imply different types of political rule and expectations. Mandates were a creation of the ill-fated League of Nations. This utopian body permitted its member states to take administrative control of other territory on the condition that it was formerly governed by a defeated, or 'backward', enemy. Article 22 of the League's Covenant provided for the mandates system in the Middle East and parts of Africa on those countries that were judged 'incapable yet of national independence', and placed them under the tutelage of a member state perceived as an 'advanced nation'. Mandated territory was divided into three categories, A, B and C, with the former Ottoman Empire falling into category A, which included countries described as having reached a 'stage of development where their existence as independent nations can be provisionally recognized subject to the rendering of administrative advice and assistance by a Mandatory until such time as they are able to stand alone' (Walters, 1952, p. 57). Article 22 also stated that the wishes of the communities in such mandated territories should be a 'principal consideration in the selection of the Mandatory', although in practice there was little evidence of this stricture being adhered to. The territories classed as category A were: the Lebanon and Syria, under the mandate of France; Iraq, Palestine and Transjordan, under the mandate of Britain.

Protectorates were territory governed but not formally annexed by a stronger state. However, as the example of Egypt highlights, the declaration of a protectorate by Britain in December 1914 was perceived by the rest of the world as a 'precedent for other expansionist bookings-in-advance' of British interests in the rest of the Middle East (Monroe, 1963, p. 26). As a British protectorate, the fate of Egypt was no less and no more closely entwined with this particular colonial power than if it had been declared a colony – appearance was the only motive behind this declaration by the British government.

Finally, colonies were semi-independent settlements of emigrants and their descendants, usually in relatively undeveloped areas distant from the homeland. The French colonization of Algeria illustrates this particular European strategy in the Middle East. From as early as 1848, Lustick (1993) argues, the French 'officially declared' Algeria 'an integral part of France', treating it as nothing more than another *département* of the country geographically removed from the European frontier (p. 81). Throughout the nineteenth century the French encountered local resistance in Algeria and defeated it through military encounter and the policy of official colonization adopted by Napoleon III, which encouraged French settlement of land. Whether it is true, as Ageron (1991) suggests, that 'Muslim society did not resist the progress of colonization; with its framework broken, it collapsed' (p. 65), has been open to debate as the relative success of local resistance to European intervention in the Middle East in the nineteenth and early twentieth century is reassessed by historians currently producing work based on archival research within the region rather than outside it.

Inter-war European decline

The inter-war period in the Middle East was dominated by the attempts by the European powers to establish their authority over almost the entire area. The task they faced was impossible more or less from the start. They faced a region-wide movement of political discontent based on the notion of the right to self-determination, a massive social and economic upheaval triggered by the modernization and development process and growing anti-European feeling that reached fever pitch by the late 1940s. The entire era was characterized by conflict, rather than stability. Even countries where Britain and France enjoyed a relatively stable colonial past, such as Egypt or Algeria, were caught up in the region-wide struggle amongst the postwar forces of colonialism, with their naked ambition, fresh and made startlingly apparent in the Paris and San Remo conferences, and in the bitter struggle of the Arabs who had been betrayed by their European partners.

Nevertheless, the British and the French went some considerable way towards shaping and moulding the political features of the new nation-states and existing protectorates and colonies. Very few escaped the impact of the Europeanization of politics, economy, culture and society in the region. As Mitchell (1988) highlights in the example of Egypt, the power of colonialism was itself a power that sought to colonize: to penetrate locally, spreading and establishing settlements not only in the shape of cities and barracks, but in the form of classrooms, journals and works of scholarship. Colonialism – and modern politics generally – distinguished itself in this colonizing power. It was able at the most local level to reproduce theatres of its order and truth. (p. 171)

The degree to which the colonizing project succeeded in the twentieth century, however, was soon affected by factors such as local resistance, economic issues, global political patterns and the degree to which the traditional state system was altered or reshaped by western forms and institutions of government. In the new states, such as Transjordan and Iraq, the British set about imposing a system of government and politics which attempted the maintenance of British control rather than helping new states towards independence. The rulers of Transjordan and Iraq, Hashemite brothers Princes Abdullah and Faisal, were generally treated with mistrust, suspicion and, ultimately, as puppets of British policy. Any attempt by either of these men to assert their independence from their British overlords resulted in difficulties. In both countries the British maintained power and influence not only by controlling the purse strings of these infant states and sending out advisers to 'guide' the Princes, but also through policies of establishing and maintaining internal security structures, controlling foreign affairs and granting incremental privileges and powers to the Arab rulers only when it suited their interests.

For the British, the inherent weakness of such policies was never acknowledged until it was too late. By promoting puppet rulers, imposing an artificial leadership on people, creating subjects in a new state, establishing new boundaries under a new flag, oath of allegiance and anthem, the British were sowing the seeds for conflict and internal instability. Underneath their benign attitude towards the Arabs, British finance, often of extremely limited means, was forwarded to pay for the new Arab armies and police of these young states. The intentions of the Hashemite rulers of these political entities were honourable: they dreamt of uniting the Arab people under the same banner that had been raised during the successful Arab Revolt. They saw themselves as leaders of the Arab nation, united by the Muslim faith and common language – Arabic. In reality, the situation could not have been further from the truth, as the Hashemites were compelled to adopt a British-inspired agenda for rule and hegemony over the region. In addition, the most common indicators of identity among the Arab people – the tribe and clan – were identified by the new state bureaucrats as the biggest obstacles to national unity under new rulers and new flags. Tribal sheikhs were often perceived as a significant hindrance to the difficult task of state-building in the new states of Arabia (Bagot-Glubb, 1948).

Sunset empire

Despite the Allied victory during World War II, the balance of external, European power began to change in the post-war period. Although Britain emerged triumphant in the Middle East, with the French marginalized and weak, policy-makers in London, while continuing to give the impression they were strong players in the region, quickly realized that the war-induced indebtedness and the rise of nationalism at a global level would hinder the pursuance of their interests in the region. From 1945 onwards Britain descended a slippery slope in the Middle East, one that would lead them to relinquish their mandate in Palestine, weaken their grip on Transjordan and abandon Iraq to the forces of Arab nationalism. In Egypt British-sanctioned independence quickly led to revolution and the Suez Crisis of 1956 (Kyle, 1991). Only in the Gulf would British influence, of sorts, endure for several more decades, but in the rest of the Middle East British prestige went into surprisingly rapid decline. New forces challenged both British and French hegemony over large parts of the region, and changes in the global balance of power in the post-war era affected the regional alliances and relationships that grew in the Middle East.

The path of disengagement which took place during this period can be easily traced (see table 1.1). It is not easy to identify a pattern – breaking away from British, French or Italian tutelage manifested itself in a variety of ways. Through *coups*, deposed monarchies, wars of independence, peaceful transition and the ending of protectorate relationships, the leaders of the region-wide movements for independence brought about a change of rule. The internal dimensions of change within the region were, of course, also reflected in other parts of the globe, where the process of independence and decolonization dominated the agenda of the Third World. A characteristic which may be identified in the process in the Middle East is the reluctance with which Britain and France relinquished their hold in the region and their failure to anticipate the change in the political environment and, as a result, their ineptitude at smoothing the path of political transition while protecting their own interests. This is all the more ironic given the fact that the original idea, at least in theory, behind the mandate system was that the colonizers would 'assist' the mandated states to independence. In reality, their presence, politically and militarily, in the states of the region hindered the smooth transition to independence. In addition, with Britain and France no longer in the frame, other external powers stepped into the region with the express desire of building spheres of influence, alliances and continued rivalry. Thus, where once France and Britain competed for power and

Table 1.1	European disengagement from the Middle East, 1945–71
Date	*Event*
1946	Transjordan granted independence, becoming the Hashemite Kingdom of Jordan
1943–6	French mandates come to an end in Lebanon and Syria
1947	UN agrees to partition of Palestine
1948	Israel granted independence
1951	Libya granted independence, after the UN rejects British and French petitions of 'trusteeship'
1952	Military *coup* in Egypt, led by Gamal Abdel Nasser, deposing King Farouk
1953	Egypt declares independence
1956	Egypt nationalizes the Suez Canal
1956	Morocco declares independence
1956	Tunisia declares independence
1957	Formal British–Jordanian Treaty terminated by Jordan, British forces removed from the country
1958	Military *coup* in Iraq: monarchy overthrown and independence established
1961	Kuwait declares independence
1962	Yemen Arab Republic declares independence
1962	Algeria declares independence
1967	People's Democratic Republic of Yemen declares independence
1971	Bahrain, Qatar, United Arab Emirates declare independence

influence in, for example, Egypt, as a means of securing strategic as well as economic interests, there now stood the new superpowers: the USA and USSR.

Independence subsequently came to mean many things to many people in the Middle East. The nature of the state system, for instance, was not always reconfigured at a local level, nor was there always a complete rejection of the colonial model of government. Indeed, in some cases new, local, western-educated elites from the military, bureaucracy or urban upper classes merely represented the colonial model as being somehow indigenous, while at the same time declaring their independence and rejection of 'all things western' on the international stage. Political independence in Iran, for example, did not necessarily mean economic independence, as the increasingly oil-based economy of the country remained under western control. The control of the sale of oil and its exploration in Iran became a foreign affair involving first the British and then the Americans. State-formation, therefore, was as much the interest of foreign capital as the local ruling elite. As Halliday (1979) asserts, 'Iran is a country whose recent development has been to a considerable degree shaped by the international ties it has had with the more advanced capitalist economies' (p. 21).

From 1945 to the early 1950s the movement towards Arab, Iranian and other forms of independence gained momentum, as more and more nationalist groups and young radical leaders emerged in countries such as Algeria, Egypt, Iran, Iraq, Palestine, Jordan, Syria, Lebanon and Libya. While the British position in the region following the war may have appeared 'unshaken and in some ways strengthened', less than a decade later this hold appeared increasingly untenable. In this respect, the same was true of France, which was weakened by the war and which found it increasingly difficult to re-establish the control over its colony, protectorates and mandated territory that it had enjoyed before the war. It is asserted that there was a change in British policy towards the Middle East during this post-war period, where there was support for 'Arab independence and a greater degree of unity, while preserving essential strategic interests by friendly agreement', but British strategic and national interests were always placed above Arab calls for independence (Hourani, 1991, p. 357). While the British may have believed that the Arabs would wait patiently for independence, they failed to recognize the signs of growing impatience in Jerusalem, Cairo, Baghdad and Amman.

The impact of Europe through colonial rule, protectorates, mandates, treaties of co-operation, business, religion and cultural ties is varied and complex. Nevertheless, the example of the Middle East does reveal a uniform pattern of colonialism which was also found in Africa and other regions that fell under European colonial rule. Economic and strategic motives were usually the prime motives in Europe's relationship with the Middle East at the end of the nineteenth century and the first five decades of the twentieth century. Europe sought to exploit the Middle East through economy, strategic position and religious symbolism. As such, Europe and the Orient engaged in a relationship of antagonism where one side was perceived as permanently strong, the other permanently weak. The relationship between faiths was also emphasized in the Middle East, between the Christian West and the Muslim East. Yet the degree to which religious character or culture really defined relations between these two regions has been grossly overemphasized and utilized consistently to create a perception of difference rather than a recognition of similarity.

The defeat of the Ottoman Empire and the European scrabble for control of the region meant that the politics of government and state in the Middle East were radically altered. The evolving indigenous social, economic and political cultures of the region were accorded little recognition in the grand plans of government outlined by the West. European policy-makers replaced old boundaries (seamless and ethnically and religiously continuous) with new nation-states, new flags, new capitals and new kings and rulers over new citizens. Institutions of state and government, which had previously evolved under five centuries of Islamic rule, were now replaced with modern European forms of government based on principles of freedom and democracy, but also on the practice of colonial and imperial rule which kept the native Arab population under foreign and European control.

Independence from European rule was rarely achieved without conflict, and this legacy would mar British–Arab and French–Arab relations for decades. In addition, the roots of much of the instability of the present-day Middle East can be found in the colonial era. Colonial rule, and by extension western intervention, is still experienced in one form or another in the present; the culture, economy and politics of the region are inextricably infused with western values, norms and standards and this in turn has played its part in creating the sense of crisis and instability which characterizes the region. It is ironic that European states such as France rail against the American assault on their culture, literature, language and mass media, while at the same time ignoring the far greater assault mounted by the colonial European powers, the French included, on the Middle East, which has led to a cultural (not national) crisis of identity which has beset the region for many decades.

The debate about the impact of colonial rule in the Middle East is still ongoing. Some analysts believe that the nature of the relationship between colonizers and colonized can best be explained by looking at economic issues, while others focus on the social structures to inform this debate. But political, social and economic issues, as well as cultural and other effects of colonialism, have all influenced the overall experience. While some believe a uniform picture can be drawn about the degrees of influence the process has had on country-specific economies, political systems and society, others concentrate on the uneven patterns of development and modernization which have emerged from the Middle East in the wake of the colonial legacy. What remains consistent, however, is the way in which, through the colonial relationship, the nature of the links between the Middle East and the West has been irrevocably altered, creating new patterns of conflict and co-operation.

Case study Egypt

Although at the beginning of the twentieth century the Middle East was still under Ottoman rule, in Egypt a European foothold in the country had been established as early as 1798, when French forces led by Napoleon occupied the country. The first decades of the nineteenth century heralded great change in Egypt, encouraged by its Arab ruler Mohammed Ali and his successors. The Egyptian economy was oriented to the European market, and cotton production, in particular, became a prime export. The building of railways and other transport routes such as the Suez Canal, which was opened in 1869, led Egypt into an increasing state of indebtedness, with large sums of money borrowed from European governments and private finance. Indebtedness and the prospects of political instability prompted the British to move against the Egyptians in 1882 to restore order, at which point the military occupation began. From 1882 to 1956 British influence and control over Egypt would dictate the development of the country.

The British occupation of Egypt was supposed to be short-lived, designed to quell a local nationalist-inspired rebellion against Mohammed Ali's successor Khedive Ismail. Yet it became rapidly apparent that the 'rebellion' was a pretext by which Britain could assert itself over the most important country in the region. For the next seven decades real power and control over the affairs of the Egyptian state rested in British hands. This in turn gave Britain economic, strategic and political control over the Suez Canal, which had been described in Whitehall as the 'Gateway to India'. From 1882 to 1914, during the first phase of British rule over Egyptian political life, control of the state and its institutions and the economy remained a largely British affair, with nominal and symbolic power placed in the hands of the Khedive and later the King (Fuad 1922–36 and Farouk 1936–52). Britain certainly preferred to promote monarchy rather than republicanism in the country and the region as a whole. This was because, as Owen (2003) points out, a 'king constrained by a constitution was seen as a vital support for the British position, since he provided an important element of continuity and could always be used to dismiss any popularly elected government of nationalists that threatened to tear up or amend the arrangements defining Britain's rights' (p. 21).

The development of the country was geared to economic exploitation, and to this end certain developments in Egypt's infrastructure were initiated by Britain. In particular, the cotton industry, which ultimately represented Egypt's entire foreign trade, led to the establishment of an agriculturally based and capital-driven infrastructure. Such developments included large-scale irrigation works (which profoundly affected Egypt's social structure), roads, railways and a trading system which sent basic food prices up and created new levels of poverty for ordinary Egyptians – the peasants (*fellahin*) involved in growing and cropping cotton for export. Wealth derived from the production of cotton and its export was largely enjoyed by the Europeans and a small class of Egyptian landowners. In 1821 the export of Egyptian cotton was just 1,000 quantars; in 1823 this rose to 259,000 and by the 1880s 2.5 million quantars of cotton were being exported from Egypt for the cotton mills of Lancashire and beyond. By 1910–14 cotton accounted for over 90 per cent of Egypt's exports and the growth of other crops, such as wheat, went into decline, as more and more acreage around the fertile Nile river was given over to the production of cotton. Colonial control over Egypt did bring some benefits to the Arab population, but these benefits were never distributed evenly and the British deliberately pursued a policy of divide and rule. Some classes or groups of Egyptians were always more privileged than others even in the distribution of benefits such as improved transportation, health care and education. But at the bottom of the social and economic pile lay Egypt's largest social group or class, the Sunni Muslim rural peasant population who toiled the land generating the profit that Britain enjoyed.

World War I added a new dimension to colonial politics in the Middle East, and in Britain the strategic importance of the Suez Canal was quickly recognized. In an attempt to further shore up its interests, Britain declared Egypt a 'protectorate' in December 1914. As such, Egypt was placed under the tighter grip of British rule, which was augmented by a large and powerful military and security system.

Opposition among Egyptians to the British grew and intensified during the war, and by 1918 an emerging nationalist movement had developed. It was encouraged by regional successes of the Arab nationalist movement during the war and its goal was to put an end to British occupation, and to establish self-determination and independence for Egypt. This desire was apparent in the formation of a new political movement or party known as the Wafd, under the leadership of Saad Zaghlul and Nahas Pasha. The British, however, were implacably opposed to Egyptian calls for independence, a reaction that served only to deepen Egyptian opposition and hostility. From 1918 to 1922 Egyptian pressure on the British for greater political freedom grew, and in February 1922 the British terminated the protectorate and declared the country a 'constitutional monarchy'. In theory, the Egyptians may well have been free, but in practice the new political order was a façade for the maintenance of British control.

While a constitution was written and promulgated in 1923, a parliament elected, a government formed and King Fuad declared head of state, Egyptians, despite many differences, remained united around one issue – that Britain should relinquish its political and military control over their country. But instead Britain persuaded the King to dissolve unpopular (for the British) government, and maintained its political and military presence over the country. Negotiations between the two sides took place sporadically and resulted in the 1936 Anglo-Egyptian Treaty which further shored up British interests.

During the Second World War, Egypt served as an important base for Britain, and military rule prevailed once more. When the war ended nationalist and Islamic groups agitated for independence. For the next five years Egyptian pressure for independence grew in all quarters of society and political stability was increasingly hard to maintain, despite the coercive powers of the British-controlled state and a malleable monarchy. The British found it increasingly difficult to resist the tide of change and pressure for independence which by this stage had gripped the rest of the Third World. In 1950 they eventually agreed to enter into negotiations with Egyptian nationalists. A deadlock in the talks by 1951 led the nationalists to abrogate unilaterally the Anglo-Egyptian Treaty. Widespread violence and attacks soon broke out against the British and by January 1952 martial law was declared over the entire country. In July 1952 Egyptian nationalist officers mounted a *coup d'état*, King Farouk abdicated, the 1923 constitution was abolished and political parties were dissolved and banned. The Free Officers, led by Gamal Abdel Nasser, had finally succeeded in ousting the British. The new military government quickly sought a settlement with Britain to withdraw its forces and in October 1954 an agreement was signed between the two declaring the termination of the 1936 Anglo-Egyptian Treaty and withdrawal within twenty months. Nasser's ultimate blow against the British was his announcement in July 1956 of a decision to nationalize the Suez Canal and thus wrest control from British hands. The import of this decision lay not just around the issue of Suez as a strategic waterway, but the ability of leaders in newly independent countries to assert their control over the superpowers. After the Suez Crisis, in which Egypt defeated the combined military might of Britain, France and Israel, colonial rule in the region would never be the same again.

Case study The Palestine débâcle

The prospects for British rule over Palestine were never very good. When Allenby conquered Jerusalem in 1917 and established military rule over the territory, the British government envisaged a new era of enlightened rule in the Holy Land. But what it failed to realize, even from the earliest times, was that it would never be able to reconcile the demands made on it by Zionist Jews keen to hold Britain to the promises implicit in the Balfour Declaration and the demands of the indigenous Palestinian Arab population for self-determination and independence promised to them in the McMahon–Hussein Correspondence. Britain's failure to reconcile these demands and its inability to govern the mandate territory of Palestine left a lasting mark on the region, altering Britain's role in the area to the present day.

Following Allenby's occupation in 1917, the area was placed under military administration (or occupation) until 1920. Palestine was divided into districts and, so far as they were compatible with the military nature of the occupation, Ottoman codes of law were applied. From 1920 onwards the British, in receipt of their League of Nations mandate, governed the country under civil administration. The indigenous inhabitants of the country, the Palestinian Arabs and Jews and the newly established Zionist Jewish community, were given no political powers by the British. A curious aspect of the mandate was the extent to which it safeguarded the interests of the Zionists, obliging Britain to 'be responsible for placing the country under such political, administrative and economic conditions as will secure the establishment of a Jewish national home', while Palestinian Arab political rights to self-determination went completely unacknowledged.

The inability of the British authorities to address the dual issue of Zionist and Palestinian nationalist aspirations over the same piece of territory ensured that the period of the mandate (1920–48) was characterized by continual conflict, revolt and political upheaval. In many respects Zionist and Palestinian Arab aspirations were the same, and the British allowed both sides to believe, at one time or another, or to a greater or lesser degree, that their dreams for self-determination and statehood would be fulfilled. Britain had promised support to both the Zionist and the Palestinian Arabs during the war and in the post-war era both sides expected Britain to maintain its side of the bargain.

The notion of a return to Zion was always present in the Jewish Diaspora but it was on the heels of the Russian pogroms and a revival of European hostility to Jews and anti-Semitism that a Jewish man named Theodor Herzl formulated a political vision of an ingathering of the exiles to Zion. In 1896 Herzl wrote and published a book entitled *Der Judenstatt* in which he argued that Jewish assimilation in Europe was a pipe dream that would never be fulfilled. He presented an alternative vision of a return to Zion, which at this point consisted of an idea rather than a place. In the years that followed, Herzl's supporters began to propose a number of locations for the new Zion, amongst which Palestine featured. Strictly speaking, however, the Jewish religion forbade a return to the 'Promised Land' until after the Messiah had returned. But Herzl was a secularist; his vision was a political solution to the growing tide of anti-Semitism sweeping Europe in the latter half of the nineteenth century.

In 1897 Herzl held the first Zionist Congress in Basle in Switzerland and his ideas found support among many Jewish intellectuals living in Europe at the time. Support was not universal, however, and many Jews complained that Herzl's endeavour to establish a new homeland undermined the attempts of assimilationist Jews. Herzl needed to find support not only from the Jewish community and for twenty years he and his followers, including the British Jewish figure Chaim Weizmann, peddled their vision round the capitals of Europe desperate for a sponsor. At various points it looked as if first the Ottomans, then the Germans and finally the Russians would support the Zionists; in the end it was the British government that adopted them. Lord Arthur Balfour befriended Weizmann and became a keen supporter of the scheme. In November 1917, in his capacity as Foreign Secretary, Balfour issued a declaration in which he stated that 'his Majesty's government view with favour the establishment in Palestine of a national home for the Jewish people, and will use their best endeavours to facilitate the achievement of this object, it being clearly understood that nothing shall be done which may prejudice the civil and religious rights of existing non-Jewish communities in Palestine, or the rights and political status enjoyed by Jews in any other country.' No one really knows to what extent Balfour intended to keep his promise, or whether the promise was just another wartime expediency in the desperate bid to win support for the British war effort. Nevertheless, the Zionists held the British government to its word and when the war had ended and the peace conferences were held it was the promises to the Arabs that were reneged on, while Britain opened the floodgates of Zionist immigration into Palestine.

Only one obstacle stood in the way of Jewish aspirations: Palestine's Arab population. Yet, from a Zionist perspective, writes Gerner, 'That Palestine had an existing population, with its own history and aspirations, was no more relevant . . . than was Kenyan history to the British or Algerian society to the French' (1994, p. 15). The Arabs, however, believed that they had been promised Palestine in return for their support against the Turks during the war, and they felt betrayed at news of Balfour's declaration in support of the Zionists. The Arabs of Palestine (Muslim and Christian) were not consulted, and their nationalist ambitions went largely unrecognized. Throughout the period of the mandate the British largely supported and allowed for the rapid influx of Jews to Palestine. British attempts at supporting the rights of Palestinian Arabs failed. Plans for a legislative assembly were never fulfilled, land sales to Jews increased and thousands of Arabs were dispossessed.

All promises to the Arabs, including those in the Balfour Declaration and the McMahon–Hussein Correspondence, seemed to evaporate as Britain established the mandate in Palestine. The mandate authorities heralded their era of rule not by establishing power-sharing institutions to prepare the path for Arab independence, but rather by adopting the classic colonial policy of divide and rule between the Jews and the Arabs. By the end of the first decade of rule it was obvious to all concerned that this policy was failing miserably. The security situation had deteriorated rapidly and Zionist immigration was rampant: in 1930 only 4,000 entered the country, yet three years later 30,000 entered in one year alone. The immigrants were also granted special privileges which were denied to the Palestinian Arab community. Land sales increased at a rapid rate, the Palestinian peasant class faced dispossession and the type of general societal upheaval that had not been witnessed in generations of Ottoman rule. Tension between the two societies, with Britain in the middle and reviled by both, increased to a violent level. In 1921, 1922, 1929 and from 1936 to 1939, any notion of public order evaporated. The Palestinians, led by religious figures, the young leaders of notable families who had founded as many as six nationalist-based political parties, staged revolts, strikes and demonstrations in a desperate bid to halt Jewish immigration, land sales and the illegal shipment of arms to the Jews.

The British responded in a typically colonial fashion, ordering one commission of inquiry after another with little meaningful political strategy in between. By 1936 British policy-makers in London were advising that Britain relinquish its mandate on Palestine and that territory be partitioned between the Jews and the Arabs. They also proposed a quota system to be imposed on Jewish immigration into the country in order to slow its flow. These proposals were contained in two documents: the Peel Commission of 1937 and the 1939 White Paper. Both proposals were rejected by the Arabs and Britain was unable to undo the web of deceit it had spun through its false promises made so easily during the war. By the end of the Palestinian Revolt in 1939 the British knew the mandate would never succeed. All they could hope to achieve was the establishment of public order in this strife-torn land, and even this was ultimately an impossible task.

The recommendations of Peel and the 1939 White Paper left no party satisfied. The Palestinian community, weakened by years of revolt, strikes and hardships and the forcible dissolution of its religious and political leadership by the British, were still denied the right to self-determination in a land which they had occupied and lived in for centuries (Gerner, 1994, p. 28). The Zionists were now forced, by the British, to slow the rate of immigration, to 15,000 a year instead of the 60,000 a year peak which had been reached in 1935, at a time when Hitler's rise in Europe had signalled a public and open campaign of anti-Semitism. British policy was characterized by containment, but from 1939 to 1945 the political situation continued to deteriorate at an alarming rate. The Zionists, led by David Ben Gurion, responded by organizing a campaign of political violence against the British. The now infamous Stern Gang, Haganah and Irgun Zvai Leumi were headed by young Zionist immigrants from Europe like Yitzhak Shamir and Menachim Begin, who would both later become Prime Ministers of Israel. The political violence was initially directed against the Palestinians, but the British authorities were soon targeted. Bombings, assassinations and other attacks increasingly characterized the period, as the Zionists attempted to hasten Britain's departure and their own independence.

By the end of World War II the British knew that continued rule in Palestine was no longer tenable. The election of a post-war Labour government struggling to reconstruct a debilitated nation quickly realized that colonial obligations could no longer be met. Palestine, along with Burma and India, was the first to be released. The chief beneficiaries would be the Zionists, and the stability of the region as a whole would subsequently be undermined by decades of conflict. Within Palestine the British authorities were already admitting to themselves that hatred and lawlessness had reached such a pitch that partition seemed the only solution. This decision was hastened by the Irgun's bombing of the King David Hotel in July 1946 which was acting headquarters of the mandatory government.

Britain was also under pressure from the Americans to give further support to Jewish immigration to Palestine (some 100,000 were waiting to be admitted). The response was to order yet another commission of inquiry – this time a British and American body deliberated over the future of Palestine. The commission's conclusions were of little help to anyone, recommending the continuation of the mandate. But by 1947 Britain was in no position to maintain the mandate on anyone's recommendation and it announced its intention to relinquish it and to leave Palestine on 15 May 1948. The fate of Palestine was put into the hands of the newly formed United Nations.

In time-honoured tradition, the UN dealt with the problem by forming a committee of inquiry to investigate the competing claims to self-determination by the Palestinians and the Zionists. In August 1947 this committee recommended the partition of the country into two states, with Jerusalem under international jurisdiction. The proposal was debated and then put to the vote on 29 November 1947, when the General Assembly accepted the partition plan. When the mandate ended the Zionists would be granted independence over 55 per cent of the territory of Palestine (previously, they had only managed to secure 6 per cent through land purchases), and the Palestinians were forced by the UN to relinquish land which they had owned and farmed and lived on for generations. It was not a voluntary, but a forcible partition: the Palestinians would be compelled to relinquish their right to statehood in their coastal cities along with hundreds of small towns, villages and hamlets. Of course they could remain, but only as citizens of the new ethnic democracy, the Jewish state of Israel (Yiftachel, 1993). While the Zionists begrudgingly accepted the partition plan, working on the principle that half a loaf was better than no loaf at all, the Palestinians and their Arab allies refused to recognize it at all.

From November 1947 to May 1948 the conflict between the Palestinians and Zionists deepened. Jew and Arab were literally at each other's throats and the British authorities were impotent in the face of yet another situation where public order could not be enforced through a British military presence. The prelude to independence was bitter and tense. Even before the British had pulled out of the country terrible deeds were perpetrated by one community against the other and vice versa. The Zionists, now with a highly organized, well-equipped and disciplined military force, prepared forcibly to wrest further territory, including Jerusalem, from the Palestinians before the mandate ended. Indeed, recent historiography by writers such as Benny Morris (1988) hint at a Zionist agenda on which ethnic cleansing of the Arab population was considered as a strategy. By April 1948 the battle for Jerusalem had begun and the Zionists inched their way from the coastal plain of Tel Aviv up the mountainous slopes of Jerusalem, capturing, securing and subsequently demolishing Arab villages such as Lydda, Biddu and Deir Yassin. The Zionists faced a constant barrage of attack from the Arabs, including the forces of the Iraqi and Jordanian armies. The Palestinians needed this support – unlike the Zionists, they had not been permitted to arm, they were not trained and were incapable of defending themselves alone. The British were still obliged to maintain internal security and protect the Palestinian inhabitants of the country, but they had given up the ghost a long time back. The events at Deir Yassin were a focal point in the conflict: when the Irgun arrived in the village, they massacred more than 200 Palestinians, mostly women and children. The impact of this event and the widespread feeling of fear that permeated the Palestinian community of the day led to an exodus, and Palestinians either voluntarily or forcibly fled their homes, fearing for their lives. Whether the exodus was voluntary or forcible, the result of Zionist massacre or Arab urging, has been subjected to academic and national debate in Israel and the Arab world ever since, with each side blaming the other for the parlous state of affairs that befell the Palestinians. However, what really mattered was the fact that when the war of 1948 was over, Israel prevented those Palestinian refugees from returning to their homes, lands, farms, shops, schools, churches, mosques and the graves of their forefathers. The Right of Return was extended by the state of Israel to all Jews, but not to those Palestinians who had fled or been expelled from their homes in 1948.

The British terminated their mandate in Palestine on 15 May 1948. On the same day the Zionists declared the independence of the new state of Israel and war broke out in earnest between the new state and its Arab neighbours. By the end of the war in 1949 (see chapter 3), Israel had secured more territory for itself and increased the size of the new state, and hundreds of thousands of Palestinians were refugees in the Egyptian-controlled Gaza Strip, Jordanian-annexed East Jerusalem and the West Bank, Jordan proper, Syria, Egypt, Lebanon and other states in the Middle East. As one diaspora ended with the establishment and independence of a Jewish state in Palestine, so another began for the Palestinian people. The refugee issue was created and remains unresolved for the millions of Palestinians who today still call for self-determination and independence.

Case study Algeria – a colony or *province outré mer?*

The prospects for French colonial rule in the North African state of Algeria were quite different from those of the British in either Egypt or Palestine. When the French first established their foothold in Algeria in the late 1820s through military invasion, the political objective in Paris was to form a settled colony that would through annexation form part of the French state. This political objective was achieved as a result of widespread colonization of Algeria and its native population by French settlers, *colons*. For some one million of these *colons* and their descendants, Algeria became home. Political legitimacy was ceded to this process when French policy-makers in Paris declared that Algeria was not a colony but simply a *province outré mer*. Algeria was not considered a territory subject to the policies of the French Ministry for Foreign Affairs but instead was placed under the authority of the Ministry of the Interior.

Algeria did have a strategic importance for the French as well. It served as an important foothold in North Africa and allowed France to pursue its rivalry with Britain as a competing colonial power in the Middle East. The later discovery of oil reserves in Algeria's southern deserts was also a further economic incentive to hold onto this particular piece of North African territory.

The annexation of Algeria by the French in the 1840s, however, was not passively accepted by Algeria's indigenous Arab and Berber population. Throughout the mid to latter part of the nineteenth century local resistance was apparent. In 1871 a local uprising against the further extension of French *colon* authority over Arab lands gripped the country. The French authorities exacted a high price from the rebels. The French had exploited Algeria's lands in a variety of ways: to own and develop for French settlers and to exploit in terms of agricultural production for French rather than local consumption and demands. Like other colonial powers, the economic imperative also meant that the French authorities and local *colons* set about a process of incipient modernization that included economic modes of production, infrastructure, industry and education. Moreover, the cultural dimensions of Algerian life were subject to the *colon* and Francophone imprint. In this way Algeria and all its inhabitants became part of the French collective consciousness.

The ruling elite developed a particular attitude towards the local Muslim population, tribes and leaders. This attitude was informed by superiority common to the metropolitan centre in any colonial enterprise as well as the romanticism associated with classic Orientalism of the nineteenth century. Hence the majority of local peoples – with the exception of particular tribal favourites and 'pets' – were regarded with suspicion and as part of a sub-sect in society to which there was little obligation or responsibility. Muslims were considered French subjects in the *province outré mer* but were not entitled to citizenship unless they converted to Christianity. Such a conversion automatically divested them of their Muslim heritage and identity. It was clear that the French state left little room for the admittance of the 'other'. Attempts by local Muslim and tribal leaders to assert rights for their own communities were brutally suppressed and political organization among such elements was prohibited and subject to severe punishment. Patronage of local elements through the well-tried colonial incentive of education and employment in the state enterprise largely failed in terms of bridging the disconnection that emerged in Algerian society in the late nineteenth century between the French-inspired ruling elite and the local Muslim population.

The Algerian national movement arose in the early decades of the twentieth century but real freedom and independence would not be won until 1962 when the war of independence finally delivered Algeria from French rule. Like those of other national movements across the Middle East at the time, the demands of the local Algerians were initially modest and centred on rights and freedoms under French rule rather than autonomy or independence. Such demands were, however, largely resisted by French power-holders wary of granting 'equality and liberty' to the Muslim subjects of Algeria. By 1939 the Algerian response was apparent in the formation of a nationalist anti-French political party called Amis du Manifeste et de la Liberté (Friends of Manifesto and Liberty) whose members included both Muslims and communists. During World War II other local political groupings arose including the Parti du Peuple Algérien (Party of the Algerian People) who, along with others, waged a growing campaign for independence.

Attempts by the French government after 1945 to incorporate local elements of the Algerian community into structures of local governance failed largely because they were viewed with suspicion and as a means of stifling or even halting the growing demands for independence. Such demands were also being met through an increasingly well-organized and armed structure of Algerians who were able to transcend religious, political and class differences to unite in their anxiety for freedom from France. The French responded by seeking to severely repress such demands but by 1954 exiled nationalists and revolutionaries formed the Front de Libération Nationale (National Liberation Front) or FLN as it became known from their base in Egypt.

In the latter part of 1954 the FLN and other revolutionary elements launched a series of guerrilla attacks that would ignite the peoples of Algeria to embark on a war of independence. The French government was caught on the back foot and rushed its troops to Algeria in a desperate attempt to put down the rising populist push for independence. In the war over one million out of a population of nine million Algerians would lose their lives. Despite the increasing French troop presence the war spiralled into a bitter conflict that pitched entire populations into resistance to the French presence. The French authorities resorted to increasingly repressive and brutal measures in their desperate attempts to put the Algerian rebellion down. Thousands were arrested, placed in detention camps, tortured and even executed. As the crisis peaked in 1958, the colonels of the French army brought the government in Paris down and Charles de Gaulle came out of retirement to lead the country as it faced the demands of the warring Algerians. A political solution to the impasse seemed an outright impossibility. De Gaulle promised that he would face down the Algerian 'terrorist' threat and restore French pride and prestige in Algeria. His method of resolution, however, angered many of his supporters on the right. He proposed a referendum on the destiny of Algeria in which Algerians themselves would decide their fate. The *colons* knew that the referendum would not deliver them from the hands of the revolutionaries and their demands for independence. In alliance with some military and right-wing elements, they formed an organization to launch attacks not only on the FLN but the French government as well. They were determined to topple de Gaulle.

By March 1962, however, the FLN and the French government had reached terms on a ceasefire in Algeria. De Gaulle's referendum was held the following July and the outcome was a foregone conclusion: independence for Algeria. Following the result the *colons* began a process of mass exodus from their positions of power as well as the lands that they had settled. The French dream that Algeria serve as the *province outré mer* had turned into a bloody nightmare and colonial disaster.

Further reading

The edited reader by Hourani, Khoury and Wilson (1993) provides a broad-based account for first-time students of the Ottoman and colonial period. Issawi (1982) is a superb introduction to the economic dimensions of European expansion in the Middle East. On France in Algeria and Syria, accounts by Khoury (1987) and Ageron (1991) are excellent. Moore (1970) provides an in-depth account of French colonialism in North Africa. Monroe (1963), Nevakivi (1969) and Marlowe (1971) review and analyse the tensions behind Anglo-French relations in the Middle East. Fieldhouse (2004) and Méouchy and Sluglett (2004) provide interesting narratives around the mandate system established by the British and French. Mitchell (1988), Owen (2003), Zubaida (1993) and Bromley (1994) all go some way towards presenting a re-evaluation of the impact of colonialism in the Middle East found in more traditional texts by authors like Brown (1984). Texts on the Third World which debate the legacy of colonialism in the Middle East include Cammack, Pool and Tordoff (1993) and Findlay (1994). For the Egyptian case study, Owen (1969) outlines a strong account of the Egyptian economy under colonial rule. Historical perspectives on Egypt under British rule can also be found in Marlowe (1954 and 1970), Woodhouse (1959) and Darwin (1981). Tignor (1984) relates state and economic development in Egypt under British rule until the Free Officers' revolution. Kyle's history (2002) and McNamara (2003) highlight the tensions between Nasser and the British that precipitated the Suez crisis. On Palestine, Abboushi (1985) presents a critical account of Britain's mandate, while Antonius (1969) is credited with authoring a nationalist-inspired account of the mandate period. Marlowe (1959), Ingrams (1972), Kedourie (1976), Tibawi (1977) and Wasserstein (1978) outline aspects of British rule in mandate Palestine. Avineri (1981) provides a superb overview of modern Zionism and its developments. Migdal (1980) gives a strong sociological account of Palestinian society under the British. Morris (1988), Pappe (1994) and Tessler (1994) all provide accounts of the birth of the conflict between Israel and the Palestinians and Britain's rule over Palestine. Gerner (1994), Khalidi (1997) and Sayigh (1997) outline histories of mandate Palestine which incorporate and assess the dynamic of change within Palestinian society and the impact this had on the politics of nationalism and anti-colonialist sentiment.

Nationalism

Introduction

ACCORDING to a variety of writers nationalism in the Middle East, and more specifically Arab nationalism, is very much a twentieth-century phenomenon associated with a variety of factors including anti-colonialism, romanticism, state-building, self-determination, socialism and religion (Tibi, 1997). To be blunt, there is no one phenomenon that may easily be described as nationalism that can be applied to the region as a whole. Instead, as much recent academic work has begun to highlight, nationalism in the Middle East has taken many forms and guises, including state nationalism, patriotism, pan-Arabism, pan-Islamism, Zionism, Islamic nationalism, Arab nationalism, Ba'thism, Nasserism, Maronite nationalism, Kurdish ethno-nationalism and so on. In addition, the very applicability of nationalism within the region was questioned after the Six Day War of 1967 when pan-Arabism was declared dead by Ajami (1979) and writers such as Zubaida (1993) began to question the saliency and utility of the concept of the nation-state and nationalism in the region. The debate about nationalism in the region, therefore, embraces a variety of perspectives and explanations – some of which focus on socio-economic issues, including fringe economies, the politics of ideology, national liberation movements, state-building and national identity, principles of self-determination and international human rights, genocide tendencies of some nationalist leaders – and the debate about the applicability of such terms in a region where religion still acts as a primary identifier for ordinary people.

Before examining the specific manifestations of nationalism in the Middle East, it is important to outline some of the most important definitions of the term in this context. More specifically, it is helpful to pose a number of questions, such as, what does nationalism mean in the context of the modern Middle East? Is it relevant and applicable, can it be historically located or associated with particular events, figures or personalities? Is it as relevant today as it was two or three decades ago? What can general theories of nationalism outlined by people such as Kedourie, Gellner, Smith and Anderson tell us about the Middle East?

First, it is worth noting that the debate about nationalism in the region, and more specifically Arab nationalism, is strongly linked to issues and analysis of political Islam and ethnicity. While these issues will be remarked upon in this chapter, it is also worth reflecting on the correlating debates which will be reviewed in chapters 5 and 8 on political Islam and ethnicity respectively. Second, there are disagreements amongst those who define nationalism in the modern age, disagreements that are extended to the Middle East when authors try to explain aspects of politics which they believe are associated with this tendency. The debate among theorists of nationalism can be divided into a number of perspectives, including the theories of scholars such as Rousseau, Fichte, Herder and Hegel who outlined a relationship between nationalism and doctrines of liberty, self-determination and statehood. Kedourie expands on this concept, outlining nationalism as a form of 'secular millenarianism' in a modern age, where religion has gone into decline and the individual enjoys greater independence. As Hutchinson and Smith (1994) argue, 'Kedourie regards nationalism as an extremely powerful, if destructive force. Its appeal is explained by social breakdown occasioned by a collapse in the transmission of traditional values, and the rise of a restless, secular, educated generation, ambitious for power but excluded from its proper estate' (p. 47). The second group of theorists is associated with the modernization thesis, and in particular the work of Ernest Gellner, who argues that nationalism is a modern phenomenon and that pre-existing nations 'can be defined only in terms of the age of nationalism, rather than, as you might expect, the other way round' (1994, p. 64). Gellner argues that the Industrial Revolution and the subsequent reconfiguration of social and economic forces breathed new life into nations, whose relationships to political units such as the state, family, tribal and clan ties create new bonds and loyalties. Thus modernization theorists, including Marxist writers such as Tom Nairn, associate the phenomenon with economic transformation and the impact this has on social and political arrangements in modern societies. Gellner also identifies factors such as culture and language as important signifiers of twentieth-century nationalism and nation identity, but this approach has its critics, including Anthony Smith (1986), who gives greater emphasis to pre-existing ethnic bonds than to the modernization process in explaining the phenomenon of nationalism in the twentieth century. Smith argues for a more nuanced approach to explanations of nationalism than Gellner. While he often concurs with Gellner's explanations, he is unhappy with the emphasis on the modern character of nationalism, arguing that 'ethnie' (the ethnic group) provides the foundation-stone on which 'modern nations simply extend, deepen and streamline the ways in which members of the ethnie associated and communicated. They do not introduce startlingly novel elements, or change the goals of human association and communication' (1986, p. 215). Smith encourages a wider, more embracing explanation of nationalism as a product both of the modern and of the traditional age, in which ethnic bonds do play a significant role.

The extent to which the ethnic bonds which Smith emphasizes are real or imagined are explored in the work of Benedict Anderson. While Anderson agrees with Gellner that nationalism is a product of the modern age, he is, according to Kellas (1998), 'concerned to explore the psychological appeal of nationalism which is close to the primordial approach' which Smith acknowledges (p. 56). Anderson (1983) contends that modern-day nationalism and nations are an imagined product, 'cultural artefacts of a particular kind'. He has also argued that from the decline of old bonding elements such as Church, Mosque and monarchical hierarchy in society, it was 'no surprise then that the search [in the modern age] was on . . . for a new way of linking fraternity, power and time meaningfully together' (in Guibernau and Rex, 1997, p. 43). As society, according to Anderson, transits from a religious-based to a secular order, the composition of nation-states must be articulated in a new way. The primary way in which identity and nationalism is now communicated is a product of the industrial age and print capitalism: 'the convergence of capitalism and print technology on the fatal diversity of human language created the possibility of a new form of imagined community, which in its basic morphology set the stage for the modern nation' (p. 51).

The development of nationalism

The theories of nationalism outlined above tend to identify its features from a Eurocentric viewpoint. With the exception, perhaps, of Anderson, the ties that bind nations outside Europe are viewed from afar and not from within, and are explained from a monolithic cultural background that is purely western or European in character. Theories of nationalism, therefore, have emerged with a particularly European hue, associated as they are with other traditions in western political thought, including the debate about liberty, democracy, individual sovereignty and secularization. As Hutchinson and Smith (1994) admit, 'the earliest nations and national states may be European but nationalism is a truly global movement and cultural system' (p. 196). Nevertheless, as we shall see in the examples below, the embrace of nationalist ideas, thinking, political institutions and economic models primarily associated with this approach, in the contemporary Middle East, occurred as a result of a specific political relationship of domination and subordination between Europe and the peoples of the region. The so-called export of nationalism, described by Brown as a form of virus from the West (1988, p. 142), and associated ideas to the Middle East impacted on religion, ethnic identities and bonds and traditional agricultural modes of production in predominantly rural rather than urbanized societies. The region, therefore, highlights the many modern forms of nationalism, exhibited in ethnic and territorial nationalisms, state nationalism, religious-nationalist thinking evident in turn-of-the-century pan-Islamism and the anti-colonial nationalism of political leaders such as Gamal Abdel Nasser of Egypt.

In the context of the Middle East in the twentieth century, the concept of nationalism or nation, or *watan* as it is called in Arabic, was explained in two ways. The first bore a strong relationship to the western notion of nation identified through the nation-state, which by the second decade of the twentieth century had been established in many parts of the region. The second concept is more indigenous in origin, drawing on Arab and Muslim notions of community (*umma*) and belonging through tribe, clan, religious or ethnic affiliation. For example, the Jordanian monarchy still refers to the people of Jordan as *Bani Hashem*, meaning from the tribe of the Hashemites, a group predating the establishment of the state of Transjordan by the British in the 1920s. The Jordanian people, however, also include among their number Hashemites, Circassians, Palestinians, Bedouins, Muslims, Christians and Turkic peoples.

Nationalism in the Middle East is associated with a number of meanings. The first is state-based, anti-colonial and dependent on western notions of state, class and ideology. This conceptualization of nationalism is described by Breuilly as 'governmental nationalism', which embraces 'policies aimed at extending the territory of the state into areas which the state claims as belonging to its nation . . . [and] internally . . . as nationalist actions taken against specific groups or individuals and justified on the grounds of the anti- or non-national character of the groups or individuals' (Breuilly, 1993, p. 8). Indeed, writers such as Tibi outline three stages in the emergence of this phenomenon from a 'literary and linguistic revival, to a transformation into political nationalism with a demand for a unified state to a form of Arab germanophilia' (Tibi, 1997, p. xiii). In the context of governmental nationalism the project was usually elite-driven, part of the homogenizing task of the state, nationalism from above imposed on the masses, rigid and narrow. The second expression of nationalism, as we shall see below, is found in the post-colonial anti-Zionist, socialist liberation movements and state elites of the 1950s and 1960s. The third expression of nationalist sentiment may be referred to as theo-nationalism or pan-Islamism, and is a product of the uneasy marriage between Islam and the West occurring both at the beginning of the twentieth century and towards the end of the century as a sustainable and politically meaningful political phenomenon. Nationalism and nationalist movements have grown from elite-based secret societies in the 1920s and 1930s through popular mass movements in the 1950s and 1960s to the realm of state-based nationalism by the 1990s. National self-consciousness has become a firmly entrenched feature of the political landscape in the Middle East, one which even the Islamists have had considerable difficulty in overcoming. National self-consciousness is expressed through many mechanisms, at both a state and regional level, and national identity is expressed at a number of levels: within the boundary of the nation-state, as an imagined community, across the region as Arabs, and in the liberation struggles of the Palestinians and the Kurds. In this context the vision of the Arab nation allows the development of a code of inter-state manoeuvre between population groups within the region.

Looking more specifically at Arab nationalism, it can be argued that it remains both an expression of nation and nationalism through the state and in individual countries as well as at a wider level of the Arab world. At the wider level it relates to attempts at great regional harmony and uniformity of political institutions or forms of government. Arabs, then, have both embraced and repulsed the notion of nation and nationalism. I will now review the emergence of the intellectual development of Arab nationalism, its bourgeois and elite roots, its importance during the First World War and the articulation of nationalism through independence from the colonial powers in the 1940s, 1950s and 1960s.

The birth of Arab nationalism

The emergence of nationalist sentiment in the Middle East preceded colonial government in the region, but did, in part, reflect growing foreign influence from the 1880s onwards in the areas of trade, education, religion, travel and culture. One argument that may be forwarded is that the first stirrings of national consciousness, and more specifically of an Arab identity, grew out of centuries-old tensions between the Arab people and their Turkish overlords. Although the Ottoman Empire was Muslim, it required its Arab subjects to learn Turkish, swear allegiance to Turkish governors and rulers and to carry the coin of the Turkish rulers. Resentment, despite reforms in Ottoman rule, grew, particularly amongst the newly educated urban Christian and Muslim elite of cities such as Cairo, Damascus and Beirut. In addition, this elite acted as an important conduit for western ideas and philosophies of democracy, modernity and nation. The role of this elite in formulating Arab nationalism as an anti-colonial expression is recognized by Breuilly, who notes that 'such intellectuals have played a prominent part in Arab nationalist politics . . . [T]he importance of nationalist intellectuals in Arab nationalism' cannot, therefore, from Breuilly's perspective, be underestimated (1993, p. 149). Aziz al-Azmeh, however, asks us to read history a little differently, arguing that Arab nationalism was the product of neither the Arab Revolt of 1917 (discussed below) nor of direct western influence. Instead he explains a more indirect root, giving credit for Arab nationalism proper to the 'product of the Ottoman reforms (*tanzimat*) of the nineteenth century . . . the incipient regime of modernity [and] . . . small elite class intellectuals' (1995, p. 7). Breuilly and al-Azmeh concur that the intellectual base of this movement was extremely important, and, in turn, would have significant bearing on the subsequent nature of nationalist ideologies within the region. As al-Azmeh ominously sounds off,

> Thus was Arab nationalism born and constituted. It was the political culture, initially of a political class which was acculturated to it and deployed it in struggles for independence, later of the entire population, through the state educational and cultural systems. It was the animating idea of a whole range of large-scale political and social forces . . . also the expression of a social fact articulating various levels of social structuration and interaction. (1995, p. 11)

In the coffee houses and salons of the urban bourgeoisie a generation of young men, educated in Constantinople, in church schools or even in Europe, raised the idea of a renaissance of Arab identity. Like so many before and after them, they shared a collective and often invented memory of a golden age of the Arabs or Islam, when the world, or at least large parts of it, was ruled by Arab leaders, when poets and artists were revered, when the Arabs achieved their greatest contributions to subjects such as astronomy and mathematics. The renaissance of the Arabs (Muslim or Christian) would embody these greater eras and result in the resurgence of the Arab nation, its people and its leaders. In addition, this notion of Arab identity would engage with Muslim identity and many of the leading scholars of the time were Muslim intellectuals. In this context nationalism was not always envisaged as embodying religion, and a role was created, by some Arab intellectuals, for the faith of Islam. As Kellas argues,

> It is difficult, therefore, to relate the rise of nationalism to the decline
> of religion, except perhaps in some mainly secular societies. In some
> cases, religion and nationalism thrive together, in others, where a
> church is strongly supranational (as ... Islam), there may be a
> tension ... However, even supranational [religions] can underpin
> nationalist movements against oppressive states which deny national-
> ism its free expression. (1998, p. 59)

Vatikiotis, however, does not perceive such an easy relationship
between Islam and nationalism, arguing that the sheer incompatibility of these two terms made things difficult from the outset.
Nationalism, imported from the outside, he argued, had to compete
against the pre-existing ideology of Islam and 'when nationalism was
linked to Islam, it failed to accommodate the different, or other, the
non-Muslims, and thus accelerated the inappropriateness and the
decline of non-Islamic nationalism as an acceptable political ideology'
(1987, p. 74). Yet, for Vatikiotis the 'exceptionalist' nature of Muslim
political culture in the Middle East meant that an imported western
ideology of nationalism would never thrive.

The Arab intellectuals, however, debated and attempted to spread
their ideas of Arab nation and nationalism by taking advantage of the
modern processes of print and publication. Small literary and
cultural societies published books, pamphlets, gazettes, newspapers,
journal articles and constitutions, and revived old texts and literature
for re-publication. Here, as Anderson (1983) argues, nationality or
nation-ness (Arab) was constructed as a specific cultural creation
emerging from print capitalism in a new era of modernity in the
modern Middle East. Here the revival of the Arabic language played an
important part in shaping the 'imagined community' that these
urban intellectuals hoped to share with the rest of the Arab world.
While language is not a prerequisite of nationalism and al-Azmeh
(1995) has a point when he states it is 'not itself the most crucial
factor', Arabic and its renaissance in the written and literary form was
a significant thread in the generation of an ideology which could be
'sold', at a later date, as authentic to a mass audience (p. 10). As a
language of communication, Arabic served the region well and played
its part in promoting a notion of unity, whether at the level of political rhetoric or humour.

The vision and aspirations that these turn-of-the-century intellectuals promoted can be divided into two themes or strands – Arab nationalism and pan-Islamism – under which authors such as Tauber and
Antonius have identified nationalist movements, personalities or
approaches, including Arabism, the Lebanese revival, the Young
Arab Society (*al-Fatat*), Syrianism, Egyptianism, Butrus al-Bustani, Jamal
ad-din al-Afghani and Abdul Raham al-Kawakibi. The two strands are

representations of the types of nationalism that theorists such as Gellner, Anderson and Smith have outlined. Some were anti-colonial in nature, others embraced a western secular outlook to nation and nationhood which grew out of a particular Eurocentric perspective on these issues. Others, as I have pointed out, reflected a literary base to the revival of Arab identity, following Anderson's 'imagined community', through poetry, the publication of classical Arabic works, newspapers, novels, music and other arts. Geographically associated with Lebanon and Syria, the intellectuals and theologians associated with this particular approach to Arab nationalism included, for example, Christian western-educated teachers such as Nasif Yaziji (1800–71) and Butrus al-Bustani (1819–83), founders of the Beirut-based Society of Arts and Sciences, who, along with their Muslim compatriots including people like Amir Mohammed Arslan, Hussein Baihum and Ibrahim Yaziji, promoted an 'incitement to Arab insurgence . . . the achievements of the Arab race, of the glories of Arabic literature, and of a future that the Arabs might fashion for themselves by going to their own past for inspiration' (Antonius, 1969, p. 54). The call was based on a desire to overthrow the mantle of Ottoman rule and fashion a secular non-sectarian future for the Arab peoples of the region based on the principle of self-determination. While the importance of these first intellectual stirrings of Arab nationalist identity and nationalism have waxed and waned according to historical interpretation, they are consistently credited with playing an important part in consciousness-raising and encouraging the growth of a secularized Arab identity which would, in theory, transcend the competing loyalties of class, tribe, religion and clan. This strand encouraged the emergence of state-centred patriotic nationalism, *wataniyya*, that would feature so strongly in the national homogenizing agenda of the new states established in the Middle East after the end of the First World War.

The pan-Islamist movement is associated with intellectuals such as Jamal ad-din al-Afghani, Mohammed Abduh and Rashid Rida, all of whom were scholars at the Islamic University, al-Azhar, in Egypt, and who reflected the association between religion and nationalism, anti-colonialism and religious resurgence that is common in other Third World contexts such as Asia and Latin America, where the Catholic Church and its priests were closely involved with nationalism. In addition, as Esposito argues, 'the development of modern Muslim nationalism was indebted to Islamic modernists as well as secular nationalist leaders' (1984, p. 60). In Egypt the emergence and prominence of such Islamic modernist-reformist thinkers was part of this new post-World War I intellectual response to the collapse of the Ottoman Empire and the Caliphate, the nation-state-building project pioneered by Britain and France, and the anti-colonial sentiment palpable by this point in history throughout the region. This response to nationalist sentiment had, however, first to deal with the issue of continuing Muslim identity in an era of global change and socio-economic transformation of society. It was this marriage of ideas that resulted in pan-Islamism.

The idea that Islam could rise to the challenge of unity presented in nationalism and at the same time provide a sense of identity that transcended national boundaries and protected its adherents was promoted by these modernists. The seeds of reformist thinking, the attempt to modernize Islam in the fields of politics, economy and society, while preserving the religious traditions established by the Prophet Mohammed himself, presented them with a formidable task. As the relationship between Islam and the West, nationalism and secularism became entrenched, this group of thinkers and writers emerged to challenge the hegemony of the western-inspired secular project, with its accompanying notions of nationalism, modernization and liberalization which so many indigenous rulers of the colonized Muslim world were adopting for their own political systems. The westernization of the Muslim political project was a significant factor, propelling the modernists to formulate a response to the political and cultural challenges posed by nationalist theories during this period. Not only was the West engaged in an economic project in the colonized lands of the Muslim world, but it sought to transform the very nature of political power, system of government and rule which had characterized the world of Islam for so many centuries.

Jamal ad-din al-Afghani

The founder of this pan-Islamic trend was an Iranian-born Muslim thinker Jamal ad-din al-Afghani (1838–97) who called upon fellow Muslims throughout the region, and beyond, to reassess the role of Islam in their lives, examine the causes of its increasing marginalization and question the benefits to all Muslims offered by the western secularist approach. Ayubi (1991) credits al-Afghani with reviving the process of *ijtihad* (interpretation) and thereby initiating 'a renaissance of Muslim philosophy, encouraging the direct study of the works themselves rather than the study, then customary, of the usually sterile commentaries or supercommentaries' (p. 57). The fragility of the 'renaissance project' dogged its thinkers, with some critics, such as Kamal Abd al-Latif, arguing that the reformers had not really accepted modernism as an integrated philosophical outlook – related to such concepts as nationalism, liberty, individualism, social contracts, etc. – but that they borrowed eclectically as it suited them, always extracting the 'modern' concepts out of their (European) intellectual and social context and trying to subsume them instead under familiar Islamic concepts (Ayubi, 1991, p. 58). Abd al-Latif's criticism seems harsh given the hegemonic nature of the European project at the time and the saturation of the Muslim body politic with western norms and values with no attempt to acknowledge Islam at the level of politics, government or leadership. As Ayubi (1991) reminds us, 'there is little doubt that the attempts by people such as al-Afghani and Abduh to initiate reform were mainly prompted by external stimuli, by confrontation with a technologically superior and politically dominant western presence' (p. 58).

Al-Afghani and his successor Mohammed Abduh (1849–1905) were modernists, however, in their own right, who wanted to formulate a response within Islam to the challenges and changes triggered by increasing western hegemony in the Middle East. They were not just responsible for promoting a call to all Muslims to return to their faith, to the 'straight path' advocated by God in the Koran and the Prophet Mohammed through example, but for recognizing the eternal and inextricable links between the regeneration of faith and the particular brand of politics that has emerged from the practice of the religion.

These men sought to reacquaint Islam with the immense political, social and economic changes that were taking place around them as a direct result of the colonial experience. As the fabric of society strained under secularizing influences, al-Afghani, Abduh and Rashid Rida formulated a response that embraced modernization – of Islam – and advocated the primacy of Muslim belief, asserting that an irrelevant and outdated interpretation of Islam, promoted by backward and old-fashioned clergy (*ulama*), was actually playing a large part, alongside colonialism, in undermining the unity of the Muslim community itself.

Rashid Rida

Rida's contribution to the renaissance of political Islam and linkage or engagement with the debate about nationalism was to develop a fundamentalist (*salafi*) approach to the modernization of Islam and its political regeneration. Throughout his life Rashid Rida led the modernist movement in Cairo and continued to win supporters for his ideas throughout the region. Through the publication of a journal-cum-newspaper entitled *al-Manar* (the Lighthouse) and his involvement with a religious school close to the traditionalist religious university, al-Azhar, Rida played his part in maintaining the momentum for reform initiated by his mentors al-Afghani and Abduh. Rida, however, was a conservative rather than a liberal reformer, rejecting the argument for liberalization of Islam through westernization of the religion. There would be no Islamic reformation where the forces of religion and the state were unleashed to depart on separate paths; for Rida, the answer to modernization lay in strengthening and further forging the ties within Islam that marry the spiritual and the political together. As Egypt modernized under British influence, Rida increasingly advocated a rejection of the West and a return to the roots of Islam, and he became the first advocate in the Arab world of a modernized Islamic state and its need to respond through inner renewal to these secularist pressures before it was too late. By the late 1920s and early 1930s Rida had become an influential figure throughout the Muslim world; his journal and associated publications were read by young men who were thus encouraged to explore and put into practice the ideas of Rida and his predecessors. In this way, the reformers planted the seed that encouraged the regeneration and defence of Islam from within.

The extent to which this revival of Islam took place is hard to measure. Although not broadly populist in appeal, al-Afghani, Abduh and Rida managed to inspire a new generation of educated Muslims, many of whom, it should be noted, were not from the *ulama* class, to rethink the role which Islam could play in their lives and the unifying nationalist role it could maintain. Whether this new generation of thinkers would actually lead peasants in rural revolts, organize new societies based on Islam or join arms with their nationalist brethren in anti-colonial struggle, they were all in one way or another at least touched or influenced by the reformers, and the implications of the political message they conveyed were not lost on them.

New identity

According to the modernists, the future of the entire Muslim nation (*umma*) lay in the ability of each member to profess a new Muslim identity based on notions of communal unity, solidarity and strength. Fear of the West or modern economic, political and social changes, the modernists argued, should be replaced with challenge and the ability of the Muslim community to offer a viable alternative to the dominance of the West and western secularized identities such as nationalism. The modernization of Islam should acknowledge and pay homage to its own important history, civilization, science, economics, art, poetry, social mores and architecture. Islam, they asserted, was capable, as a political as well as a religious force, of addressing the issues raised by western modernization processes in the Middle East and their impact at all levels of society. Of course, in recent years, the debate about the authenticity of this particular reconstruction of the Islamic past has been questioned at length. But, in the context of the time, this political response was inevitably anti-colonial and anti-western, while at the same time pro-Arab and pro-Islam. It embraced a nationalist pan-Islamist philosophy which promoted liberation from colonial rule through localized and regional political agitation.

This pan-Islamist emphasis on unity and reform encouraged many supporters throughout the region. Revolution or jihad (just war) against illegitimate rule, no matter what form it was manifested in, the modernists argued, must be undertaken. If the ruler of a country was corrupt and a westernized enemy, then his rule must be resisted. It was with these beliefs that al-Afghani supported attempts to end the rule of the Khedive in Egypt. The jihad against unjust and corrupt Ottoman rule and domination was launched in Arabia by Sharif Hussein of Mecca in the early years of World War I. In other Arab capitals young Muslim men formed secret societies based on the new dream of pan-Islamic thinking which put the unity of the Muslim Arab peoples before loyalty to territory, nation-state or ruler. If such unity could be achieved, the liberation of Muslim lands from corrupt rule and foreign usurpation would naturally follow.

Throughout the first decades of the twentieth century the young Arab nationalists and pan-Islamists formed groups, societies and literary circles to promote their message. The first Arab Congress of nationalist groups was convened, however, outside the region, in Paris in June 1913. The Turkish authorities had been alerted to the threat latent in Arab nationalism to their authority to rule over the region and had tried to stop the Congress. In addition, by this point the Ottoman powers were admitting to themselves that the earlier policy of Turkification of the region, through changes in school syllabi, language and business, had failed. In their failure, the Ottoman authorities resorted to violence to quell the new force of nationalism. In the province of Syria, for example, the Ottoman ruler of Damascus, Jamal Pasha, ordered the imprisonment, exile and public execution of Arab nationalists. Throughout the region the intellectual swing to Arab nationalism and pan-Islamism of a particularly Arab nature away from Ottomanism was perceptible.

The Arab revolt

An important watershed or turning point in the movement for Arab nationalism and, in particular, in the linkage to a form of territoriality or the nation-state (al-Azmeh's criticisms notwithstanding) was the First World War. Following the decision by the Ottoman rulers in Constantinople to side with the Germans against the British and the French, the Middle East became an important arena for battle during the conflict. Colonial aspirations over the region by this point were intense and, as highlighted in chapter 1, a significant feature of the war was the rivalry between Britain and France to gain influence over local Arab leaders in the region and to secure a foot-hold over particular territories. During the war the greatest symbol of Arab nationalist aspirations was the Arab Revolt. The revolt was organized by Sharif Hussein, and the liberation of Damascus was led by his son Prince Faisal of the Hashemites, assisted by T. E. Lawrence, 'Lawrence of Arabia'. Although not a mass movement, the revolt was the clearest sign that the Arabs and, more specifically, their leaders wanted both political and territorial independence after the war no matter who won. As Antonius (1969) remarks, 'after the revolt the Allied cause had become identical with the cause of Arab independ-ence; and . . . the triumph of Allied arms would bring freedom to the Arab people' (p. 225).

The ruthlessness of Ottoman governors like Jamal Pasha in Damascus helped fire Arab nationalist fervour and turn them against their Turkish overlords. The deployment of Turkish troops com-manded by the Germans in southern Arabia also alarmed Arab leaders. It was Sharif Hussein who subsequently lent his support and that of his sons, Ali, Faisal and Abdullah, to the allies in their military campaign against the Germans in the deserts of Arabia. The particular ally which became embroiled with the Hashemites were the British who, as part of war policy, were keen to establish local Arab support. The British assured Hussein of their support for Arab nationalist claims in return for Arab support during the war. In a letter dated 24 October 1915 Sir Henry McMahon, High Commissioner in Egypt, had declared to Hussein that Britain was 'prepared to recognize and uphold the inde-pendence of the Arabs in all the regions lying within the frontiers proposed by the Sharif of Mecca'.

In June 1916, following the British assurances, Hussein and his sons led a revolt against the Ottoman rulers and raised the first Arab force for independence. Military success, although limited, was forthcom-ing and Hussein was able to oust the Turkish garrison force from Mecca and other surrounding settlements. By November, Hussein was declared 'King of Arabia'. The British and French, however, who were engaged in further negotiations to secure their own, rather than the Arabs', interests over the area, only agreed to recognize him as King of Mecca. The secret Sykes–Picot Agreement contained an arrangement for the territorial carve-up of the region after the war between the French, British and imperial Russia. The agreement would have remained secret had the Bolsheviks not released the papers to the Turks following the Russian Revolution in November 1917. For the Arabs, the implications of the agreement were plain: the document was a direct contradiction of nationalist aspirations. As Antonius

(1969) remarks, 'The . . . Agreement is a shocking document. It is not only a product of greed at its worst, that is to say, of greed allied to suspicion and so leading to stupidity: it also stands out as a startling piece of double-dealing' (p. 248).

Throughout 1917, however, Hussein and his sons continued with their plan to unite the Arabs of Arabia, Transjordan and Syria under the banner of Arab independence and nationalism. They organized their supporters around certain themes or concepts which Hudson (1977) identifies as 'hallmarks of modern Arab identity . . . Arabic language and culture and Islam' (p. 38). They plotted the conquest of Aqaba on the coast of the Red Sea, Karaq in Transjordan and Damascus, which was still under the rule of Jamal Pasha. Following the Turkish defeat in Arabia, Jamal Pasha had ordered a bloody crack-down on the secret nationalist groups that had flourished in Damascus and Beirut, and throughout the early spring public executions were stepped up. Hussein, by this point, had charged his son Faisal with the task of liberating the north, including Damascus. Faisal faced a formidable challenge and it has been argued that victory would have eluded the Arabs under Faisal's leadership had they not been supported by the British through arms, money and the legendary Lawrence of Arabia. Faisal succeeded in uniting the tribes of Arabia against the Turks, while Lawrence managed to secure British military approval of the revolt against Damascus. Notably, however, the British were not prepared to deploy their own troops to Alexandretta to support the Arab effort, for fear of a rift in relations with their French allies.

On 1 October 1917 Damascus fell to the Arabs. Although a contingent of Australian troops had occupied the city, it was Faisal, with Lawrence at his side, who entered popular myth as the liberator of the city which had for so long quivered under the grip of Jamal Pasha's iron fist. The conquest of Damascus was important to Hussein and his sons in the quest for Arab nationalism and independence. Their claims to the leadership of the Arab world were bolstered by the victory and acted as an important counterbalance to the growing perception that the allies, whether British or French, were untrustworthy partners. The British triumph in Palestine, with the fall of Jerusalem to Allenby in November 1917, and the revelations of the Sykes–Picot Agreement that soon followed, alerted the Arabs to the possibly duplicitous character of the British in particular. The conquest of Palestine was also coupled with the revelation that the British had announced their support of the fledgling Zionist movement. The Balfour Declaration sealed Britain's role in Palestine and sowed the seeds of double promise and betrayal for a long time to come. This commitment to support the Zionists in their quest to settle Palestine would create significant political and strategic problems throughout the mandate period. Although authors such as Mansfield (1992, p. 159) maintain that the declaration was 'apparently unsensational' at the time, the ripples in Arab nationalist circles at the news of Balfour's promise were immediately evident. While the Arab peoples celebrated their liberation from the Ottoman authorities and savoured the very real prospect of independence, the Arab leadership was already facing up to the prospect that their European allies would not live up to their promises.

Arab independence over territory was short-lived. Faisal ruled Damascus until 1920 when the British supported prior French claims over Syria and stood by as Faisal was expelled. The shamefaced British offered Faisal the leadership of Iraq, while his brother Abdullah claimed control over the newly created state of Transjordan with its capital in Amman. The Arabs received the minimum when they had demanded the maximum. New nation-states under the mandated authority of either the British or the French – puppet kingdoms – were created for the Hashemites in Iraq, Syria and Transjordan. As a British official maintained, 'London's support for Arab claims should not be pushed to the point of conflict with France' (Dockrill and Goold, 1981, p. 153). The import of this Arab autonomy over territory in Iraq in particular cannot be underestimated, as Kedourie (1992) argues:

> Like its short-lived predecessor in Damascus, the Kingdom of Iraq would become the base whence Arab nationalism would be spread over the Arab world . . . attempting to create a unified Arab state: as Arab nationalists repeatedly reaffirmed in the 1930s, Iraq was to be the Prussia or the Piedmont of an Arab world . . . It was in Iraq that a fully-fledged doctrine of Arab nationalism was articulated. (p. 295)

Arab autonomy under the mandate system instituted after the war, however, was not enough to satisfy the growing and increasingly mass-based identity of Arabism which emerged throughout the region. From this point onwards Arab nationalist demands increased and political change placing more power in Arab hands was inevitable.

Arab nationalism and revolution

In 1932 Hans Kohn, one of the founders of the study of nationalism, noted that the Middle East was entering an 'epoch in which nationalism is the highest and most symbolic social and intellectual form and sets its stamp upon the whole era' (1932, p. 32). Yet, less than twenty years earlier religion had been the determining factor in the region. Nationalism was not ousting religion, but was more or less rapidly taking a place beside it, frequently fortifying it, beginning to transform and impair it. National symbols acquired religious authority and sacred inviolability. As Kohn again noted, 'the truth which men will defend with their lives is no longer exclusively religious, on occasion it is no longer religious at all, but in increasing measure national' (p. 35). The Arab Revolt had fuelled the popular imagination and helped shape national consciousness throughout the region. The single most significant factor, however, which accounted for the ascendance of Arab nationalism was the perceived betrayal of the colonial powers, in particular Britain and France. During this period Arab nationalism became, in Breuilly's words, symbolic of 'one sort of modern anti-colonial nationalism', where Arab identity was forged in opposition to the colonial West (1993, p. 149).

The effect of the post-war settlement of the Middle East between the colonial powers on Arab nationalist ideology and sentiment was perceptible throughout the inter-war period. As western interests in the region expanded, the Arabs gained a new sense of unity and direction, this time against the West rather than the Ottomans. They were increasingly hostile, and populist agitation for change became a major feature of the region. They still maintained their claims to independence and agitated for change under the mandate system run by the British and the French. The European powers responded by trying to split the Arab nationalist movement, weaken it and discredit it. They were not successful. By the late 1920s and early 1930s public order in Palestine, Transjordan, Iraq, Syria and Lebanon had been severely undermined by localized revolts, demonstrations, strikes and disturbances.

Throughout this period, however, it can be argued that the movement for Arab nationalism was characterized by the emergence of two strands: pan-Arabism or unification nationalism and Arab nationalism or patriotic/state nationalism. The first was based on grand visions for Arab unity across the region, transcending the new boundaries of nation-states, which were viewed as a temporary measure or step towards the creation of one whole Arab nation that did not recognize state boundaries. Indeed, one governing factor in the fight for independence based on pan-Arab aspirations during this period was that this approach could make most regimes 'look small and petty, just disembodied structures headed by selfish rulers who resisted the sweeping mission of Arabism and who were sustained by outside powers that supposedly feared the one idea that could indeed resurrect the golden age of the Arabs' (Ajami, 1978, p. 361). The emergence of thinkers such as Sati al-Husri, first in Iraq and then in Syria, described by Kedourie (1992) as the 'first ideologue of Arab nationalism' (p. 296), and Salah ad-din al-Bitar and Michel Aflaq, founders of the Ba'th Party, promoted the idea of anti-colonial resistance which involved pan-Arab unity. Inherent, however, in the appeal of unification nationalism was patriotic or state nationalism, which Owen (2003) describes as presenting or creating the paradox of 'the contradictory necessities of state-building versus Arabism' which was reflected in the region from the 1920s onwards as the struggle for independence grew (p. 86).

The second strand reflected the difficulties that would be associated with state-building and creating new national identities within certain boundaries during the inter-war period and which in turn would propel revolutionary movements throughout the Middle East. In this context a new generation of Arab leaders repeatedly made an appeal for unity within the boundaries of the new states, playing their part in shaping the national agenda – in school curricula, radio, television, arts, literature and so on – which would combine to construct, as Anderson has highlighted, 'imagined' Syrian, Iraqi, Egyptian, Tunisian 'communities' and identities. The success, therefore, of patriotic/state nationalism is inextricably linked to the decade of revolution and independence which befell the region after World War II. With revolution, a *coup d'état* or independence achieved in Egypt, Lebanon, Syria, Iraq, Libya, Tunisia, Morocco, Sudan, Palestine/Israel, Transjordan, Algeria and Yemen by the mid-1960s, a new era had been proclaimed in the region. With independence, however, the new political elite of the Arab states of the region were forced to address the pressing issue of creating new bonds in old boundaries, while at the same time balancing the demands of old bonds in new boundaries.

The extent to which this delicate balancing act resulted in the emergence of stable democratic nation-states is subject to intense debate and, of course, varies from one example to another. In addition, other factors need to be addressed, including the swing within the Third World as a whole to revolutionary regimes, the emergence of Arab/African/Latin American Marxist, socialist and revolutionary movements. The impact of global capitalism on emerging oil economies in the Arabian Gulf must also be factored into any assessment of the nationalism issue within the region as a whole. In Iran, for example, the apparent failure of Mossadeq's nationalist government of the early 1950s can partly be explained by internal factors and failure to appeal to the masses but the *coup* of 1953 in which Mossadeq was ousted from government can only fully be explained by highlighting the role of America and the CIA in supporting the *coup* as a means to protect their oil interests and overall regional security strategy (Halliday, 1979, p. 25).

A final factor which has been identified in the attempt to explain the competing pulls and pushes of nationalism within the region is the Palestine issue. As Owen (2003) explains it, the 'Palestine issue also possessed the same ability both to unite Arabs and divide them' (p. 88). Evidence of the degree to which this issue united the Arab people is easy to find in the annals of official organizations of the region, like the Arab League, in the financial pledges made by wealthy Gulf states, the countless petitions of Arab states in international organizations such as the UN and the military encounters between the Arab states and Israel which, until the 1990s, had locked the region into a cycle of conflict. All this, however, has to be contrasted, as we shall see, with the national, rather than regional, agendas of individual states such as Jordan, Libya, Syria, Iraq, Tunisia or Egypt, with the animosity between Arab states which has led to conflicts and even wars, and ultimately with the inability of the Arab people to achieve the self-determination and independence of some two million of their brethren. There can be no doubt, therefore, that the emerging force of nationalism in the Middle East which would characterize the politics of the region in the 1960s was a double-edged sword on which so many ideals and principles which had assisted the people of the region to independence would flounder.

Unification nationalism: the United Arab Republic and beyond

Following the successes of the various movements for Arab independence in the 1940s and 1950s, one might have expected to witness the decline of Arab nationalism and the rhetoric which supported such aspirations. Instead, Arab nationalism was further strengthened as the new regimes of the Arab world used the ideology of nationalism to pursue the unification agenda more strongly. It could be argued that the success of Arab nationalist movements in achieving independence at the level of nation-states encouraged some tendencies to promote the nationalist agenda to supranational levels. As Breuilly (1993) argues, 'one would have expected Arab nationalism to recede in the face of increasingly important territorial nationalist movements, especially once these had acquired independence' (p. 283). Breuilly and others have pointed out that, alongside the Palestinian issue which unified the Arab nation, the emergence of Egyptian leader Gamal Abdel Nasser was the other significant force explaining the durability of pan-Arabism in the Middle East.

In Egypt, after the 1952 Free Officers *coup* led by Gamal Abdel Nasser, a programme of pan-Arabism and the unification of states was pursued. In the context of the Cold War and superpower rivalry in the Middle East, any form of co-operation between Arab states under the banner of pan-Arabism was perceived within the region as positive.

During the years following Egypt's nationalization of the Suez Canal, Arab nationalism became increasingly popular in the Middle East and pan-Arab ideas were at the base of political mergers between states. It was believed that pan-Arabism would allow the leaders of the Arab world to transcend state boundaries, many of which had been artificially imposed during the colonial period, to obtain the ideal of Arab unity. The Arab state system became defined as 'first and foremost a Pan system. It postulates the existence of a single Arab nation behind the façade of a multiplicity of sovereign states. In pan-Arab ideology, this nation is actual, not potential' (Khalidi, 1997, p. 181). Although initially proposed by Syrian Communists, such a political, economic and social dream was pursued by Nasser from 1958 to 1961 following Egypt's union with Syria in the United Arab Republic (UAR). Ironically, the UAR is often understood as the classic example of the Arab Cold War rather than pan-Arab unity, characterized by two central themes: the centrality of Egypt in the region for strategic and political reasons and the flexibility of alliance based upon existing core Arab concerns. Pan-Arabism was identified as possessing six attributes which combined to make it an evocative ideology with mass appeal. The six features were: universalism, Arab nationalism as an intellectual force, the decline of the colonial powers, a mobile trans-state Arab elite, the 1948 Palestine débâcle which 'forced Arabs to unite against Israel and the power of pan-Arabism [from 1956 to 1970] derived from Nasser's charismatic leadership of the movement' (Ajami, 1979, p. 368). As Drysdale and Blake (1985) point out, however, 'the discrepancy between hope and reality is immense and a source of anguish to all Arabs' (p. 224).

The growth of Nasser's power base in the region was simultaneous with the rise of Arab nationalist Ba'thism, particularly in Syria and Jordan where Ba'thists had reached the highest levels of government by 1956–7. In Syria it was the Communists and later the Ba'thists who first raised the issue of union with Egypt. In spite of the pan-Arab rhetoric, Nasser was initially cautious about the Ba'thists' proposal, fearing the immense differences between the Egyptian military authoritarian regime and the Syrian system of parties, parliament and a free press. Nasser met his fears by announcing that he wanted 'internal union of the countries' citizens', that Syria should dissolve its parties to make way for a unitary state. The Ba'thists accepted these conditions, believing that they could still dominate Syrian political life. Thus, on 1 February 1958, the UAR was proclaimed.

However, the new Republic was almost strangled at birth and proved to be both a political and economic disaster in the making. This historically important attempt at Arab unity based on pan-Arabism failed primarily for three reasons: first, because Nasser was not prepared to share power with the Syrians, the UAR became an experiment in Egyptian imperialism. Second, the union strengthened the Egyptian state but only by weakening the Syrian state at an institutional level, and as a result there was no parity of political power. Finally, the most significant weakness of the UAR lay in Nasser's attempt to introduce rapid social and economic change and his failure to find a suitable political framework to support this process.

The experiment in Arab unity illustrated by the UAR outlines a depressing picture whereby Egypt remains central to the region and eschews relationships of parity with other Arab states. The centrality of Egypt in the region throughout the period 1958–70 was ultimately instrumental in the conduct of inter-Arab politics and attempts at unity or integration. A number of factors strengthened Egypt and Nasser's position during this period, including Egypt's strategic location, its national identity, its pre-existing military and social infrastructure and modernized economy. Egypt and its leaders, however, failed to establish the 'superstate' that would threaten the hegemony of the superpowers. The demise of the UAR, the establishment of the Baghdad Pact resulting in conservative versus radical Arab states and the defeat of the Arabs in the Six Day War of 1967 were all factors which played a part in what Ajami (1979) refers to as the 'end of pan-Arabism'. Ajami and others exposed the myth of unification nationalism or pan-Arabism, arguing that by the end of the 1970s it had been replaced by local nationalisms, patriotism and the resurgence of Islam. This coincides with the argument that by the 1970s and 1980s there was a triumph of state over nation in the region. In the past it had been possible to examine the Arab nation as a 'unit of analysis' (Hudson, 1977, p. 83) and authors like Esposito (1983) had regarded the Arab nation as a fairly homogeneous unit (p. 59). In the modern-day Middle East, however, it became increasingly apparent that unification nationalism was not enough on its own to sustain the power of any Arab regime. The loads on the hypothetical system of the Arab nation were far too great and, as Hudson (1977) contends, 'the rapid modernization of the state as a unit of analysis has been at the cost of the nation' (p. 83). State and territorial nationalism is no longer regarded as a transitory phenomenon on the path to unification nationalism; today it is regarded as a permanent feature of politics in the region. However, as Hudson reminds us, 'if the Arab state is stronger than it used to be, it is not just because their populations are more harmonious and supportive of the system. More important is the fact that the system itself can exert increasingly pervasive influence (both positive and negative) over individuals and society' (p. 83).

The defeat of the Arabs in the Six Day War of 1967 against Israel, and the further loss of Palestinian territory, was thus considered by most writers on the Middle East to be the watershed or turning point in pan-Arabism and Arab nationalism. The rout of Nasserite Egypt and Ba'thist Syria in the war shattered the image of radical power in the region, as revolutionary Arab politics suffered its most crushing defeat (Dessouki, 1982, p. 322).

Arab unity around the Palestinian issue did enjoy a brief revival during and shortly after the war with Israel of 1973. A new sense of triumph emerged, but triumph was not associated with the lofty ideals of pan-Arabism but with the economic strength of the oil-producing economies of the region. From this point onwards a threshold was crossed: the radical nationalist regimes had failed to unite, but the clout of the petrodollar had increased regional interdependency. Oil and its multiplier effects led to a greater interdependency among the Arab states as a new order turned previous positions of regional leadership on its head. As money from the Gulf states, and migrant labour from Egypt, Syria, and Jordan, flowed in more or less opposite directions, relations changed. The end result of this new order was an Arab Cold War in which the radical and conservative states of the region found themselves locked in the most bitter of disputes behind closed doors.

The rhetoric of Arabism was still broadcast across the region by radical states like Iraq, Syria and Libya, but their calls largely fell on deaf ears and were discredited by bitter experience. The mask of Arab nationalism could no longer conceal the personalized political agendas of Arab leaders throughout the region. Clearly, the system of regional relations which rose from the ashes of the 1967 defeat, known as the 'new Arab order', was no bright new dawn for politics in the Middle East. In the era of crisis which followed 1967 the field of politics was open to the appeals of other forces, in particular political Islam and Islamist movements. The contested ground of ideology grew, with many declaring nationalism the loser and Islam the victor. Yet the picture which has emerged is far more complicated than this, as Tibi (1997) reminds us: 'Now the claim of Islamic fundamentalists is universal, but the realities they are operating within are related, among others, to ethnic, sectarian and national strife. Thus, in Islamic fundamentalism we can observe a mix of ethnicity, nationalism, and sectarian rivalry' (p. 220). In addition, there are no strict differences to be found between Islam as Islamic state and nationalism as nation-state. As Piscatori (1986) observes, in some respects there is no tension between the nation-state and modern political Islam – the nation-state is a fact of life in the current global order and Islam has learnt to accommodate and live with it.

The interdependency and co-operation, however, which Islamic fundamentalism fostered until August 1990, when Iraq invaded Kuwait, stood in stark contrast to the adversarial and ideologically pan-Arab and Arab nationalist politics of the Cold War period that preceded it. Despite the distinct lack of rhetoric surrounding the changes, the inter-Arab links forged by millions of migrant workers and the millions more who depend on their earnings adds up to an interdependence and integrating force far in excess in real terms of anything that was enacted between the formation of the Arab League in 1945 and the defeat in the Six Day War of 1967. Importantly, the two myths upon which Arab nationalism, pan-Arabism and the Cold War relied became irrelevant. The first myth stated that the Arabs constitute one nation, the second that the needs and desires of millions of people could be neatly summarized in slogans such as 'unity, liberation and revolution' (Kerr, 1971, p. 3). In addition, other factors added to the demise of Arabism during this period, including the ascendancy of Palestinian nationalism, the emergence of Syria and Saudi Arabia as regional power players, the Maronites in Lebanon who opted out of the Arab state system and the new value and emphasis put on the development of nation-state nationalism and patriotism over other nationalist ideologies.

Case study Egyptian nationalism

The rise of Egyptian nationalism at the turn of the twentieth century was associated with an urbanized, anti-colonial, educated elite which was determined to end Britain's hold over the largest country in the region. During World War I London proclaimed Egypt a British protectorate and the country was subordinated to British strategic, military and political interests. Opposition among Egyptians to the British centred on mobilizing opinion and developing strategies to oust the British from their country. Egyptian consciousness-raising centred on the belief in the unity of the Arab people in the face of damaging foreign interference. The goal of the national movement was an end to British control, independence and self-determination. This vision was articulated by the leaders of a new political group led by prominent Egyptians and named the Wafd. The British basically refused to legitimate the call for independence and instead pursued policies of suppression. This refusal to allow greater political freedom for Egyptians only served to intensify hostility towards them in the aftermath of the war. From 1918 to 1922 Egyptian opposition increased, through Arab nationalist and pan-Islamic political platforms. Pressure was so great that eventually the British were forced to concede some ground for fear of full-scale national revolt. In February 1922 the protectorate was terminated and the British decreed that Egypt was a 'constitutional monarchy'. Technical independence may well have been declared, but Britain still remained firmly in control.

This technical and titular Egyptian head of state did not satisfy nationalist demands. While many differences existed within Egyptian society, for example between the peasant population and land-owning classes, all were agreed on one thing – that Britain should relinquish its political power over the country and let the Egyptians rule. Negotiations did take place, but by and large the position on key issues changed little and British influence remained significant. A new Anglo-Egyptian Treaty signed in 1936 shored up Britain's interests.

The Second World War proved a turning point in Anglo-Egyptian relations. Britain used the war situation to impose its security apparatus over the Egyptians, and military rule was supported by press censorship, suspension of the Egyptian legislature and government as well as the further imposition of martial law. All this took place in a country acting as an important base and ally for the British. In post-war Egypt the nationalists and their Islamic counterparts took advantage of the relaxation of various war restrictions to push their agenda into the public arena. Indeed, during the period from 1945 to 1950, mass-based demands for independence from the British were articulated throughout the country, ultimately making British rule increasingly untenable. The movement for independence in Egypt was difficult to withstand, and public protest and demonstration became an almost daily occurrence. Although Britain extended its coercive powers, it was compelled to enter into talks with Egyptian nationalists to determine the country's future. By 1951, however, the talks had stalled and the Egyptians broke the treaty with Britain. Public demonstrations and disorder became the rule of the day, as ordinary Egyptians took to the streets in cities and towns throughout the country. By early 1952 even the Egyptian police, who were employed by the British, had turned against their overlords and, once again, the British announced martial law across the whole country. In July 1952 a military *coup d'état* led by Gamal Abdel Nasser took place. King Farouk abdicated, the constitution of 1923 was abolished, political parties were dissolved and banned. A new political era was born and British days were numbered.

Gamal Abdel Nasser, the Egyptian nationalist leader, ranks as one of the most significant political figures in the Middle East in the twentieth century. His sustained vision of a united Arab world was rapidly translated into populist support which spread throughout the region in the 1950s and 1960s. For better or for worse, Nasser and his supporters shaped the future of Arab nationalism both within the region and in the international arena. Indeed, the ideology of nationalism which became associated with this era became known as Nasserism. It was largely an expression of the marriage between revolutionary socialism and pan-Arabism on Egyptian, or rather, Nasser's terms. The Suez Crisis of 1956, despite the military defeat of Egypt, projected Nasser's vision of pan-Arab unity and nationalism throughout the region and encouraged him to promote further his agenda for Arab unity. It can be asserted that from this point 'Nasser himself made Arab nationalism his personal message, especially in the sense that he was its natural leader and Egypt the nucleus state of the Arab world' (Hopwood, 1985, p. 98).

The reality of promoting the Egyptian state as the 'nucleus' of the pan-Arab model was somewhat different from the ideas developed by Nasser and his supporters. While it is true that Nasser did enjoy widespread mass and popular Arab support, the same could not be said of levels of support for Nasser's pan-Arab ideals among the political elite and leaders of a variety of Arab states. Indeed, while on one hand Nasser promoted unity in practice, on the other his unwillingness to compromise and his quest for Egyptian supremacy in any regionally integrated order created new tensions and fissures between the leaders of Arab states, which would ultimately kill the unity dream from within and leave the Arabs, post-1967, in a state of disarray. Nevertheless, by the mid-1960s even the leaders of the conservative Arab regimes found it increasingly difficult to resist the tide of change which Nasser appeared to have inaugurated within the region. Pressure and populist sentiment was so great that conservative regimes whose governing ideology represented the antithesis of Nasserism were goaded and compelled into siding with Nasser in his decision to wage war against Israel in the name of the Palestinians.

The greatest illusion created by Nasser on the eve of the Arab war against Israel in June 1967 was the myth of Arab unity in the face of a common enemy – Israel. In reality, there was no sense of unity among the Arab states of Egypt, Jordan and Syria which would lead the attack against Israel. Nasser, for example, taunted and goaded Jordan into the war and again used the notion of Arab unity to legitimate his aggressive stance vis-à-vis other Arab states. The defeat became Nasser's defeat, and the illusion of unity which had prevailed in the region was shattered for ever. While Nasserist movements are still present in the regional landscape of politics, the 1967 watershed effectively ended the dream associated with Nasser's rhetoric. Pan-Arab political integration would never deliver the Palestinians from Israeli rule, nor act as a bulwark against superpower rivalry in the region. Arabness, post-Nasser, would be reconstituted according to a different agenda.

Case study Ba'thism – unification or state nationalism?

For more than thirty years Ba'thism (Renaissance) has played a pivotal ideological role in the states of Syria and Iraq. Ba'thism has subsequently become associated with one-party rule, a lack of democracy, militarized society, dictatorship and decline. It is not just an expression of an Arab nationalist identity, but calls for a wider unity among the Arab people under a socialist agenda.

The Ba'th Party was founded by two Syrian intellectuals, Michel Aflaq and Salah al-din al-Bitar, in the early 1940s. Aflaq, a Christian, and al-Bitar, a Muslim, drew up an agenda based on the principles of secular, nationalist socialism which would unite all Arabs throughout the region irrespective of religion, nation or class. Their ideas were crystallized in the establishment of the Ba'th Party when it held its first congress in Damascus in 1947. In addition to the party establishing itself in Syria, branches soon followed in Iraq, Jordan and Lebanon by the early 1950s. The objectives of the party were based around the theme of pan-Arab unity under the banner of 'one nation' with a policy of socialism and national revival. This call found a large audience in a period following the decline of the colonial powers, which included the departure of the French from Syria and Lebanon, the British from Iraq, Egypt, Palestine and Jordan, the phenomenon of pan-Arabism and pan-Islamism which had been established in other parts of the region and the example of other post-colonial socialist movements in the Third World. Ba'thism would promise the liberation and subsequent freedom of the Arab people from communal, religious and ethnic loyalties as well as loyalties to artificially created nation-states, which had been the product of western interference in the region. Aflaq enshrined these aspirations in the slogan 'unity, liberation and socialism'. Freedom was envisioned in a personal as well as a national sense.

Socialism was the ideological facilitator for the aspiration for freedom and Arab unity, outlining a social and political order designed to eliminate confessional and class difference. The problem that the Ba'th Party faced, however, was how to achieve the necessary political change to reach its objectives. The solution presented itself in the form of *coup d'état* rather than reformist change, along the path advocated by many other national liberation movements throughout the region and the Third World in general.

A *coup d'état* rather than society-wide revolution was the path which eventually allowed the Ba'thists to obtain power in both Iraq and Syria. Thus, the link between Ba'thism and militarism was established and some of the earlier ideas advocated by Aflaq were abandoned. In Syria the Ba'thists had been significant political actors throughout the 1950s and by 1963 were major players in the military *coup*. However, it was not until the second *coup* of 1966 that the Ba'thists were able to consolidate their power over the state and its political institutions. By 1966 the Ba'th Party was firmly in the hands of the young military Alawites – an Islamic sect, in the minority in Syria – and Aflaq and al-Bitar had become marginalized figures. Although leadership of the country changed again in 1970, when General Salah Jadid was defeated in a third *coup* led by Hafiz al-Assad, an Alawite, the generally Ba'thist ambitions for Arab unity and socialism were maintained, although in a more symbolic function. The failures of the UAR in 1961 and the defeat of the Arabs in the Six Day War of 1967 had resulted in the maintenance of the competition for Arab leadership between the Syrians and Egyptians in particular but had also severely dented popular support and belief in a united Arab nation, even when it was called to rally round an issue as important as the Palestinian–Israeli conflict.

After 1970 Hafiz al-Assad established what Hinnebusch (1990) describes as an 'authoritarian presidency': pluralism in politics almost vanished, Alawite sectarianism came to dominate the ethnic and religious mosaic of the country, a socialist state-planned economy failed, intransigence over the conflict with Israel was maintained and politics became meaningless unless played out under the rubric of the party through recruitment, membership, policy, the military, elections and participation. The death of Hafiz al-Assad in June 2000 led to the succession of his youngest son, Bashar. Bashar al-Assad's attempts to open up the political system have largely been quashed by the ever important triumvirate of the Ba'th Party, the military and the Alawite powerhouse. Nevertheless al-Assad faces new opposition in the form of the trade sanctions regime imposed by the United States of America in 2004, the vulnerability of Syria's borders to events in Iraq since 2003 and the resurgence of Islamist movements such as the Muslim Brotherhood.

The same defeat of the principles of Ba'thism became largely true of Iraq where, following the Ba'thist *coup* of 1968 and the reign of Saddam Hussein, who became President in 1979, one-party rule, and 'authoritarian presidency' were prevalent. In Iraq, however, the pretence of party leadership, according to Owen, was soon dropped by Hussein, who 'made it clear he was no longer interested in an image of collective leadership but one of personal power' (Owen, 2003, p. 263). The Ba'th Party was eclipsed by this drive for dictatorship, and the military/security apparatus rather than the party, despite its million-plus membership, was the vehicle employed by Saddam Hussein to maintain power. The call to Arab unity was merely a foil for his personal ambitions in territorial conflict with Iran and Kuwait, or Jordan and Syria. Arab unity in Hussein's lexicon implied his personal dictatorship through military control and fear. The visionary calls of Aflaq and al-Bitar for a pluralist socialist state were abandoned and Saddam Hussein succeeded in ostracizing the state from its Arab brethren in the region and internally.

Iraq's economy was ravaged by a combination of war and UN sanctions, its population living in the apocalyptically named 'Republic of Fear'. Unity, liberation and socialism were largely lost in both Syria and Iraq, replaced by a slogan for the twenty-first century, 'fragmentation, subjugation and capitalism'. These three factors represent not just the failures of those who claimed to harness the ideas of Ba'thism as an expression of Arab nationalism, but the profound political and economic changes in the global environment: the fall of the former Soviet Union, the death of Marxism, the resurgence of Islamist movements, ethnic conflict and worldwide recession. These wider global changes compounded the paradox of the Ba'thist tendency to authoritarianism; the primacy of continued dictatorship being more desirable than further ethnic or religious fragmentation and political change in these two countries. In Iraq Ba'thism was put to death as Saddam Hussein was toppled from power in April 2003 and the country fell under the military and civil occupation of Allied forces led by the United States of America. The immediate collapse and dismantlement of the Ba'thist state – including the political party, its various committees, military, police and security apparatus –

plunged post-war Iraq into a security vacuum which foreign military forces have struggled to fill.

It cannot be argued that nationalism epitomized by the Ba'th Party in either Syria or Iraq represents or expresses an inclusive sense of nation. In this respect, if Ba'thism represents a nationalist ideology it has truly, to paraphrase Gellner, 'come before a nation' and has also failed to unite or create a sense of nation among a disparate group of peoples divided by tribal, ethnic and sectarian difference. In these cases nationalism has failed in its unification function and its success lay only in allowing minority interest (Takriti – the clan within Iraq from which Saddam Hussein comes – or Alawite) to be promoted and consolidated as national interest in the task of state-building. In post-war Iraq nation-building and the discourse on Iraqi nationalism has begun all over again. The state remains susceptible to new debates and divisions over what it means to be an Iraqi national in the twenty-first century.

Further reading

General theoretical accounts of nationalism can be found in Smith (1979), Gellner (1983) and Breuilly (1993). Eric Hobsbawm's (1990) account of nation and nationalism is also particularly useful for a general overview of debates and Benedict Anderson (1983) pays particular attention to the construction of national identities. Kedourie (1993), who has also written about Arab political culture and issues of democracy, gives his own insights into the debate on nationalism, setting out a unique context for the reader to then apply to the Middle East. Kellas (1991) is useful in clearly setting out main themes and approaches to the subject. On Arab nationalism, historical overviews from Provence (2005) and Abdul-Jabar and Dawod (2003) are helpful. Tibi (1997) provides a comprehensive account of contemporary theories and approaches associated with thinking on the subject. Choueiri (1989) presents a critical analysis of Arab nationalism and related debates of historiography. Suleiman (2004) reflects on issues of nationalism, national identity and language in the Middle East. Tauber has produced two texts (1993a and 1993b) which provide a strong historical account of the emergence of Arab nationalism and Arab nationalist movements in the Middle East at the turn of the century, while Khoury (1983 and 1987) examines more specific features of colonialism, nationalism and its elite base. The anthology of Arab nationalist literature in Haim (1969) provides an accessible account of nationalist thinking in the Arab world. Tibi's (1997) in-depth account of Arab nationalists such as Sati al-Husri should also be reviewed along with Haim. Debate on the import of Arab nationalism and historiography is covered by Khalidi et al. (1991), Abu-Khalil (1992), Firro (2003) and al-Azmeh (1995) and should be contrasted against more traditional accounts such as those of Antonius (1969), Brown (1984) and Fromkin (1989). The nationalism and Islam matrix is reviewed in texts such as Moaddel (2005), Piscatori (1986), Vatikiotis (1987) and Tibi (1987), and further reading on this subject can also be found in chapter 5. On early Egyptian nationalism and Nasserism, a number of books abound.

Coverage of early Egyptian nationalism can be discovered in Coury (1982), Khoury (1983), Warburg and Kupferschmidt's edited collection of historical insights (1983), Wilson (1983) and Dawn (1988). Stephens's (1971) biography of Nasser is extensive in its account and provides detail to the more general accounts found in Mansfield (1969) or Hopwood (1985). More recently, Gordon (1992) and Abdel Magid (1994) have both produced cogent and interesting books on the Nasser era. For accounts of Ba'thism in Iraq, Devlin (1976), Batatu (1979), Farouk-Sluglett and Sluglett (1990) and Baram (1991) examine the impact of this philosophy on state-formation and political life. Khalil (1989) outlines an account of life in Ba'thist Iraq with chilling clarity. Tripp (2002) and Dodge (2003) both demonstrate the problems inherent to nation and state building in Iraq and the impact of Ba'thist ideology and rule under Saddam Hussein. Moreover they highlight the many problems that lay in the colonial roots of this newly forged nation and state created in the early part of the twentieth century. Kienle (1990) achieves a similar feat in his text on Ba'thism, which takes a comparative approach to the Syrian and Iraqi examples. Hopwood (1988) provides a good overview of politics and society in Syria from 1945 to 1986 and Seale (1988) offers the most comprehensive and in-depth account of the country under Hafiz al-Assad. Perthes (2004) has produced a new work on Syrian politics under the new president Bashar al-Assad that demonstrates the issues besetting this President of the Arab republic.

Political Economy: Riches of a Region

Iᴛ is tempting to believe that the issues affecting contemporary economics and politics in the Middle East revolve solely around oil and the revenues (rents) derived from its production. While oil is important to any understanding of political economy in the region, there are a number of other issues which are worth examining, such as water, and the conflicts over its distribution and usage, debates about import-substituting industrialization, urbanization and the region's poor economic performance in global markets. Nevertheless, our popular conception of the region and its wealth is dominated by the issue of oil. Cheap caricatures of an oil-rich region populated by wealthy Arab sheikhs who gamble away millions at the casinos in Cannes or Monaco feed our perception of the area. The region's large oil reserves (66 per cent of the world's supply) have resulted in the rapid creation of wealth for some states and an often near total dependency on oil revenues. The region's relations with the West (and, formerly, the Soviet East) have also been significantly affected by the oil factor. It has eased integration into the world trading system and papered over some inherent economic weaknesses.

Is there a 'pan-Arab' economy internal to the region which is united by the above factors? The group of countries that the term seeks to cover are disparate entities and separate economic units with diverging economic policies and different historical and political foundations. Can we speak of an oil economy? Here, as this chapter illustrates, the ripples in the oil pool are easy to discern. Irrespective of economic policy, political orientation or historical antecedents, there are very few if any economies in the region that are not altered or affected by oil, its production and its revenues.

Other issues evolve out of these debates, including the impact on economies of other natural resources in the region such as gas and water and related questions about excessive energy use. Political and economic development in Algeria, for example, could never be adequately understood without first analysing the impact of the gas industry and the wealth associated with it. The Algerian FLN's (Front de Libération Nationale) success in state-building and consolidation was significantly bolstered by the wealth created by gas. Mismanagement, the constriction of state control of the industry and declining prices in the world market all played their part in the economic crisis of the late 1980s and early 1990s which provoked the political crisis that led in turn to the civil war that devastated the country for most of the 1990s. Similarly, the resolution of the Arab–Israeli conflict can only be achieved when disputes over water have also been dealt with.

Other issues important in understanding the relationships between politics and economics in the region are rentier economies and states, the development/decline of agriculture, migrant labour and its impact within the region, and state ideologies which have shaped the nature of economic policy and development. The importance of all these issues is reflected in and illustrated by the cases studied in this chapter. The first case of Kuwait is a prime example of oil dependency and is also an example of rentier economies – i.e. a state increasingly dependent on unearned income. The second case of Egypt highlights the issues of migrant labour, dependency, distortion of agriculture and raw materials, and of how water affects the economic and political development of the region's largest country.

Rich man, poor man, beggar man, thief

Located in the Middle East are some of the world's poorest and richest states. This fact raises an important question relating to development and development studies. Is the Middle East part of the Third World? If countries such as Egypt or Yemen are cited from such diverse perspectives as Gross Domestic Product (GDP), Gross National Product (GNP), infant mortality, literacy rates, national debt and International Monetary Fund (IMF) loans, it might lead us to conclude that it is. In Egypt, for example, while the overall economic situation improved throughout the 1990s, with GDP per capita growing around an average of 1.5 per cent per year, unemployment remained as high as 9.9 per cent (World Bank, est. Egypt). In Yemen the economic situation has deteriorated since unification of the country in 1990 with inflation running, by 1994, at 71 per cent, declining to single digit levels at 6 per cent by 1997 but reaching 10.9 per cent in 2000. Poverty, development crises, disease and economic stagnation are, therefore, not unknown in the region. Other characteristics of colonial and post-colonial society, proximity to other developing regions, the former Cold War theatre and polarized development strategies, all support inclusion in the Third World category. The mega-wealthy states of the region, however, would, one might imagine, make it harder to generalize and apply the Third World label. But there are a number of ways in which even those wealthy states are somehow still denied membership of the First World club. Here, all the economic clout in the world can still be ignored in favour of ascribing Third World characteristics to political systems, governments, institutions and the law. Saudi Arabia may be a First World player economically, its citizens may enjoy per capita GDP as high as $7,000, but its conservative, anti-democratic and authoritarian state structure and rule still condemn it to Third World status in popular and global perception.

There is still merit in exploring the patterns of economic similarity within the region that characterize states as either rich or poor. What kind of wealth one is talking about is also worth reflecting on. Is migrant labour-rich Egypt, with a population of 68 million and average daily wage rates of $3, for example, any more or less dependent than labour-poor but oil-rich Kuwait, with a population at just 2.4 million in the twenty-first century? Is wealth distributed equally among citizens, or is it the property of the few, and what is the nature of state and class relations in the rich and poor states of the region? How relevant, for example, are other indicators of economic development, such as expansion of industry, a strong agricultural sector or the access to essential natural resources such as water, in telling the story of economic development in the region? Wealth, then, becomes a relative term depending on which perspective one takes. For example, Saudi Arabia may be able to buy an agricultural sector that grows its own wheat and breeds its own cattle for milk and beef, but at what cost and level of sustainability? In Egypt agricultural diversification in the Nile delta has evolved over centuries and currently includes more than half of the cultivated land in the country, yet it has struggled with import dependency issues for decades (Held, 1994, p. 261). These issues assume as much importance in the eastern states of the region as the preoccupation with oil does in the western states of the area. The issue of water, for example, may become increasingly important in assessing the relative wealth of states in the region and their capacity for future economic development. Water wealth, then, will become vital in the economic, political and territorial future of the region, as well as a source of conflict (Allan and Mallat, 1995, p. 15). Economic development has been affected by the rapid population growth witnessed across the region – the Middle East has some of the highest rates of population growth in the world, combined in states like Yemen with some of the highest rates for infant mortality (87 per 1,000 live births). The consolidation of post-colonial economies through programmes of national development, diversification and sustainability has not always been successful. National debt and public spending deficits, for example, in countries like Egypt, Syria and Jordan, have economically enslaved them to the dictates of foreign government aid programmes such as those from America to Egypt. The US has granted Egypt $1.3 billion a year in military aid since 1979, and an average of $815 million a year in economic assistance. All told, Egypt has received over $50 billion in US aid since 1975.

In addition, planning and economic policy are also dependent on international lending organizations like the IMF and World Bank on which, for example, in the 1990s Yemen was dependent for $80 million as part of the International Development Association's (IDA) economic recovery programme and an IMF 'stand-by arrangement' (World Bank, Yemen). The impact of such relationships is widespread, as Ehteshami and Murphy (1996) note: 'While there may be popular consensus over the need for reform, there is decreasingly so over the strategy of economic liberalization, and particularly IMF-negotiated structural adjustment programmes, the benefits of which are usually "deferred, uncertain and diffused" ' (p. 766).

The political implications of such relationships are not difficult to discern. They explain, for example, Egypt's role in the American-sponsored Arab–Israeli peace process, Jordan's path to political liberalization and, until 1990, Syria's military alliances with the Soviet Union. Real economic independence, then, whether in rich or poor states in the Middle East, remains something of a holy grail. In the so-called sanction countries of Iran and Syria the same problems of wealth creation, distribution and sustainability occupy policy-makers, economists and citizens alike. Economic crisis or instability of any sort can be identified, irrespective of relative wealth, in any state in the region as potentially explosive. Explosive, because citizens remain consistently weakened by the vagaries of Arab economies and marginal or excluded from the political leaders who decide policies of resource allocation within their societies. This is particularly true in the case of those Arab states such as Egypt, Syria, Algeria or Tunisia, where nationalist single-party regimes instituted classic Third World policies of import-substitution industrialization (ISI) in the modernization and development of state and national economies. The policy of ISI implied a decline in dependence on the export of raw materials and basic commodities and dependence on imported goods. Imported goods would be produced by the economy at home and raw material, such as cotton, which had previously been exported would be manufactured into cloth in the domestic economy. The economic benefits of ISI were a reduced dependence on the world market and independence from costly foreign imports.

The associated state model of corporatism has created new class interests associated with the state elite (industrial bourgeoisie) and widened the very gap between the state and working classes that the populist appeals of such regimes initially attempted to narrow. Such exclusion, as noted in other chapters, has led to growing economic discontent, food riots and price rise demonstrations in an increasing number of economies, consequently emphasizing the vulnerability of claims to legitimacy by political leaders. This particular phenomenon has been highlighted by the failure of the corporatist model throughout the single-party states in the region in the mid- to late 1980s and the concurrent waves of popular protest which accompanied programmes of economic liberalization that these states were encouraged to adopt. Indeed, the very failure of ISI by the 1970s led to an era of recession and economic adjustment throughout the region. In Tunisia, for example, the direction of the economy under socialist principles had already failed by 1970 and the state began an inexorable path towards decentralization, liberalization and a reduced role in the economy. By the mid-1970s a similar economic path had been adopted in Egypt, as illustrated in this chapter's case study. The process highlighted the paradox for state elites who on the one hand knew that their very survival depended on policies of liberalization, but on the other were unwilling to relinquish control over the economy (Ayubi, 1995). In addition, like many nationalized industries throughout the globe, the process of privatization did not always guarantee economic success. The pressures of economic events regionally and globally, especially by the 1980s when oil prices reached an all-time low and recession gripped the advanced industrialized economies, inhibited the momentum for adjustment and expanded capitalism. Thus, conversely, the further the economy was restructured to promote profit, deregulation and a reduced role for the state, the more indebtedness grew. Political movement did not occur in a broad-based liberalized form and opposition to these economic changes continues to grow.

Endemic corruption, poor planning of resource allocation and misappropriation of state funds in Middle Eastern economies also reflect the chasm between state and citizens and opaque mechanisms of state control over the economy. Attempts at economic adjustment appear only to have succeeded in widening the gap between rich and poor in nearly every country throughout the region. Yet this need not be the case, as Stewart (1995) argues: 'while increasing poverty is the norm for countries undergoing adjustment, *this is not necessary; poverty can be reduced during adjustment* . . . governments can make choices . . . which offset, or accentuate any ill-effects of adjustment on the poor' (p. 193). In addition, the state elites which redistribute national wealth, revenue and funds to their own pockets are found in nearly every capital city in the region. Irrespective of whether they are Arab, Israeli, Wahabi, Maronite, Ba'thist, Alawite or Takriti, their 'theft' of national wealth has severely undermined economic confidence in the region. In the Gulf states, business people are wary of trading with Arab governments, given the vast level of bribes needed to secure contracts. Debt is becoming a common feature of these wealthy regimes and, as in the case of Saudi Arabia, budget cuts of around 20 per cent in 1994 did 'not affect the royal family' but only the rest of Saudi society, leading to dangerous political antagonisms (Aburish, 1994, p. 304). Moreover per capita GDP in Saudi Arabia has, in the twenty-first century, begun to dip below the $10,000 mark. In the autonomous Palestinian West Bank and Gaza Strip corruption became a currency as a form of reward for Fatah loyalists who supported Yasser Arafat's Palestinian National Authority (PNA), whose $326 million in foreign aid was subject to persistent allegations of misuse amid accusations of poor mechanisms for financial accountability and rumours of extortion by Palestinian public officials. The same stories are repeated in Damascus, Riyadh, Kuwait city, Tunis, Algiers, Cairo, Baghdad, Tripoli, Beirut and Manama – while the Arab world burns, their leaders dance, eat and make merry on profits from state industries, revenues from state assets and investments, bribes from the business community and loans secured in the name of poor and destitute populations. The remedy is linked to the political argument for increased democracy: open government and an end to authoritarianism – both economic and political – which currently characterizes the region. This particular assessment of the Middle East economy is highlighted in the work of Richards and Waterbury, who stress the symbiotic nature of the relationship between politics, state development, modernization and the transformation of societies from traditional agricultural modes of production to the ISI-corporatist and authoritarian models of rule and economic planning. These authors want to refocus the lenses of analysis: 'what we have in mind is the formulation of public policies that shape the allocation of resources within societies *and* the political consequences that flow therefrom' (Richards and Waterbury, 1990, p. 2). This particular lens, looking at the economy and its impact on the political, is particularly useful in explaining the growth and nature of the rentier economies in the contemporary Middle East.

Many models make poor work

A variety of economic systems and interpretations of economy have been practised in the Middle East with varying degrees of success, and there has been no single uniform pattern of economic relations across the region. Too often the nature of economic systems and practices has been affected by political, religious and cultural considerations which often impact at the same time. Talk of purely Marxist, socialist or capitalist economies in the Middle East, therefore, is difficult; even in those rare attempts to develop 'pure type', ideology-based economies, other factors have soon muddied the waters. In addition, as Gran (1990) highlights, the way in which political economists and Marxists look at the Middle East is still grounded by orientalist assumptions and the unique supremacy, for example, of western-inspired liberal trade theory:

> They argue that when British industrial goods reached the Middle East in the nineteenth century, people bought them because they were cheaper. But why should pricing, taste and access to market have been such simple matters in the Middle East when studies of working class culture elsewhere suggest how complicated such matters were? (p. 231)

Indeed, the way in which most economies of the region are distinguished, identified and differentiated is along western lines of analysis, taking little account of traditional patterns of commerce, trade, ownership, religious belief (Muslim, Christian or Jewish) or gender relations. What becomes clear, however, is that while a particular economy may be described in broadly, say, capitalist terms, for comparison's sake, the local patterns of economic relations must be reflected in the discussion of specific economic indicators such as GDP, export or foreign earnings.

Capitalist economies in the region have flourished with limited success and few notable examples. In Lebanon, however, the economy has always been market- rather than state-led. Indeed, Lebanon is a notable example of a free market economy and its resulting impact on the state and political system. The state is weak in a variety of ways but particularly in terms of directing the national economy. A lack of natural resources in Lebanon, a small, largely urbanized population of 3.5 million and a significant refugee and migrant population have all contributed to the development of economic practice based on a large service sector (which used to serve the whole of the region) and commercial interests. Yet, as a result of a weak state and the perennial problem of corruption in the 1970s, the government wrought its own downfall and the commencement of a civil war which would last for fifteen years. The revival of the capitalist economy in the 1990s has been characterized by many of the features from the 1970s, and attempts to introduce a mixed approach to the economy are few and far between. This leaves the country facing the same political fallout from economic policies as it did in the 1970s, with anti-government protest focusing on demands that Lebanon's leaders change their economic policy. In May 2004 protesters filled the streets of Beirut in dispute over rising fuel prices with five killed by Lebanese armed forces. In addition, reconstruction of the country has compelled its leaders to seek loans from international lending organizations such as the World Bank and regional lenders including Kuwait.

Examples of socialist- or Marxist-based economies in the region are Egypt, Syria, Iraq, Yemen, Libya and Algeria. The political linkage between these economic types and the emergence of one-party states in the 1950s, 1960s and 1970s is strong. The socialist economies of the region, based on the ideological agenda of Arab nationalist and state-led development, has included land reform, industrialization, nationalization (e.g. the Suez Canal in 1956), planned economies, state-centred development policies and limits on private capital and commercial interests or land ownership. The success of such economies, however, particularly by the late 1970s, has been called into question. Since that point crisis has precipitated a move in such economies towards liberalization or *infitah* (open door policy). In the case of Syria this has led to economic reform which has included a greater role for the private sector, cuts in public expenditure, reduction of foreign trade imbalances, but avoidance of large-scale privatization or major expansion of the merchant sector in Syria's economy. Nevertheless, Syria has avoided incurring debt or seeking loans from the World Bank or IMF, but much of its economy still remains highly dependent on income derived from oil. Further economic reform, however, is dependent on the willingness of the regime to engage in political liberalization at the same time. To date, the Ba'thist government has avoided this particular issue and by taking an incremental and selective approach to reform it has avoided the widespread alienation and legitimacy crisis which accompanied the problems of the 1980s (Perthes, 1995, p. 251). Syria, like the other primarily socialist economies of the region, is engaged in a delicate balancing act between economic reform and the maintenance of state power amid pressures from external players like the US that have resulted in the imposition of trade sanctions. Central to this balancing act is the ability of the state elite to manipulate the process of change rather than allow the masses to determine the pace and extent of political empowerment. In sum, as Ehteshami and Murphy (1996) observe, 'Middle Eastern socialism has almost always in reality been a combination of *etatism* and welfarism' rather than the real revolutionary economic principles associated with the concept by its ideologues (p. 758).

Islamic economic practice is found in multiple locations in the region, from the Islamic banking systems of Cairo to the levy of a charity tax (*zakat*) by Islamic movements like FIS (Front Islamique du Salut) in Algeria. Islamic economic principles include the following measures: a hostility to socialism, 'approval of certain aspects of capitalism, including private ownership of the means of production, profit maximization as a motor force in economic behaviour and free market competition in products, service and labour' (Pfeifer, 1997, p. 157). In addition, the religion prohibits usury – interest on money loaned. Following the 1979 Revolution in Iran, the theocracy established by Ayatollah Khomeini attempted to Islamicize the economy in a number of ways, including state confiscation of privately owned businesses and industries and the introduction of Islamic banking, involving the abolition of interest. For most of the 1980s the creation of an Islamic economy in Iran was hindered by the war with Iraq, sanctions levied by the international community and a decline in oil prices. In the 1990s, however, the advent of a moderate and pragmatic government led by Rafsanjani encouraged economic development, including a free trade zone in Qeshm, reprivatization of some industry and a more stable oil economy and production. Iran accounts for 7 per cent of world oil reserves. Moreover, a slow but gradual rehabilitation in international economic markets had also encouraged some foreign investment. Iran, like other Islamic states or economies, has acknowledged the power of the international market and faces the challenge of reaching economic arrangements which meet religious as well as international requirements. Islamic economic principles, therefore, are neither wholly capitalist nor socialist/Marxist; rather, they reflect a unique marriage of economic principles and ideas which are familiar to economic theorists across the globe.

In the case of Iran, developments in the 1990s and early twenty-first century highlight the advent of a certain approach to economic policy in the contemporary Middle East which is associated with liberalization. Specific aspects of this approach are examined in the case study of Egypt at the end of this chapter, but at this point a few general remarks are required. Economic liberalization occurred in the region from the 1970s onwards and was further entrenched in the early 1980s as many states of the region faced vast foreign debts, the collapse of their own currency, rampant inflation and crisis in their economies. While modernization and ISI policies had encouraged a rapid population boom and demands for higher living standards from the newly urbanized population of the region, the economy could no longer deliver. While it was true that the region enjoyed varying degrees of wealth generated from oil reserves, the plummeting price of oil and recession in the world economy began seriously to affect the amount of rent enjoyed from this source. As has already been noted, the region could no longer feed itself, had become increasingly aid-dependent and had a poor record in global export markets. There were few diversified economies and even so-called stable democratic Israel was suffering severe economic problems with survival dependent on huge American loans and aid and other forms of financial support from the diaspora community.

One path out of this economic meltdown, for both oil and non-oil states, was a policy of structural adjustment and liberalization of aspects of the economy. Liberalization eventually occurred, in one form or another, in most countries of the region as a response to poverty and growing international pressure in the form of institutions like the IMF and World Bank. It is also important to remember that this state-led planning of the economy was a way in which the elite could preserve its power and continue to maximize its share of the national profit. In many respects, structural adjustment and liberalization was a compulsory 'no option' trend which would characterize the region from the 1980s onwards. The aim of such an approach in Algeria, Syria, Tunisia and Egypt was to create a new base for sustainable growth, even if this meant a cut in state provision in terms of social expenditure (it is worth noting that defence expenditure often remained stable), thus exacerbating the problems of poverty which economic crisis had created. Macro-economic liberalization resulted in a negative effect on the distribution of income and issues of social equity and welfare. Indeed, when the leaders of Syria or Jordan announced price rises or cuts in welfare spending in the name of 'national belt-tightening', it was the poor who suffered more.

Nevertheless, the forced agenda of economic liberalization, relinquishing state control over the economy, encouraging new economic actors, foreign investment and capital, and diversification of industry, has resulted in limited economic improvement in some states of the region. For example, Egypt's economy was recognized as holding real promise, with macro-stabilization efforts which Egypt undertook in the early 1990s a success and longer-term structural reforms under way (Global Agenda, p. 13). The political consequences of even such faltering and minor improvements in disparate economies of the region have been serious and are characterized, as discussed at length in the chapter on democratization, by an increasing tendency to reassert state authority through coercion. Ultimately, economic liberalization in the region, unlike other areas of the Third World, has not ushered in democracy; rather, as Ehteshami and Murphy (1996) argue, 'political liberalism is in retreat ... economic liberalization creates a restructuring' of interests which only consolidate and benefit the power-holders rather than the powerless (p. 768).

Evolution of oil-based economies

For as long as the Middle East is host to some 66 per cent of the world's oil reserves, the fascination of economists, politicians and policy-makers with the region will remain. The presence of such large oil reserves in Saudi Arabia, Kuwait, the United Arab Emirates, Iraq and Iran alone have ensured the domination of the Middle East in the world oil market and producer organizations such as the Organization of Petroleum Exporting Countries (OPEC). As Hudson (1977) remarked, 'oil is beginning to transform the Arab economy in fundamental ways . . . oil is certain to be increasingly linked with politics – internal, regional and international – as Arabs debate who shall control the oil and how the revenues should be used' (p. 140). Since the discovery in the 1920s of major oil reserves and the establishment of oil-producing fields in the Gulf area, the unseemly scrabble to cash in on Arab (and Persian) oil carried on for the best part of the twentieth century. The oil epoch is littered with alarming episodes, among which are the European and American exploitation of reserves, price-fixing through the 1973 oil boycott, the Iranian Revolution, and the débâcle of three wars in the Gulf: the 1980–8 Iran–Iraq war, the 1990–1 Gulf crisis and Operation Desert Storm led by America following Iraq's invasion of Kuwait, and the 2003 American-led invasion of Iraq. It is these episodes as much as the startling but rather dry economic calculations of wealth, price per barrel, production costs, sales, production capacity and OPEC quotas which illustrate the impact of oil on the economy, development and modernization and politics in the region. Oil production, then, has shaped and influenced the nature of most states in the region, in particular the Gulf states. It does this through the impact on state revenue of income derived at home and abroad (Luciani, 1990, p. 70). By the twenty-first century oil prices steadily rose and experts were warning that prices could even rise as high as $100 per barrel.

The story of oil and its production within the region is inevitably rooted in the colonial era. The role played by British companies, particularly in Iran and other parts of the Gulf, in the exploration of oil resources coincided with British government attempts to strengthen its foothold in the region – as an old joke illustrates, BP stood for 'Bugger Persia' not 'British Petroleum'. The first decades of the twentieth century witnessed the discovery and exploitation of the region's oil resources by various foreign powers. In Iran, for example, from 1920 British influence and control of the country was consistently linked, until the 1950s, to the production of oil and monopolized by the Anglo-Iranian oil company later known as British Petroleum (BP). Iran possessed and still possesses substantial oil reserves, making it the second largest oil producer in the Middle East. By the 1930s, however, Britain became a minority player in foreign oil production in the region, as a number of American oil companies – Exxon, Mobil, Texaco, Gulf and Socal – moved into the region and, more specifically, the oil-rich Gulf. The Anglo-Dutch company Shell completed the picture, and the operations of the 'Seven Sisters', as they became known, ensured a complete foreign monopoly of oil in the region. The impact on the political systems of the region at this time was significant. The oil companies worked in co-operation with each other and resisted demands from local leaders and rulers for greater royalty payments or control over their own oil fields. Control by the Seven Sisters of the oil business extended from reserves through exploration and production, to the petrochemical industry and oil refineries (Almulhim, 1991, p. 14). The Seven Sisters encouraged political growth only in so far as foreign patronage would allow, and more often than not the Arab and Iranian rulers of the region were surrounded by foreign advisers on military, foreign, economic and political affairs.

By the 1950s and early 1960s increasing resentment over the ratio of royalty payments (50/50), the impact of political radicalism and the rise of nationalism and pan-Arabism in the region provided an impetus for the first Iranian and Arab challenges to the monopoly of economic (and therefore, political) power that the Seven Sisters enjoyed. Iran was the first to undermine the status quo when it announced the nationalization of its oil resources in 1951. The government seized BP's installations, and oil production was halted for three years. The Americans gained a vital interest in the country by brokering the agreement in 1954 which allowed the resumption of production, and licences were granted to a consortium of oil companies to work in Iran.

The Iranian dispute was the first of many that would characterize the period. Nationalization was the goal of most Arab oil-producing states at that time. Some wanted to nationalize so as to direct their revenue from natural resources to their radical, socialist agendas, while others wanted to resist the pressure for change and preserve traditional dynastic rule and conservatism. The Seven Sisters, however, were not passive bystanders to these events and did their utmost to stem the tide of change. Iraqi nationalization of its oil industry in 1961, for example, led the major players to strike back and tighten their stranglehold on the oil market (Halliday, 1974, p. 397).

The ultimate expression of localized resistance to the domination of the oil market and price-fixing by the Seven Sisters came in 1960 with the formation of OPEC. Within the decade, the power of this newly founded organization became apparent, as further nationalization combined with the OPEC agreement to take more control over fixing the price of oil per barrel and greater control over the running of their oil industries. Collective action had bolstered the Seven Sisters, and the Arab oil-exporting countries, along with states like Venezuela, discovered that their collective rather than individual weight could be brought to bear to win bigger and better concessions for themselves over their natural resources. By 1972, despite nationalization, the formation of OPEC and concessions over control, the price per barrel of oil was still low, at only $1.4, and the Seven Sisters continued to dominate the market. The political changes in the region and the new-found confidence of the oil-producing countries would, however, precipitate the energy crisis of 1973, the oil weapon, the growth of the petro-dollar and the political clout wielded by the region.

Sheikhdoms and petro-power

The energy crisis of 1973 was the result of a number of factors, including the preceding pattern of nationalization, the internal battle between radical and conservative elements in the Arab world, foreign involvement in the region and the Arab–Israeli conflict. Indeed, it was the 1973 war between Israel and the Arabs which prompted the oil-producing states to announce production cuts which would send oil prices sky high. The Arab oil producers, with the exception of Iraq, and led by Saudi Arabia, asserted their power by punishing America and Holland, as well as other European countries, for supporting Israel during the war. The impact of this decision was profound. The American economy, for example, was rocked by the 'oil weapon'. America had felt secure in its supply of Arab oil, as companies like ARAMCO in Saudi Arabia had spent decades discovering and exploiting some of the largest oil fields in the world and so believed that it had the support of Saudi Arabia. In addition, the American economy, despite its own oil resources, was increasingly dependent on the profitable exploitation of Saudi oil fields. Low production costs, the post-war economic and manufacturing boom and domestic oil price quotas all propelled the Americans into a relationship of weakness which the Saudis and other Arab oil producers both exploited and exposed in 1973–4.

The production cuts announced in 1973 as a result of the Arab boycott led to a series of startling oil price increases. First, in October when the price per barrel shifted from $1.40 per barrel to $5.90. By December 1973 the price had risen again to $11.60 per barrel, heralding an energy crisis in western Europe and America. Petrol in Britain, for example, was suddenly subject to rationing, and power cuts became a frequent reminder of the impact of the 'oil weapon' in the Middle East on the distant lives of ordinary people. By 1971 oil had replaced coal as the most important source of energy and the crisis of 1973 made the economy vulnerable. However, it did prompt British politicians and policy-makers to exploit fully their country's own reserves in the North Sea oil fields so as to decrease the dependence on oil from the Middle East (Odell, 1981, p. 222). In the Middle East the effects of the production cuts and subsequent price rises were staggering: revenues derived from the sale of oil quadrupled and the power of the petro-dollar was felt throughout the world economy. In Saudi Arabia production cost per barrel of oil was just 1 cent while, as already noted, the price of sale was $11.60, leaving the Saudis to make huge profits (Wilson, 1979, p. 41). Countries like Saudi Arabia and Kuwait were transformed almost overnight into major players in the world economy, and they gained the power within their own countries to pursue their own conservative and anti-democratic agendas without requiring the political fealty of their citizens. Indeed, the tax-free economies of rentier states showed little inclination towards expanding or even establishing a democratic base in their societies (Luciani, 1990, p. xxiv).

The oil price bubble was burst by the Arabs themselves, again led by Saudi Arabia, which moved in 1974 to end production cuts and restore some sense of stability to the oil market. After all, the long-term interests of the Arab oil producers would not be served by the perpetuation of high oil prices associated with the oil weapon. Nevertheless, five years later the oil industry was shaken again following the events in Iran which brought about the fall of the Shah and the rise of Ayatollah Khomeini and the establishment of the Islamic Republic of Iran. Economic growth in Iran under the Shah had largely been dependent on the revenue from the country's oil fields. Much of the politics of the country under the Shah and his father before him had been shaped by first British and then American interest in exploiting these resources. Indeed, the Shah's quest for power had been supported by the Americans and the CIA on a number of occasions. The 1979 Revolution and its political stand of intense hostility to foreign power and the USA in particular gave rise to fears that Iran's oil production would cease, and as a result some two million barrels a day disappeared from the international market (Richards, 1993, p. 69). These fears of further price rises as a result of political instability in the region were further compounded by the war which broke out in 1980 between the revolutionary mujahideen of Iran and Ba'thist Iraq. Not only were both countries oil producers, but their strategic location, in and around vital Gulf shipping lanes, alarmed the oil market once again. This time, however, although price rises occurred, the market soon stabilized as a result of the pragmatic outlook by all parties involved.

The economic fortunes and the political clout of the oil-producing states were maintained in the early 1980s. However, by the end of the decade the effects of the world recession were hard to ignore, particularly in the rentier economies of the Gulf which were dependent on income from oil revenues and their substantial investments in a number of by now recession-ridden western economies. This decline in revenue coincided with the rise of political and economic discontent within a variety of oil-producing states. Political protest and opposition to the spending policies and rampant corruption apparent in Saudi Arabia, for example, was manifest in a series of workers' protests throughout the decade, which were brutally suppressed by the Saudi military (Aburish, 1994). While international human rights organizations and exiled dissident groups tried to highlight the poor political and human rights enjoyed by citizens in the oil-rich Gulf, the majority of western governments, including the Americans, were prepared to turn a blind eye so long as the flow of oil remained unhindered and prices remained stable. Any threat to that precious stability was worth opposing. The political nature of such states, whether progressive nationalist socialist, or conservative religious-dynastic, was immaterial to the equation in which oil prices and production were kept stable. Yet, this preoccupation with authoritarianism, in whatever shade it was expressed, as a form of protection in the capital-led market of the world economy, would ultimately have its price in the Middle East. That price was the Gulf crisis of 1990–1. Debates about oil and their revenues have also been key to the toppling of the regime of Saddam Hussein in Iraq and the costs of reconstruction in post-war Iraq. Before the war, US Deputy Secretary of Defence Paul Wolfowitz had confidently asserted to the US Congress that oil production, post-war, would derive revenue for Iraq of between $50 and 100 billion in a three year period. Post-war, the reality is a little different. Despite US protection, oil production has been subject to persistent sabotage by Iraqi insurgents and production has declined, leaving a major shortfall of promises for the national budget.

Rentier futures, profit in decline?

Since the emergence of the argument that oil is the single most important factor in determining the nature of the economy in the Middle East, a variety of writers have contributed to the reassessment of appropriate economic models and their impact on the political systems and nature of the state. As Beblawi (1990) has argued, 'the whole of the Arab world, oil rich as well as oil poor, is becoming a sort of oil economy with various undertones of rentier mentalities. This development has affected the role of the state in the whole Arab world' (p. 88). In turn, the nature of relations between the economy and the state can best be understood in association with a number of other themes, including rentier economies, distortion of agriculture and raw material uses, the problems of urbanization and excessive energy use, dependent development and the relatively poor economic performance of the region in global markets. These themes will be examined in the rest of this section.

The emergence of oil economies dominating the region has encouraged certain political economists to engage with the rentier model. In particular, both Luciani and Beblawi use this approach to explain the nature of state and politics in the region. The primary argument put forward by these theorists is that unlike other states, which derive income from taxation or internally generated sources, many states in the Middle East derive their revenues from rent and more specifically, according to Mahdavi (1970), from external rent. This rent is defined as the wealth generated from ownership of natural resources such as oil or gas, and, as Beblawi (1990) highlights, 'in rentier states only the few are engaged in the generation of this rent (wealth), the majority being only involved in the distribution or utilization of it' (p. 87). In a rentier economy the state has a monopoly on rents and employs a policy of expenditure around this revenue. Benefits are distributed to citizens, and the state demands nothing in return in terms of economic revenue. As Luciani (1990) remarks, 'allocation is the only relationship that they [the state elite] need have with their domestic economy' (p. 76). The outcome of this situation politically is a relationship between state and citizen that takes a new perspective on legitimacy, citizenship and loyalty to the state, which in this case becomes the 'crucial mover of economic activity' for a whole country (p. 79). In addition, the extension of rentier logic is not confined to those countries within the region which possess oil reserves, export it and live off the rents derived from this resource. Peripheral states (so-called semi-rentiers) have also been identified, with the claim that in countries like Jordan, Syria, Egypt and Yemen external rent has bred 'a chain of second-order' rentiers which in turn has affected, as we shall see in the discussion of migrant labour and the case study of Egypt, the nature of state and politics, government policy and demands from citizens (p. 79). There can be no doubt, despite the criticisms of the approach by some authors, that the rentier model ignores 'history' and differences in the political features of oil-producing states themselves and that 'too much emphasis is placed upon the role of oil', that the model has proved durable, particularly in the 1990s following the decline of oil prices on global markets, the Gulf crisis, the growth of internal opposition in many rentier states, budget cuts and decreasing rents due to world recession (p. 79).

One aspect of economic activity that has been severely dented in the contemporary Middle East by the decline of hydro-based and emergence of hydrocarbon societies has been the agricultural sector and production of raw materials. Until the advent of oil production in the region, the net export of raw materials derived from agriculture had accounted for the largest part of economic activity in the majority of countries across the region. Today, the 'food gap', whereby the region cannot produce enough from agriculture to feed its population, has made the area 'the least food self-sufficient region in the world' (Richards and Waterbury, 1990, p. 139). Indeed, Held claims that by the 1990s at least fifteen countries in the region were importing more than 50 per cent of their food (Held, 1994, p. 99). This is not to say, however, that the agricultural sector has not remained an essential or important feature of a variety of states in the region. What is also worth examining is the decline in production and price of raw materials such as cotton for export, as oil export profits have filtered to all economies in the area. In addition, agriculture and the use of raw materials throughout the region has been affected by government planning in terms of ISI policies and increasing urbanization, both of which have, by and large, resulted in a negative effect on rural areas. As Richards and Waterbury admit, 'Of course, ISI strategies are indeed "biased" towards industry; their entire rationale is to increase the percentage of national output coming from industry' (1990, p. 161).

The agricultural sector and production of raw materials have also gone into decline in terms of GDP and, understandably in the Gulf states, their contribution to GDP has become insignificant. Yet even in states like Syria or Egypt, where the agricultural sector remains significant, providing employment for 30 and 42 per cent of the economically active population respectively, these figures represent a decline on earlier decades, particularly the 1950s and 1960s when the agricultural sector of these countries was significantly altered by the respective populist policies of Nasserism and Ba'thism. Despite initial optimism in Egypt, for example, that land reform might increase the wealth of the agricultural sector, Nasser quickly ran into problems, including rapid population growth, expansion of per capita income, increasing defence expenditure and ISI policies. Indeed, by the 1970s the government was forced to introduce a scheme of generous food subsidies on basic commodities such as flour and bread, resulting in 10–15 per cent of government expenditure and contributing to the large budget deficit the country had generated (Stewart, 1995, p. 88). Agrarian change, therefore, has become a significant feature of the region, contributing to the economic decline or crisis of many countries, particularly from the 1980s onwards, and leaving certain states increasingly prone to a number of features: externally earned remittances from a workforce which in the past had been employed in domestic agriculture, indebtedness and austerity programmes requiring intervention from the IMF and World Bank, increasing unemployment particularly in the newly urbanized areas, following migration from rural areas, and concurrent episodes of political protest, food riots, demonstrations and pressure on government from its people. As a percentage of GDP, agriculture in Egypt has declined from 19.6 per cent in 1983 to 16.1 per cent in 2003 (World Bank, Egypt).

By the 1990s these debt-ridden economies began the slow process of adjustment, management and limited change. Nevertheless, the prospects are not overwhelmingly favourable, particularly given the comparatively poor performance of the region in terms of economic recovery. Unlike Latin America's emerging markets and slow but healthy economic recovery on the global stage, the Middle East, despite its huge wealth, has not shown the same potential to integrate with the world economy at a variety of levels or sectors. Thus, although the Third World debt crisis persists, some regions have had more success in coming to terms with the situation than the indebted countries of the Middle East. Indeed, rather than freeing themselves from debt, countries such as Yemen, Tunisia, Algeria, Egypt, Iraq and Morocco seem to be tied even further to the diktats of their creditors in the IMF and World Bank. In the twenty-first century these debates about debt have been fuelled by pressures for greater globalization and internal economic adjustment within the Middle East to meet such demands.

On the wings of a dove: the migrant workforce

In many ways the phenomenon of a large migrant workforce in the Middle East is linked with the development over the past century of the oil industry, the patterns of distribution of wealth in the region and other issues such as the increasingly high rates of birth and population growth, the Palestinian refugee population and the poor natural resources of countries such as Yemen. The impact of Arab migrant labour on the economic well-being of the region should not be underestimated and indeed reflects a complex system of economics that has reigned over the region for decades. These issues of migrant labour also highlight the economic relationships of dependency, dependent development and interdependency that exist in the contemporary Arab world. These relationships are sometimes voluntary but at other times they reflect the internal balance of power within the region, whereby – and perhaps uncharacteristically – both geographically and demographically, larger states are dependent on smaller states. It reflects the inability of some domestic economies to develop and sustain their populations and the concurrent political problems of legitimacy that this bestows. In Egypt, for example, Dessouki (1991) has noted that workers abroad had become a significant foreign income source: 'their remittance constituted a major source of Egypt's hard currency' (p. 162). With low levels of regional trade and capital flows (particularly when compared with flows outside the region), migrant labour from capital-poor to capital-rich states represents one of the most significant indicators of inter-Arab economic relations. The import of this should not be ignored and whether this represents a positive or negative development in the region should also be questioned. What is certain, particularly in the wake of the Gulf crisis, is the vulnerability not only of this migrant population but of the states to and from which it moves to the vagaries of regional political events. This is particularly true in relation to Yemen and Saudi Arabia. During the Gulf crisis of 1990–1 some 700,000 Yemenis were repatriated from their jobs in the area and the government of states like Saudi Arabia suspended aid programmes to the country. This resulted in serious economic crisis and mounting political instability. Throughout the 1990s, as a result of this rapid decline in relations, Saudi Arabia has experienced a wide variety of problems with its Yemen neighbours and the relationship between the two countries has been significantly altered, adversely affecting the stability of both states. Saudi Arabia, however, still pays more of its workers as migrants (80 per cent of the workforce) than any other country in the world.

Labour shortages, particularly although not exclusively in the oil-producing states of the Arab Gulf, became a significant developmental issue from the 1940s onwards. Labour shortages arose for a variety of reasons, including small native populations in oil-producing states like Kuwait and a lack of skilled and educated labour among the existing native population. Labour skills were not just related to oil and development of the petrochemical industry in the Gulf but also bore a direct relationship to the development of infrastructure (building, water, electricity, health, education) as well as administrative and governmental skills – technocrats and administrators. Thus, from the earliest development of the oil-producing states a pattern of dependence on migrant labour emerged. During this period, skilled labour was imported not just from within the region. The first wave of Palestinian skilled workers arrived in the early 1950s in Kuwait, Saudi Arabia, Abu Dhabi, Dubai, etc., and was accompanied by American and European workers associated with the major foreign-owned oil companies which were exploiting the oil fields of the region. The patterns of dependency which emerged during this period were not only broadened but also strengthened following the 1973 oil crisis and the quadrupled revenues that the oil-producing states enjoyed.

Now the oil states could pay the costs of importing skilled workers and states like Iraq, which was labour-rich, could even afford the luxury of importing labour for a variety of unskilled and menial jobs. By 1975 Arab labour was a significant factor in the economic development of a variety of Gulf countries. In Saudi Arabia, for example, the native population was swamped by a migrant population of more than one million, the majority of whom were drawn from Yemen to the south, Jordan (including Palestinians) to the north and Egypt to the east (Findlay, 1994, p. 106). Even the economic recession of the 1980s failed to curb the appetite for imported labour and the problem of encouraging native labour into the domestic economy was recognized. The Gulf crisis, however, did alter these patterns significantly, resulting in the wholesale deportation of some labour groups, including Palestinians, Jordanians, Egyptians and Yemenis.

For the labour exporters, including those mentioned above, the impact of this pattern of economic relations was manifest in a number of ways. First, there was a variety of negative factors which were never really considered, among which were the cost of educating a population and then facilitating the export of its brightest and most talented workers. The Arab brain drain to the Gulf states has been identified as a serious socio-economic consequence of governments like Egypt encouraging migration. In addition, migrant labour from Jordan, Yemen and Egypt has left many households without a male head for prolonged periods of time, significantly altering social relations within society. In addition, patterns of birth, marriage and education of children have all been altered by a migrant-led economy. Family resources were often collectively directed to the education and subsequent professional employment of one child, who in turn would support others in the family through remittances sent from the Gulf. Remittances in themselves have been a mixed blessing. They have promoted consumer booms and private capital projects such as house-building and funded large dowries for weddings, but they have not increased the health of national economies in Egypt, Yemen or Jordan. In addition, the abrupt loss of remittances plus the forced and wide-scale return of labour, as witnessed during the Gulf crisis in Jordan, had a severe dislocating effect on their economy, the effects of which are still being felt. More than 300,000 Jordanians (including Palestinians) were forced to leave the Gulf and millions of dollars in remittances were lost. In addition, the Jordanian economy now faces serious economic problems including an over-stretched infrastructure, high unemployment, lack of housing and pressures on health, education and other welfare provisions. Remittance economies, then, are not a paradigm to be encouraged in the Arab world.

The political and economic implications of these arrangements within the Arab world are clear, leading to new patterns of economic development and dependency, exploitative relationships between receiving and sending economies, and affecting issues of democratization, citizenship and Gulf-based aid packages to the rest of the region. Patterns of migration have been altered within the Arab world, with a switch by Gulf economies from Arab- to Asian-based labour, which was accelerated by the fallout of the Gulf crisis. Those Arab migrant labour groups which have endured enjoy few if any political or labour rights within the host country. Labour unions are prohibited, working conditions, rates of pay, etc. remain largely unregulated internally. Integration of long-term migrant communities is not particularly apparent and, again, those communities, such as the Palestinians in Kuwait, who had perceived their migrant status as long term, permanent and economically viable, discovered the opposite when 100,000 of them were ejected from the country in 1991. Settlement, hopes for naturalization or even citizenship are largely illusory and have proved costly for all sides – the migrants, the receiving state and the sending state. Such illusions, for example, have inhibited migrant workers from investing their remittances and capital in home-based industrial, commercial or agricultural enterprises. Future prospects for migrant labour remain unpredictable and uncertain, to say the least. As oil economies face the task of economic diversification, demands for increased political participation and the threat of further conflict with their neighbours, the issue of migrant labour must be balanced against these factors. Within the labour-rich states of the region the balance between the quest for foreign earnings and the actual developmental impact these have on national economies must be reassessed, patterns of dependence must be questioned and inter-Arab relations, integration and economic development need to absorb the economic changes wrought by a combination of the recent war in the Gulf and global recession.

Case study   Mega-economy Kuwait-style

The key to any examination of the Kuwaiti economy is the reliance of that country on the revenue from the production of oil. Oil is Kuwait's main natural resource and is exploited to the extent of creating an imbalance within the economy vis-à-vis other sectors such as industry or agriculture. The importance of oil is firmly underlined in the report of the Central Bank of Kuwait for 1979, which states that oil receipts in the period 1969–79 made up, on average, 86 per cent of total government revenue, 'thus facilitating the establishment of a modern state, the development of productive potential and the import of various commodities and services necessary to satisfy development and consumption needs' (ad-Dekhayel, 1990, p. 164). In short, Kuwait as a classic rentier economy exhibited all of the features outlined by theorists such as Beblawi (1990) and Luciani (1990). Other generally accepted features of a rentier state such as Kuwait are that only a small percentage of the population is engaged with wealth production and that state revenues derive predominantly from external sources.

In Kuwait oil revenues are appropriated by the state. Although a latecomer in this respect, the state's major move to control the oil industry came in January 1974, when it bought up 40 per cent of the Kuwait Oil Company, and in the same month it acquired a 60 per cent share in the Arabian Oil Company. By late 1979 the state had gained control, either by purchase or decree, over the whole of the country's oil sector and, with a view to improving sectoral cohesion and efficiency, the state sought to centralize crude oil production and its associated downstream activities. Naturally, as the state consolidated its hold over the oil sector, it appropriated an increasingly large share of oil revenues. The effect of its increased presence in this area stimulated state involvement in other sectors of the economy; in public, joint stock and private companies.

The state has complete control over the Kuwaiti public sector, bestowing a variety of benefits on its citizens (citizenship in Kuwait is the privilege of the few rather than the many). It has taken great interest in the fields of education, health, water and other infrastructure resources, such as electricity and roads. Among other state-owned enterprises is the Kuwait Fund for Arab Economic Development, which is the largest institution for the financing of economic projects in the Arab world. It began with a capital of 50 million Kuwaiti Dinar (KD) rising to KD1 billion in 1974 – after the oil price rises – for the sole financing of projects. Thus, the state has played an important role in the public and the private sector, establishing a formidable hold over the country. Levels of dependency on state help in the private sector are also high. Perhaps during the state-building era this might have been more understandable, yet the state continues to direct a major proportion of national wealth towards the private sector via expenditure policies and the merchant class. Perhaps the clearest and best-known example of the economic results of political coalition between the ruling al-Sabah family and the merchant class is the Land Acquisition Programme (LAP).

The LAP is, in fact, a misnomer, since the idea behind it had very little to do with acquisition of land. First instituted in 1951, the programme allowed the state to purchase land from citizens at a price higher than the market value and then resell the land for a nominal fee. LAP was originally conceived as a system of incentives to encourage citizens to move from the old city to the new suburbs, but since the 1960s it has become the means by which the Kuwaiti state places a substantial proportion of oil revenues directly into the hands of the upper classes – the ruling family and the merchant class. Apart from the open political transfer of funds, the LAP had two main effects: first, to pump money into the private sector and, second, to inflate land prices artificially to as high as $700 per square foot and to direct investment away from industry and into real estate (al-Sabah, 1980, p. 55).

Why has the state maintained such a strong hold over the Kuwaiti economy and what are the results of such a policy? In the public sector, particularly through heavily subsidized services and utilities, the most obvious result of state expenditure has been to create a climate of dependency among the Kuwaiti people and resident migrant workers, who rely strongly on such indirect handouts. If this is the result of widespread economic intervention it can equally be said to have increased the relative autonomy of the state vis-à-vis those whom it governs. Given Kuwait's oil rentier economy, the state had a head start in this process, particularly once it had gained control of the means of oil production. Such vast wealth accruing to the state has allowed it to be entirely financially independent of those outside the ruling class. Yet, it is not the wealth itself which allows the state political autonomy but the way in which it is spent. The programmes outlined above, whether in terms of services, investments or outright political transfers, created a popular dependency on the state which would not have been possible without its strong role in the economy. In the 1980s the recession did not hinder the Kuwaiti state in the maintenance of dependence. Even the Gulf crisis, which was financially costly for the Kuwaitis, ultimately failed to establish any radical reform or transformation of the country's political economy. Although the al-Sabah family was pressured into instituting minor political reforms, including limited franchise Assembly elections, some lifting of censorship on the media and other minor freedoms, the promise of further reform of the economy or government has yet to be realized and, as Peck notes, 'fundamental decisions about the future of Kuwait remain to be taken. Mistrust of other Arabs has led Kuwaiti leaders to declare that Kuwaitis will never again be a minority in their own land (1995, p. 124). In the twenty-first century Kuwait is still relatively bolstered by its oil-derived wealth. The state still controls and owns most of the economy and employs more than 95 per cent of its own citizens in jobs that are guaranteed for life. Kuwait has not relinquished its demand from post-Saddam Iraq for reparations but it also remains one of the most generous aid donors in the region.

Case study   Econo-dependent development Egyptian-style

This profile of Egypt's economy will date from 1952 following the Free Officers' *coup d'état* and the advent of Gamal Abdel Nasser as leader of the country. Until this time the Egyptian economy had been largely governed and directed by the demands of the British economy, in particular, and other global forces. Economic development and modernization in the country in the first half of the century had been directed by the British, who had secured the political system under their control and sat at the top of the pyramid of wealth (Issawi, 1982, p. 8).

Nasser's revolution took time to establish a populist base and appeal, but through a socialist economic agenda, announced in the decrees of 1961, Nasser hoped to achieve a new economic dawn for the country. His policy of economic reform was influenced by socialist ideology as well as elements of Arab nationalist interpretation. In addition Nasser engineered the slogan *'al-adl wa-l-kifaya'* – justice and sufficiency for everyone – which he hoped to achieve economically through mechanisms of nationalization, land reform and industrial as well as agricultural expansion (Richards, 1982, p. 176). Such policies required a strongly centralized economy which inevitably moved away from strict socialist principles to state-led capitalism. The first five-year plan led to only partial economic successes and the second five-year plan was never implemented. Nasser's commitment to the social contract – including rights to basic provision of food, health care, education and housing – would also require large amounts of capital. By the early 1960s Nasser's populist-driven economic policies had run into trouble, the military defeat of 1967 and a leadership crisis that led many to question the viability of the socialist Arab nationalist experiment.

When, following Nasser's death, Anwar Sadat assumed power in 1970, the nature of Egypt's economy changed dramatically. Indeed, Ayubi (1995) goes as far as to state that, 'Egypt can be said in a certain sense to be the "mother of Arab liberalization". Just as she was the first Arab country to champion a leading public sector . . . she also became the first . . . to experiment with economic liberalization and privatization, from the mid-1970s onwards' (p. 339). As part of his programme of 'de-Nasserization', Sadat was to reshape Egypt's ailing economy, address indebtedness and depart from the socialist-led pre-planned economy developed by Nasser and the Revolutionary Command Council. The socialist-led, planned economy had faltered under Nasser, as can be illustrated by the fact that the second five-year plan (1964–5) never materialized. In one respect it might be argued that Sadat was hoping to bring a new era of prosperity to the country. Nevertheless, the programme of economic restructuring known as *infitah* (open door policy) or liberalization announced by Sadat in April 1974 would prove to be hasty and ill-conceived. In addition, *infitah* was as much about politics as about economics and, although Sadat announced political reforms to accompany economic change, they were largely empty of real political import and left the executive authority of the President untouched.

Sadat's policy, however, would also have to address a series of major problems affecting the Egyptian economy by the early 1970s, including 'stagnant productivity in the (overwhelmingly public) industrial sector, lagging agricultural growth and growing food imports, a serious imbalance of trade and a large resource gap' (Richards and Waterbury, 1990, p. 240). A policy of economic liberalization was designed to affect the Egyptian economy in a number of ways. First, it was believed that state-approved liberalization would attract foreign investment capital into Egypt – that capital came from the West as well as oil-rich Gulf states. Billions of dollars of Arab, European and American capital flowed into the country throughout the 1970s, eventually totalling $4.4 billion. Second, liberalization also encouraged increased rates of bilateral aid to the country, with the Arab Gulf states contributing $5 billion between 1973 and 1976. The state introduced legislation which protected new investors from nationalization and confiscation and which bestowed favourable tax benefits as well. Third, the public sector, the largest employer of labour, would be reorganized to increase productivity and regulate prices for utilities to a profitable level. Finally, the region-wide oil boom promoted an era of prosperity leading to a high level of remittances being received from Egypt's army of workers in the Gulf states. By 1985, for example, remittances from Egypt's migrant workers contributed $3.3 billion to the country's foreign exchange earnings, making it the top contributor in this field.

Has liberalization profited the Egyptian economy? In the 1970s there was no question that the policies associated with *infitah* increased the wealth of the country and contributed to economic growth. For example, per capita GDP grew by 8–9 per cent per annum. By the 1980s, however, with the advent of Sadat's successor Hosni Mubarak, growth had slowed down and economic crisis still prevailed over the economy. Mubarak introduced only limited economic reforms and as the economic crisis worsened the government instituted wide-scale austerity measures to try and address issues such as its foreign debt, which by the mid-1980s had reached more than $30 billion. Foreign debt has left Egypt increasingly dependent on US aid, the IMF and World Bank strictures vis-à-vis economic planning. This relationship was emphasized during the Gulf crisis, which brought both negative and positive aspects to the economy: 'On the negative side it (*the Crisis*) exacerbated financial and economic problems. . . . On the positive side external aid (mainly grants) worth about $3.9 billion was rushed to Egypt' (Ayubi, 1991, p. 346). Some foreign debt was cancelled and new agreements favourable to Egypt were negotiated with the IMF. What seems certain is that the process of economic recovery in Egypt will always be slow in coming, that indebtedness and dependency on foreign imports, even for basic foodstuffs, will be a long time in declining or even disappearing altogether. Wealth creation as a result of liberalization has not been evenly spread and the emergence of the wealthy elite only serves to heighten economic and political tensions in the country. In addition, 'the state retains a dominant role in the economy, and the basic problems of providing food, jobs, and basic consumer goods for the mass of the population continue to cast a shadow over the Valley of the Nile' (Richards and Waterbury, 1990, p. 244). Further economic uncertainty will be provoked by any succession crisis that takes place in the wake of the passing of Hosni Mubarak. In the twenty-first century there is still everything to play for in the development of Egypt's economy.

Case study **The great globalization debate**

In the spring of 2004 an article appeared in a leading Arabic newspaper outlining the economic and developmental woes of the Middle East in the twenty-first century. Much of the statistical evidence cited drew on a UNDP Report on Development (or its lack) in the Arab world. Illiteracy – particularly among women – youth employment rates, unemployment rates, poor GDP performance, growing poverty rates, mediocre access to technology, risible participation of women in legislative systems and the articulation of a desire by the majority of Arab youth to work in economies other than their own, highlighted the formidable challenges facing the state system in the Middle East and its populations.

An emergent explanation for this state of affairs indicated that globalization – the process of economic (and other forms of) integration across the globe as a result of free trade policies – was impacting negatively on the Middle East (with a few notable exceptions) and in fact making it harder for the region's populations to keep up with the new global tempo set by multinational enterprises in North America and Europe. This critique of globalization in the Middle East has emerged both inside and outside the region. It forms part of the discourse of the anti-globalization movement as well as of some Islamist popular movements.

Before I analyse these debates, it is first useful to outline some general trends within the Middle East as well as some key components of the globalization debate. As the sections above have indicated, the impact of a changing global economy has already been significant in the various states of the Middle East for more than several decades. The accelerating push for free trade, liberalization, and investment and capital flows has not only impacted on the economies of the region but has been accompanied by expectations of change within political systems as well. Yet the emergent economic conditions and the responses of state elites in many Arab countries have resulted in lagging economic and political reform. In the AHDR (Arab Human Development Report) of 2005, 22 Arab countries were criticized for failing to meet local aspirations for development and political freedom. 'The impending disaster scenario is that in the absence of peaceful and effective mechanisms to address injustice and achieve political alternation, some might be tempted to embrace violent protest', the authors warned (UNDP, 2005). In terms of development and economic profiles, the UNDP reports statistics that indicate that the population birth rates in the Middle East are higher than other parts of the globe – the demographic time bomb becomes an increasing reality. Earlier reports highlighted that economic growth, despite the perception that many Arab countries were wealthy, was generally weak throughout the region. A report stated: 'Overall GDP at the end of the twentieth century (US $604 billion) was little more than those of a single European country such as Spain (US $559 billion) and much less than those of another European country, Italy (US $1,074 billion).' The best that could be said about GDP in the Arab world in the last twenty-five years of the twentieth century was that it was 'extremely modest' (UNDP, 2004, p. 137). Other economic indicators were far from healthy either. The clear linkage between economic development, human security and political reform has been established in debates about globalization and the Middle East by world organizations such as the World Bank, the United Nations and the European Union. The issue often at stake, however, is whose definition of globalization the peoples of the Middle East should be working with.

Although globalization is commonly understood as a term for the economic integration of the contemporary world, its meanings have been interpreted as having significance in the fields of technology, society and politics. Nevertheless, the term does imply connection and integration across 'border' and 'barriers' that have previously existed. Globalization can have both negative and positive connotations. As Noam Chomsky has argued, ' "globalization" used in a neutral sense just means "international integration" . . . The term has come to be used in recent years as a kind of a technical term which doesn't refer to globalization, but refers to a very specific form of international economic integration namely based on the priority given to investor rights, not rights of people' (Danilo, 2005, p. 1). Globalization cannot be rolled back or easily resisted for it is a complex process with a number of dimensions to it that involves such factors as good governance, migration, ethnic integration, the removal of trade barriers, popular protest and the centrality of issues such as the knowledge economy. The limits of integration inherent to the definition of globalization are contested and challenged. Culturally globalization has established a cosmopolitan culture that is simultaneous and similarly enjoyed and experienced by elites in Mumbai, New York, Moscow and Paris.

As an economic experience the process of globalization optimizes profit making in the free-market economy. For the proponents of economic globalization the larger that market, the fewer barriers to trade and the greater the efficiency of the process, the better the profits. Market competitiveness, low inflation, foreign investment and new technologies spur this economic process. It is reported that such economies grow quicker than others (Lukas, 2000, p. 2). But for the majority of economies in the Middle East there has been a state-led resistance to such changes and globalization penetration by actors from outside the region has impacted negatively. Moreover it is argued that 'the drama of globalization is a continuation of the colonial dialectic played out by earlier generations of the indigenous elite' (Henry and Springborg, 2001, p. 15). Many contend that in fact the problem of resistance lies with the elites of the region and the dominant cultural trend of Islam. Elites are persistently blamed for failing to allow the state to relinquish control of the economy and ergo the rest of society, including the political system. Outside agencies are variously accused of double standards in calling for reform but standing by or propping up states that resist such changes. Islam is perceived by western economic experts as a major restraint on the market forces behind globalization. Recent research demonstrates, however, that although Islamic economic practice has elements that are distinct from western free-market principles, they have not actively hindered the globalization process as an economic mode: 'do not presuppose that Islam is inherently inimical to economic development' (Kuran, 2004, p. 146). The challenge for the whole of the region remains undiminished.

Further reading

Richards and Waterbury (1990) is a solid introduction to the political economy of the region. A number of chapters in Luciani (1990), including Chatelus, Makdisi and Luciani himself, give broad analysis and perspective to this subject. A number of Marxist-based interpretations of political economy of the region were produced in the 1980s, among which Amin (1982), although dated, remains pertinent about a number of issues. The comparison between European and western economic models at work in the Middle East can be found in two texts by Rodinson (1977 and 1979). On debate about the efficacy of Islamic economics, see Roff (1987), Nasr (1989) and Pfeifer (1997). Issues of rentier economics are explored by Luciani (1990) and Beblawi (1990), by Luciani again in 1995 where he assesses the rentier model, in Brynen, Korany and Noble (1995) and in Mahdavi (1970) where the concept was applied to the case of Iran under the leadership of the Shah. More recently, Niblock and Murphy's (1993) edited text on aspects of the liberalization debate provides good general coverage. Richards and Waterbury (1990), Owen (2003) and Bill and Springborg (1994) all cover the debate about economic restructuring in the Middle East. Murphy's chapter in Nonneman (1996) on Algeria and the political implications of economic liberalization is also recommended, as is Brynen, Korany and Noble (1995) on this topic. The issue of migrant labour is discussed in Owen (1995), R. Adams (1991) and by Sabagh and Russell in their contributions to Luciani (1990). Aspects of the economy in Kuwait are analysed in Crystal (1990), Hindley (1993), Collett (1994) and Sadowski (1997b). Overviews of the Gulf economy can be found in texts such as Wilson (1979 and 1995), Hardy (1992) and Held (1994). A number of interesting works on Egypt and political economy are available, including the edited text by Tripp and Owen (1989) looking at developments under Mubarak, Vitalis (1995), Hinnebusch (1985), who examined aspects of economy under Sadat, McDermott (1988) and Baker (1990), who provides an overview of politics and economy from Nasser to Mubarak. In addition, political economist Waterbury (1983) authored a strong account of developments under the rule of Nasser and Sadat, while Kerr and Yassin (1982) along with Hopwood (1985) give a useful introductory overview to developments in Egypt's political system and economy. Henry and Springborg's (2001) alongside Dodge and Higgott's (2002) texts on globalization and the politics of development in the Middle East region is worth looking at for an insight into the continuing issues that beset economic development in the twenty-first century. Kuran (2004) takes a wider perspective on the debate about Islam and economy but it is one worth pursuing for further reading.

War and Lack of Peace

Introduction

THE Middle East has been characterized as a battleground. From this region – more than any other – opinion in the West has crystallized around the issue of war and conflict. In the twenty-first century the region has become synonymous with war and terror. This chapter will examine the nature of conflict in the region and examine why peace and political stability have often been so difficult to achieve. Conflict and war in the region have taken place at a number of levels: first, long-standing regional conflicts; second, short-lived conflagrations within the region; third, localized disputes; and finally, wars waged by external actors. There have been conflicts between states as well as between ethnic groups at all levels. Regional conflict has been primarily shaped by the Arab–Israeli conflict, while conflict between actors within the region and outside it is illustrated by the Suez crisis of 1956, when Nasser of Egypt challenged both the French and the British, or the Allied attack on Iraq in 2003. Intra-state conflict is epitomized by the sectarian dispute of Lebanon which led to fifteen years of civil war from 1975 to 1990. All of these aspects of conflict in the region will be analysed in this chapter.

Debates about conflicts in the region have examined such factors as traditional state-to-state rivalries, conflicts over natural resources such as oil or water, sectarian and ethno-national disputes and the role of external factors such as international actors and climate (i.e. context of conflict in the Middle East during the Cold War). In addition, academics have raised questions over the legitimacy of certain regimes whose leaders have attempted to create a sense of cohesion by playing the nationalist card in times of crisis – an example of this is Saddam Hussein. Although this chapter is not specifically about the military but about conflict in more general terms, the prevalence of the military in the politics of the region, the nature and process of state-formation and nationalist tendencies have all been utilized to explain the apparent and widespread phenomenon of unrest across the Middle East. Wars have broken out between Arabs and Israelis, Palestinians and Israelis, Arabs and the states of Europe, Arabs and Arabs, Arabs and Iranians, Sunni and Shi'a Muslims, Muslims and Christians, Kurds and Arabs. There have been civil conflicts in Iraq, Syria, Algeria, Yemen and Lebanon, a feature of intra-state conflict identified by Bromley as 'the main source of conflict in the Middle East . . . concerned with the internal pacification and repression of domestic populations' (1994, p. 116). Border conflicts have occurred between countries such as Egypt and Libya, Morocco and Algeria, Jordan and Syria, Israel and Lebanon, Iraq and Kuwait, and Iran and Iraq, all reflecting the contested nature of boundaries in the contemporary Middle East – a certain legacy of the nature of colonial-inspired state-formation from the turn of the twentieth century.

The arms race in the region has played a part in perpetuating conflict. Arab states, Iran and Israel have all built up significant arsenals, including conventional weaponry, chemical weapons and nuclear capability – hence the real fear, particularly in the late 1970s, of a nuclear Armageddon in the area. Western and eastern support for the arms race has been ill-disguised and has been used to maintain vital economic contrasts within the region. The nuclear issue has arisen once again in the twenty-first century as Iran continues to develop nuclear capability. National spending on arms and the military in the region is higher than in any other developing area in the world. While in the Middle East spending on arms and the military is cited on average as 15 per cent of national income, it is only 5 per cent in the rest of the developing world (Fischer et al., 1993, p. 2). In Syria, for example, defence expenditure is as high as 18 per cent and the army constitutes 3.9 per cent of the total population, compared to 0.8 per cent in America (Picard, 1990, p. 192). The Middle East also remains the largest single market for weapons produced by the United States of America (SIPRI, 2002). The role of the military in the political systems of the area cannot be underestimated: military *coups* and revolutions have been a significant feature of the Middle East and military-based regimes are characteristic of states such as Syria, Algeria, Libya, Egypt and even Israel. There can be no doubt that these close political links between the military, power and politics help explain the nature of the conflicts. As both Picard and Owen highlight in their own debates about the role of the military in state-building, they have been increasingly independent political actors and an important force in the region in terms of modernization. While Picard goes on to discuss the stable nature of the military regimes in the region, it is still important to remember that regimes posited on such power will depend on the military to support the state – this can often only be done through war. Although it is true that the emergence of the soldier-politician and the praetorian nature of the state in the region has a direct cause-and-effect relationship on the political process of countries like Syria, Libya and Iraq, this does not, according to some authors such as Bromley and Picard, mean that the Middle East is an exception. Cammack, Pool and Tordoff (1993) lend support to this assertion, highlighting the pervasive presence of the military across the Third World (p. 165). In addition, while in the 1960s, as Richards and Waterbury suggest, the role of the military in the politics of the region was perceived as a positive development heralding progress, technological efficiency, modernization and the promotion of the nationalist agenda, a dramatic volteface had occurred two decades later. The true nature of conflict and military in society had convinced many that the negative effects of this feature of politics in the region were too much to bear. The pervasive nature of factionalism and internal strife within the officer class, the lack of economic development, economic crises, widespread corruption, coercion and lack of democracy convinced many that 'whatever degree of order and discipline the military has been able to provide, it has been outweighed by the chocking off of the free flow of information and ideas, and the blocking of the assumption of responsibility on the part of ordinary citizens for their economic and political affairs' (Richards and Waterbury, 1990, p. 359).

While the role of the military has been debated extensively, other explanations of conflict also need to be highlighted. Ideology, religion, resources, state-formation and nation-building are all factors that have been cited to one degree or another in explanation of conflict in the region. In the past, particularly before the end of the Cold War and during particular historical epochs such as the decade of Arab nationalism during the 1960s, it was argued that most disputes were the result of ideological differences. Such disputes between pan-Arabism and Zionism were given added impetus by the role of other actors in the international community, particularly the extension of superpower rivalry between America and the Soviet Union to the shores of the Middle East. These factors have been explored and examined extensively in works by Taylor (1991), Efrat and Bercovitch (1991) and Freedman (1991), all of whom have highlighted the impact that these particular actors had on the nature of conflict, the military and the perpetuation of arms in the region. The end of the Cold War and the apparent resurgence of Islam has been identified by authors such as Huntington (1993) as a new force for conflict both within the region and with the West. Moreover the declaration by the government of the United States of America in the wake of the 9/11 attacks of a 'war on terrorism' and the naming of such Middle Eastern states as Iraq and Iran as part of an 'axis of evil' has led to increased confrontation and war. In addition, the rise of competing ethnic identities in states such as Iraq has created a new axis for tension and conflict and undermined the apparently stable edifice of the nation-state. This is particularly so in the case of Israel, where the rise of religio-ethnic tension within the state has been identified by authors such as Rouhana (1997), Bulmer (1998) and Shafir and Peled (1998) as creating not only conflict within the state but a crisis of the very nature of the state-building project itself. In sum, then, a variety of conflicts characterize the region in the contemporary era and hamper the maintenance of stability and development, create further dependency and encourage authoritarianism in an age where other regions of the globe are slowly evolving from these negative political, social and economic forces.

The problems of peacemaking are examined in the case studies of this chapter, with a focus on the Camp David Peace Treaty between Israel and Egypt in 1978 and the peace negotiations between Israel and the Palestinians which resulted in the Oslo Accords signed by Israeli Premier Yitzhak Rabin and PLO President Yasser Arafat in Washington in September 1993. The following section will signpost the different paths to peace which have been adopted in the Arab–Israeli dispute, the importance of external or international influence or mediation and the coalescence of other factors such as political leadership, economic and social conditions and the power of diplomacy. The final case study in this chapter focuses on the war in Iraq that took place in 2003 and the subsequent western occupation of the country following the toppling of Saddam. It analyses the controversies surrounding the decision by western powers to engage in war in the Middle East twenty-first century style.

The bigger battle: Arab–Israeli hostility

The conflict between the state of Israel and the Arab states has dominated the political life of the Middle East for decades. As Sahliyeh claims, 'the Palestinian–Arab–Israeli conflict is potentially the most lethal and volatile . . . and the most difficult to resolve' (1992, p. 381). Although the conflict originally centred on the establishment of a Jewish state in Palestine and the subsequent dispossession of the Palestinian Arab population, over the years the dynamics of the conflict have resulted in a character often far removed from the original Palestinian issue. At a wider level the Arab–Israeli conflict has come to symbolize the internal competition for leadership of the region, the phenomenon of Arab nationalism, the disputes between Islam and Judaism, colonialism and independence, East versus West, the nation-state versus the boundaryless aspirations of Arabness or Islam, and the conflict between Arab and Jew.

The origins of the conflict, the explanation for its longevity, its history, its seeming intractability and difficulty to resolve, have all been subject to a variety of explanations and often fierce political discourse. Particular events, such as the war of 1948 or the role of the Americans in the conflict, are subjected to controversy, interpretation, reinterpretation, revisionism and accusations of fabrication. For sure, there can be little else in the realm of contemporary Middle Eastern politics that is more hotly contested than the explanation of this particular conflict, for in any explanation there is also, explicitly or implicitly, an accusation of blame and responsibility, an 'auditing of antagonism', which is mutual and often inflexible. Some have crudely limited the explanation of these interpretations as either pro-Arab or pro-Israel with no other residual category. Like any other deep conflict, there is always pressure to be on 'one side or another'. Such reductionism, however, does not help explain the dynamics of the conflict or the multitude of factors involved, including important debates about the nation-state, self-determination, the arms race, the international community, forms of political violence, genocide, partition, civil disobedience, negotiations and economics. Suffice to say, any 'reading' of the conflict must be placed in this wider context of politics in the region throughout the twentieth century. For example, the ambitions of the Iranians post-1979 cannot be understood without reference to the Arab–Israeli conflict, which resulted in the 1982 Israeli invasion of Lebanon to oust the PLO, which in turn led to the formation of a radical Shi'a militia Hizb Allah, the kidnap of Americans, the US Irangate scandal, arms to Nicaragua and support extended by the Iranians throughout this episode.

The Palestinian issue, then, has done more both to unite and divide the Arabs than any other issue. The conflict between the Arab and Muslim states with Israel has been dominated by war rather than reconciliation. Since the establishment of the state of Israel in May 1948 there have been five major wars, and every Arab/Persian state from Morocco to Iran has been engaged at some point in an economic, political and diplomatic boycott of the country designed to deny its existence in the region. Only two Arab countries have made peace with Israel. The first was Egypt under the Presidency of Anwar Sadat in 1978, the second in November 1994 when King Hussein of Jordan signed a peace treaty with Yitzhak Rabin, the Prime Minister of Israel. Since 1978, Egypt, isolated and punished by the rest of the Arab world, has maintained a 'cold peace' with Israel. Sadat was assassinated in 1981 and Egypt ostracized by the rest of the Arab community for many years; Jordan has yet to experience the dividend of peace or, despite the historical references to the Hashemite–Yishuv pact, warm relations with its new peace partner.

The wars of 1948, 1956, 1967, 1973 and 1982 have resulted in both Arab defeats and Israeli victories, Arab victories and Israeli defeats. They have perpetuated the massive arms race which has characterized the region, the superior role of the military in politics, the politics of attrition, authoritarianism, national unity and emergency – often providing the excuse for the praetorian politicians of the region to practise authoritarian measures at home by promoting states of emergency, national service, perpetuation of the uniform culture, obsession with internal and national security threats, censorship of the press, extended police powers and a culture of hostility to the 'other', which is disseminated in the national media and educational curricula.

Territory, its acquisition or loss, has also been a major feature of the hostility between these state actors. The land of the region is subject to competing claims, battles and disputes. Antagonism of rights to territory, self-determination and sovereignty have led the Israelis and the Arabs into a seemingly intractable conflict. While at a state-to-state level there have been attempts and limited successes, as noted above, between Israel, Egypt and Jordan at resolving conflict, region-wide resolution of the Arab–Israeli dispute remains an elusive goal even given the relative strides in peacemaking achieved at the beginning of the 1990s. The territorial claims of one side over another are alternately bolstered by political, historical, economic and even religious claims. For example, the Zionist claim to Eretz (Greater) Israel, bolstered by the notion of being 'Chosen People', is countered by the Muslim claims of custodianship of the Holy Places (Hashemite and Saud) and the covenant of *waqf* maintaining eternal Muslim ownership of land for future generations of the Muslim faithful.

The first war, as the second case study in chapter 1 explained, between Israel and the Arabs broke out on 15 May 1948, the day after Israel announced its independence. The armies of Egypt, Jordan and Syria, backed by those of Lebanon, Saudi Arabia and Iraq, attempted to regain Palestine for the Arabs by force. In theory, the combined military might of the Arab armies should have made short work of the poorly equipped Israeli Defence Force (IDF). In practice, the Arab armies lacked a united command or unity of war aims, and proved weak in combat. By the end of the summer of 1948 the Arabs were facing a defeat and by July 1949 they had signed an armistice with Israel.

One direct outcome of the conflict was a mass of Palestinian refugees and the creation of a new factor in this conflict: a dispossessed population which would demand the right of return and the right to self-determination. By 1949 some 700–800,000 Palestinian Arabs had either fled or been forced to leave their homes. Whether the mass movement of Palestinians out of Israeli territory was part of a Zionist policy of transfer has recently been the subject of passionate debate among Israeli and Jewish historians, with some, such as Karsh (1997), claiming that his colleagues, including Benny Morris and Avi Shlaim, have 'fabricated' Israeli history, coining it a 'new Israeli distortiography'. Whether or not the Zionist leadership, including David Ben Gurion, was 'predisposed to nudge the process along, occasionally with the help of expulsions', these refugees ended up in the Jordanian-controlled West Bank, Egyptian-supervised Gaza Strip, Egypt, Lebanon, Jordan, Syria, the Arab Gulf states and elsewhere across the globe (Morris, 1998, p. 81). The effects of the war and the increasingly long-term nature of the Palestinian refugee sojourn in other Arab states were palpable throughout the region, largely radicalizing Arab leaders and the masses around the symbol of Palestine, a symbol that would persist as a motif for wars between Israel and the Arabs in 1956, 1967, 1973 and 1982. For sure, the presence of large numbers of Palestinian refugees and successive generations in countries like Jordan, Lebanon, Syria, Kuwait and Saudi Arabia irreparably altered the dynamics of internal and regional politics in those states. In Jordan, for example, by 1970 the large Palestinian population represented a very real threat to the Hashemite monarchy, leading to civil war and the expulsion of the PLO. Regionally, the Arab advocacy of the Palestinian cause was a double-edged sword, encouraging both inter-Arab rivalry, particularly between Nasser and the conservative Gulf states, as well as unity, as demonstrated during the 1973 war when the Arab oil boycott brought the international community to its knees.

Israel was declared the enemy of the Arabs, and an agent of the widely despised western powers, in particular the USA. Israel's strategic and military alliance with the West during the Suez Crisis of 1956 confirmed Arab perceptions. The Six Day War of 1967, which resulted in a massive military defeat, again, for the Arab states of Egypt, Syria and Jordan, only served to consolidate a cycle of conflict between Israel and the Arabs which often lost sight of the Palestinian issue and assumed its own specific Arab–Israeli character. The careers of statesmen like Gamal Abdel Nasser, Hafiz al-Assad and Saddam Hussein were often dominated by the Arab conflict with Israel, while in their own countries they persecuted their own Palestinian populations, imprisoning, torturing, expelling and even executing them.

Even the defeat and despair which followed the débâcle of 1967 did not release the Israelis or Arabs from further battles. Sadat's attempt to recover Arab pride – the October War of 1973 – assisted by Syria, resulted in temporary and small-scale Arab victories. The recovery of Arab pride, however, was not enough to promote peace, and Israeli belligerency also intensified. American brokerage in the region, born out of superpower rivalry against the Soviets, the oil embargo and western fears about the 'oil weapon', resulted in the signing of a peace treaty between Israel and Egypt in 1978. In the same year Israel invaded south Lebanon. In 1982 Israel launched another offensive and, under the codename 'Peace for the Galilee', declared war on the PLO in Lebanon. The Palestinian refugee community and the Lebanese citizens of the country and Syrian military forces present in Lebanon were inexorably tied into the war; even those sectors of the Lebanese community (the Shi'a in the south) that initially welcomed Israel's invasion turned against them as the truth of the civilian casualty and death tolls emerged.

The war in Lebanon had now become another episode in the Arab–Israeli conflict. This time, however, Israel began to flounder when, following the PLO's departure, its continued occupation of the country enraged the Shi'a community of the south. The war aims of the government were questioned by the Israeli people, Israeli casualties grew, the PLO had gone but the conflict with the Arabs remained (Schiff and Ya'ari, 1984). It can be confidently asserted, therefore, that the Arab–Israeli conflict established a dynamic of its own which was often explicable, not by reference to the status of the Palestinian issue, but to the individual ambitions of certain Arab leaders at home, the relative success or otherwise of their domestic policies, the concurrent nature and status of superpower rivalry, the common agenda of Third World states, the price of oil on the world market, the current status of arms contracts, strategic developments and nuclear capability and the ability of diplomats to win concessions in international forums such as the United Nations or World Bank. In sum, the Arab–Israeli conflict has created pockets of profit for the Arab elite built on the maintenance of authoritarian power, the wealth derived from arms and the military industry and associated economies, as well as the political prestige associated with any form of victory (real or otherwise) over Israel. In turn, Israel in its defence of itself has established a state consistently concerned with its security, the poor relations with its neighbours and the maintenance of further territorial claims as a result of past conflicts, begging the question, 'What price for peace in Israel?' Israel and its Arab neighbours still face an uphill struggle in the search for peace treaties and enduring peace-building between its peoples.

Killing dreams: the Israeli–Palestinian dimension

The Israeli–Palestinian conflict has assumed a nature and dynamic all of its own, particularly from the late 1960s when aspects of the pan-Arab dimension diminished and a culturally and politically specific

Palestinian nationalism was ascendant. While the roots of nationalist conflict between Palestinian and Jewish nationalists lay in the Yishuv and Zionist colonization of Palestine at the turn of the twentieth century, the transformation of Palestinian national consciousness, translated into their own political movements for liberation, emerged after the débâcle of 1967 and Israel's occupation of the Palestinian populated territories of the West Bank and Gaza Strip. Indeed, from this point onwards the conflict between the Palestinians and the Israelis changed, altering the political objectives and strategies of both parties and leading to the Palestinian terror campaigns of the 1970s, Israel's illegal settlement movement and a further entrenchment of views on both sides which would remain unaltered until the Palestinian uprising (Intifada) in 1987. The dimensions of this conflict reflect political, ethno-national, class, colonial, religious and economic antagonisms that have proved difficult to resolve. This conflict, however, is primarily one between two peoples over one territory, of competing nation visions and nationalism and of the varying religious, ethnic, historical and moral issues used by both sides to support their case in the domestic, regional and global theatre of politics.

It is apparent how quickly the lines of conflict between the Palestinians and the Israelis had become seemingly intractable during the period of the British mandate (1920–48). From 1948 to 1967, political solutions to this conflict were limited. Conflict characterized relations as Israel embarked on a period of successful state-building, creating an ethnically Jewish state in which its Arab citizens were not treated equally. The Palestinians, meanwhile, formed national resistance movements and through the strategy of armed struggle sought self-determination for their nation. In addition, after 1967 the Palestinians realized they could no longer depend on their Arab brethren for liberation, that their fate now rested firmly in their own hands. The number of factors that prevented integration or reconciliation between the two communities grew rather than diminished. Among the factors were politics, religion, language, culture, social values, economy and ethnicity. Yet, the two communities could not be completely segregated and the conflict was characterized at a day-to-day level by the way in which individuals related to one another. As Israel's occupation continued throughout the 1970s, the rate of illegal Israeli settlement in the West Bank, East Jerusalem and Gaza Strip increased in one direction: by 2004 over 400,000 Israelis lived in more than 150 settlements on Palestinian land confiscated or purchased by the Israeli government. Cheek by jowl, settler and Palestinian were forced to reside in the same small densely populated areas. In the Gaza Strip some 7,500 Jewish settlers were living in 21 settlements on three-quarters of the entire territory of the area – over 1.2 million

Palestinians lived on the remaining quarter of the territory. The attempt by Israel to link its economy through internal markets, subcontracting day-labour in the other direction, resulted in hundreds of thousands of Palestinians entering Israel over the Green Line (the border created in 1967) on a daily basis to earn so-called 'slave' wages in the unskilled manual sector of the Israel economy. Although Israelis may have shopped in Arab market towns like Bethlehem, and Palestinian labourers worked on building sites in Tel Aviv, true integration never occurred, mixed marriages were and remain almost unheard of, housing remained strictly segregated and the mentality of distrust and mutual antagonism characterized both sides. For decades Palestinians and Israelis sought ways to distinguish themselves from each other, creating difference, whether religious (Muslim, Christian, Jew), ethnic (Jew and Arab), social, linguistic, cultural, through cuisine, dress code, social values, art, literature, media and any number of social rites, rather than mutual bonds to promote compromise.

The Palestinian–Israeli conflict was not just confined to the occupied territories. The culture of hostility spread to all corners of the globe, wherever Israelis and Palestinians resided. In Lebanon, Cyprus, Munich, Entebbe, Rome, London and Algiers, the battle between the PLO and Israel's Mossad wore on for decades. The 1960s, 1970s and early 1980s, while characterized by creeping annexation and political violence within the West Bank, Gaza Strip and Israel, were also marked by bombings, hijackings and assassinations abroad. Following Israel's rout of the PLO from Lebanon in 1982, the Palestinian nationalist movement was weakened and an era of internal dispute and fissure beckoned as the factions of the PLO squabbled among themselves and blamed each other for the Lebanon débâcle (Sahliyeh, 1988). In addition, within the West Bank and Gaza Strip a new political force was encouraged by Israel to counter the secular appeal of the nationalists. The Palestinian Islamists, including the Muslim Brotherhood, Islamic Jihad and the Mujama, waged a campaign for political power in Palestinian universities and professional associations against the nationalists. They quickly established themselves, particularly in the Gaza Strip, as contenders for local power (Milton-Edwards, 1996a; Abu Amr, 1994).

By the mid-1980s there was growing resentment within the Palestinian community against the Israeli occupation authorities. Any form of political activity was criminalized, the PLO was outlawed, membership of political organizations was punishable by long prison sentences, people were banned from free assembly and public meetings were forbidden. Within Israel, Labour or Likud hegemony in government, which had been established by the 1984 elections, was often immobilized through squabbles between these two sides, while the leftist peace movement which had become so strong during the Lebanon war tried to maintain momentum on the Palestinian issue. The government, however, led by Yitzhak Shamir, remained implacably opposed to the idea of any peace moves towards the Palestinians and remained content with the status quo (Arian, 1989). The settlement by right-wing Likud-voting Israelis continued almost unabated and international censure was ignored. The outbreak of the Intifada on 9 December 1987 was, therefore, inevitable. Throughout the Gaza Strip, the West Bank and Jerusalem, the residents of refugee camps, villages, hamlets, towns and cities rose up in a spontaneous protest against the occupation. The Palestinian community was gripped by one of the most significant social and political revolutions in its history (Peretz, 1990).

The long-term goals of the Intifada were articulated as a desire to end the Israeli occupation of the West Bank and Gaza Strip and the establishment of an independent Palestinian state (Lockman and Beinin, 1989). In the short term, hundreds of thousands engaged in activities designed to disengage in any way possible from the structures which supported the occupation and to achieve a much greater level of Palestinian self-reliance and independence from Israel. Separation would take a variety of forms, from resignations in employment with the Israeli authorities, boycotting Israeli-produced goods, displaying the Palestinian flag, organizing marches and demonstrations, sit-ins at human rights organizations, alternative education committees which drew up Palestinian rather than Israeli teaching curricula and any form of popular culture which celebrated the existence of Palestine as a nation (Nassar and Heacock, 1991).

The Intifada was the most significant indicator of the depth of malaise that had set in during the Palestinian–Israeli conflict. Palestinians, through the framework of the Intifada, indicated that they were rejecting anything that represented Israeli rule or domination over their lives; they were no longer willing to pay taxes without representation, to fund the military occupation of land which they perceived as their own. Until the Intifada there was every indication that Israel might annex the occupied territories. There is no doubt that the Intifada led Israel to question its hold over the West Bank and Gaza Strip. In 1993 Israel and the Palestinians signed the Declaration of Principles; a timetable for negotiations and interim limited autonomy for the Palestinians ensued. The Oslo, Cairo and Wye Accords did not guarantee peace, nor were they a peace treaty in themselves, but they irrevocably altered the dynamics of conflict and peacemaking between Israel and the Palestinians for ever. By 2000 the momentum for peace was stopped as a result of both Israeli actions and the outbreak of the second Palestinian uprising – which became known as the armed Intifada.

By 2001 the peace process had stalled entirely. The extent to which these events have altered the nature of the conflict between Palestinians and Israelis is further explored in the case study at the end of this chapter.

East against West in the Suez crisis

The Suez crisis of November 1956, following Nasser's decision to nationalize the Suez Canal on 26 July, was a unique conflict in a number of ways. Involving Egypt, Britain, France and Israel, it irrevocably altered regional and international relations. A number of factors have to be borne in mind when reviewing the crisis, including the impact of political personalities such as Gamal Abdel Nasser the Egyptian President, Anthony Eden the British Prime Minister and President Eisenhower of the USA. The particular personalities of all three men were largely at odds with each other. Other factors include the international nature of this particular Middle East dispute which brought an Arab state into direct conflict with former colonial superpowers Britain and France. In addition, the Cold War climate in which the war occurred inevitably drew directly and indirectly both the USA and the Soviet Union into this 'local conflict', which in turn had implications for the Hungarian crisis of 1956 (Thomas, 1986, p. 12). Within the region, Nasser's decision to challenge the previous hegemony of the West, or, more specifically, Britain (and France), changed the pattern of Arab politics, bolstered notions of pan-Arabism and encouraged the nascent movement for Arab independence in states such as Iraq and Algeria.

The prelude to the war over Suez was characterized by Nasser's increasingly belligerent attitude towards the West and Britain in particular. The special relationship between Britain and Egypt had been under severe strain since the Free Officers *coup* led by Nasser in 1952. Until that time the politics and government of Egypt had been dominated by Britain, not Cairo. Under Nasser, however, a quest for neutrality, followed by a challenge to Europe and the rest of the world, would occur. That challenge resulted in the departure of one set of players from the Middle East (Britain and France) but further encouraged superpower rivalry over the region. The challenge to Britain also became personalized, as Nasser attempted finally to sever the knot between Cairo and London, and the British Prime Minister Eden perceived Nasser as 'the new Mussolini or Hitler whose ambitions needed to be curbed, just as Hitler's should have been at the time of the Rhineland crisis in 1936' (Fraser, 1995, p. 68). Yet Egypt, Nasser had determined, was carving a new role for itself both on the regional and the international stage.

Whether Nasser was able to formulate a clear policy on Egypt's regional and international role is disputed, but he was determined to make an impact on the international stage by promoting his leadership of the largest Arab state in the Middle East, his quest for leadership of the Arab world and by forwarding Egypt as a lead state under the collective and burgeoning non-aligned movement. He was particularly influenced by the Third World context, and impressed by Tito of Yugoslavia's concept of non-alignment – a policy which avoided anti-Russian or pro-western pacts, but did not debar them from receiving aid or purchasing arms from either side. Nasser embraced the concept, found himself a celebrated hero at the 1955 Bandung conference of newly independent Third World states and was encouraged to undertake his next step – the nationalization of the Suez Canal, the final step in Egypt's liberation from British colonial rule.

The Suez crisis, however, was not just about nationalization, a policy decision taken in light of the funding crisis caused by American refusal to support loans for the building of the Aswan Dam. The decision to nationalize the Suez Canal, which potently symbolized the West (Britain and France) in Egypt, also reflected Nasser's attempt to carve out a fully independent non-aligned role for Egypt on the international stage. As the Egyptian government faced the tripartite alliance between Britain, France and Israel, the rest of the world waited with bated breath for the outcome of this first direct challenge by a Third World state to the Great Powers. As a result of a secret agreement between the tripartite alliance known as the Protocol of Sèvres, it had been agreed that, under the pretext of an Israeli invasion and occupation of the Sinai and Suez region, British and French air strikes would be launched against Egypt on 31 October 1956, with a land offensive planned for 5 November (Kyle, 1991, pp. 314–31). British and French incompetence and deception, however, had resulted in the isolation of America and the Eisenhower government, which was up for re-election. Eisenhower was outraged at the British and French deception and the attention it was taking away from the revolution taking place in Hungary. He urged Eden to act with moderation, stating in a letter to the British Prime Minister, 'you are making of Nasser a much more important figure than he is . . . and where we apparently do not agree is on the probable effects in the Arab world of the various possible reactions by the western world' (Thomas, 1986, p. 77). Britain ignored America and paid a high price, its future as a major power in the Middle East effectively halted by the Suez débâcle.

The Egyptian victory, however, was largely due to the intervention of three external parties: the United Nations, America and the Soviet Union. American pressure on British currency reserves, for example, compelled the Chancellor of the Exchequer to advise an end to the

British war against Egypt. The United Nations, meanwhile, played an important part in brokering ceasefire agreements and the subsequent deployment of UN forces in the Sinai region. In effect, while Nasser rid himself of one superpower, he saddled himself with another. US policy in the Middle East following the Suez crisis resulted in an ascendant role, while Britain and France engaged in a bloody departure from the region in Iraq and Algeria.

The Suez crisis, however, still left Nasser in a fairly strong position internationally and proved extremely useful in his pursuit of domestic and regional policies. The ideology of Nasserism turned out to be highly popular at home, and across the region radical nationalist Nasserist groups sprang up to challenge the hegemony of British-supported rulers in Iraq and Jordan as well as elsewhere. Irrespective of his failures in the coming decades, the apogee of Egyptian power under Nasser during the Suez crisis was never forgotten. As Hopwood remarks, following Suez, Nasser 'stood as a man who had successfully defied the two old colonial powers on behalf of Egypt and the Arab world' (1985, p. 49).

Arab–Arab: brothers at arms

Inter-Arab rivalry is no stranger to the politics of the Middle East. Since the turn of the twentieth century, the leaders of a variety of Arab states have found themselves in competition with each other for political power, territory and control of the region's vital natural resources, including oil and, just as importantly, water. Even in the heyday of Arab unity in the 1950s and early 1960s, when Nasser of Egypt championed the Arab cause and urged his 'brothers' across the region to unite, rivalry characterized relations between most Arab states and even resulted in war in the case of Yemen. While political rivalry within a region is not unusual or unique to the Middle East, the occurrence of conflict between Arab states has allowed an insight into the regional balance of power, the major issues of tension and the illusion of unity in the face of a common enemy – Israel – which has been used to mask the individual ambitions of political leaders from Gamal Abdel Nasser of Egypt, Saddam Hussein of Iraq, Hafiz al-Assad of Syria, King Hussein of Jordan and King Fahd of Saudi Arabia. Behind the façade of unity a usually more personal or national ambition may be discerned, as Hourani remarks about Nasser: 'the events of 1956 and subsequent years turned Abd al-Nasir into the symbolic figure of Arab nationalism, but behind that there lay a certain line of Egyptian policy: to make Egypt the leader of an Arab bloc so closely united that the outside world could deal with it only by way of an agreement with

Cairo' (1991, p. 411). While it is true that much has united and promoted the integration of the Arab world, two factors in particular have led to divisiveness and even conflict. The first has already been alluded to: the competition for regional rather than just national leadership. The helm of the region, or even a significant coalition of states, has been a prize which many Arab leaders have fought over and to a greater or lesser degree continue to dream of. This was the case in Yemen from 1962 to 1967, when the competition for power within the region embroiled both Egypt and Saudi Arabia on opposing sides during civil dispute. The second factor is linked with the decline of pan-Arab unity and the emergence of greater economic ambitions among Arabs, as demonstrated by the Iraqi invasion of Kuwait in 1990. Indeed, this event could truly be dubbed the 'Mother of all Economic Wars' in the region.

When President George Bush of America opposed Iraq's invasion of Kuwait, he declared that the economic stakes were high. Iraq already possessed the world's second largest reserves of oil and had more than one million men under arms, making it the fourth largest military force in the world. With America dependent on imports for half its oil, it literally could not afford to let an authoritarian leader of a Third World state monopolize control of the world's oil supply. Despite the many other factors cited for the invasion, Iraq's sole goal was economic. Overproduction of the OPEC quota, Kuwait's decision to recall loans to Iraq which had been extended to the country during the war with Iran, accusations of oil-stealing and border disputes all contributed to a list of grievances which Khalidi (1991b) argued 'indicate[d] the existence of a three-decades long background of tension in Iraqi–Kuwaiti relations constituting an extended prologue to the invasion' (p. 64).

Within the region the war ended any illusion of Arab unity as, for the first time in a century, the conservative regimes of the Gulf found themselves supported by radical states such as Syria against their radical nationalist brethren in Iraq. Indeed, the war confounded so-called normal patterns of inter-Arab politics with, for example, the normally conservative monarchy of Jordan compelled by its own population to side with Iraq. Such short-term decisions had profound long-term consequences for Jordan and its relations with the Gulf Arab states, affecting aid and employment issues, creating a refugee problem and putting pressure on an already weak infrastructure and new domestic political issues at home (Milton-Edwards, 1991). The Arab world appeared to be split fifty–fifty down the middle in either siding with or opposing Saddam Hussein and, as Khalidi (1991a) notes, the invasion 'retard[ed] the prospects for the progress and advancement of the Arab world. It squander[ed] the patrimony of the Arab world and divert[ed] attention from the real challenges facing it' (p. 162). The Allied military operation in the early months of 1991, known as Desert Storm, ousted Saddam Hussein's troops from Kuwait, encouraged Shi'a and Kurdish uprisings in both the north and south of Iraq, freed the Kuwaiti oil fields, restored the al-Sabah monarchy and led to UN sanctions against Iraq and to war being waged for the first time ever in its name. The war changed the status quo, with mixed effects felt throughout the region. For the Gulf states, stability was only achieved by the intervention of foreign military support, and the hopes of idealists that democracy could gradually be attained were dashed. In Egypt and Syria the financial rewards were immediate. Yet, more than anything, as Owen notes, the fundamental result of the war was fissure and division within the Arab world, a gap not just between states but within states, with elites and leaders holding different views from those of the Arab masses (Owen, 1991). By the late 1990s the effects of the Gulf débâcle were still palpable throughout the region: Saddam Hussein remained in government in Iraq, inter-Arab relations were still soured by the events of 1991 and by the pressures for peace, driven by US ambitions for stability to protect oil in the region, and there was little movement for democratizing forces in the Gulf or Egypt, Jordan, Tunisia or Algeria. Memories of unfinished business between Iraq and the USA were revived after 9/11 when the neo-conservatives of the earlier Bush administration began to press his President-successor son to set his sights on Iraq. By the spring of 2002, George W. Bush openly declared that regime change in Iraq was now a priority for his administration.

One indirect casualty of the Gulf War has been Algeria. The civil conflict in Algeria in the 1990s highlighted the changing regional climate and the ideological clash between the forces of secularization and political Islam together with the pressure applied from the international community, with disastrous consequences. Since the Algerian war of liberation against France in 1962, secular national government in the hands of the ruling FLN (Front de Libération Nationale) had dominated politics and promoted authoritarian one-party rule. An economic crisis in the late 1980s and the forces of democratization in the early 1990s, however, promoted political change and challenge to the rule of the FLN. A referendum in 1989 permitted the foundation of new political parties, allowing Islamists in FIS (Islamic Salvation Front) to gain victories in municipal elections and the first round of national elections in 1991. The fear of an Islamist victory in national assembly elections proved too much for the ruling FLN elite, which postponed (indefinitely) the second round of elections and declared a state of emergency in February 1992. The leadership of FIS was arrested, the new president Lamine Zeroual was drafted from the army and from that point onwards the country was plunged into a brutal and bloody civil conflict between Islamists and state security forces, including the police and army.

Thousands of Algerians lost their lives in a conflict which the political leadership seemed powerless to halt and in which the international community was reluctant to intercede. Islam had been identified as the 'cause of the conflict', but Tahi (1995) questions this, arguing:

> the main obstacle to democratization in Algeria is not so much the Islamists as the persistence of old ways of thinking. Islamism . . . [is] the logical outcome of a regime which, having failed to respond to people's material expectations, sought to base its legitimacy both on Islam and the buried bones of the martyrs of the Algerian war of independence. (p. 197)

Radical Islamic guerrilla groups, including Algerian Hamas and Gama Islamiyya, have conducted a ruthless campaign against ordinary Algerians, including journalists, singers, schoolgirls who did not wear the veil and the entire population of villages in remote rural areas (Willis, 1996). The concepts of right and wrong in this civil conflict were lost, and both sides stood accused of human rights violations and atrocities. The battle remained as ideological as ever, with the two sides engaged in a dispute that was of importance for the rest of the region, challenging as it did the authoritarian rule of one-party systems with political rule premised on a version of Islam that was avowedly anti-democratic and anti-plural. In April 1999, a new era was signalled with the election as President of Abdelaziz Bouteflika, the military's preferred candidate and the country's veteran Foreign Minister under President Boumediènne in the 1970s. Under the new President violence declined and some reforms were promised. But in the twenty-first century Algeria still remains scarred by violence and a lack of security, radical elements of the Islamist movement disrupting attempts to restore stability to the country.

The lion and the peacock: Arab–Iranian relations

There is a history of Arab–Iranian conflict in the region which dates back to the power struggles which took place between the Persian and Arab empires of Islam's Golden Age. Through conquest by the Arabs, the Persians adopted Islam. From that point in the eighth century to the rise of the Ottoman Empire in the sixteenth century the Persians played a minor political and major cultural and religious role in the region. From the sixteenth century, however, the first Persian challenge to Arab authority emerged under the leadership of Ismail Safavi. Safavi was not only successful in challenging the rule of Constantinople in Persia (Safavid rule 1501–1732) but he associated his rule with Shi'ism to forge a sense of identity different from Sunni Arab Ottomanism. Islam, then, has acted as a paradoxical force between the Arab and Persian empires, serving on the one hand to unite and on the other to result in important doctrinal splits, such as the Sunni/Shi'a split that has led to enduring tensions over the centuries.

In the contemporary era the Iranians and the Arabs fell under the authority of the colonial powers after the collapse of the Ottoman Empire. But the colonial experience was not uniform and resulted in further tensions between these two ancient peoples. Under the influence of the Russians, the British and, later, the Americans, Iran became identified with the West, as an agent of imperialism in the region, harbouring expansionist ambitions which were a threat to Arab and other states. The rule of the Pahlavis, from 1925 onwards, was largely perceived as anti-Arab, as the Pahlavi dictatorship increasingly depended on the promotion of a Persian rather than a Muslim sense of national identity to legitimate its rule over an ethnically and religiously diverse population. In addition, the political independence of the Shah was consistently called into question, yet, as Halliday (1979) remarks, 'the Shah has been neither as independent as he himself claims, nor as reliant on foreign [mainly American] assistance as most of his enemies allege' (p. 21). In the neighbouring Arab state of Iraq, the experience of rule through a British mandate served to radicalize the minority Sunni population and reject colonial interference. Following the first Ba'thist *coup*, which overthrew the pro-British monarchy in 1958, Iraq promoted itself as a major regional player and secular Arab nationalist state. Holding at bay its majority Shi'a population, as Zubaida (1993) highlights, for the Sunni minority 'whose traditionally dominant position is threatened by the entry into national politics of Shi'is and Kurds . . . the appeal of Arab nationalism is that it relates the Sunnis to an Arab world in which Sunnis are the predominant majority' (p. 92).

Significant political change in both Iran and Iraq in 1979 led, almost inevitably, to a major war between the two states that would last for nearly a decade. In Iran the Pahlavi regime, headed by Reza Shah Pahlavi, was brought to a sudden end during the revolution of 1978. By early January 1979 the Shah had fled Iran and in his place the Shi'a clergy of the country, led by the charismatic Ayatollah Khomeini, announced the establishment of the Islamic Republic of Iran. The world was shaken by this revolutionary change and the USA bemoaned the loss of one of its most important client states in the region. The threat of an Islamic revolution washing up on the shores of other states in the area, and the instability and threat to Gulf oil states, were deliberated in the West as Iran declared its anti-western and anti-imperialist credentials. In Iraq, the Takriti military leader so closely associated with the rise of the Ba'th, Saddam Hussein, became President following the unceremonial ousting of Hassan al-Bakr who had led the *coup* of 1968. Saddam Hussein's imprint on politics was immediate: rivals and opposition were immediately imprisoned and executed as rule by dictatorship was almost established. Within a year the hard-won treaties between Iraq and Iran over sovereignty in the Shatt al-Arab waterway and mutual borders and boundaries would disappear, as Saddam Hussein set his sights on neighbouring Iran.

Conflict seemed the only option between these neighbouring states. Ba'thist Iraq represented the antithesis of Islamic Iran. Politically, economically, religiously and culturally, the breach between the two states appeared insurmountable. Bolstered by western, including American, support, Saddam Hussein ridiculed Iran, and on 20 September 1980 sent his troops to invade the country. Saddam Hussein's war aims were ambitious: first, the battle with Iran was promoted as ideological, the forces of Arab nationalist secularism against Iranian Shi'a Islam; second, there were economic benefits to be derived from wresting control of the Shatt al-Arab waterways from the Iranians and placing them in Iraqi hands and acquisition of territory in the Khuzistan province of Iran to Iraq's south-eastern border would guarantee additional oil reserves; third, Saddam's actions were supported by the West, which hoped that Iraq could defeat Iran and thus kill the expansionist ambitions which Islamic Iran was perceived as harbouring.

Whatever Saddam Hussein's ambitions, the defeat of Iran would not be achieved as easily or as swiftly as he and the West imagined. The war, as one journalist wrote in the *Guardian* newspaper, became the 'most expensive and futile' in the contemporary Middle East and lasted for some eight years. The figures are frighteningly eloquent: it was estimated that the two countries were responsible for more than one million civilian and military deaths. According to the most realistic estimates, the two belligerents must have spent between a third and a half of their national budgets on the war. In all, additional military expenditure, losses in GDP and non-invested capital would reach $500 billion between the two countries. For all that, was this war as futile as the *Guardian* journalist claimed? The absurdity of it did become all the more apparent once deadlock set in from 1982 onwards, following Iranian territorial gains and a repulsing of Iraq forces. Only one sort of logic prevailed, as an Orwellian state of mind descended on the combatants in which the war became a purely 'domestic affair', the object of combat no longer to make or prevent territorial conquest but to keep the structure of society intact. Both regimes used the situation to weld a diverse and increasingly discontented population together to face an external and common enemy.

Although the UN tried repeatedly to broker a ceasefire agreement between the two sides, the deadlock was not broken until 1988. The movement came from Tehran, where Ayatollah Khomeini finally announced his acceptance of a ceasefire on 20 August. There are four clear reasons why Iran finally 'bit the bullet': first, although Iran had successfully occupied the Shatt al-Arab waterway and Fao in 1986, the military burden and string of defeats in early 1988 were becoming increasingly hard to sustain, particularly in the face of international support for Iraq. Second, domestic morale was reaching an all-time low, civilian casualties were high after the 'war of the cities', in which Iraqi forces had targeted Tehran and other major population centres. Additionally, the threat of chemical warfare was particularly potent. Thirdly, within Iran's political elite the ascendancy of the pragmatists, symbolized by President Rafsanjani, and the concurrent decline of conservatives, symbolized by the death of Ayatollah Khomeini himself in June 1989, augmented the new sense of willingness to accept the inevitable. Finally many argued that the main motivation for suing for peace lies with the recognition that with the US as a co-belligerent against Iran in the latter stages of the war, this was a battle that could never be won. Iran's acceptance of the ceasefire left Iraq declaring itself the official victor of the war, the effects of which would be easily discernible some two years later. Encouraged, to some extent, by the victory against Iran, and by a variety of other factors, on 3 August 1990 Saddam Hussein ordered his troops to invade Kuwait. Three days later, in a dramatic volte-face, Saddam Hussein announced that he would return Iranian territory seized in the war of 1980–8 and respect previous agreements over the Shatt al-Arab waterway. This grand gesture made a mockery of one of the region's most destructive conflicts, nullifying the loss of life, prosperity and peace.

Lebanon: the politics of a deeply divided society

Sectarian conflict is found throughout the Middle East. Religious conflicts between Christian Copts and Sunni Muslims in Egypt, Alawites and Sunni Muslims in Syria, Jews and Sunni Muslims in Israel, Shi'a and Sunni Muslims in Iraq, Shi'a and Wahabi Muslims in Saudi Arabia may all, to a greater or lesser degree, be characterized as sectarian. Indeed, given the importance of the region to the three great monotheistic religions, Judaism, Christianity and Islam, it should not be surprising that an element of sectarian conflict or rivalry has always existed and continues to be found within the region. Religious minorities of all types have existed in communities scattered throughout the Middle East but in the twentieth century there was a tendency to believe that the secularization of the state system and society had diminished these tensions to a large extent. This belief, however, has always been challenged by the politics of confession which has dominated the structure of the state in Lebanon and had also resulted in significant conflict in 1958 and from 1975 to 1990. Civil war in Lebanon was the product of the failure of confessional and consociational arrangements in state and politics to account accurately and fairly for religious minorities.

Sectarian conflict in Lebanon, however, is not purely a product of the confessional state system which was established under the French mandate in the 1920s. This system incorporated the principal religious groups of the country into a state which, in matters of personal status, allowed individual communities to decide, but maintained an artificial Christian political majority position and in the pact of 1943 allotted government posts according to religious group, with a Maronite President presiding over government. As Gresh and Vidal highlight, the drawbacks to this system of politics are significant, while the 'presidential nature of the regime has accentuated the large hegemony of the Maronites. The country has thus been divided into virtually homogenous cantons, each cosily withdrawn into its own communal solidarity' (1990, p. 30). A diverse representation of religious groups has always characterized this territory and has, as a result, attracted further minorities to seek shelter there (Shehadi, 1988). To date, the following confessional groups may be identified in Lebanon: Christian – Maronite 25 per cent, Orthodox 10 per cent, Greek Catholics 5 per cent, other Christians 5 per cent. Muslim – Sunnis 20–25 per cent, Shi'ite 30–35 per cent and Druze 6 per cent. In addition, Lebanon is host to other immigrant communities, including Armenians, Kurds, Syrians and, since 1948, a Palestinian refugee population within its border. Each of the seventeen confessional communities is distinguished by a differing identity – Arab, Lebanese, Palestinian, Muslim, Shi'ite or Armenian – and political loyalty has been generated from these factors and brought the citizens of the same state into violent conflict with each other.

The political system of Lebanon had been designed to take account of difference, by a process of consociationalism with the classic features of grand coalition, mutual veto, proportionality and segmental authority (Lijphart, 1977). Thus personal and community identities remain autonomous from the state and within the community. Under this system the President is a Maronite, the Prime Minister a Sunni Muslim, the speaker of the National Assembly a Shi'ite and the cabinet is made up of Greek Orthodox and Druze membership. The state, as a result of the large amount of autonomy enjoyed by the different communities, is also perceived as weak. This assemblage, however, was predicated on a Maronite majority and Christian dominance, with a subordinate Muslim community. Throughout the late 1950s and 1960s, as the Muslim population rate grew, particularly among the Shi'ites who were also the poorest of the Lebanese, regional factors impinged on the conduct of Lebanese politics, exacerbating the already deep divisions within this society. The nature of the civil conflict which broke out in 1975 was also altered by the presence of Palestinian, Syrian and later Israeli, American and Iranian factors in this war in Lebanon.

From 1975 to 1990 and the implementation of the Taif peace agreement, the war in Lebanon would spiral through a number of phases. The first phase, from 1975 to 1977, was a mainly Lebanese affair, with battles between the militias of the Lebanese Front and the National Movement. The Palestinian factor had, however, sparked the conflict and the formal entry of the PLO into the war occurred quickly. In 1976 the Syrians arrived and remained in Lebanon until their withdrawal of troops and other personnel in 2005 after they were accused of involvement in the assassination of former Lebanese Prime Minister Rafik Hariri. In 1982 the Israelis invaded to oust the PLO, and when this was achieved Israel remained, and still remains, as an occupying force in the south of the country where the majority of the Shi'ite population live. American forces had supported Israel but withdrew from Beirut in 1982 following the departure of the PLO. An American presence in the rest of the country was maintained and was only ended after the car bombs of 1983, when hundreds of US service personnel were killed by a Shi'ite suicide bomber. The human toll of the war is of tragic proportions, marked only by the apparent ceaseless catalogue of murder, massacre, kidnappings, suicide bombings and destruction of an entire country and its people. Attempts at peacemaking were thwarted as much by internal as external factors and the ceasefire phenomenon was always short-lived (Hiro, 1993).

Since 1990 Lebanon, however, has lived under a fragile peace. The 1989 Taif Accords, set up under the auspices of the Arab League (initiated by Saudi Arabia, Algeria and Morocco), formulated an agreement whereby limited reforms to Lebanon's political system were designed to weaken the Maronite monopoly of power and increase Sunni Muslim representation in the National Assembly. Here again parity in favour of Christian political dominance was the primary concern of the architects of this modest agreement (Hollis and Shehadi, 1996). There was also some consensus that the Syrian presence in the country should eventually be withdrawn. The Taif Accords, however, have not and did not solve Lebanon's political problems. The Christian army leader General Aoun refused to recognize the agreement, and the Shi'ite community was still unhappy at the relatively low level of power accorded to them and further strengthened their links to Iran.

In 1990 Beirut was reunited, many of the militia groups withdrew from the city, elections to the National Assembly and Presidency were held, and under Syrian guidance Lebanon has been in the process of reconstruction and reconciliation. This process is fraught with dangers, not least of which is the fact that the political system has remained largely unchanged, the state remains weak and the politics of confessionalism – which played such a large part in the conflicts and wars of the past – have remained enshrined in a system of government and politics which encourages segmented autonomy and a variety of cleavages along ethnic, religious, class, rural, urban and geographical lines. The presence of Syrian troops in Lebanon until 2005 further inhibited the prospects for lasting peace in the country. The inauguration of a multilateral peace process in 1991, bringing the Lebanese and the Israelis to the same negotiating table for the first time, should have been cause for optimism, but the reality remains that any notion of Lebanese autonomy in the peace process is mythical as long as Syria continues to influence Lebanese politics. Subsequent elections to the 128-seat Lebanese Parliament have confirmed the old confessional balance of power, with the Maronites securing the highest number of seats. The new Lebanon has a long way to go before the reconstruction of national identity which all citizens feel they can share is achieved. The assassination of former Prime Minister Rafik Hariri in February 2005 directly contributed to a new call and momentum to deliver a Syrian withdrawal from Lebanon. Within a month the Syrian President had agreed a military and intelligence withdrawal but many of the uncertainties that had prevailed in the civil war period appeared to re-surface as the country's government fell amidst the fallout of Hariri's death.

Case study Egypt and Israel – the Cold Peace

The Camp David Peace Treaty signed by the leaders of Israel and Egypt on 29 March 1979 marked a significant turning point in the Arab–Israeli conflict and for peacemaking in the Middle East in general. Of equal importance was the fact that the treaty signed between Israeli premier Menachim Begin and Egyptian President Anwar Sadat was the first sign of peace in the conflict between Israel and the Arabs, and indicated significant movement in a six-year period from war to peace. The consequences of the treaty would be momentous, and it was heralded by some as the 'end of adversary relationships in the Middle East'. Yet the treaty did not produce the comprehensive peace settlement to the Arab–Israeli conflict that other forms of negotiations might have. Instead, it represented yet another stage in a long drawn out dispute. The treaty was a document mapping out the future of negotiation between Israel and the Egyptians and provided a timetable for part of them. Issues that were deliberately avoided were to be addressed in the future. Little wonder, then, that fourteen years later commentators would remark on the resemblance between Camp David and the Oslo Accords signed between Israel and the Palestinians. Obviously, strategies for peacemaking between Israel and the Arabs would have a particular character and pattern, choosing the most minor concessions as a starting-block for a protracted, difficult and oft-stalled negotiated settlement. Common security should be the goal that all sides seek in negotiations, but this definition of security between Israel and its allies has been fiercely contested, making any form of negotiation difficult.

The three parties involved in the evolution of this particular treaty, America, Israel and Egypt, each had their own idea of how negotiations should be conducted and what issues should be placed on the agenda. In particular, the aim of a peace treaty was seen by Israel and Egypt in particular in very different lights. It was the self-appointed job of the Americans, under President Carter's leadership, to seek a workable compromise when it was needed. Indeed, the Camp David Treaty was described as 'the only case so far in the Middle East in which successful crisis management and resolution ultimately led to conflict resolution' (Yariv, 1992, p. 144). From 1973 to 1976, under US Secretary of State Henry Kissinger, a process of 'step-by-step' diplomacy resulted in disengagement agreements between Egypt and Israel. The US administration, fearing the resumption of general hostilities between Israel and the Arabs and the continuation of the oil embargo, was aiming to create a role for itself, while at the same time excluding Soviet influence. America had vital oil interests in the region – by the 1970s a third of its oil consumption had to be imported. Kissinger promoted himself as an 'honest broker', but there was considerable criticism of his role in pressurizing Sadat into concessions in Israel's favour. The American agenda, however, lay in getting Israel and Egypt to make peace without getting mired in the issue of a 'comprehensive' agreement that would have to take account of the Palestinian issue as well.

Sadat's decision to enter into peace negotiations was influenced by the impact of the military defeat of 1973. Although Egypt had scored early military successes, Sadat still had to face up to the loss of Egyptian territory to Israel and the fact that at one point during the war Israeli tanks had reached the suburbs of Cairo. In addition, Sadat believed that Egypt's regional role would be better served with support from the Americans. He knew that in terms of diplomatic settlement only the Americans could deliver Israel to him, only America had enough influence over the Israelis to pressurize concessions out of them. Sadat wanted to lure the Americans into a more active role in resolving the dispute. Luckily for him the pressure of the oil embargo, and the orchestrations and moderation of his stated goals, were conducive to the realization of at least some of his American-orientated aspirations. His objectives were twofold: first, he wanted a rapid peace settlement because Egypt was becoming increasingly unstable and opposition was mounting from all sectors of society. Second, he wanted to cement an alliance with America and was willing to turn all Nasser's policies on their head in pursuit of this goal. This was demonstrated when in November 1977, against the advice of his fellow statesmen, Sadat travelled to Jerusalem and addressed the Israeli Knesset and declared his objectives for peace. Sadat's gesture was treated as one of betrayal among his Arab brethren. For them, every step taken towards Israel was a step further away from the Arab regimes and their economic and diplomatic support. Nevertheless, throughout 1978 Sadat pursued his peace agenda and in August President Carter invited him and Israeli Prime Minister Begin to Camp David to discuss a peace settlement.

In contrast to Egypt, the Israeli position from 1973 to 1979 grew from a position of defeat and low morale to power, with Israel eventually holding the predominant position in negotiations. A large part of this achievement was due to the political and diplomatic skills of Israeli premier Menachim Begin and three of his cabinet colleagues – Moshe Dyan in particular. The Begin–Dyan plan was premised on time: they were willing to draw out the peace process, negotiate each point separately, avoid so-called comprehensive packages and would not countenance, under any circumstances, a Palestinian state in the West Bank and Gaza Strip. There would be a complete diffusion of the peace process, splitting it into three parts: territory, the nature of peace and the Palestinians. For the most part the plan succeeded, although the Israeli government was placed under US pressure to make certain concessions. Israel, nevertheless, sought American-guaranteed compensation including supplies of oil, an increase in economic and military aid and guarantees that Egypt would not break a peace treaty.

The peace treaty was a success in some ways. A state of conflict between Egypt and Israel was halted, territory was relinquished and Israeli settlements in the Sinai were dismantled. Diplomatic relations, including embassy and consular representation between each country, were established and limited trade agreements signed. Since 1979, however, a cold peace between the two countries has existed. Sadat paid dearly for the peace agreement, assassinated by Islamist extremists opposed to the treaty. Egypt has spent many years regionally isolated by its Arab neighbours and it was only by the 1990s that Sadat's successor Hosni Mubarak was able successfully to embark on a process of reintegration into the Arab world. For Israel, the treaty did not lead to peace with other Arab states; the domino effect did not take place. Instead, Israel became embroiled in the conflict in Lebanon and later faced a full-scale Palestinian revolt on its own borders. The lessons in peacemaking and negotiation, on both sides, however, have not been forgotten and many of the tactics and strategies employed in the past can be seen in evidence in the present, as other peace agreements between Israel and its neighbours are forged.

Case study The Oslo breakthrough

Negotiations concerning the Israeli–Palestinian and wider Arab–Israeli conflict have, in recent years, gone some way to resolving the disputes that divide these groups. Since 1991, the Gulf crisis, the collapse of the Soviet Union and its influence in the region, the pressure for peace – of a sort – has been steadily growing. The precedents set as part of this wider peace process are considerable and the unthinkable has, to a certain extent, been achieved. Since that time Israelis and Palestinians have, for the first time ever, met together at the negotiating table, the PLO has, for the first time ever, formally recognized the state of Israel and renounced terrorism. Israel has, for the first time ever, passed legislation in the Knesset, permitting its citizens to have official contacts with the PLO. It has, for the first time ever, agreed to the limited redeployment of Israeli troops in the West Bank and Gaza Strip and limited autonomy for the Palestinians. Together, for the first time in the history of the Palestinian–Israeli conflict, the two sides have agreed an agenda for negotiation for a durable peace settlement. The difficulty has lain in the obstacles that have arisen in the path to peace, from the assassination of Yitzhak Rabin, the establishment of new settlements including Har Homa, the acceleration of Hamas violence, the collapse of the Likud government in 1998, the assassination by Israel of Palestinian leaders, the election of Ariel Sharon to government in 2001 and the decision by the Israelis to re-occupy Palestinian territories in 2002.

The 1990s were characterized by a peace process of sorts. The first years of the twenty-first century were characterized by no peace process of any sort. The Palestinians and Israelis engaged in negotiations and have been governed by a variety of strategies, formulas, options, demands, highest stakes, lowest concessions and compromises. Negotiators and political representatives have had to be responsive not only to their partners in peace and the international community, but also to the constituency they claim to represent – legitimacy has, therefore, become a key factor in this peace process.

The implications of the Gulf crisis for the Palestinian–Israeli conflict were profound. The Palestinians, in their alleged support of Iraq, had alienated vital Gulf Arab support, including financial assistance, and their population in Saudi Arabia and Kuwait was expelled. A crisis of legitimacy beset the PLO as Yasser Arafat struggled with the financial implications of the war and growing Islamist popularity in the West Bank and Gaza Strip. Israel had been denied any part in the conflict and was forced to adhere to American strictures, protection and assistance, while Iraqi Scud missiles dropped on Tel Aviv. Yet after the war American re-centring of power in the Middle East plus economic pressure on Israel would be brought to bear in its attempts to bring its vision of peace and stability to the region. It rapidly became apparent that, 'in the aftermath of the war, the United States reassessed its strategic priorities . . . and decided that maintaining the new and stronger links with the Arab states was of an importance at least equivalent to that which it had previously put on US ties with Israel' (King, 1994, p. 60). America envisaged a peace process that would bring all sides together in bilateral and multilateral meetings. Yet bringing the Israelis and the Arabs together was a formidable task.

The breakthrough came when the Madrid conference was convened on 3 October 1991, with the following parties in attendance – Israel, Lebanon, Egypt, Syria, a joint Jordanian–Palestinian delegation, European Community observers and American and Soviet sponsors. From 1991 to August 1993 the Madrid process would result in Israel and the Palestinians (in joint representation with Jordan) engaging in eleven sessions of negotiations. This was a significant process in the trouble-ridden Middle East where countless peace initiatives had resulted in failure. By late 1992, however, the Madrid process increasingly became an obstacle rather than a facilitator of negotiation. Substantive issues were constantly obscured by the mechanics of negotiation, yet at the same time it alerted those involved to the truth about finding political solutions to conflicts in deeply divided territories. As Crick argues, 'Problems (especially political problems) can either be said to have many possible solutions, or no solutions, only resolutions, settlements, compromises or even ameliorations; none perfect, but several, perhaps many, ranging from the more or less agreeable to the more or less acceptable' (1990, p. 268).

The Oslo negotiations (in 1993) were remarkable in their own right and politically unique from the Madrid process. The Oslo channel was secret, it involved only a few key negotiators, it consisted of compromise and recognition and was facilitated by the Norwegians. As Gerner claims, both sides needed Oslo – the Israeli government had 'lost faith in the Madrid process [and] became convinced that they had to deal directly with the PLO', while Arafat, conscious of internal political problems, 'needed a concrete achievement to restore his credibility' (1994, p. 187). The outcome of Oslo was not ambitious in terms of a peace treaty but it was in the sense that it brought an end to a state of conflict which had kept Israelis and Palestinians divided for decades. Secrecy was the key to the Oslo channel; negotiators were free from external pressures and interference allowing those involved quickly to draft a declaration of principles which would be a document that would set out the agenda for future negotiations (Corbin, 1994). In addition, the declaration would allow Palestinians limited autonomy in the West Bank and Gaza Strip with Israeli troop redeployments.

Since the signing ceremony of September 1993 the Oslo Accords and the experiment of limited Palestinian self-rule have lurched from one crisis to another (Usher, 1995). Israeli troops did redeploy, Israel transferred certain civil powers to the new Palestinian National Authority (PNA), headed by PLO President Yasser Arafat, who returned from exile to establish himself in Gaza. Elections were held for the Palestinian Council, the legislative wing of the PNA, and the timetable for negotiations would remain. Political violence, however, marred the process, along with significant opposition to the way in which negotiations were carried out from both sides of the political divide. In November 1995 Israeli Prime Minister Yitzhak Rabin was assassinated by an Israeli extremist opposed to peace, and the following year Israelis elected Binyamin Netanyahu as the country's new premier on an anti-Oslo agenda. Since April 1994 Islamic extremists opposed to the Oslo Accords and Israel's continued occupation of the West Bank and Gaza Strip have waged a war of suicide bombings in Israel which have killed hundreds (Milton-Edwards, 1996b). The rule of the PNA over the Palestinian community of the West Bank and Gaza Strip has been called into question on countless occasions, as a variety of voices have expressed concern at the authoritarian tendencies of the PNA and its massive security forces which have been destroyed by Israel, accused of failing to protect Palestinians and failing to contain the Islamic security threat to Israel (Milton-Edwards, 1998).

The timetable for final status negotiations fell along the wayside as the outbreak of the armed uprising in 2000 brought renewed enmity between Israel and the Palestinians. Each side blamed the other for the breakdown of the peace process, the lost opportunities and the outbreak of violence. A glimmer of hope was revived in 2003 around the announcement of the Roadmap which recognized a new timetable for a two-state solution and included American recognition of legitimate Palestinian demands for statehood. Ariel Sharon announced a unilateral plan to disengage from the Gaza Strip and a few settlements in the West Bank but still refused to enter into peace talks with PNA and PLO President Yasser Arafat. In November 2004 Yasser Arafat died and in January 2005 Palestinians elected a new President, Mahmoud Abbas (Abu Mazen). The prospects for a revived peace process were temporarily better but the terms of the peace were far from agreed by either side. The election of a Hamas government in 2006 appeared to push peace even further to the margins.

Case study Back to Iraq

The war in Iraq in 2003 that led to the toppling of the regime of Saddam Hussein has been mired in international controversy and once again placed the politics of the Middle East centre stage in international affairs. The reasons for the war, as cited by the US and UK governments hinged on a belief that Saddam Hussein possessed weapons of mass destruction that were a direct threat to the West; that Iraq had links to al-Qaeda which in turn had been responsible for 9/11; that Saddam Hussein presided over a regime where the majority of Iraqis lived in a permanent state of fear; and that with western support Iraq could turn itself into a model of democracy that the rest of the region could emulate. The war animated the whole of the international community in ways that were previously unheard of. Millions demonstrated against the western plan to wage war on Iraq, certain European governments publicly opposed the US/UK plan; the work of the western intelligence services, the mission of the

UN arms inspectors in Iraq, the legality of such actions all appeared to throw the international community into temporary turmoil.

The war in Iraq is understood by many commentators as an arena in the American-led and defined war on terrorism that was formulated as a response by the administration of George W. Bush in the wake of 9/11 (Halliday, 2005). According to this thesis Iraq was quickly identified by American policy-makers and politicians as part of a threat defined by President Bush as 'the axis of evil'. Iraq represented a threat because of the aforementioned links with WMD and al-Qaeda. Moreover, others argued that economic factors also had their part to play as Iraqi oil resources were important to the US energy agenda and hence they remained vulnerable in Saddam Hussein's hands. The wider geo-strategic import for the US lay in the message that a military success in Iraq would convey to other states and actors that they considered a threat. As Hersh has noted in reflecting the view of one US intelligence official, 'This is a war against terrorism, and Iraq is just one campaign. The Bush Administration is looking at this as a huge war zone' (Hersh, 2005, p. 3).

In the Middle East itself the prospect of the western intervention in Iraq to topple Saddam Hussein was greeted with almost universal hostility at a popular level and with mistrust and suspicion by the leaders of many regimes in the region. A year after the war Muslim opinion surveyed highlighted that, 'opposition to the war remains nearly universal' (Pew, 2004). The war in the spring of 2003 was a relatively short-lived affair; the Ba'th regime was easily defeated by the combined military prowess of the US and UK but there was a sense of disappointment that the western liberators were not greeted with open arms by the people of Iraq. In the wake of the war the extent of Saddam Hussein's crimes against his own people was revealed; the reality of western occupation and the scale of reconstruction made itself felt; security for ordinary citizens diminished; and the political wrangling over the future of the state commenced.

The official mandate of occupation for the American-led Coalition Provisional Authority was short-lived and its head, Paul Bremer, departed from Iraq in June 2004, leaving power in the hands of a transitional government headed by Iyad Allawi. During the one year of official occupation, however, the security situation, despite the presence of over 100,000 western troops, spiralled out of the control of the governing authorities. Significant parts of the country fell into a security vacuum over which the western military authorities had no power. Sabotage, looting, kidnappings, suicide bomb attacks on crowded streets, religious shrines and ceremonies, gun attacks on occupation and local police and military forces quickly became the reality of post-war Iraq and hampered reconstruction efforts. Allawi's power, however, remained dependent on the continuing military presence of thousands of western forces stationed throughout the country. They, in turn, were viewed as the real tools of power in Iraq and insurgency quickly marred the post-war landscape. The insurgency has flowered in many forms including among both Sunni and Shi'a elements in Iraq. The prevailing environment of insecurity, however, did not decrease Iraqi demands for free elections. Free elections for all Iraqis were seen as an important mechanism for increased sovereignty and independence for all Iraqis. In particular the prospect for elections was viewed positively in both the majority Shi'a community and among the sizeable minority of Kurds living in the north of Iraq.

When elections were held in January 2005 the majority of Iraqis participated in the poll. Only in the Sunni areas where security fears were at their highest and the greatest antipathy to the western presence has been expressed was turnout poor. The elections were an achievement in themselves but they would not be sufficient for political or other forms of stability to emerge in Iraq nor to serve as a much-touted model for democracy for other states enduring authoritarian regimes elsewhere in the Middle East. It took many months of negotiation among the winning parties to agree on the formula and balance of power among Iraq's many ethnic and religious elements before the formation of the new Iraqi government and legislature was announced in late spring 2005. Ahead of the new government lay the task of agreeing on a new constitution which would be ratified in a referendum that would be put to the Iraqi people. The continuing presence of western troops in the country with little indication of the exit strategy proposed by UK and US government also led many sceptics to conclude that the war in Iraq had more to do with the wider agenda of the US war on terrorism and the military tactics employed to pursue that war. In June 2003 a senior American official argued that 'the liberation of Iraq is a triumph for American forces' and went on to outline the US commitment to the country in the wake of the war. He noted that the majority of the burden for reshaping, building and redefining Iraq as a modern democratic state lay with the Iraqi people themselves and affirmed that 'the long-term future of Iraq depends on the establishment of rule of law, representative government, and sustainable economic development' (Larson, 2003). The issue that only time will resolve is whether the US and UK role in Iraq, before, during and after the war of 2003, helped or hindered in the achievement of that goal. Further legislative elections in December 2005 came on the heels of the ratification of the new constitution. In this poll, Sunni rates of participation increased but voting patterns revealed an increasingly ethnic and sectarian breakdown of the country, pushing it ever closer to civil war.

Further reading

Debate on the causes of conflict in the Middle East can be found in a variety of texts, many of which are written from a particular perspective – for example politics, international relations, peace studies, economics, history or anthropology. Many accounts of the Arab–Israeli conflict can be found. A number of introductory historical accounts are worth citing, including Smith (2004) and Fraser (1995), who give concise overviews of the conflict between Israel and the Arabs since 1948. Deeper historical analysis of the origins of conflict and the wars between Israel and the Arab states of the Middle East is provided in Morris (1988 and 1998), Lukacs and Battah (1988), Bailey (1990), Shlaim (1990) and Pappe (1994). More recent Israeli historiography can be found in Karsh (1997). Specific accounts of the Palestinian–Israeli conflict are available in books such as Aruri (1989), McDowall (1989), Gerner (1994) and Tessler (1994). The work of Morris and Tessler should also be contrasted with Khalidi (1997), who has written a strong historical account of developments in Palestinian nationalism. Avineri's (1981) work on Zionism is particularly interesting and, along with Avishai (1985) and Cohen (1987), provides refreshing insight into this very modern nationalist movement. Lukacs (1992) provides a good documentary account of the conflict. Said has written a personal account of dispossession and Palestinian national struggle (1995a) and this should be read in conjunction with Sayigh's (1997) comprehensive account of Palestinian nationalism. A variety of accounts on the Palestinian uprising have been published and a broad spectrum of views can be garnered from Schiff and Ya'ari (1989), Peretz (1990), Nassar and Heacock (1991) and Milton-Edwards (1996a). Worthwhile accounts of the Suez conflict can be found in Thomas (1986), Louis and Owen (1989) and Kyle (1991). No one definitive account of inter-Arab conflict exists, yet details of such disputes may be found in individual country studies, such as Stephens (1971), Hopwood (1985) and Gordon (1992) on Egypt and conflict in Yemen, Tahi (1995), Spencer (1996) and Willis (1996) on Algeria. Hundreds of texts were published in the wake of the Gulf crisis of 1991, including Gowan (1991), al-Gosaibi (1993) and Gow (1993); valuable readers include Bresheeth and Yuval-Davis (1991), Brittain (1991), Sifry and Cerf (1991), which includes texts of speeches, documents and opinion pieces, and Bennis and Moushabeck (1995). A particularly chilling and compelling account of the war and its aftermath in the region has been authored by Makiya (1993). Freedman (1993) is commended for contextualizing the events of 1990–1 in relation to the concept and politics of the New World Order. The war between Iran and Iraq is the subject of literature on the region, including Cordesman (1987 and 1988), in which the military/security dimensions of the conflict are examined. Evans (1988) and Creighton (1992) examine the political implications of this conflict, with Creighton in particular comparing the war between Iran and Iraq with the 1990–1 crisis. The sectarian and civil dimensions of the conflict in Lebanon between 1975 and 1990 are examined in Shehadi (1988), Fisk (1992), Hiro (1993) and Salem (1995). The future of Lebanon after conflict is discussed in Collings (1994) and Hollis and Shehadi (1996). Books on peacemaking in the Middle East, including the Camp David peace treaty, include Quandt (1986 and 2005), Rabinovitch (1991) and Feste (1991). General debates can be found in Boulding (1994) and Spiegel (1992) and the economic effects of peace are discussed in depth in Fischer et al. (1993). Accounts of the Palestinian–Israeli peace process are dealt with in a variety of texts, including Kaufman et al. (1993), King (1994), Said (1995b), Usher (1995), Cordesman (1996), Flamhaft (1996) and Makovsky (1996). The collapse of the Oslo peace process is debated in Rothstein et al. (2002) and by Usher (1999). There have been a huge number of books authored about the war in Iraq. They cover topics ranging from weapons of mass destruction to ethnic issues and ethics. Among the more thought-provoking and informative texts are Dodge (2003) and Tripp (2002) which should be read in conjunction with books such as Feldman which discusses the ethics of war and nation building by the West in Iraq (2004). The future of Iraq is outlined and analysed in Anderson and Stansfield's book (2004) while more polemic arguments feature in Clark (2003) and Ali (2003).

Past, Present and Future Politics: Political Islam

Introduction

WHEN the muezzin at the mosque call faithful Muslims to prayer five times a day they do so in step with a tradition established in the seventh century by an Arabian merchant's son known as Mohammed. Islam is one of the three monotheistic religions founded in the Middle East. As a religion, way of life and practice of politics, it has made its presence felt throughout the globe; from Belfast to Beirut the Muslim community remains true to its faith, culture and often its politics. The politics of Islam constitute a myriad phenomenon apparent in many guises, and are the product of varied social bases worldwide. Political Islams rather than political Islam best describes the different kinds of political movement which have emerged throughout the past 100 years to contest politics in domestic, regional and international settings. Such movements can be found in the formal as well as in the informal worlds of politics – in the home, where domestic politics between men and women are often shaped by the faith. On the street, whether in Nairobi, Cairo, Jakarta or Islamabad, Islamic ideologues have influenced responses to Third World populism, problems of dependency, indebtedness and poverty. In addition, political Islams have consistently tussled with their political opposites – notions of secularized nationalism, which have held the ideological sway over the globe. Islam, in response, has gone some way both to accommodate – through notions of pan-Islamism and Islamic nationalism – and to reject this very real challenge. The two sides to this particular argument are presented by Juergensmeyer, who contends that political Islam has been presented as a form of religious nationalism – 'many Muslim movements are indeed nationalist . . . most Muslim activists seem happy to settle for Islamic nationalism' (1993, p. 47) – and by Tibi, who argues the opposite by claiming that the call of contemporary fundamentalists 'becomes a call for an Islamic order opposed to the order of the secular nation-state' (1992, p. 183). Al-Azmeh, however, points out that the distinctions are less than clear: 'Be that as it may, a number of conceptual features common to the ideologies of Arabism and Islamism rendered possible the association between them and their occasional power of mutual convertibility' (1993, p. 69).

It would be unthinkable to study the politics of the Middle East without examining or taking into account the impact that Islam has made on the dynamics and interchange of policy, politics and the state in the contemporary era. In almost every Middle Eastern state, the majority of the population is Muslim. In the twentieth century Islam has been recognized by both state and non-state actors as an increasingly important political force, whether in terms of the promotion of alternative revolutionary agendas, sanctioning existing state rule, reformist social activities, the political rights of women (as I discuss further in chapter 7), the kidnap of foreigners, the mistreatment of religious minorities or suicide bombings. While Islam has always acknowledged the political as well as the spiritual, many authors argue that in the twentieth century a resurgence of Islam as a political force for change, reform and even revolution has taken place in response to the westernization of society as a result of colonialism, the struggle for independence and establishment of the post-colonial nation-state. The resurgence of Islam, argues Esposito (1992), however, is about its 'higher profile' in political life rather than its absence during previous eras (p. 11). The revival in political life has also been accompanied by a resurgence of interest in all things Islamic, from the five pillars of the faith, to its literature, societal and social programmes, relations to folk and Sufi Islam, orthodox literature, law, economic practices, differences and commonalties between Shi'a, Sunni, Druze and Ismaili', and popular and street Islam. Often the clash between popular folk Islam and the reforming movements of political Islam has occurred, as Zubaida (1993) points out, when fundamentalists reject secular nationalism and reclaim Islam in the 'original': 'their construction of "original" Islam, however, would exclude most of the beliefs and practices of popular culture, including religio-magical practices, which would be seen as corrupt' (p. 118). In sum, political Islam is as much an internally as an externally driven dynamic force in the modern age.

Political Islam, described by Dessouki as 'an increasing political activism in the name of Islam by governments and opposing groups alike' (1982, p. 4), then, is one part of the larger resurgence of Islam and other religions that many authors have argued has taken place in the Middle East since the 1970s. The re-emergence of Islam as a potent political and social force came at a time of immense change in the Arab world, following the defeat of the Arabs in the war of 1967 and what has been termed by Fouad Ajami as the 'end of pan-Arabism' (1979). As the Arab secular nation-state and pan-Arabism were discredited and legitimacy undermined, the crisis which emerged 'contributed to the end of pan-Arabism and the rise of an alternative: political Islam', claims Tibi (1997, p. 218). Whether or not one accepts the argument that 1967 was a watershed in the competition between secular nationalism and political Islam in the Middle East, what is certain is that the subsequent relevancy of political Islam, the varying interpretations of its ideologues and thinkers and the formation of many new movements for change became increasingly salient and noticeable. The oft-quoted 'revival', 'resurgence', 'rebirth' or 'return' of Islam as a response to the crisis of identity and legitimacy in the face of the 'humiliating defeat in the war, the loss of Jerusalem, and the occupation of the West Bank, as the western secular model of government failed, was Muslims' only hope' (Esposito, 1984, p. 215). A new generation of political players emerged, challenging the legitimacy of the nation-state and its rulers throughout the Middle East and beyond.

This chapter will examine the impact of Islam as a political force, its earliest proponents at the turn of the century, its reformist agenda of the 1920s and 1930s, the crisis of identity following the war of 1967 which many argue accounts for the current resurgence of Islam, its radical and revolutionary manifestation and its challenge to prevailing conservative, secular, nationalist and capitalist ideologies in the Middle East. The case studies will focus on distinct manifestations of political Islam in the latter part of the twentieth century: the Iranian Revolution of 1979 which was successfully harnessed by the Shi'ite clergy of the country and transformed into a state system of government and politics; and the emergence of the Palestinian Islamic activist movement Hamas (Islamic Resistance Movement), a non-state actor engaged in a political campaign to end Israeli occupation of the West Bank and Gaza Strip.

Islam and politics

The participation of Muslims in the political life of a community is perceived as embedded in the religion itself. The Prophet Mohammed set the first example when, following his flight from Mecca in the seventh century, he directed his political energies to the government of the city-state of Medina, establishing the rules for a political as well as religious community which would later extend its power over other parts of Arabia, and eventually beyond. The growth of Muslim rule in the seventh and eighth centuries promoted a principle not just to win the souls of converts to the faith, but also their hearts and minds. The political expansion of Islam was inextricably linked with the spread of the religion itself, encompassing not just the act of worship and the mosque but all aspects of life – political, legal, economic, cultural and social relations fell under this universalist form. Islam provided an inherent sense of unity (*tawhid*) to the Muslim and his or her community (*umma*). Under this arrangement, it has been argued, religion and politics became fused, with no separation between the state and the mosque, in the same way that there was no separation between the state and church before the reformation in Europe.

This view of the inextricable ties between faith and politics has, however, been challenged by Eickelman and Piscatori, who contend that, historically, such linkage was just not present. In addition, Muslim thinkers have always held a 'variety' of views about the relationship between Islam and politics; nevertheless, 'the indivisibility of the two realms persists in the study of Islam', creating three significant obstacles, 'exaggerating the uniqueness of Muslim politics, inadvertently perpetuat[ing] "Orientalist" assumptions' and, finally, 'contribut[ing] to the view that Muslim politics is a seamless web' (Eickelman and Piscatori, 1996, p. 56). The religion, however, has always accepted a tradition of interpretation (*ijtihad*) and innovation (*tajdid*), and doctrinal differences and schisms have resulted in differing political practices and approaches. The difference, for example, between Sunni and Shi'a Muslims is reflected in their political practices and traditions. The Sunni/Shi'a split emerged during the contest for succession and political authority following the death of the Prophet (AD 632). While one faction of the Muslim community was determined to follow the Prophet's most trusted companions, the 'rightly guided Caliphs', under the authority of Abu Bakr, Omar, Othman and Ali, others preferred the offer of rule by the Prophet's cousin and son-in-law Ali. A battle between the two camps followed the power struggle which emerged after the death of Othman (AD 656). Ali's (Shi'a) supporters believed that authority should rest with the descendants of the Prophet, not with his companions. Ali's rule, however, met resistance and revolt, led by the Muawiyah of Syria, and eventually resulted in Ali's assassination. Nevertheless, the split, which resulted in the first war between Muslims and further splits within Ali's camp (the Kharijites, for example) established modes of rule and political power which represented differing approaches to authority, leadership and the system of politics within the religion. With their own school of law and a core of faith in which a charismatic leader – Imam – leads, it is claimed that the denominational differences have shaped Shi'a Islamic political thinking – particularly in areas of leadership, politics of opposition and the role of the *ulama* (clergy) in the political as well as the spiritual life of the community.

This period provided the example of many experiences and visions of the new religion which would guide its followers for many centuries, encouraging different paths to rule through the example of the

Prophet himself (creating the *sunna* – accounts of his acts), the Medinan state, the development of Islamic rule through appropriate political and legal structures and the success of the rightly guided Caliphs in establishing the rule of Islam over vast territories in the region. Indeed, from the seventh century onwards Islam was established through successive dynasties that ruled over the region until the 1900s. The Ummayads, Abbasids, Mamluks, Safavids and Ottomans assured the legacy of Islamic rule and its linkage to a tradition of political rule incorporating many styles of leadership and system, from reformist to fundamentalist, scripturalist to interpretative, benign to despotic, liberal to conservative. The religion acted as a foundation stone for political systems that were widespread and varied. Islamic law remained the legal basis of many of these states, the ruler ruled in the name of Islam and politics evolved under a system of consultation (*Shura*) and councils (*Majlis*) in which Muslims could claim representation. Above all, Allah, not the particular leader or sultan of a dynasty or community, remained sovereign and demanded total submission from his followers.

The impact of the political on the religious and vice versa resulted in a complicated history where the political hue of Islam assumed greater importance, often in response to a challenge or contest for authority, yet none of this was unusual. The history of Islam and, therefore, of political Islam, is one of ebb and flow. Islam's followers have challenged corrupt authority and rebellion against apostasy is a significant feature of the political landscape. Dynamic, turning and reaching out to respond to the passing of history, the followers of Islam have contributed to the development of political systems which embrace modernity, rule, institutions and government, human rights and political economy. Political Muslims have been rulers, the ruled, in government and in opposition, claiming legitimacy in the name of the faith, contesting and protesting it. The utopian vision of Islam's thinkers, theologians and politicians has led to the development of schools of thought and practice which advocate particular paths or visions of Islam, while also challenging traditional orthodoxy.

At the dawn of the twentieth century the Ottoman Empire reached over the territories of the present-day Middle East, the rule of the Ottomans had endured for more than four centuries, yet the impact of global political changes had weakened its defences and its grasp on the Islamic way of life and the example of the past. The security of Islam was weakened as western political ideas were imported almost wholesale along with the colonial experience which had been established in the region. While the British and the French may have exported Egypt's cotton, in return they imported ideologies and ways of thinking that challenged the traditional orthodoxy of Islam to its very core.

The tradition of western political thought that had been established over many centuries encouraged the secularization of society, the breaking of bonds between religion and politics, the notion of rule by the people for the people and the promotion of capitalist and other economic agendas, all of which clashed jarringly with the hitherto-held notions of political, religious, economic and social norms which had governed the Islamic world. Muslim thinkers responded by calling for reform, and set about the modernization of Islam with an increasing sense of urgency.

Thoroughly modern Muslims

The modernist trend within political Islam, led by al-Afghani, Abduh and Rashid Rida, had an important impact on the emergence of a new generation of thinkers and activists who embraced many of the ideas and approaches advocated by these men. Indeed, the very notion of Islamic modernism as opposed to traditionalism was in itself revolutionary and acted as a catalyst for change in a number of political arenas. While the pan-Islamic import of the message promoted by the modernists has already been recognized, there are other areas of their work, in particular on the relationship between Islam and the state, theology and politics, modernism and the rights of women, which were also significant in altering or reshaping the political landscape in which Islam would re-emerge as a potent force. Indeed, as Esposito (1984) highlights, 'Unlike conservative Muslims, however, Islamic modernists asserted the need to revive the Muslim community through a process of a reinterpretation or reformulation of their Islamic heritage in light of the contemporary world' (p. 47). They created a new space within Islamic circles for new approaches and thinking and, all the more remarkably, as Ayubi (1991) contends, 'whereas the earlier "Islamic reformers" such as Afghani and Abduh were striving to modernize Islam, the following generation of Islamists such as al-Banna and the Muslim Brothers were striving to Islamise modernity' (p. 231).

Although al-Afghani, Abduh and Rida are linked together through brotherly bonds and a sense of sharing the same intellectual roots, the ideas and careers of the three men also reflect the differing approaches they took to the modernist project and in turn its impact on the political establishment and emergence of a new Islamic project which would change the face of Islamism in the region forever. Al-Afghani was a noted activist seeking to turn his ideas into deeds which would help shape the approach of modern Muslims to the impact of modernization through the vehicle of colonialism. While it has already been noted by Ayubi that al-Afghani called for the regeneration of the faith by returning directly to the text of the Koran and casting off the customs of tradition, he also promoted a confidence about the religion as a whole to meet the demands and challenges posed by the new western-based order in ascendance over the Middle East. Kedourie (1992), however, levels a bitter attack against al-Afghani, accusing him of being a charlatan, neither Sunni nor Afghani: 'he cultivated a reputation of Islamic zeal, while he was in fact a secret unbeliever' (p. 80). Yet, Kedourie misses the essential point of al-Afghani's appeal; irrespective of whether such accusations were true or not, national identity, schism or sect were entirely irrelevant to al-Afghani's conceptualization of the modern Muslim project. For him, the politics of identity lay not in nation, state or tribe, or in the difference between Sunni or Shi'a Muslim. The route out of oppression, subjugation and dependence lay, in al-Afghani's opinion, in a rediscovery of a true and pure Muslim identity. The tainted past and decline of Islam was explicable only by acknowledging that the time had come for change, resistance and a return to the faith.

If al-Afghani represented a more activist approach, Abduh's scholarly demeanour and intent allowed the representation of modernist expressionism to filter through the hallowed halls of al-Azhar University. He is described as a 'rationalist who influenced and inspired not only a whole school of thinkers and reformers . . . but a number of non-Egyptians and even non-Muslims as well' (Ayubi, 1991, p. 57). Nevertheless, although Abduh was never the political activist of the al-Afghani mould, and although from the late 1880s onwards it is understood that he 'accepted the existing political framework [colonial Egypt] and channelled his energies into religious, educational, and social reform rather than politics and agitation against political rule', it would be disingenuous to assume that he was an apolitical creature without influence (Esposito, 1984, p. 49). If, for example, politics is about power, and power can be represented at the level of state and society, then much can be made of Abduh's considerable contribution to the debate about the rights of women according to Islam. His work on women and Islam was predicated on reform of outdated practices which, while representing the spirit of the faith, did not respect the original intent. Hence, on the issue of polygamy, while there is a conventional belief that Islam actually encourages as well as permits the taking of more than one wife, Abduh, according to Jawad (1998), argued that if Islam was a faith based on principles of justice, then 'the ban on polygamy becomes imperative to prevent any injustice towards the wives' and that, in addition, modern social, economic and political circumstances 'means that the practice of polygamy is no longer a necessity or requirement' (p. 45). If a linkage between this reformist approach to Islam and the state was required, then the impact of Abduh's new perspective on issues of arbitration during marriage breakdown and divorce on legislation in Muslim countries is important. This is the case in Tunisia, which 'was one of the few Muslim countries which decided to introduce legal reform based on Abduh's view of judicial divorce . . . Thus, all divorce actions were prohibited, henceforth, from taking place outside the domain of the court', and women were accorded greater legal representation than hitherto had been the case (Jawad, 1998, p. 77). Abduh's fresh approach was a direct result of the modernists' approach to the faith, making it relevant to a modern age, referring directly to the source (the Koran) and moving away from the ornamented traditions and mystique which surrounded the *ulama* and over-dependence on the authority of the *hadith* rather than the word of God. This process, embraced by al-Afghani and perpetuated by Abduh, is acknowledged by Brown (1996), who notes that 'Abduh was willing to depart from traditional approaches to *hadith* in certain cases', but, he is quick to note, 'nowhere does he offer a systematic approach to the criticism of the *hadith*. Abduh was more at home with questions of theology than of jurisprudence, and more speculative than scripturalist in his method' (p. 37). Abduh can certainly be credited with a contribution to modernizing the boundaries of modern Muslim scholarship and for a fresh approach to his faith which led his own disciple Rashid Rida to further work under the modernist rubric.

Rida, however, can be categorized as a scripturalist modernist representing a trend called *salafi* Islam, meaning or pertaining to the good 'ancestral' example and tradition of Prophet Mohammed, his companions and the first four caliphs rather than the centuries of Muslim rule which followed. Those who invoked *salafi* principles wanted a return to the fundamental principles which underpinned the faith. In this respect the *salafiyya* were not primarily political animals, as al-Azmeh (1993) argues: '*salafiyya* reformism engaged in theorising the reconstitution of civil society in terms of itself rather than in terms of politics' (p. 65). Rida, as was noted in chapter 2, was the fundamentalist modernist who directly influenced young Muslim activists in Egypt and beyond, and who went on to play such important roles in the reformist wing of modern political Islam. While it is argued that 'Abduh is not normally identified as a fundamentalist but rather as a liberal reformer with a nineteenth-century faith in progress through enlightenment', the same cannot be said of Rida who promoted a less liberal and more strict version of the modernist approach, and who, although the heir to the modernist throne, 'developed his own distinctive position and legacy during the thirty-year period after Abduh's death' (Esposito, 1984, p. 62). Rida's own work reflected more political matters and examined the decline of Islam in relation to the nature of the state and balance of power therein. He recognized that any regeneration of the faith had to be underpinned not only through a revitalized spiritual community but by the state and through the instrument of the legislative process as well. From this starting point, the logical outcome, according to Rida, was a call for a restoration of true Islamic government and the caliphate, as Esposito (1984) notes: 'for Rida the true Islamic political system is based upon consultation between the caliph and the *ulama*, who are the guardian interpreters of Islamic law' (p. 63).

While it has already been acknowledged that the modernists failed to inspire a mass movement of Islamic reform, it would be wrong to underestimate the influence of their ideas on future generations. It is also important to acknowledge the fundamentally important part they played in opening up new fields of debate within Islam at a time in the region where great changes were being wrought. Here, Rida's analogy to the lighthouse, which he used in the title of his journal, proves useful, as modernist thinking, while reflecting diverse and individualist approaches, exposed the perilous path of unquestioning acceptance within Muslim societies of the modernization project and accompanying political principles, and revealed Islam as the guiding light for Muslims who were believed to have lost their faith and were out of touch with its true meaning.

Muslim Brotherhood

The organization founded by Hassan al-Banna in 1928 would have an immense impact on the revival of Islam and the resurgence of Muslim political thought. As Zubaida (1993) points out, 'This is the movement, which, in one form or another, has been the most prominent fundamentalist current in Sunni Islam' (p. 47). Hassan al-Banna and his ideological successor Sayyid Qutb would help shape the political response of Muslims throughout the region (and beyond) to the forces of capitalism, materialism, colonialism and secular nationalism. A network of Muslims would be established to unite co-religionists in Algeria, Morocco, Kuwait, Palestine, Pakistan and Britain. The Muslim Brotherhood has survived attempts by such ruling regimes as Egypt, Israel and Syria to eradicate the force of political Islam which they represent. The movement founded in 1928 persists to the present day and has continued to promote a message which has won many hundreds of thousands of supporters.

The idea behind the organization was very simple and as such this may explain the endurance of its populist appeal for the better part of seventy years. Hassan al-Banna and his followers preached a message that promoted Islam politically, religiously, economically, socially, legally and culturally as the only alternative to the forces of westernization, secularization and materialism that had penetrated Muslim society in the Middle East. They argued that the menace of the West and its supporters could only be conquered by the wholesale adoption of Islam. The strategy for promoting this message would be influenced by the hugely charismatic al-Banna until his death in 1949 and would change following the ideological split within the Egyptian movement. Under al-Banna's leadership the Muslim Brothers' strategy focused on a gradualist-reformist approach which continued to emphasize the need, previously advocated by Rida, to return to the roots of the religion, to the Koran, the Prophet and the Golden Age of rule under the 'rightly guided caliphs'. The strategy was not modernist in the sense that Islam should embrace western political thought, innovation or technological expertise and reformulate itself; rather, its response lay in the rejection of these alien tendencies and in the promotion of traditional Islam. The Muslim Brotherhood eventually incorporated politics into its strategy as well as the option of jihad as an act of defence against aggression. Following al-Banna's assassination by Egyptian secret police, the strategy of the movement was reassessed. In addition to the loss of al-Banna, the movement as a whole was deeply affected by the tragedy in Palestine and the region-wide movement towards Arab nationalism. Throughout the 1950s and 1960s internal debate and dispute centred on these issues and resulted in a split, with one tendency supporting the radical agenda of Sayyid Qutb and another pursuing the gradualist approach promoted by al-Banna in the first years of the Brotherhood and carried on by his successor Hassan al-Hudaibi.

When Hassan al-Banna and his supporters established the movement, their aim was to create a mass-based populist organization that would encourage Egyptian Muslims to renew their interest in the faith of Islam. The principal aims of the society at this time were not political but religious, although politics could not but help influence and shape people's ideas. Thus, through a rapidly expanding network of mosques, clubs, reading and discussion groups, public prayer meetings and sermons, clinics, hospitals, schools and income-generating projects, the Brotherhood impacted on Egyptian society and its individuals; the politics would follow later. This strategy, as Zubaida (1993) highlights, was innovative, looking to the populist base, 'the common people'. The networks established by the Brotherhood in the 1930s and 1940s earned the title 'state within a state', and in countries like Egypt they withstood the radical changes of government, persisting through many decades to survive to the present. As Kepel (1994) asserts, these networks (now apparent throughout the Middle East) 'play an essential part in assimilating those elements of the population who aspired to taste the fruits of modernity and prosperity but could not get them' (p. 24).

The first step taken by the Brotherhood was to persuade people to return to the practice of Islam and to educate them in its ways. Al-Banna, who had been exposed from an early age to the impact of colonialism, started on an anti-western premise that Muslims must return to their faith in its fundamentalist context. Thus, his first message was one of preaching and education (*da'wa wa tabligh*) to encourage people back to Islam, to teach them how to appreciate its message and the alternative it promoted. For ten years the Brotherhood established hundreds of branches throughout Egypt, Palestine, Jordan and Syria, with the principal aim of educating people in the ways of Islam. The illiterate were taught to read, learning from the Koran. In each mosque that the Brotherhood was able to preach, their activities also included lessons in Islamic practice, the pillars of the faith and debates about politics, law, social issues and economics. The young were identified as an important target, especially those recently educated men who aspired to liberation from colonial rule. No distinction was made between class, background (urban or rural) or education, as the Brotherhood sought new recruits to its movement.

The second step, later advocated by al-Banna and adopted by many but not all branches throughout the region, was to agitate for political change, to undermine the existing political order and contest the legitimacy of those who claimed to rule in the name of Islam. While the strategy of education and social reform was maintained, some within the movement, including radical thinkers like Sayyid Qutb, argued for a more politically proactive path to bring about the revolutionary societal change which was needed to banish western influences and resurrect the force of Islam. This step met with resistance from the radical post-colonial nationalist governments of the 1960s and 1970s which ruled over large parts of the Middle East. The potential of the movement to destabilize powerful Arab states like Egypt was precipitated by the Six Day War of 1967 and the crisis of identity which subsequently swept the Arab world.

Sayyid Qutb had promoted this approach within the Muslim Brotherhood. A prolific author, he was imprisoned by the Egyptian authorities in 1954 and executed in 1966. Influenced by Hassan al-Banna and the Pakistani Islamist Mawlana Mawdudi, Qutb made a major contribution to contemporary Islamic thinking and inspired a number of region-wide Islamic groups. As Ayubi (1991) notes, 'Qutbian discourse . . . tends to influence people's thought and action in a psychologically tense way that creates in the individual not the ability to reconstruct reality but rather the dream of breaking with that reality' (p. 141). These groups fuelled an important change in the direction of Islamic politics, propelling it into an activist revolutionary realm based on change through jihad. Qutb's analysis of Egyptian society focused on the nature of decline to a state of chaos, paganism and disorder known within Islam as *jahiliyya*. The only route out of the decline, argued Qutb (1988), was revolutionary and sometimes violent. He advocated jihad as the method of liberation: 'The truth of the faith is not fully established until a jihad is undertaken on its behalf among the people . . . a struggle to remove them from this state (*jahiliyya*)' (pp. 8–9). Qutb's call reflected a change in the ideology of political Islam. As Kedourie (1994) remarks, for Qutb it is Muslim rulers, above all, who are 'infected with the spirit of idolatry . . . They are apostates from whose deadly clutch Muslim society has to be saved' (p. 333). While Hassan al-Banna had argued for gradual change from within society, Qutb called for jihad, revolutionary disengagement and the overthrow of power to establish the Islamic state. The Qutbian perspective proposed an Islamic order, established through military struggle and the politicization of the religion. Change, according to Qutb, has a radical appearance and is best achieved through struggle and striving. There are many interpretations of Qutb's impact on Islamic politics. Sivan (1985) argues that his message contained 'violence of tone and urgency . . . to his fellow Muslims who were tempted and even brainwashed by western ideas' (p. 24). This particular liberation theology has been classified as fundamentally violent, with an Islamic order established by the sword. Yet Qutb himself is more circumspect, neither ruling violence out nor actively advocating it. What is certain is that, contrary to much academic opinion, for Qutb the call to jihad was made in its broadest sense – striving for the liberation of the soul, of the individual through education, a return to faith and disengagement, where possible, from a state system of contested legitimacy. The martyrdom of Qutb only served to emphasize the durable nature of his message which has persisted and inspired Islamic groups in the contemporary era. The radical agenda which eventually characterized Qutb, its hostility to the West and fear of tyranny from within, became the starting point of many radical groups. As Esposito (1992) points out, Qutb's influence (along with others) can be seen in 'the two options – evolution, a process which emphasises revolutionary change from below, and revolution, the violent overthrow of established systems of government' (p. 129). The Muslim Brotherhood remains an important element to political Islam in the Middle East in countries such as Egypt, Jordan, Syria, Lebanon and Iraq. Its leaders are convinced that they will continue to play an important part in shaping political discourse in the twenty-first century.

Radical and fundamentalist Islam

From the 1970s onwards the phenomenon of political Islam was perceived as veering to the path of revolution rather than evolution. The political character of the religion was increasingly portrayed as fundamentalist or radical, the product of what Sayyid identifies as five issues, including the already cited 'end of secular Arabism', an increasing tendency by governments towards authoritarianism, the impact of economic crisis in the region (as discussed in chapter 3), the 'crisis of the petty bourgeoisie' and the culminating cultural effects of the West on Muslim societies. As Sayyid (1997) remarks, 'these five arguments are those most often deployed to account for the rise of Islamism', yet, as he continues, why have 'these problems met their response in the form of Islamism' (p. 26)?

The answer was never going to be easy, and was made all the more difficult by the fact that 'Islam and Muslims are portrayed as the instigators and protagonists in fourteen centuries of warfare. Islam is the aggressor . . . Islam and the acts of Muslims are described as aggressive – responsible for attacks, jihad and conquest – while the West is described as defensive, responding with counterattacks, crusades, and re-conquests' (Esposito, 1992, p. 178). Fierce debate and controversy has also surrounded this process of 'naming' Islam in its contemporary condition. To date, a number of definitions have emerged which in turn indicate particular views of Islam. These perspectives are variously described as orientalist, neo-orientalist and apologist. There are a number of definitions which may support one particular perspective over another.

Fundamentalist Islam is defined by Beinin and Stork as a phenomenon that may be 'compared to politically activist, socially conservative movements mobilized by revivalist Christian, Jewish and Hindu identities'. In addition, they argue that it may be defined as representing 'the restoration of a pure unsullied, and authentic form of religion, cleansed of historical accretions, distortions and modernist deviations' (1997, p. 3). Despite this definition Beinin and Stork reject it as inappropriate to Islam. They prefer a definition of political Islam which writers like Ayubi (1991) suggest 'tend[s] to emphasize the political nature of Islam and to engage . . . in direct anti-state activities' (p. 69).

Other conservative authors, however, prefer to ascribe the following explanation: radical Islam, 'the radical end of the spectrum [of Islamic revivalism] (which encompasses more than just "extreme radicals" or terrorists) . . . is only a part of a whole, but being the cutting edge of the Islamic resurgence – its most creative and consistent expression – it may also tell us something about the revival movement as a whole'

(Sivan, 1985, p. xi). This view sees all Islamic politics as being radical, associated with violence and terror; as Miller (1993) claims, 'in Islam's war the end justifies the means. Radical political Islam placed atop these societies in the Middle East has created a combustible mixture' (p. 33). An Islamic state, meanwhile, represents theocratic, conservative, radical, anti-democratic and violent politics. Islam, from this perspective, became commonly associated with a threat to the international order, as Muslims engaged in a jihad against the West. Lewis (1990) echoes this perspective, declaring that, 'the Muslim world is again seized by an intense – and violent – resentment of the West. Suddenly America has become the arch-enemy, the incarnation of evil, the diabolic opponent of all that is good, and specifically for Muslims, of Islam' (p. 53).

Many solve the dilemma by opting for the broader term of 'Islamist', which encompasses recognition of the political role of such activists: Islamist/Islamism – 'the conscious choice of an Islamic doctrine in political action . . . a political phenomenon that has only recently developed and spread in the Muslim world, must not be confused with Islam, a much broader concept referring to the Islamic religion and civilization as a whole' (Guazzone, 1995, p. 4).

To suggest, therefore, that something called Islamic fundamentalism exists is both right and wrong. It is right, in the context of a literal sense, that, as authors such as Zubaida argue, any Muslim who is a believer is a fundamentalist because by believing they accept the fundamental tenets or principles of their faith. But is it right to categorize all politically active Muslims as fundamentalist in the sense that it is commonly understood in the West? Since the early 1980s thousands of articles, news items and books have appeared in Europe and the USA describing a phenomenon known as fundamentalist Islam. This fundamentalism is manifest in the news pictures of self-flagellating Shi'a in Lebanon and Iran and is associated with the violent atrocities carried out by Islamic organizations such as Islamic jihad, Hizbollah and Hamas. It is portrayed as inextricably linked with violence and, more particularly, terrorism. Bearded fanatics, wielding guns, punching the air with their fists populate this particular fundamentalist landscape. Iran, Afghanistan, Algeria, Sudan and Bosnia are the backdrop for a supposed tidal wave of fundamentalism washing up on the shores of the Middle East since 1979. Some authors, such as Halliday, remind us, however, that it has also suited some Islamists to encourage such fear, doing much to create and perpetuate mutual suspicion and hostility between, to quote Anderson, two 'imagined communities' – the neo-Crusader West and the Muslim fundamentalist East (Halliday, 1996, p. 110). The fear of fundamentalist Islam was stoked by the al-Qaeda attack on America in September 2001 and subsequent bomb attacks in Bali and Madrid. The war on terrorism has led to the toppling not only of Saddam Hussein's regime in Iraq, but regime change in Afghanistan, political unrest in Pakistan and Yemen, Saudi Arabia and other locations across the Arab and Muslim world. A new understanding of political Islam has emerged that has a specific focus on a group of fundamentalist thinkers and organizations known as *salafi* (original follower of Islam). The *salafi* advocate an orthodox and literal interpretation of Islam and this has inspired politically active Muslims and thinkers such as Sayyid Qutb.

The stereotype of the twenty-first-century Muslim has been constructed with little acknowledgement of the true breadth of activity and opinion in a movement for political change which has spread throughout the Middle East and beyond. While stereotypes do have their uses, in this particular case it only serves to reinforce generation after generation of orientalism, representing the 'other' as completely negative. As Said (1981) angrily declares, 'All discourse on Islam has an interest in some authority or power' (p. xvii). While Said alerted people to the dangers of orientalism, the resurgence of Islam and the interest in this phenomenon expressed in the West serves to remind us that the debate is far from over. Indeed, Said argues that *homo Islamicus* does not exist, that it is nothing more than a western invention, in an era in which 'Islam is defined negatively as that with which the West is radically at odds and this tension establishes a framework radically limiting knowledge of Islam' (Said, 1981, p. 155). What issues, therefore, does the debate centre on?

The first issue is focused on the terminology associated with describing the political phenomenon that has emerged from the revivalist period. Debating the issue has resulted in the emergence of at least two distinct approaches which can be found in the current literature on the subject. What might, at first, appear to be a debate about semantics or 'political language' (Eickelman and Piscatori, 1996, p. 11) in truth turns out to be far more political than one might have imagined. Islam, or more specifically radical or fundamentalist Islam, is thus consistently portrayed as a negative 'signifier' (Laclau, 1996). Islam is represented in contrast to the West – as Sayyid reminds us, there is a danger in this approach: 'it makes an understanding of these movements difficult by making them look simple' (1997, p. 267). Equally significant about this debate is the impact that this has on general perceptions of political Islam and the specific impact that these views have on the policies of governments involved with the Middle East. Since 9/11 a great disconnection has emerged between western governments and the Middle East.

The debate about fundamentalism, therefore, has an extremely important bearing on trade policy, arms sales, counter-terrorist strategies, diplomatic relations and the balance of power in the global order. The West, far from appearing indomitable, is vulnerable to a perceived threat from the fundamentalist Arab heartland and this weakness is exploited on all sides. Islamophobia is fuelled by western governments, the media, particularly in America, and popular culture in Hollywood films such as *True Lies*, *Executive Decision* and *The Siege*.

The broad brushstroke view of Islam promoted by the neo-orientalists, however, obscures the different voices of Islam, which are variously described as radical, militant, Islamism, modernist, cultural, Islamist, political, liberal, *salafi* and moderate. As a body of post-orientalist writers emerges, so too does a difficulty in accepting funda-mentalism as a useful label for describing a political phenomenon manifest in the Middle East. Aware of the diverse nature of the current Islamic revival, authors like Guazzone, Ayubi, Esposito and Piscatori embrace the more narrowly defined terms to describe the movement of political Islam whether referring to the Wahabi state of Saudi Arabia, the Muslim Brotherhood in Jordan or the government of Iran. These terms aid us all in more accurately representing other polities, cultures and traditions, while going some way to avoid the trap of neo-orientalism.

In returning to the original issue, then, it can be argued that Islamic fundamentalism does exist, but in a highly circumscribed form rather than as it is currently portrayed. The prefixing of fundamentalism when describing political activity is also associated with a particularly orientalist view of the Middle East which has been politicized by two decades of debate following the publication of Said's book. To date, the debate remains as current as it was in 1978 and has led scholars into fierce combat with each other. While the battle has been resolved in other spheres of the discipline, the debate in the study of Islam rem-ains as pertinent today as ever. Islam has been and remains, in its polit-ical dimension, a widely varied and important phenomenon. Neo-orientalists have sounded the alarm at the new threat to global peace and harmony, that is the 'Green Peril' of fundamentalist Islam. As Turner (1994) points out, however, this version of Islam is 'defined by a limited, but highly persistent, bundle of interpretative themes which have the effect of bringing into question the authenticity of Islam as religion and culture' (p. 67).

Twenty-first-century Muslim

Has the debate about political Islam in the twenty-first century been any different? Certainly there is room on both sides for a reassessment of the impact of Islam on the political activities in which people and states are engaged in the Middle East. The landscape is still largely populated by the radical version, and the tendency to fixate on fundamentalists, particularly in America, is gradually lodging in the popular consciousness. Increasingly Americans have come to believe in the threat that political Islam poses to America. This has been underscored by the al-Qaeda bomb attacks on America in 2001.

In the decades since the Iranian Revolution the stability of the region, however, has not buckled under the Islamist threat; the governments of Sudan and Somalia may have 'gone Islamic' but the tidal wave that was predicted in the early 1980s has not manifested itself. This is not to say that Islamists have not had a tremendous impact on the politics of the region, rather that the impact has not been uniform, specific or rigid in agenda. In each state of the region political Islam, as part of a religious revival and a common source of identity, has played its part in influencing government policy (for better or worse) and, perhaps more importantly, in the regeneration of grassroots populist politics that impact on the lives of people in a very real way. Within the region political Islam, in opposition rather than as a legitimating force, has been identified by the state as a threat to the prevailing order, designed to topple governments and generate revolution.

Yet, at the heart of this issue lies a dilemma. While Arab governments and the West support the battle against political Islam, the genuine issue of popular grievances against corrupt authoritarian dictatorship remains peripheral. Instead of understanding why Muslims object to tyranny, authoritarianism and lack of pluralism, they are condemned for the formation of a variety of political organizations that resist such corrupt practices. When Syrian troops massacred 10,000 members of the Muslim Brotherhood in 1982 in the Hama rebellion, there was little regional or international outcry about the death of innocents at the hands of their government. Many forget the real role that Islamists are committed to. In Jordan, for example, the Muslim Brotherhood has spent decades arguing for reform of a state governed by an absolutist monarch. The agenda has been political and the Brotherhood has never engaged in acts of violence against the state or its citizens. Within Jordan, however, and outside the country, the Islamists are tarred with the same brush and are variously described as 'zealots and fundamentalists' burning with revolutionary vision. These views play on the fears commonly expressed in the West by counter-insurgency and terrorism specialists whose contact with such movements is minimal and whose lack of criticism of the corrupt regimes of the region is questionable to say the least.

Within the Middle East there is a very real likelihood that in the twenty-first century some regimes will collapse through succession crises and the forces of political Islam will play an important part in shaping the future direction of such states. However, many Islamist groups are weakened when faced with the prospect of real power; their political agendas appear shaky on key elements of economic policy in particular. Thus, while it is true that Islamists will have a role in future polities and governments, the spectre of a Muslim theocratic Middle East does not loom. The reality is more likely to resemble present-day Lebanon where pragmatic Islamists, including Hizbollah, have entered the political fray, becoming part of the fabric of parliamentary consociationalism, by standing for elections and winning seats to the Lebanese parliament (Jaber, 1997).

Already there is evidence of the emergence of a new generation of Islamists who seek to grapple and engage with the current global order – modernists, liberals, democrats and pragmatists in Egypt, Jordan, Tunisia, Kuwait, Iran and so on – who politically and theologically recognize the importance of these concepts to present-day expressions of political Islam. As such, these writers, thinkers and activists represent a fringe element the like of which the West is unprepared for. For them, the fringe is the realm of the radicals and militants, yet, increasingly, as popular support for those strategies wanes, the 'new fringe' is populated by writers such as Khalid Muhammad Khalid, Muhammad Amara and Muhammad Khalafalla in Egypt, who have spent decades seeking a new articulation of Islam that continues to recognize the specific principles of the faith while at the same time calling for new interpretations of general practice of government. Even in Iran, in the Ayatollah-dominated theocracy, there have emerged modernists who have gone some way in democratizing or providing for minority rights in a Shi'a-dominated state. In addition, much new scholarship has also begun to recognize the importance of the 'new fringe', the articulation of 'Muslim politics' rather than Islamic fundamentalism and the growing influence of those Muslim thinkers who tackle globalization, modernity, postmodernism and the unipolar capitalist order with words not terror. Indeed, in many respects Muslims have now resolved the 'crisis of identity' which beset the Middle East in the 1970s at a time when Americans and Europeans are embarking on their own crisis of identity and cast around them for new identities and beginnings.

Case study **The Iranian Revolution**

The mass-based revolution in Iran in 1978–9, which culminated in the exile of its monarchical ruler the Shah in January 1979, is commonly described as an Islamic revolution. In addition, the new political order which followed the departure of the Shah, led by the Shi'a leader Ayatollah Khomeini, has been characterized by theocracy rather than democracy or other types of rule. The establishment of the Islamic Republic of Iran in 1979 also heralded a new era in Islamic politics across the Muslim world. Whether Iran served as a model for Islamic revolution is debatable, because, as Ehteshami (1995) reminds us, 'the emulative potential of the Iranian "Islamic" revolution model was stunted. This does not mean, however, that at some future date and under the right circumstances it could not offer, at the very least, inspiration to other "Islamic" revolutions in Africa or Asia' (p. 199). These factors – revolution, theocracy and the Iranian model – have been perceived as important in understanding the nature of political Islam, the politics of the Middle East and the political character of the region in the twenty-first century.

The Iranian Revolution was the culmination of decades of misrule, abuse of power, modernization for profit not welfare, increasing foreign, particularly American, interference in the politics, culture and economy of the country and spiralling economic and social problems compounded by the Shah's increasing propensity to coercion as a means of rule. Iranians, irrespective of class, ethnic or religious background, political or religious differences, were increasingly aware of the immense wealth the country was generating and the growing indebtedness of ordinary people who failed to benefit from the Shah's programme of economic expansion and westernization. In addition, as Esposito (1984) highlights, 'Military and economic dependence were matched by progressive westernization of Iranian education and society. Religious and lay people shared a common concern about cultural alienation' (p. 188). From this body of concerned citizens a number of 'thinkers' would emerge, including Mehdi Bazargan, Ali Shariati and Ayatollah Khomeini – the 'symbol and architect' of the revolution. The contribution by figures such as Shariati in giving a voice to the discontented of Iran should not be underestimated. His thinking and ideas straddled the secular and sectarian worlds of Iran, combining reformist thinking with pure Muslim ideals, and he has been described as 'an innovative Islamic thinker who stood in sharp contrast to the traditional religious interpretation of the *ulama* and the westernized secular outlook of many university professors' (Esposito, 1984, p. 193). Following Shariati's death in 1977, however, it was Ayatollah Khomeini who would harness Iranian opposition and determine its Islamic character in revolution.

The religious character of the revolution makes it unique and distinguishes it from other revolutions in the contemporary era. In addition, other features such as its 'reactionary, non-materialistic and anti-history' character mark it out from the so-called ordinary business of overthrowing one existing political order and replacing it with another (Halliday, 1996, p. 44). Khomeini offered a new vision for politics, advocating the abolition of the monarchy and political rule and government by the Muslim clergy. This conception of leadership set Khomeini apart from other Islamists throughout the Muslim world. He believed that the political rule best suited to an Islamic state included the clergy in key positions, a rule 'of Divine Law as interpreted and applied by the Just Faqih (clergy)' (Zubaida, 1993, p. 17). Not only did this conception of rule empower the Shi'a clergy, but it also involved the Muslim people in the matter of rule and government and required their total obedience. Khomeini and his supporters succeeded in promoting this vision, and although the revolution involved all sectors of Iranian society in ousting the Shah, it was Khomeini who won the battle to direct the political future of the country after the event.

The state system which emerged from the revolution was Islamic in character. In addition, it was anti-western, anti-Soviet, anti-Israeli, opposed the claim to Islamic rule by leaders in Gulf states such as Saudi Arabia and Kuwait and embarked on the entire reform of Iranian society. Whether Iran itself qualifies as an Islamic state is considered by some as questionable. As Zubaida (1997) asserts:

> We shall see that the basic processes of modernity in socio-economic and cultural fields, as well as in government, subvert and subordinate Islamization. The Islamic authorities are often forced to adapt their policies and discourses to practical considerations. 'Secularization' has not been reversed, but disguised behind imposed symbols and empty rhetoric. (p. 105)

Nevertheless, an Islamic state ruled by Islamic leaders was the goal for which Khomeini (until his death in 1989) and his supporters strove. The first decade of the republic was characterized by the zealous rhetoric and Islamic agenda-setting which would set Iran apart within the region, isolate it from the international community, lead it into war with Iraq and the quest to export the so-called revolutionary model to other contexts such as Lebanon. It is worth remembering, however, as Abrahamian (1989) highlights, that in many respects the real revolutionaries of 1979, the mujahideen, have all but been eliminated by Khomeini's 'populist version of Islam' (p. 1). The agenda was met with varying degrees of success, but what became increasingly clear, particularly following the death of the revolution's symbol, was that revolutionary zeal, rigidity and isolation would not be enough to secure the future of this particular Islamic project.

Indeed, the era following Khomeini's death has been termed by writers like Ehteshami as Iran's 'Second Republic', one characterized this time by the following features: accelerated economic and political reform, improved international and regional relations, and better culture and social conditions. Evidence of such changes can be discerned in 'the leadership style of Khomeini's heirs, the content of the policies of the post-Khomeini leadership and the ways in which their policies differ from those of the Khomeini era' (Ehteshami, 1995, p. xiv). This change in affairs, however, should not be mistaken for a 'second revolution' or a change in the outwardly Islamic character and image which the Iranian republic seeks to promote both at home and abroad. Iran's leaders still struggle internally to balance the call for theological purity and improvements in real economic terms among the country's population. Increasingly, Iranians are demanding greater democratic practice and economic benefits, but the ability of the political authorities to deliver is highly questionable. Difficulties at home can only mean difficulties abroad. The fears of the international community in the 1980s that Iran would inspire a tidal wave of Muslim revolution sweeping the entire Middle East have proved fallacious. The model has proved far too unique to inspire the majority Sunni Muslim population of the Middle East. The echo of Muslim discontent at corrupt rule and the continued impoverishment of entire populations as in Iran in 1979 can, however, be heard, but this has as much to do with Iranian-inspired calls for revolution as the continued policy of the West in supporting tyranny in the Middle East. Iran, however, has fallen under the studied gaze of the second-term administration of George W. Bush. In 2005 George Bush described Iran as the 'world's primary state sponsor of terror' as he delivered his State of the Union address to Congress; an immediate military response was ruled out, however, while US forces remained entrenched in the Iraqi quagmire.

Case study Palestinian Islamists – Hamas

In 1987, following the outbreak of the Palestinian uprising against the Israeli occupation of the West Bank and Gaza Strip, a new Islamist movement was established by a charismatic sheikh and his followers. The organization was called the Islamic Resistance Movement, its Arabic acronym was Hamas (Milton-Edwards, 1996a). Since 1987 Hamas, led by Sheikh Ahmad Yassin, has proved a formidable political actor and has played an important role in shaping the Palestinian–Israeli conflict and the way in which it can be resolved (Milton-Edwards, 1996b). Hamas became known as the most violent of the terrorist movements of the 1990s; its suicide bombers have claimed hundreds of Israeli lives and undermined prospects for peace between Israel and the Palestinians. Thus, in a little over a decade this Islamic organization transformed itself from pragmatic non-violent support for an end to Israeli occupation to acts of political violence directed against defenceless Israelis in Tel Aviv.

The agenda of this Islamic movement, initially encouraged by the government of Israel as a foil to the popular support engendered by the PLO in the occupied Palestinian territories, is Islamist and nationalist at the same time. Like the PLO, Hamas calls for an end to Israeli occupation of Palestinian land in the belief that Palestinians have the right to self-determination and independence; unlike the PLO, Hamas is not prepared to compromise or give up its claim over the whole of historic Palestine (Abu Amr, 1994). Hamas is as much a movement against Palestinian secularism as against Israeli occupation; where the two sides differ is over the nature of a future political entity – the PLO wants to establish a secular non-sectarian state, Hamas wants to establish an Islamic nationalist state.

When Hamas was first formed it wanted to compete on an equal basis for popular support under the framework of the uprising. The movement organized strikes, special committees for education, welfare, policing and first aid. Its activists were able to utilize an Islamic welfare network which had been established by Sheikh Yassin and his followers in the early 1980s throughout the Gaza Strip. Hamas was able to mirror the activities of the nationalist movement while making a bid against the PLO's claim to be the 'sole legitimate representative' of the Palestinian people. It effectively challenged the last bastion of effective nationalism in the Middle East, in its Palestinian guise in the occupied territories.

Over the years Hamas has established a large organizational structure. The political, military, welfare, educational, religious and fund-raising activities of the organization have spread throughout the Gaza Strip and the West Bank. Hamas supporters are found in most schools, universities, hospitals, professional associations and businesses and the organization also builds and runs its own mosques which also serve as libraries, sports centres, classrooms and kindergartens. As many observers are fond of stating, Hamas provides something for everyone, from the cradle to the grave. Political support for the organization has fluctuated, largely shaped by external changes, such as the Gulf Crisis of 1990–1 and the Declaration of Principles signed by Israel and the PLO in 1993. Nevertheless, the organization has become a part of the political fabric of Palestinian society, and won elections to government in 2006.

The agenda of the organization has, however, changed over time. Hamas is the product of the Islamic revival that took place in the Gaza Strip and West Bank in the early 1980s. From that period to 1987 the Islamic movement preached a reformist agenda and concentrated on activities in social, education and welfare issues. Its political wing concentrated on discrediting the secular nationalist ambitions of the PLO and by and large was absent from those political circles that called for an end to Israel's occupation. The Islamists were more likely to wage a campaign for the re-Islamization of society than organize demonstrations against the appropriation of Palestinian land or the building of illegal settlements. The creation of Hamas did, however, signal a change in the political agenda of the organization which was, by and large, the result of popular sentiment at the time. Hamas leaders recognized that the survival of the movement for political Islam depended on their responsiveness to anti-occupation sentiment expressed in the popular demonstrations of the uprising. The leadership quickly harnessed this energy for change and directed it towards an Islamic-nationalist rather than secular-nationalist goal. The recognition of nationalist aspirations and their marriage to an Islamic message proved a potent combination in the battle against the PLO for popular support. Conversely, however, this ability to respond to the sentiment of the street has left Hamas at the mercy of popular opinion, which vicariously swings from one side to another on a regular basis.

The strategy of an armed campaign (or jihad) against Israel has also been criticized and questioned in an era when the nationalist movement has eschewed the gun for the olive branch and started along the long path to peace with Israel. Indeed, the issue has turned on whether the organization is now innately predicated on violence and terror or whether such activities have been a strategy in a campaign for liberation from foreign rule. As such, it touches upon the more philosophical debates about religion and violence as well as armed struggle as part of liberation campaigns. The nature of violence which Hamas has engaged in has mutated from attacks on Israeli soldiers, to armed settlers, to unarmed civilians waiting at bus stops or sitting in open-air cafés. In defence of its actions, Hamas leaders claim they are waging a legitimate war against a foreign occupation and that a Hamas attack on a woman or child is no worse than Israeli soldiers who killed Palestinian women and children during the uprising. Their armed campaign, however, cannot be justified in an era of peacemaking when the acceptability of violence is questioned as much within the Palestinian community as outside it. To date, Hamas has not relinquished the gun, and its leaders have been elected to govern, in defiance of international opinion. Although largely perceived as pragmatic in nature, the war of defence (jihad) against Israel as occupier has not ended. The release of Hamas leader Sheikh Ahmad Yassin in late 1997 prompted a new era for the by then largely weakened movement. For Israel and the PNA the joint objective was the total containment if not the elimination of this particular Islamic challenge. By 1998 the PLO had even been compelled to accept FBI assistance (under the Wye agreement) in thwarting the terror threat posed by Hamas. The outbreak of the second uprising altered the landscape with a return to suicide attacks against Israeli targets by Hamas. The Hamas leadership was targeted and assassinated by Israel. Yet, in terms of popular support the organization had maintained a large constituency of followers among Palestinians. They support Hamas because of the endemic corruption and lack of legitimacy in the PNA. They support Hamas because it, along with other armed elements, is 'resisting the occupation'. This backing has translated itself into a potent presence in the Palestinian arena that is likely to be sustained for the foreseeable future. By 2005 Hamas had declared it would contest Palestinian legislative elections and was to become part of a Palestinian committee to reform the structure of the PLO. Moreover, the withdrawal of settlers and soldiers by the government of Ariel Sharon in August 2005 was claimed by Hamas as a victory. Attempts to ignore the power of Hamas were weakened after their electoral successes.

Case study al-Qaeda

The presence of a violent radical Islamic group called al-Qaeda which emanated from the Middle East only really entered into global public consciousness in the wake of the attacks on major American targets such as the Pentagon in Washington and the World Trade Center in New York on 11 September 2001.

The dimension of political Islam that al-Qaeda was rooted in, however, had been experienced in many parts of the Middle East before that time.

Dimensions of political Islam have been expressed in the Middle East through political violence or terrorism that has been inflicted by organizations such as al-Qaeda, al-Gama al-Islamiyya in Egypt and FIS in Algeria against ordinary Muslim civilians as well as agents of the state or state elites. Such elements arise out of a political context that is often characterized by conflict and struggle against the state but their worldview of society is significantly different from other radical or resistance elements of political Islamism such as the Muslim Brotherhood or Hamas groupings. They are different because they reject society in its entirety.

Some authors, such as Hafez, contend that this notion of radical rejection or 'exclusion' has much to do with the nature of the societies in which such groupings have emerged but this is somehow insufficient explanation in accounting for al-Qaeda and its ideology of hate and terror (Hafez, 2003). Al-Qaeda can be classified as a movement of transnational force across the Middle East and beyond that is predicated on a strategy of terrorism. The expression of terrorism is a symbol of the outright rejection of the contemporary Muslim and other contexts that the leadership of al-Qaeda promotes among its ranks. It is argued that 'al-Qaeda (modern in terms of educational profiles, knowledge and use of modern technology [. . .]) represents a new form of terrorism, born out of transnationalism and globalization. It is transnational in its identity and recruitment and global in its ideology, strategy, targets, network of organizations, and economic transactions' (Esposito, 2002, p. 151).

The ideologues of al-Qaeda – and in particular the Egyptian Ayman al-Zawahiri – premise their view of the contemporary context as un-Muslim or pre-pagan. They refer to this context as *jahilli*. They advocate withdrawal from this context and denounce others – including fellow Muslims – as apostates. This radical worldview has meant that the al-Qaeda target list is almost limitless and includes those regimes of the Middle East such as Saudi Arabia and Egypt whose leaders they accuse of being apostate supporters of the West. The ideologues of al-Qaeda then provide a theological justification (included in certain *fatwa*) for their particular brand of terrorism.

While it is true that al-Qaeda has been responsible for a great many acts of terrorism committed throughout the Middle East, there may be a danger post-9/11 in putting the blame on them for all such violence. The 'idea that a single man and a single group are behind the current threat is convenient and reassuring . . . the creation of "al-Qaeda" as a traditional terrorist group constructs something that can be defeated using traditional counter-terrorist tactics' (Burke, 2004, p. 15). In some respects traditional counter-terrorist tactics employed more recently in states such as Saudi Arabia, Egypt and Morocco have gone some way in dealing with and identifying al-Qaeda elements. But conversely in the wake of the dispersal of al-Qaeda from Afghanistan in 2001 the movement has become more diffuse and difficult to identify across the Middle East. Al-Qaeda elements are now considered to be present in states such as Saudi Arabia, Yemen, Kuwait, Algeria, Lebanon,

Morocco, Egypt and other countries such as Iraq. Although such elements are not directed in their individual acts by Usama bin Laden, it is alleged that such people, 'look up to bin Laden as a symbolic leader [and] are acting in the style of al-Qaeda, along the agenda of al-Qaeda, but are not controlled in any meaningful way by al-Qaeda' (Burke, 2004, p. 14). In this sense the symbolic power of al-Qaeda stands in significant contradistinction to acts that are now truly perpetrated by operatives under the direct orders of the al-Qaeda leadership – wherever they may be. Al-Qaeda and al-Qaeda-affiliated attacks in Saudi Arabia have not just seen westerners being targeted. In Saudi Arabia Muslim workers as well as westerners have been targeted in suicide bombings, beheadings, and shooting sprees across the country. The legitimacy of such violence has been questioned widely within and among Muslim ranks.

Al-Qaeda is accused of having a *salafi* perspective that legitimates such acts of terrorism by relying on the 'Quran and authentic hadiths, citing pieces of evidence according to the Salafi *manhaj* and praising publications by other well-known Salafis' (Wiktorowicz, 2001, p. 22). While it is true that scholars associated with *salafi* thinking in Islam, such as Sayyid Qutb and Ibn Taymiyyah, are alleged to influence the ideological imprint of al-Qaeda, this accusation fails to account for the breadth of influence that these thinkers have across the canon of contemporary Islamist thinking. As Doran notes: 'when it comes to matters related to politics and war, al-Qaeda manoeuvres around its dogmas with alacrity' (Doran, 2002, p. 178). This manoeuvrability means that al-Qaeda has come to represent more than the sum of its parts. Much that represents political Islam in the Middle East is now interpreted – both within the region and outside it – within a paradigm over which al-Qaeda dominates. The statements, actions, ambitions and inspirations of countless Islamic movements are now measured against al-Qaeda to determine the ways in which the governments of the region (and their allies across the globe) should now respond. The issue here is whether this is the right yardstick for the political expression of a faith system which accounts for the identity of the majority of the region's citizens.

As such al-Qaeda remains as a marker on the landscape of the contemporary Middle East through its actions in the form of terror attacks in vulnerable states across the region; through its ideas in influencing debates within Islam about the future of the faith in the Middle East; and in terms of a symbol of antipathy and hatred against that which is considered un-Islamic and sympathetic to the West. While the terrorist threat may be contained, it is in the realm of ideas and symbols that the biggest battles in the region may yet take place.

Further reading

Currently, there is a huge amount of literature on the phenomenon of Islam and politics in the Middle East. The most comprehensive introductory accounts can be found in Esposito (1984), Ayubi (1991) and

Halliday (1996). The accounts by Eickelman and Piscatori (1996) and Zubaida (1993) of Muslim politics are particularly useful, as they analyse popular forms of politics as well as government and institutions. These should be contrasted against accounts of Islam and politics found in Lewis (1974, 1976, 1993a, 1993b), Kramer (1980), Gellner (1981), Pipes (1983a, 1983b) and to a certain extent the material published in association with the fundamentalism project by Marty and Appleby (1991 and 1993). Much of the work by authors such as Lewis and Pipes has been debated or criticized by Edward Said (1995c, 1981), Abaza and Strauth (1988), Daniels (1993) and Halliday (1996). The state and politics dimension of Islamism has occupied many writers, including Piscatori (1986), Jaadane writing in Luciani (1990), and Tripp in Sidahmed and Ehteshami (1996). Beinin and Stork's (1997) reader on political Islam covers a diverse range of subjects from economy to Rai and Rap music, civil society to Shi'ism in Lebanon and parallels Guazzone (1995). Roy (1994) on political Islam questions its saliency in the contemporary Middle East. Ahmed (1992), Ahmed and Donnan (1994) and Sayyid (1997) debate extensively the impact of Islam on postmodern thinking, including cultural and post-colonial theories. Aspects of this subject are also covered in Choueiri (1988 and 1990), al-Azmeh (1993) and Salvatore (1997). Coverage of the modernists can be found in Adams (1968), Enayat (1982), Arjomand (1984), Roy (1994), Abu Rabi (1996) and Tibi (1996). On the Muslim Brotherhood, Hassan al-Banna and the Qutbists, interesting insights can be garnered from Mitchell's classic study of the Muslim Brotherhood (1969), Ansari (1984), Baker (1991), who examines the role of the centre, and Abed-Kotob (1995), and in any of the main texts on political Islam cited above. Specific discussions of Qutb are explored by Haddad in Esposito (1983), Sivan's text on Islamic radicalism (1985), Ayubi (1991) and Nettler (1996). Contemporary thinking on Islamic fundamentalism and the debate on Islamism and the threat it either does or does not pose may be found by comparing Sidahmed and Ehteshami (1996) with Kramer (1996). In addition, aspects of this complicated debate are explored by AbuKhalil (1994) and Faksh (1997). On the Iranian example a number of excellent texts can be found, including Afshar (1985), Arjomand (1988), Abrahamian (1989), Zubaida (1993) and Ehteshami (1995). Aspects of Shi'a politics are also examined in Keddie and Hooglund (1986), Kramer (1987), Richard (1995) and Malek (1991). Further reading on Hamas and the Palestinian Islamic movement can be found in Legrain (1991a and 1991b), Taraki (1991), Abu Amr (1994), Barghouti (1996), Milton-Edwards (1996a and 1996b) and Hammami (1997). There are numerous books on al-Qaeda that have been written since 2001. There is much material and analysis in Burke (2004), Bergen (2001) and by extension the debate in Esposito (2002) and Gray (2004) pushes the issues in comparisons to wider issues in modern society. The debate about Islam and democracy is explored in Abou El Fadl (2004) and Moussalli (2003).

Democratization: Old Politics, New Problems

Introduction

DEMOCRATIZATION, political liberalization and the promotion of liberal democracy in the Middle East became the catchwords of the 1990s, reflecting a new crisis of legitimacy for many regimes and pressure from the masses for change and progress. Also it has been a way in which the West has once again used its economic and political influence in the region: 'in virtually every case', as is argued in *MERIP* (Middle East Report), reforms (liberalization or democratization) 'have been abetted by the intervention of institutions representing international capital' (1992, p. 4). The drive towards democratization has presupposed the absence of democratic trends in the region and the incompatibility of Arab and Muslim ideologies with accompanying notions of freedom, pluralism, participation, equality of opportunity and justice. As Bromley (1997) notes, the conventional view is that 'democracies are strangers to the Middle East . . . The limited post-independence experiments with democratic politics did not survive the rise of nationalist forces seeking modernization and independence, or were thwarted by monarchical rule and oil wealth' (p. 329). In the 1990s the path of democratization was seen as a positive phenomenon with accompanying social and economic preconditions which should be encouraged in the region, albeit in a piecemeal rather than wholesale fashion. In reality, however, many have ruled out any prospect for democracy, arguing that the combined forces of Arab and Muslim political culture promote the region as an exception to the global movement. These culturalist arguments then lead to a concept of exceptionalism: 'the idea of an Arab or Islamic exceptionalism has thus re-emerged among both western proponents of universal democracy and established orientalists, and this in turn has encouraged a great many local apologists of "cultural authenticity" in their rejection of western models of government' (Salame, 1994a, p. 1). An example of the orientalist perspective can be found in Lewis (1993a) who has argued that the gap between western and Arab notions of 'freedom' highlights the antipathy of this particular culture to accompanying notions of democracy.

Indeed, it has been judged by a variety of authors (Pipes, 1983a and 1983b; Huntington, 1984; Perlmutter, 1992; and Kedourie, 1994) that the political, economic and cultural conditions prevalent in individual states of the region (bar Israel) did not go any way towards encouraging the development of liberal democratic models of government and politics. The countries and political cultures of the region were largely viewed as weak, unstable, lacking in unity, authoritarian and lacking political legitimacy. The processes of modernization, which authors such as Lerner (1958) and Rustow (1971) had recognized as conducive to democracy, had broken down, encouraging only limited opportunities for political participation. Indeed, even within the modernization approach there was still room to air doubts over the Arab or Muslim temperament in notions of pluralism and democracy. An example is the following claim by Lerner that a 'complication of modernization' in the Middle East is 'its own ethnocentrism – expressed politically in extreme nationalism, psychologically in passionate xenophobia . . . wanted are modern institutions,' he continues, 'but not modern ideologies, modern power, but not modern purposes' (Lerner, 1958, p. ix).

In the decades, therefore, that followed the collapse of early democratic projects in the region, and the era of authoritarianism and dictatorship, orientalist scholars found all the evidence they needed to doubt the chances of democracy. Even the process of economic liberalization from the 1970s onwards was not considered as significant in promoting political change and democracy as it had been in other parts of the developing world, and in Latin America in particular. Yet, there has been a critique of this approach argued by Bromley, who declares that, 'seen in comparative perspective, the Middle East may only be exceptional in the timing and fragility of its democratization rather than constituting a wholesale departure from patterns found elsewhere' (1997, p. 329). Since the 1990s this view has altered both within and outside the region. Many states have been seen to engage in some form of political liberalizing process such as the more open elections in Jordan, Yemen, Egypt, Algeria, Israel and Iran, to name a few. The early rush to declare democratization as a process in the Middle East, however, has to be tempered with the important distinction between liberalization and democratization – as Brynen et al. (1995) point out, liberalization 'involves the expansion of public space through the recognition and protection of civil and political liberties', while democratization 'entails an expansion of political participation . . . to provide citizens with a degree of real and meaningful collective control over public policy' (p. 3). The two terms, however, are not one and the same thing, nor are they reflective of the same structural changes in government, politics, economy or society.

A number of important themes, therefore, have emerged from the debate about democratization and liberalization in the Middle East. The first theme, as I have noted above, has rested on the critique and counter-critique that Arab/Islamic civilization is uniquely exceptional in its undemocratic tendencies, and has created a political culture which means that the Arab world can never democratize in a meaningful manner. This debate has raged for a number of years, resting largely on Huntington's 'clash of civilizations' thesis, and on work on Arab political culture by authors such as Vatikiotis and Kedourie. A number of other authors, however, refute this approach and contend that there is room within Arab and Islamic political culture for a meaningful discourse on democracy. They point to both past traditions and present trends to highlight the accommodation of concepts, noting, for example, that 'elements of Islamic culture are both congenial and uncongenial to democracy', with a variety of political contexts in the Middle East proving variation rather than exception of a theme (Ayubi, 1997, p. 362). The second discernible strand is the emergence of a democratization thesis that is distinct from the discussion about political liberalization in the region. This discussion focuses not just on the theoretical dimensions of the concept of democracy but the manifestations of democratization that can be identified within the region. The third strand of this debate looks at the impact of so-called economic liberalization on the democratization and political liberalization theses, exploring whether or not a particular approach to the development of economy in the region is a prerequisite feature of any experiment in democratization. The fourth motif focuses on the relationship between democratization and civil society and questions whether Ayubi was right to assert that in light of the democratization and liberalization debate it would be better to refer to civic society. In contrast to Ayubi, Richards and Waterbury argue that civil society has not reached the appropriate level of development in the region to support a process of 'redemocratization' (1990, p. 329). The fifth motif looks at the relationship between democracy and Islam and analyses the continuing dispute within the discipline over this issue. The final theme of this debate will focus on the so-called anomaly of Israel as the region's only 'fully fledged' democracy and the impact this has on the development of the discourse within the region, whether at the level of state elites or the population in general. Why is Israel the only democracy in the region and what features of the state inhibit the promotion of this internal model within the area? Some answers to these questions will be immediately apparent, but others require a further analysis.

Clash of civilizations

In the late 1980s and early 1990s a series of events around the world occurred which encouraged the promotion of the democratization agenda even in many Middle Eastern states. The collapse of the former Soviet Union, the fall of the Berlin Wall, the rise of democracy in Eastern Europe and the Gulf Crisis of 1990–1 all contributed to the apparent rise of a new world order, where the USA would dominate the world stage and political change was inevitable. The end of the Cold War and America's triumph gave the victory to liberal democratic values and market capitalism, without which, it was argued, the world was doomed to dictatorship and tyranny. Within the Third World in general the mantra of democratization was preached by western governments, international corporations, aid agencies and development experts. In the Middle East, in particular, the message was broadcast loud and clear: democratization was the only way forward, a path out of the legitimacy crisis, a vehicle by which failed economic policies, the demands from the masses and external pressures could be harnessed by a variety of regimes of differing political hues to promote democracy by diktat. As Norton (1993) explains, 'No doubt, the defining concept of the 1990s is democracy. Like *Coca-Cola*, *democracy* needs no translation to be understood virtually everywhere. *Democracy*, however, is easier to say than to create' (p. 206).

A difficulty was apparent in this mantra of democratization that the alarmists who were associated with the culturalist and neo-orientalist school of writing were quick to point out in relation to the Middle East. The difficulty, in particular, was highlighted by Huntington (1993) in his thesis of the 'clash of civilizations'. In brief, the thesis argued that 'the fundamental source of conflict' in the present day and future will rest on a 'clash of civilizations that will dominate global politics' (p. 22). Huntington, believing that identity from civilization was more important than other types of identity, admits that religion is the most important feature contributing to this new identity: 'even more than ethnicity, religion discriminates sharply and exclusively among people' (p. 27). The basis for conflict, he argues, lies in the 'fault line' between civilizations and, in particular, the one between Islam and the West. For Huntington, the relationship between the West and Islamic civilization has always and will always be based on military conflict. Muslims and, by association, Arabs are an aggressive civilization, Islam has 'bloody borders', violence is repetitively cited as an indiscriminate way of life against Serb, Jew, Hindu, Buddhist and Catholic. This theme had been developed from Huntington's earlier reflections in an article written in 1984, in which he declared: 'Islam has not been hospitable to democracy . . . the prospects for democratic development seem low.

The Islamic revival, and particularly the rise of Shi'ite fundamentalism, would seem to reduce even further the likelihood of democratic development' (1984, pp. 208, 216). The combination of violence, Islam and anti-democratic tendencies highlighted by Huntington painted a picture of the Middle East (with Israel as the notable exception) in which Arab/Islamic civilization was portrayed as backward, static, barbaric and vicious. The shift to democracy, in whatever form, could, therefore, be immediately ruled out in Huntington's book. Huntington leads us to conclude that democratization is a non-starter among the peoples of this particular civilization. In echo of this approach, Waterbury (1994) adds that, 'whether Islam and Middle Eastern culture are separable phenomena the two work in ways that do not augur well for democracy. I believe that basic tendencies in regional culture and in religious practice must be overcome rather than utilized in any efforts to promote pluralism and democracy' (p. 33).

Other authors have gone a considerable way in supporting Huntington's thesis. Lewis and Kedourie have both suggested that within the Arab world the prospects for democracy are weak. The relationship between Arab and Muslim identity is cast in stone, perceived as one and the same thing and as such democracy is declared 'alien' to such a mindset. Whether Arab or Islamic, Kedourie declares that democracy will always fail. Representative government and other features associated with democratic society and government are, he writes, 'profoundly alien to the Muslim political tradition' (1994, p. 6); political tradition, whether Arab or Muslim, is based on a form of 'oriental despotism' which has dominated the region for centuries. This tradition of rule, which survives to the present day, whether in the form of Ba'thism, pan-Arabism or Islam, remains, argues Kedourie, hostile to any form of democratic government through popular and constitutional representation as practised so successfully in the West. Thus, even those Arab states which claimed a populist, nationalist base were regarded as highly dubious by writers such as Kedourie, who stressed the region's proclivity to anti-democratic political practices. In addition, the appalling human rights record of many Arab regimes casts further doubt on the professed claims to pluralism and freedom for all in their societies. Yet, as Abdallah (1992) reminds us, 'human rights, in their vast range, can be protected under non-democratic regimes and violated under democratic ones' – Islam and Arab culture could not just be guilty by association (p. 6).

The future for promotion of democracy within the region, according to such writers, then, is far from rosy. The despotic orientalism school also fails to make a distinction between types of state and government in this respect. All regimes, irrespective of whether one is talking about Wahabi Saudi Arabia, consociational Lebanon, populist Yemen or monarchical Jordan, are the same in this respect. The predominantly Muslim basis from which most, if not all, Arab governments within the region work therefore inhibits the development of liberal democratic rule. This approach, however, has not been adopted wholesale by scholars of the region. Many writers believe that both Arab and Islamic political culture are open to expressions of democracy.

Democratization or liberalization?

Democracy and liberalism, democratization and liberalization are related terms, but in the context of our particular analysis should be scrutinized very carefully. While it is the case that democratization cannot truly take place without liberalization of political systems, government and institutions, the same cannot be said of liberalization. Indeed, in the Middle East it is true to say that the processes of reform that have taken place in countries as politically diverse as Syria and Saudi Arabia, Tunisia and Oman are more akin to a trend towards liberalization than democratization. Indicators which in the early 1990s were seized upon as signs of the wave of democracy sweeping the Middle East were, in reality, a series of minor and major acts of liberalization prompted by factors as diverse as the Gulf Crisis, the rise of ethno-national discontent, religious persecution, changes in the global economy and the deepening crisis of identity within the Arab world as it faced pressure from the outside to change and emulate 'other' foreign western cultures.

The trend towards liberalization in the Arab world and the Middle East in general even predates the momentous political changes which swept the former Soviet Union and the communist states of Eastern Europe in the late 1980s. Glasnost Arab-style was manifest in the *infitah* (open door) policies of Egypt and Tunisia in the late 1970s and early 1980s. As the state opted for reform through liberalization, Syria and Egypt's citizens saw the 'open door' as an opportunity also to press for greater political changes and liberalization. The trend towards liberalization, however, should always be treated cautiously, as Hinnebusch points out in the case of Syria, where the shift is limited in nature,

> as the regime adapts its rule to a revival of civil society dictated by exhaustion of statist development. The private sector is being encouraged, Asad is broadening his base beyond the party, government controls over society are being incrementally relaxed . . . This will not produce democratization any time soon, but it may permit a more autonomous and developed civil society, creating the base for future political pluralization. (1993, p. 244)

Thus while the leaders of the Arab world hoped that policies of economic liberalization would strengthen the role of the market and capital in the economy, the economic aspects of such developments could not take place in isolation. Political and social changes occurred concurrently, having important effects on the general economic experiments that were under way. As Niblock and Murphy note, 'economic liberalization generally widens the gap between rich and poor, at least in the short term, increases regional disparities, and deepens dependence on external powers and institutions . . . the social discontent unleashed . . . may create political dynamics which undermine regimes, and perhaps even tear the state apart' (1993, p. xiv).

Conceptually, the debate about democratization and liberalization must focus on the differences inherent in the two terms. Liberalization, for example, may be taken to mean any activity which generates greater individual freedom in societies. Individual and collective freedoms are separate constructs and the process of liberalization enhances one, the individual, over the other, the collective. Such perspectives are, in turn, related to the tradition of liberalism that has dominated western political thought. As such, the works of John Stuart Mill remain as relevant to current thinking on liberalization as Margaret Thatcher's aggressive liberalism of the 1980s. At the heart of this approach is an emphasis on and protection of the individual, economically, socially and politically, and on a weakened state. Liberalism and liberalization, then, are essentially western constructs which have been promoted in the Middle East for a variety of reasons. In theory, this approach relegates the state to the periphery; state interference in economic activity, social issues and other areas is to be avoided at all costs. In reality, however, the picture is a little more complicated, as Zubaida explains in the case of Egypt, where liberalization has led to the withdrawal of the state in some spheres and yet the 'active intervention' of it in others. As he remarks on the issue of economy:

> Sadat's *infitah* was meant to end state control of economic activity. State bureaucracies, however, in the form of the 'public sector', remained firmly in control of the commanding heights of the economy. Private enterprise was at its most successful in partnership with or under patronage of these bureaucracies and their personnel. (1992, p. 8)

This example highlights the paradox and limits of liberalization from above. In the Arab world much of the political and economic change of the 1970s and 1980s, in countries like Egypt, Tunisia and Syria, did not promote freedom, liberalism or democracy; instead, as Farsoun and Zacharia note:

> the social movements of political liberalization . . . suffered not only internal state control and repression but also international isolation.

> Indeed during the mid-1980s, the intensification of the socio-economic
> and political crises triggered popular and civil associational opposition
> *and* increased regime repression and state terror. (1995, p. 269)

Democracy, meanwhile, as I have discussed above, enjoys a relationship to liberalism and processes of liberalization but remains a different creature. Democratic socialism, for example, promotes an agenda
which is often largely at odds with liberal democracy as it is currently
understood. Nevertheless, the generic term, particularly in relation to
the Middle East, is currently understood or interpreted in a number of
ways. As we shall see in subsequent sections, democrats in Algeria are
very different from democrats in Israel. In the contemporary era, then,
democracy largely reflects on the process of electoral politics or press
freedoms and human rights. Yet, larger structural impediments relating to the process of state formation, allocation of resources, state
bureaucracies and citizenship have been ignored. As Bromley remarks,
'the relative absence of democracy in the Middle East has little to do
with the region's Islamic culture and much to do with its particular
pattern of state formation' (1994, p. 169). The failure of the secular
nationalist state system in the region is thus cited as an important
constraint on the emergence of truly democratic life and liberal democratic states.

Processes of liberalization, however, are well under way in the
region. As such, they allow for greater degrees of political participation in existing political systems without necessarily embracing widespread democratic reforms such as universal suffrage, increased citizenship rights, a multi-party system and pluralism. Political changes
in many of the Gulf states since 1991 illustrate this point. For example,
in March 1992 in Saudi Arabia the ruling al-Saud family announced
the establishment of its first significant political institution for
decades, the Majlis al-Shura (Consultation Council). The sixty-member
council has widened the base of participation and consultation in a
largely symbolic sense and cannot, despite Saudi assertions, be seen as
either an Islamic parliament – indeed, as al-Sayyid (1995) has asserted,
'the ruling monarchy in Saudi Arabia is adamantly opposed to any
attempt by any other group to share with it the legitimating use of
Islamic concepts' (p. 144) – or a precursor to something along western
democratic lines. In another example, Iran, rates of electoral participation have been significant in the second Islamic republic. Opportunities for participation in the political system are provided for
according to the rules of *Shari'a* law, and since 1979 there have been
more than twenty-six elections in the country for government,
President, Majlis representatives and ratification of the constitution,
with a high level of electoral participation, which Ehteshami declares
is a 'fledgling democracy' by anyone's standards. Both cases illustrate

the faltering steps towards liberalization either as a result of internal or external pressures for greater change, as in Saudi Arabia, or as a means of interpreting Islam in a modern age when the demands of participation are high, as in Iran.

Liberalization, through increased individual freedoms of participation, allows a marriage of convenience between the nation-state and Muslim cultures which has developed into an important trend in the region. How these factors are balanced by demands for democracy and the continued socio-economic changes which have characterized the area are explored below.

Socio-economic indicators

The relationship between economic, social and political factors in a discussion of liberalization is complex and cannot be said to represent a particular type in relation to the Middle East. Nevertheless, there does seem to be a meaningful relationship between economic changes, or more specifically economic liberalization, and the social and political factors which precipitate it and accompany it. Since the 1970s, forms of political liberalization have occurred within certain states in the region, primarily because of some form of domestic economic crisis. As the case studies of both Jordan and Algeria illustrate, the path to liberalization and democratization has often been heralded by an unfortunate coincidence of spiralling inflation, high levels of unemployment, massive food prices on basic foodstuffs and so on. In other words, the decision to undertake new economic programmes, moving from a centrally state-planned economy to the privatization of state assets and removal of state controls, is normally a result of crisis rather than a change in government through election, and, as Richards (1993) asserts, 'economic imperatives dictate heightened political participation in the region. Since Middle Eastern states began gaining independence, industrial technologies and development strategies have fundamentally favoured centralization and autocracy. Today the opposite is true' (p. 217). Once again, the reasons for political opening have more to do with preservation of the status quo than real change:

> the main purpose of liberalization from above is system maintenance in a situation of acute socio-economic crisis, by co-opting wider circles of political public, distributing responsibility for future austerity policies more broadly, directing political and religious organizations into controllable channels and excluding all those outside the 'national consensus' defined by the regime. (Kramer, 1992, p. 24)

The rapid and uneven pattern of economic development and modernization which has gripped the Middle East since the 1990s has played its part in the economic and widespread societal crisis that has affected many of the region's countries. The difficulty, politically, with the new path of economic liberalization has been, as Deegan (1993) comments, that 'economic reform, then, would seem to suggest a diminishing role for the state and by implication, the role of the present political leaderships' (p. 131). Hence the reluctance by political leaderships in the Arab world to opt for limited economic liberalization and a limited path of political reform. As we have already discussed, in some cases the liberalization has little if nothing to do with economic reform and in others, despite huge economic problems, the path to political reform or democratization is strongly resisted and even reversed.

Indeed, the nature of economic reform, i.e. liberalization of Middle East economies, has been viewed by some authors as nothing more than another indication of the pressure for change according to a predetermined western-based agenda, rather than an economic agenda which is best for individual Arab states or the region as a whole. In a bitterly worded attack, Vitalis suggests:

> Beneath the last fashionable rhetoric, 'democracy' in the hands of the AID (US Agency for International Development) serves as an instrument for the pursuit of other ends – specifically, more market-friendly economies . . . [development practitioners] should show why contemporary political engineering projects by US agencies are any less likely . . . to retard indigenous democratic currents and institutions. (1994, p. 46)

In addition, this perspective might help explain why liberalization has been limited and why it has not been a resounding success vis-à-vis the economic problems it is supposed to address. Finally, this model of economic activity takes little account of the prevailing social conditions of the region. The process of state-formation, independence and state-consolidation that has occurred within the Middle East over the last fifty years has wrought significant social changes, such as decline of rural for urban life, widespread immigration and migrant labour patterns, changes in levels of education, a drop in infant mortality rates and so on. The issue here is whether these social changes and new patterns of life, with the creation of new class interests which often abut family, tribal, religious and other pressures, can withstand the liberalization process both in terms of economic and political change.

As Pool writes:

> at the present conjuncture there is an uncertain and unpredictable balance between the two processes. Economic crises have brought some degree of economic liberalization, and the latter has been a factor in

> establishing a process of political liberalization. Yet, the introduction
> of political liberalization under conditions of economic reform can
> sustain or re-introduce authoritarian forms of rule. (1993, p. 53)

One might add that such limited economic liberalization only widens
the inequalities within society, keeping the underclass down and
removing it even further from whatever state assistance is available.
This has been apparent in Egypt, where the liberalization of the economy since the 1970s has, among other things, resulted in a huge
bureaucracy but declining state provision in terms of welfare assistance and health care. The crippling poverty and new social as well as
economic inequalities that have been created as a result of the partial
liberalization of the economy through *infitah* have not been resolved
through the limited process of political appeasement. For example,
the introduction of a multi-party system in Egypt has had a minimal
impact on the continued authoritarian nature of the state and has not
made it any more accountable to its citizens. Instead, the sense of frus-
tration grows and the tendency to authoritarian rather than democratic rule becomes strengthened.

After all, the process of economic liberalization is a double-edged
sword which can both weaken and strengthen the state. As Richards
and Waterbury assert:

> Paradoxically liberalization can thus be seen as the only means by
> which the state can regain control over the direction of the economy. It
> is unlikely, however, that the state in most Middle Eastern societies will
> ever again enjoy the same degree of autonomy as it did in the past from
> major interest and classes that constitute civil society. (1990, p. 428)

Democracy and civil society

Civil society, the amalgamation of non-governmental and autonomous social organizations such as trade unions, women's groups,
professional associations, trade guilds, religious groups, chambers of
commerce and voluntary associations associated with issues such as
children, disability or welfare rights, are perceived as a prerequisite
of democracy and democratic life in any society and its relations to
the state. As Turner (1994) notes, 'The theory of civil society was part
of the master dichotomy of nature/civilization, since it was within
civil society that the individual was eventually clothed in judicial
rights of property, possessions and security' (p. 25). The existence of
civil society protects the individual from a monopoly of state control.
The individual lies at the heart of this concept, as do individual
rights, notions and concepts which are regarded by scholars such as

Kedourie and Huntington as anathema to the collective *umma* ever present in Arab and Muslim societies. Since the late 1980s, however, the promotion of democratization in the Middle East has been strongly associated with the study of whether civil society exists in the region, together with its strengths and weaknesses and future prospects. One of its most passionate proponents writes: 'a vibrant and relatively autonomous civil society is integral to democracy . . . no discussion of political change in the contemporary Middle East will be complete unless it takes into account the status of civil society' (Norton, 1993, p. 203). The issue of autonomy from the state has been debated extensively, with little resolution of the issue. As Zubaida (1992) writes in the case of Egypt, it requires regulatory legislation from other arms of the state to maintain civil society. Civil society, in Egypt, Zubaida counters, is 'not autonomous from the state, but depend[s] on another of its facets: the corrupt bureaucracies' (p. 3).

It should be noted from the outset that certain battle lines are drawn around the issue of whether civil society exists in the Middle East or is likely ever to exist in the region. A number of writers, identified by Sadowski (1997a), including Patricia Crone, Daniel Pipes, Samuel Huntington and Bernard Lewis, have rejected the possibility of any form of civil society existing in the Arab countries of the region. According to these authors, civil society cannot exist because Arab and Muslim societies are despotic in nature and despotic rule presupposes the absence of any social institutions between the individual and the despot. Others, including Augustus Richard Norton, Muhammad Muslih, Michael Hudson, Bryan Turner and Asad AbuKhalil, believe that evidence of civil society can be found in the region and that as states weaken these groups have grown in strength, acting as an important check on a number of regimes. In addition, this flourishing sector supports the case for localized routes to democratization and greater pluralism in Arab and Muslim societies. Muslih, writing about the Palestinian context of civil society and its relation to the PLO as 'state surrogate', outlines evidence of a flourishing civil society existing 'in the absence of a democratic state' where 'it is precisely because the state surrogate has sustained political pluralism that it may be inclined to sustain a pluralistic civil society if independence is achieved' (1993, p. 272). While evidence of civil society is clear, Muslih is perhaps slightly over-optimistic about the maintenance of autonomy. Since the establishment of the PNA in 1993 there has been growing evidence of a squeeze by PLO bureaucrats on the relatively autonomous activities of Palestinian non-governmental organizations, trade unions and other sectors of civil society. Indeed, many of the gatekeepers of democratic traditions among the Palestinians remain at large, continuing their work in the large civil society sectors of welfare, human rights, education and professional associations.

For the neo-orientalists, however, as Sadowski points out, civil society in the Middle East is the harbinger of authoritarianism, not democracy. They 'assert that the proliferation of social movements will discourage any trend toward power sharing and greater tolerance in the region, if it does not breed civil war and anarchy' (1997a, p. 42). Either way, as far as the neo-orientalist perspective is concerned, democracy cannot be linked positively with either the absence in the past or the contemporary growth of civil society in countries such as Egypt or Lebanon and among such communities as the Palestinians of the West Bank and Gaza Strip.

In contrast, however, there is a growing body of writers, some of whom are mentioned above, who believe that there is strong empirical evidence among, for example, the Egyptian and Lebanese cases, that supports the argument for an important link between the birth of civil society and the promotion of democratization. In Egypt, for example, since the early 1970s liberalization of the economy by the state through the process of *infitah* has resulted in the unintended by-product of a growth in civil society which in turn has made governmental concessions to some forms of democratization impossible to resist. Since that time the Egyptian state has not managed to relinquish its control over the economy, yet the limited impact of liberalization has had profound effects on the political scene. Under President Mubarak the regime has sought a balancing act between pressure for reform of the political system, the creation of pluralism and a space between the state and the individual for civil society to flourish and a deep-seated fear within the regime concerning any relinquishment of political power to the people or their representative associations. What they fail to see is the reluctance of the people to recognize the legitimacy of state power as it is currently constituted, even as they do accept the legitimacy of the work of professional associations, guilds, chambers of commerce and voluntary associations (Zubaida, 1992).

In the example of Lebanon, the relative autonomy of large sectarian sectors of civil society undermined the capacity of the state for a considerable period. The strength of civil (or civic) society in Lebanon (sustained by vertical lines of kinship, confessional allegiance and other affinities) weakened the state in a dramatic manner. Because loyalty to the state and identity with political elites in control of the consociational arrangements were continually denied or questioned, trade unions, professional associations, religious communities, women's organizations and charities often replaced the state in serving the citizens. Indeed, as Drysdale and Blake (1985) conclude, 'The Middle East and North Africa can provide no better example of a country without an effective state idea than Lebanon' (p. 195). The question that needs to be raised, however, is to what extent civil society has survived the new peace arrangements and resurrection of consociational government since 1989. The answer, of course, is far from clear, but, as Norton (1997) contends:

> while some restructuring of the political system has occurred, there is little prospect for comprehensive political reforms while power remains in the grip of a coterie of politicians on good terms with Damascus. Instead, the government operates like a giant patronage machine, enabling newly entrenched political bosses to create networks of clients and grow richer on 'sweetheart deals'. (p. 9)

In Lebanon the prospects for political liberalism are surely promoted by the respect for economic liberal practices for which so many of its people are infamous; as the economy of Lebanon is reconstructed according to capital and free-market principles, the inevitable pressures for political reform have become increasingly difficult for either Lebanese leaders or their Syrian overlords to suppress. In this context, civil society, as it is currently constituted, could play a contradictory, ambiguous and confused role in political reconstruction, particularly as civil society has had the power in the past to play its part in the collapse of the Lebanese state (Brynen et al., 1995, p. 12).

It remains clear, the objections of the neo-orientalists notwithstanding, that the existence and promotion of civil society is an important component of democratization in the Middle East and of attempts by the state to act in an authoritarian and despotic fashion. Civil society remains stronger in some states than others in the region and it is no surprise that those states – Egypt, Lebanon, Tunisia, Jordan and among the Palestinians – are places where the greatest hopes for political liberalization are held. As al-Sayyid (1994) comments, 'what took place in the Arab world [is] at best a process of political liberalization, limited by its dependence upon the agreement of ruling groups to extend certain civil and political rights that had hitherto been denied' (p. 181). In addition, therefore, it is no surprise that civil society in hand with democracy seems remote in authoritarian regimes that have resisted the tide of change as much as possible. Finally, much of the debate about civil society, democratization and political liberalism has spun on the axis of Islam. As the next section highlights, the addition of this particular ingredient to the debate has provoked fierce passions.

Islam and democracy – an oxymoron?

In most monotheistic religions a tradition of monolithic interpretation is not present. Whether one reflects on Christianity, Judaism or Islam, the diverse expression of one faith is always apparent. The history of these religions is one of schism, denomination and other differences. Islam, therefore, like Christianity and Judaism, is capable of having multiple and major ideological interpretations or orientations. Political Islam has been used both to oppose and legitimate a variety of political models and state types. It has been used to support both democracy and the despot. Ayubi, while challenging Huntington's approach, reiterates this point by asserting, 'I would argue myself that Islamic culture contains elements that may be both congenial and uncongenial to democracy, depending on the particular society and on the historical conjuncture' (1995, p. 399). Democracy, or *shura* (consultation) as many Muslims prefer to think of it, is part of a contemporary practice of politics that is used by both opposition and ruling groups to state their political case. It is important to recognize that within the diverse body politic that is Islam there are Muslim thinkers, intellectuals, lay preachers, spiritual leaders and ideologues who believe that democracy is incompatible with Islam, while others argue for a new approach to a concept so thoroughly equated with modern political progress that it cannot be ignored. Whichever side of the spectrum opinion falls on, there is no denying, as Esposito and Piscatori (1991) point out, that 'whether the word *democracy* is used or not, almost all Muslims today react to it as one of the universal conditions of the modern world. To this extent it has become part of Muslim political thought and discourse' (p. 440).

The school of thought within Islam, rather than those outside it, that rejects the idea that Islam and democracy could be compatible fears for the future of the faith in the same way that European clergy feared the impact of the Enlightenment and the rise of secularism in Europe. There is a genuine spiritual desire to protect the faith, rather than a predilection for conflict with the traditions of western political thought that champion democracy as part of the great secular experience. The hostility to this type of democracy that is found in Islam is not unique and can be found in the fundamental impulse of evangelical Protestantism in Northern Ireland or Jewish fundamentalist movements in Israel. Like their Muslim counterparts, the political wings of such movements, however, have no fear of participating in democracies through the electoral process as a means of communicating their message. Indeed, some writers even see a deep compatibility between religious revolution and democratic values, arguing that 'the pattern of political change followed by most religious revolutionaries fits exactly the guidelines for "democratizers" that Huntington . . . offers as the prescription for democratically overthrowing authoritarian regimes' (Juergensmeyer, 1993, p. 149). In theory, then, the Islamic intellectuals who voice their opposition to democracy do so because of its secular associations. They question how a believer can embrace a secular notion of equality that is associated with democracy when Islam already encourages believers to accept equality as part of their faith. This debate has been examined by Ismail (1995), who points out that the 'confrontation' between Arab secularists and Islamists 'is not without its links to the protagonists' hopes and fears regarding democracy', yet it takes place, she adds, at a time when 'the interpretation of divine sovereignty . . . is not agreed on among the various thinkers of the Islamist movement' (p. 102). Issues of sovereignty are rejected for the same reason; the efficacy of Westminster-style legislative bodies is questioned because Islam is supposed to *legislate* for all aspects of life and ultimate sovereignty rests not with the people, as is common in secularized democratic practice, but with God (Esposito, 1983, p. 79).

Most Muslims have, however, accepted some notion of democracy, but as I have already stated, they do have differences over its precise meaning. Muslim interpretations of democracy, which are currently understood to mean *shura*, place varying degrees of emphasis on the degree to which *the people* are charged with power and are able to exercise their duties. This can only be done in the context of acknowledging the higher authority of God, who remains the supreme ruler of the people. Nevertheless the people do have some authority over their earthly rulers, leaders or caliphs who guide the community according to Islam. A corrupt, unjust or un-Islamic ruler does not have to be tolerated by the people and the assent of the community should be regularly sought by the ruler whoever he may be. All members of a community should be treated equally and bias must not be shown because of race, class or creed. This approach recognizes the importance of consensus within the community (*umma*) of believers, for without the *umma* Islam cannot flourish. It is not democracy per se, then, that is problematic within Islam, as Halliday (1996) reminds us: 'If there are in a range of Islamic countries evident barriers to democracy, this has to do with certain other social and political features that their societies share' (p. 116). While many focus on the rejection by fundamentalists of the democratic impulse, others have discovered the important debates taking place within Islam which encompass not just the problems of democracy but the role of Islam in a world of nation-states, capital-led economies, multi-party national and transnational corporations and the technological boom. These new modernists and reformers, Islamic democrats and advocates of human rights are embarking on the formulation of an authentic Islamic response to the issues of our age. They do not engage with soundbite populist quick fixes which unravel as quickly as they are formulated, the kind of fix-it-all response which many wish the Middle East would undertake; rather, they form the backbone of the truly intellectual response which must evolve through important discourse and problem-solving (Baker, 1991). As Abou El Fadl (2004) contends, 'democracy is an appropriate system for Islam because it both expresses the special worth of human beings . . . and at the same time deprives the state of any pretence of divinity by locating ultimate authority in the hands of the people rather than the ulema' (p. 36). In practice, the formation of political Islamist parties such as al-Nahda in Tunisia in the 1980s is evidence of a liberalization of Islamic thinking on issues of plurality, democracy, partisan politics and elections (Kramer, 1995, p. 122). In the meantime, the picture does indeed look bleak, as tyranny, anti-intellectualism and authoritarian dictatorship continue to dominate the region, and when the opportunities for change are avoided in favour of stability no matter how anti-democratic that stability is. Yet, this fascination with the extreme at the expense of the moderates tells us more about our own perceptions of the relationship between Islam and democracy than it does about the long-standing debate which currently grips the Arab and Muslim communities of the region.

Evidence of fascination with the 'extreme' in Islamist discourse on democracy has dominated the work of orientalist and neo-orientalist authors. As discussed earlier in the chapter, their hostility to Arab and specifically Muslim political culture leads them to rule out any form of meaningful discourse or co-existence between Islam and democracy. How compelling is their case? Is it true, as Martin Kramer asserts, that Islamic fundamentalists only embrace democracy in an instrumentalist and short-term fashion as a strategy for Islamic statehood which is both authoritarian and anti-democratic? 'Democracy,' he writes, 'diversity, accommodation – the fundamentalists have repudiated them all. In appealing to the masses who fill their mosques, they promise, instead, to institute a regime of Islamic law, make common cause with like-minded "brethren" everywhere, and struggle against the hegemony of the West and the existence of Israel' (1993, p. 41). Ayubi believes the picture to be more complicated than this, particularly at a time in the Arab world where Islamists form the main base of opposition. While he admits that there is some currency in the argument that, 'in the immediate instance, most "fundamentalist" groupings act as a counter-democratic force', he concludes that, 'whereas some of the factors that explain the delay of democratization in the Middle East are purely economic or technological, rather than religious or cultural, there is little doubt that the refusal by ruling elites to allow an element of participation for Islamic movements is an added cause for the slow pace of democratization in many Muslim societies' (1997, p. 364).

Nevertheless, for writers like Martin Kramer and Kedourie the attempt to impute democratic qualities to Islamic culture is the dangerous and naive preoccupation of apologists who fail to recognize the threat implicit in all Islamist movements in the region. According to this school of thought, therefore, there is no place or hope for democracy in the region. Yet, this approach fails to distinguish between the many mechanisms of Islamic politics which operate within the Middle East – Wahabi Saudi Arabia, consociational Lebanon, populist Yemen or monarchical Jordan are all the same from this perspective. The predominantly Muslim basis from which most governments within the region work, therefore, is identified as inhibiting the development of liberal democracies; other socio-economic, structural and strategic considerations are largely ignored. It is Islam which makes the Middle East the exception to the democratizing rule. In Iraq, however, it has been Islamic forces – principally the Shi'a spiritual leader Ayatollah al-Sistani – that have maintained the momentum for democracy in the post-war era. The holding of democratic elections in January 2005, delivering the majority Shi'a vote to steer negotiations for the country's constitution and future arrangements of power in the emerging political system, was down to the mobilization of a constituency identified as religious and sectarian.

The process of post-war democratization in Iraq is emblematic of the centrality of this issue to US foreign policy-making towards the region since the early 1990s. It is emblematic because it illustrates the dilemma that the promotion of this policy of democratization has thrown up for both the Clinton and Bush administrations. Since 9/11 the Bush administration has been an active promoter of democracy within the Middle East as a vehicle for the resolution of the many problems the region faces. The Bush administration has framed a significant new focus of its policy towards the region around resolving the democracy deficit. But there are fears that, as in the past, in those regimes of the Middle East where lack of democracy but plenty of oil or goodwill towards the US is apparent, the Bush administration will baulk at insisting on change. President Bush went some way to acknowledging past mistakes by declaring,

> Sixty years of western nations excusing and accommodating the lack of freedom in the Middle East did nothing to make us safe because in the long run, stability cannot be purchased at the expense of liberty. As long as the Middle East remains a place where freedom does not flourish, it will remain a place of stagnation, resentment, and violence ready for export. (Bush, 2003)

In practice, with American hopes pinned on Iraq as a beacon that might then shine its light over the rest of the region, American-sponsored efforts at democracy-promotion elsewhere are viewed as continuing to fail, working on assumptions of double-standards with pro-western allies, and at best ambivalent about Islamist participation and success in democracy processes across the region. American policy-makers have found the region receptive to notions of democracy but suspicious of American sponsorship to this end. The solution to this problem of promoting democracy in a region where authoritarianism is dominant is for US policy to reflect the debate in a vocabulary that is of the region and from the region rather than to be understood as coercing nations into democracy down the barrel of the gun as has been the case in Iraq. Such pronounced changes in policy may be nigh impossible to achieve.

From democracy to ethnocracy in Israel

The debate about democratic exceptionalism in the Middle East has regularly cited Israel as the only truly representative example of a democratic polity in the region. For a number of decades this claim remained unchallenged and the benefits of the Israel model were regularly explored. When in May 1948 the modern nation-state of Israel was established it was founded as a Jewish one, with the express objective of encouraging the ingathering of Jews from around the world, an ideal set around concrete political and legislative functions such as the 1950 'Law of Return'. Israel, however, is not a uni-ethnic state; its majority Jewish population (of 82–3 per cent) is extremely diverse and demographically multi-cultural, and the remaining Arab minority (17–18 per cent) often remains excluded from the privileges or benefits of citizenship because of its ethnic difference (Rouhana, 1997). The political system is largely western in structure, reflecting consociational approaches to plural society and coalition politics, if not, perhaps in practice. More recently, however, a number of critics have emerged to challenge the notion of liberal democracy in relation both to Israel's 'other' ethnic population – the Arabs – and within the Jewish community of the country itself. There is, however, little agreement over the alternative definition or the degrees of democratic or non-democratic tendencies exhibited by the system. Sammy Smooha, for example, prefers to classify Israel as an 'ethnic democracy' – exhibiting a dual character that is democratic by the usual standards, such as electoral politics, participation and so on, and yet where 'the dominance of a certain ethnic group is institutionalized along with democratic procedures . . . minorities are disadvantaged but can avail themselves of democratic means to negotiate better terms of co-existence' (1990, p. 412). Ghanem and Rouhana, however, both prefer the appellation of 'ethnic state': 'Israel . . . is not a democracy, if our criterion is the ethnic preference it shows for Jews. It is, instead, a textbook example of an ethnic state, applying sophisticated policies of inclusion and exclusion toward the Arab minority' (Ghanem, 1998, p. 443). Peled and Shafir take the issue of semantics one step further by concluding that Israel is best described as an 'ethnorepublic' inclusive of an approach to citizenship which is discriminatory in gender as well as religion (Shafir and Peled, 1998, p. 415). Finally, authors such as Yiftachel have presented the case for classifying Israel in yet another manner: eschewing claims to democratic credentials according to territorial and ethnic organization, he argues that 'the Israeli polity is governed not by a democratic regime, but rather by an "ethnocracy" which denotes a non-democratic rule for and by a dominant ethnic group, within the state and beyond its borders' (1999, p. 5). What remains clear in this debate is not definitions but the criticism of Israel's hitherto untarnished democratic credentials as an island of liberal democracy in the Middle East.

Israel's Jewish foundation is a major element in the political system and has consistently acted as a factor in the huge internal differences which exist within the Israeli political scene. Thus, although government is secular (despite claims by its critics, Israel is not a theocracy), the state is often under considerable and sometimes exceedingly influential pressure from its various Jewish ethnic communities (Ashkenazi, Sephardic and Russian), and its religious and orthodox communities. This relationship is exacerbated by an electoral system of single-constituency proportional representation, which allows minority parties to attain positions of power in precarious coalition governments.

The country is a parliamentary democracy. The parliament (Knesset) is a unicameral rather than bicameral legislative institution, with 120 seats. Through proportional representation candidates are elected on party lists every four years to serve their term of office. Universal suffrage allows Israel's citizens (Arab and Jewish) to stand for the Knesset and vote in the elections. The President of the state is a largely symbolic role and is subject to election every five years by the Knesset. As head of state, the President plays a largely ceremonial or rubber-stamping role, although the extent to which certain 'political' activities are tolerated has depended on the individual personalities of those who have taken this title (Arian, 1989). The government has normally been formed by the dominant group in the Knesset. From 1948 to 1977 the Israeli Labour Party dominated the government, led by successive Prime Ministers – David Ben-Gurion (1948–53, 1955–63), Moshe Sharett (1964–9), Golda Meir (1969–74) and Yitzhak Rabin

(1974–7). After 1977 the Labour stranglehold was broken by the ascendancy of right-wing parties such as Herut (Freedom) and, later, the Likud Party. In 1996 Israel held its first direct election for Prime Minister, and the first victor was Binyamin (Bibi) Netanyahu, the leader of the Likud Party. In May 1999 Labour's Ehud Barak snatched control back from Netanyahu in a landslide election victory which put the peace process back on track. This process was overturned in February 2001 when Likud leader Ariel Sharon won the national election against the Barak government.

The Prime Minister selects appropriate candidates (from both the Knesset and outside it) to form a government which must win a vote of confidence from the Knesset. The formation of government is usually a highly complex process dependent on tactical alliances, with minority parties gaining undue influence over the selection of particular cabinet posts. This is because of the large number of political parties that compete in the elections, as well as other factors such as the system of proportional representation which make it exceedingly difficult, if not impossible, for any one party to form a majority government. By and large, this process of political horse-trading is a significant indicator of Israel's claim to a robust democratic life. This is also reflected in the independence of the Supreme Court, the independence (nominally at least) of the government from the army, a free press and media (which is only subject to military censorship), a lively party system in which tens of political parties proliferate, a powerful trade union (Histradrut) and, until recently, a diaspora community that was largely supportive (politically and financially) of the vibrant political life of the country.

By much-vaunted western standards, Israel closely replicates a system of political life, government and institutions which has evolved in Europe and the USA, and as such the democratic path chosen by the state is largely alien to the region in which the state is sited. There are, as we can see, many characteristics of liberal democratic life present in Israel which are largely absent from the Arab states of the region. In Arab states such as Syria there are no free or plural elections in which a multiplicity of parties may compete. In Egypt there is relatively little freedom of the press and the independence of the judiciary is constantly called into question. In Lebanon government was largely determined by Syria, and the delicate balance of confessional politics has, in the past, been very difficult to maintain through the practice of representative democracy. In Jordan, as we shall see, monarchical rule often excludes the possibility of truly participatory democracy. Why, then, have the Arab states of the region resisted the lure of the Israeli example? Why has Israel not been able to encourage its neighbours to adopt its style of government?

The answers to the above questions are manifold. First, resistance to democracy Israel-style stems from the exclusive religious nature of the state. As I have discussed, Israel as a Jewish state actually privileges some of its citizens above others and clearly does not treat them all equally either in terms of the law or in practice. Citizenship is closely related to the fierce debate about 'who is a Jew?' and this in turn reflects on notions of equality that should be at the heart of any modern liberal democratic nation-state. Second, through the whole-sale adoption of a western system of government and institutions, the development of the state and indeed the Zionist movement itself is perceived within the region as an artificial entity reflecting a political culture and traditions far removed from those indigenous to the area which has evolved over hundreds of years. By and large, however, the biggest problem associated with the Israeli democratic model is the continued military occupation by Israel of Arab lands. For the Arab states of the region, this has meant that Israel, while protecting and preserving the rights of its Jewish citizens, ignores or abuses the rights of millions of stateless Palestinians in an exceedingly undemocratic fashion. Democracy in Israel is inextricably chained to the notion of security for its Jewish citizens. Thus, there are no good neighbours, only bad neighbours, as Israel struggles to secure its borders against the perceived threat of Arab hostility, fanaticism, authoritarianism and conflict. Israel is not perceived as the model democracy for others to emulate and its democratic character is constantly overshadowed by the larger conflict with the Palestinians and the other Arab states of the region.

Case study Jordan – a façade democracy

At the beginning of the 1990s, Jordan was often cited as the most encouraging example of democratization in the region. By the middle of the decade, however, more circumspect analysis emerged, calling for a proper assessment of the conditions of change that were prevailing in the country. Jordan has not democratized successfully, but there is strong evidence to suggest that democratization was never truly the aim of the ruling regime. Rather, appropriate conditions were created to maintain a 'façade democracy', satisfying both local demands for greater participation and international and particularly American conditions of democracy for aid-giving and other financial assistance (Milton-Edwards, 1993). In addition the process of political liberalization in evidence at the beginning of the decade was met with a series of reversals, as the kingdom faced further internal crises due to factors such as peace with Israel, the continuing political fallout of the Gulf crisis and the succession debate prompted by King Hussein's episodes of cancer throughout the late 1990s, and his death in 1999.

According to its constitution, the Hashemite Kingdom of Jordan is a constitutional monarchy with a bicameral system of parliament, including an elected legislature known as the House of Representatives. The Senate makes up the other institution of parliament and its members are appointed by the monarch. The Prime Minister and government are also appointed and dismissed by the monarch, who has the right to exercise this power as frequently as he chooses. In practice, until 1989, the government and politics of Jordan were severely circumscribed by the power of its monarchy through King Abdullah and then his grandson King Hussein. Although there has always been a formal provision of plural and democratic institutions of government and legislation, Jordan, particularly since the period of intense political instability of the late 1950s when the monarchy looked precarious, has not been famous for its unfettered practice of democracy. Indeed, the ethnic make-up of the state – a majority Palestinian population ruled by a Hashemite monarchy – and a history of intense conflict, including the civil war of 1970 (Sayigh, 1997), has been used to legitimate coercion to create stability at any price.

For more than twenty years (from the late 1950s onwards) full elections were suspended, political parties were banned, the press was censored and the internal security service (the *mukhabarat*) imprisoned hundreds if not thousands on political charges. Allegations of human rights abuses and tortures were widespread and consistent. These conditions highlighted a tradition of autocratic rule which was described by Finer (1970) as a 'façade democracy', one where 'historic oligarchies govern from behind a façade of liberal-democratic forms which serve as a screen for their rule' (p. 124). The palace, rather than the people, ruled the political roost in Jordan for many decades. The legitimacy derived from King Hussein's Hashemite lineage to the Prophet Mohammed was used to bolster the monarchy of this troubled state. Oligarchy rather than democracy prevailed, and the opposition remained largely circumscribed, forced underground by the security network which hounded it. In this shackled political arena only one other political actor stood apart from the palace and those tribal leaders whose fealty lay with the king, and that was the Islamic movement (Milton-Edwards, 1991). The Islamic movement, primarily the Muslim Brotherhood, however, acted largely as a body of loyal opposition, doing little if anything to actually threaten the status quo of Hashemite hegemony.

The status quo was radically shaken in early 1989 following a series of riots throughout the country against IMF-imposed price increases on basic foods. King Hussein, aware of the increased pressure from below for political concession of some sort, announced that full elections would be held. In addition, it was widely believed that the monarch had decided to embark on a process of democratization that would encourage greater plurality of opinion, increased opportunities for participation, greater freedom of speech and assembly and an end to the high levels of corruption which had almost paralysed the business of government. Economic crisis had severely weakened the king's coercive powers, as Jordanian citizens demanded greater freedoms at a time when the IMF was making it clear that any assistance would be dependent on a certain liberalizing of political control. The events since 1989 have gone some way to meeting expectations but are still more likely to be treated with scepticism.

Indeed, Jordan's path to democratization in many ways reflects Ayubi's (1997) manifestation of cosmetic democratization 'for the Yankees to see' and must be viewed as a continuing process in which the destination – full democracy – is still a long way off. The election that was held in November 1989, however, was treated and regarded as an unheralded spectacle and a roaring success. The campaign and polling day were the freest ever experienced in the country, although it should be noted that political parties were still prohibited, the press was still censored and human rights abuses were still reported by organizations such as Amnesty International (Milton-Edwards, 1996c). The elections to the eighty-seat House of Representatives, the lower house of parliament, resulted in an Islamist victory, delivering thirty-four seats and a high participation rate of some 60 per cent of the eligible electorate. The Cabinet and Senate, the upper house of parliament, however, still remained subject to appointment by the king himself, who has also maintained the power to dissolve parliament and call the election when he so chooses.

Since 1989, aspects of political liberalization have been episodic in nature, combined with an almost inexorable deterioration of certain freedoms once granted. The monarch continued with plans to push for greater political and economic liberalization of society at a pace dictated by the palace not the people. The schedule for change has been step-by-step and reformist, with high-ranking figures such as the former Crown Prince Hassan selling this strategy as a need to recognize that 'change in the Middle East must be gradual and sensitive to the political, cultural and social needs of the population. It must develop organically and not be imported wholesale; with the will to change coming at once from above and below' (Bin-Talal, 1992, p. 5). Further advances were signalled by announcement in 1992 of the National Charter, which called for greater freedom for the individual and equality in society including the establishment of a multi-party system and greater freedom for the press. Notably, particularly in relation to the debate about the compatibility of Islam and democracy, the Jordanian charter also enshrined the principle of Islamic law by declaring that *shari'a* (Islamic law) would be the source of all law in the kingdom. Opponents complained that such steps would serve to inhibit democratic mechanisms rather than encourage them. In the same year, the king permitted the legal formation and registration of political parties and announced that further elections to the House of Representatives would be held in 1992. Those elections resulted in the undermining of the Islamist vote and a further consolidation of the traditional tribal allegiances to the king.

Since 1992 the pace of reform in the country has slowed and curbs on the press and informal political bodies such as professional associations have been reintroduced. Freedom of speech is not widely evident, protest against official government policy – whether it be domestic or regional – is not tolerated and when it is permitted is largely circumscribed by the continual presence of the secret police. While the formal process of elections has been maintained, with a third general election in November 1997, popular confidence in the democratization process has been undermined by the continuing grip on political life exerted by the monarchy. In addition, while Jordan has gone some way towards addressing its economic difficulties and restructuring the economy in terms of the liberalization agenda, it has been less successful at rooting out corruption, absorbing the thousands of Gulf returnees following the débâcle of 1990–1 and, finally, in evincing the much-vaunted peace dividend out of its treaty with Israel in 1994. While a trend towards some form of liberalization in Jordan has been discernible (and may even be the best example within the region), it was motivated by the monarch's skill for pragmatism, pressure from the middle classes for greater political freedoms and international pressure linked with economic aid. By the end of the 1990s all of these variables became increasingly difficult to predict, particularly the nature and form of monarchical rule in the kingdom following the demise of King Hussein, and the accession of his son King Abdullah II. The new king has been forced to constrain further the forces of political liberalization and democracy as he grapples with the severe economic conditions in his country and pleads for debt forgiveness from the big-power players in the international community. Subsequent elections have seen participation rates drop and boycotts by certain political elements. Of greatest significance is the fact that Jordan's Islamist elements – including the Muslim Brotherhood – found themselves increasingly on the margins of parliamentary and governmental power. The parliamentary elections of June 2003 illustrated this change in the balance of power: independents known for their loyalty to King Abdullah II won the majority of the 110 seats to the parliament. Not one single woman was elected and the Islamic Action Front (the political party of the Muslim Brotherhood) won only 16 seats or 15 per cent of the votes across the country. Democracy Jordanian style has taken a long time in terms of reflecting a plurality of political voices in the country.

Case study Algeria – the wrong kind of democracy

This case study presents one of the worst scenarios for the proponents of democracy within the region and the way it has been manipulated to serve certain political ends. Indeed, events since the late 1980s have typically been presented as the 'wrong kind of democracy', where political liberalization and electoral freedoms only encouraged Islamic fanatics bent on manipulating the system to their own undemocratic ends. In many respects the events in Algeria and the democratization debate were precipitated by all the usual suspects on the economic and political front – including a financial crisis which bankrupted the country and led to spiralling foreign debt and IMF strictures on economic restructuring. On the political front, the 'crisis of legitimacy' was evidenced by widespread disillusionment with the Front de Libération Nationale (FLN) among the majority of the population. The outcome has been bloody to say the least, with the country, by the mid-1990s, mired in massacre, carnage and civil conflict. At the heart of this conflict has been a battle in which 'on the one hand, the state is characterized by illegitimacy and divided by "hawks" and "doves". On the other hand, Islamists with a goal of total hegemony – and who themselves are torn between "radicals" and "moderates" – are fighting to replace the existing regime' (Tahi, 1995, p. 219).

After Algeria achieved its independence from the French in 1962, it was governed by the revolutionary populist forces of the FLN. The military-dominated Council of the Revolution, led by President Hourari Boumedienne, inaugurated decades of quasi-military one-party rule along populist socialist lines. State consolidation resulted in the end in the abolition of any form of plural parliamentary life or democracy for the country's citizens. The National Assembly and other parliamentary institutions were suspended. Nevertheless, through this process of state control the economy of Algeria prospered, living conditions and other economic indicators rose and the state maintained its socialist political agenda. When Boumedienne died in 1978, his successor Chadli Benjedid embarked on a process termed by Entelis and Arone (1992) as 'de-Boumediennization' through his own consolidation of state, economy and the all-important military. Yet, the changes and reforms which Benjedid pursued came at a time of contraction in Algeria's economy, when the usually buoyant energy prices from the country's gas and oil industries dropped dramatically and the impact of global recession was felt. Instead of success, Benjedid floundered and compounded the problem by pursuing economic liberalization policies that benefited external rather than domestic capital and investors. By the late 1980s the country was gripped by an economic and political crisis which the president, despite the support of the military, was unable to prevent. The turning point came in October 1988 when demonstrations against the regime and continuing economic crisis swept the country. Whether the demonstrations were about economic crisis, poverty, demands for democracy or 'internecine power struggles within the body politic . . . and rejection of political and economic monolithism' is debatable, and does not detract from the significance of these events in the democratization discussion (Cheriet, 1992, p. 9).

Benjedid responded to the widespread and violent protest by promising political reform – democratization and a greater say in the political system and its economy. In 1989 a national referendum ended the FLN's and Benjedid's single-party system and paved the way for the formation of new political parties. The first democratic test for these new parties came in the municipal and provisional elections of June 1990. The poll resulted in a victory not for the forces of socialism but for a new political movement and party – the Front

Islamique du Salut (FIS) – promoting an Islamic political agenda, including the establishment of an Islamic state in Algeria. The victory gave the FIS control of most of Algeria's local authorities, sending shock waves through the Maghreb and beyond. As Jansen noted at the time, 'The FIS victory has a much greater impact than the establishment of the so-called "Islamic Revolution" in Iran because it is a manifestation of majority Sunni Islamic devotion, not that of the schismatic Iranian Shi'ite minority' (1992, p. 8).

It was feared, within the regime as well as the international community, that if the success of the FIS were repeated in the elections to the National Assembly planned for December 1991, it could well represent the first democratic accession to power by a militant or fundamentalist Islamic party. On 26 December 1991 the fears of the government and its supporters were proved in the first round of the elections, when the FIS took a commanding lead, wiping out most of the other 49 parties contesting the election, winning 3 million votes and 118 seats. At the end of this first round the FIS needed only another 28 seats in the second round scheduled for 16 January 1992 to control the National Assembly. The prospect of democratization producing a victory for Islamic fundamentalists alarmed the government and its supporters, who would not tolerate the utilization of the democratic process to replace one form of totalitarian government with another. As Hermida (1992) pointed out, 'Few are convinced that the FIS, once in power, would respect the multiparty system. The party has in the past described democracy as blasphemy' (p. 7).

The government was faced with growing pressure internally and externally to intervene. The pressure certainly had its effects. The scheduled second part of the election was 'postponed', and remained so. A state of emergency was declared in February 1992 and the leadership of the FIS was arrested. The authorities were determined to eliminate the FIS as a political movement with populist support. From 1992 fierce battles raged between a defiant array of Islamic groups, including the FIS, its supporters and government forces. Hundreds of thousands of lives were lost and terrible terrorist atrocities perpetrated by all sides to this civil war. The army effectively seized control of the state, and the new president Lamine Zeroual, drawn from army ranks, failed to consolidate his rule, despite a presidential poll in 1995 and support from the West in his campaign against the Islamists. Democratization was dead; the experiment in Algeria had been a resounding failure. The 'grand bargain' offered by Algeria's rulers in the early 1990s 'granting new elites some access to authority in exchange for restored regime legitimacy and the prospects of future economic improvements and political liberalization' came far too late to appease any sector of society and proved problematic to the end (Eickelman and Piscatori, 1996, p. 161). Algeria became paralysed by the civil war, and the prospect of some negotiated democratic resolution to the conflict appeared remote. The economy was floundering, the liberalization process collapsed as foreign investors fled the country in the face of the Islamist campaign of violence which often directly targeted them. The battle lines had been drawn between the forces of secularism and Islam, Muslims and the state, the military and the people. Any common ground, any shared sense of Algerian identity, had been lost, and attempts to formulate resolutions sponsored by the international community were slow in fruition. Even Algeria's former colonial ruler, France, battled desperately to remain aloof and apart from the conflict, wary that its own Algerian immigrant population might turn the country into a further battlefield in this bitter war. The vocabulary and sentiments of democracy – pluralism, freedom and representation – had been lost in the bloodshed that has touched every corner of Algeria since 1992. In 1999, as energies for conflict dissipated, the state declared a Civil Harmony Law as a means of moving to amnesty and increasing the prospects for a resumption of democratization. But it wasn't until 2005 when President Bouteflika was elected as President for a second term that Algeria's military declared itself 'neutral' in the polling process. The referendum of September 2005 saw the adoption of a Charter for Peace and National Reconciliation that provided a form of amnesty for both sides to the conflict in Algeria. Promoted by President Bouteflika as a means of moving from conflict to peace, it was regarded with suspicion in some quarters. Nevertheless nearly 98 per cent of those voting in the referendum supported the Charter and the state acknowledged a turnout of 80 per cent of 18.3 million registered voters. The Charter is clearly seen as one way in which Algeria is beginning to come to terms with issues of transitional justice as a means of dealing with the deadly experiment in the democratic politics of the early 1990s.

Further reading

Debates about democratization in the developing world are covered extensively in Potter et al. (1997). On the more general level, Held's (1996) text on models of democracy outlines classical theory to contemporary debates about democracy and democratization. Other texts on Third World politics, including Cammack et al. (1993), examine the subject with special reference to the Middle East region. Deegan (1993) provides an introductory overview to some of the themes associated with the debate in the Middle East. Owen (2003) gives an historical account of the emergence of political parties, aspects of electoral politics and the emergence of one-party political regimes in the earlier half of the twentieth century. The work of modernization theorists in relation to issues of democracy and pluralism is represented in the somewhat dated works of Lerner (1958) and Rustow (1971). The resonance of certain arguments promoted by the modernization theorists, however, is reflected in Huntington's (1993) article, which provides a contentious starting point for the subject in relation to the political culture of the Arab and Muslim world. Such themes are further explored in Saikal and Schnabel (2003), Diamond, Plattner and Brumberg (2003) and Ottway et al. (2002). This can be contrasted against the positions outlined by Hudson (1988, 1991 and 1995),

Esposito and Piscatori (1991) and, more recently, the civil society project publications from al-Sayyid (1994 and 1995) and Norton (1995 and 1996). Ayubi (1995), following the civil society–democracy discourse, discusses these issues at length, while Vitalis (1994) and the *MERIP* (1992) special issue point to the role external intervention has played in encouraging this phenomenon. Schwedler (1995) covers some useful ground, and can be contrasted with Moussalli's contribution (1995). Muslih and Norton (1991) emphasize the need for democracy within the Arab world. Brynen et al. (1995) examine democratization and liberalization across the Arab world and would make an interesting companion to Salame (1994a),
which features worthwhile contributions by Waterbury, Leca, Luciani and al-Azmeh. Ibrahim (1993) focuses specifically on the role of elites. The issue of compatibility between Islam and democracy is debated extensively by Pipes (1983a, 1983b) and Perlmutter (1992) as well as Vatikiotis (1987), who in turn links the debate to aspects of plural politics, secularism and nationalism. Gudrun Kramer's (1992) contribution to this issue contrasts with that of Martin Kramer (1993). This theme is also addressed by Juergensmeyer (1993), who takes a comparative approach with other religious fundamentalist movements. Ismail (1995), Gudrun Kramer (1995), Nasr (1995) and the edited text by Salvatore and Eickelman (2004) discuss both aspects of the Arab and Muslim discourse on this theme. On politics in Israel, Arian (1989) articulates a clear outline of the liberal democratic character of the country. The ethnic dimension is articulated by Cohen (1983) and this should be analysed in conjunction with the material by Smooha (1990), Rouhana (1997), Ghanem (1998) and Yiftachel (1999). On Jordan, the debate about democracy can be found in Amawi (1992) and Milton-Edwards (1993), while politics in general in the country are discussed in Wilson (1991), Salibi (1993) and Satloff (1994). The issues of Islamism and democracy in Algeria are covered extensively in Abraham (1990), Brumberg (1991), Mortimer (1991), Addi (1992), Entelis and Naylor (1992), Howe (1992), Reudy (1994), Roberts (1992), Deeb (1994), Zartman (1994), Kapil (1995) and Willis (1996). Joffe (1993) and Stone (1993) provide useful political histories of the country.

Women: The Invisible Population

Introduction

Muslim and Arab women in the Middle East have traditionally been relegated to a minor role in the dominant patriarchal system of religious, social, economic and political relations. Women remain a largely marginal force who are often absent from the public and political domain, literally hidden from view. As the themes in this chapter highlight, however, women have been and remain an important influence in society, their apparent marginal role as much to do with Eurocentric orientalist and feminist views on the subject as other factors (L. Ahmed, 1992). In the contemporary era, their battle for rights has been linked with the early twentieth-century anti-colonial Arab nationalist movements which achieved independence in the 1950s and 1960s. Arab independence, state-encouraged or directed feminism, state socialism and social reform have, however, impacted in unexpected ways on women's rights. One aspect of this impact is reflected in the important debate about the status of women in the laws of various states, including their rights to education, work, relations to men, inheritance and property rights. In addition, many would argue that the root of women's oppression in Arab society lies in the Islamic religion and its attitude to women.

Both western and Arab feminist authors have been critical of Islam for further enslaving and imprisoning them in their own homes. Arab feminist authors such as Fatima Mernissi, for example, have developed a thesis which not only questions the way in which Islam (or Muslim men) have created a particular place for women in the social order, but the way in which certain orthodox interpretations of the religion perceive women as actively threatening sexual beings undermining Muslim male order and authority (Mernissi, 1985). But as Judith Tucker reminds us, 'there is actually little agreement on what the central texts of the religion have to say about gender. The Quran . . . is rather vague or so all-encompassing on most gender questions as to offer only very general guidance on the subject' (Tucker, 1993, p. ix). Debate within the Arab world, then, has focused on Islam in relation to gender issues and is used as a guide. Issues of marriage rights, polygamy, inheritance and dress are not as fixed as many associated with one perspective or another might have us think, and are open to the same methods of interpretation as other issues. As Leila Ahmed (1992) has outlined, there is no single blueprint of behaviour for Muslim women, rather, an accretion of roles determined as much by faith as by history, class, culture and economic context. Indeed, the Islam–women debate has created two distinct approaches, the first promoting the argument outlined above that Islamic culture has created significant problems for women in the Middle East. The second approach, discussed further in this chapter, claims that Islam and the current revival of the religion is actually responsible for the liberation of women, protecting and respecting their status and role rather than objectifying and denigrating them as has occurred in the secularized West. The ideological impulse behind both positions is not difficult to discern and reflects the ways in which women's issues have become an extension of the battlefield between secular and Islamic forces in the region.

Islam, however, is just one factor contributing to the current status endured by women in the Middle East today. It is important therefore to address indicators of socio-economic status – work, the domain of the home and associated issues – to gain a deeper insight into women's lives as they are currently experienced across the region. In societies that have prospered and remained largely static politically, like the Arab states of the Gulf, women have remained powerless, marginal and excluded. Issues of citizenship, suffrage, economic independence, violence and education for women are rarely addressed. While some states have made a few advances more than others, the political patriarchy of these states has ensured the continued control of women and debates about their status, rights and political roles in society. The creation of wealth in these societies, therefore, has not empowered women. Finally, this chapter will examine the future frontiers of scholarship on these issues. Feminist debate and discourse has played an important part in the way in which not only women but the region as a whole is viewed. An increasing number of writers are reflecting on the import of Eurocentric feminist debates, the dominance of liberal feminism or state feminisms and have contributed further to the debate about the 'other' initiated by Said in the late 1970s. As such, the gendering of the Middle East is under way, constructing the 'other' not just in the post-orientalist sense but in terms of gender and the rights of women, whichever perspective this issue is taken from.

The two case studies in this chapter, concerning Palestinian and Iranian women, reflect the diverse nature of women's lives in the region. The continued progression of such women and their movements will not be uniform but will reflect the differing political, social and economic cultures they are located in. As Kandiyoti remarks, 'If some women's response to their vulnerability is a retreat into the protective certainties of religious conservatism, others may be motivated to struggle for a social order in which they no longer need the veil to legitimize their public presence and to fend off male aggression' (Kandiyoti, 1991, p. 18).

The role of women in nationalist movements

The rise of Arab nationalism, anti-colonialism and the independence movement in the Arab world has a strong link with women's rights. The earliest stirrings of the women's movement coincided and involved women who were also engaged in national struggles against colonial powers in the region. The history of the women's struggle during this period, then, may be reflected through the lens of nationalism, be it Egyptian, Iraqi, Syrian or Palestinian. As such, the independence, development, progress, setbacks, concrete gains and perceived losses of the movement for women's rights can only be understood by understanding the political climate of the time, which dictated the role that such individuals and movements would have.

This climate also ensured that although the issues of women's rights, suffrage, political participation and so on were given attention, the agenda for action was male-dominated – very few women, if any at all, were able to achieve real positions of power and the political activities which women began to engage in were often associated with traditional female occupations such as education, or through the burgeoning networks of women's charity associations which were established during this period. Arab nationalism was largely an expression of patriarchy, and although the leaders of such movements appealed to women to support their cause, it was as mothers, daughters and wives, not as women of independent rights. As Botman (1987) notes, using the example of Egyptian nationalism, 'With few exceptions, political work was performed by Egyptian men who, through family prominence, wealth, political connections or the patronage system, rose up the legislative ladder. Women participated in public affairs only sporadically, essentially because Egyptian society was socially traditional and highly conservative' (p. 14). These national movements for independence presented women with an opportunity to play a role on the margins of their own history and society and a double-edged dilemma in the quest for their rights in the legal, social and religious spheres. As such, they were consistently reminded that while their struggle must take second place to the larger fight for national independence and freedom against colonial rule, their freedom would come only when the people were freed from the yoke of colonialism and imperialism.

It might have been assumed that the national independence movements of the Arab world would achieve the social, political, economic and legal reforms that some women dreamed of when independence was achieved. In reality, however, the outcome was somewhat different. First, it has to be remembered that although some women did play an important role in independence movements in countries like Algeria, their involvement was never a primary objective or the result of a widespread social revolution that had taken place as nations struggled against colonial powers. Indeed, in Algeria, despite the fact that as many as 10,000 women played a role in the revolution, the leaders of the Front de Libération Nationale (FLN) and the Armée de Libération Nationale (ALN) absorbed many of the reactionary ideological positions on the subject of women that were prevalent in Algerian society at the time. As Knauss (1987) has highlighted, patriarchy and control of women after French attempts to define their role was one way of resisting the colonial onslaught. Fanon, as quoted by Gerner (1984), sums up the French colonial position: 'If we want to destroy the structure of Algerian society, its capacity for resistance, we must first conquer the women; we must go and find them behind the veil where they hide themselves in their houses where men keep them out of sight' (p. 76). The women heroes of revolutions were a minority, predominantly drawn from the Arab bourgeoisie and leftist forces. The goal of the Arab nationalist movement was independence from foreign rule, not the transformation of society. While it was inevitable that the transition from one order to another would incorporate some changes, traditional patterns of social and power relations within society between men and women would remain unchanged. During the Algerian war of independence (1957–62) women did play a role in the ranks of the FLN, mainly in a gendered service function such as cook or cleaner, yet the legends of women fighters, such as Djamila Bouhired, Djamila Bouazza, Zahia Khalifah and Djennet Hamidoh, and the nature of the role they played, are reassessed, as Minces (1978) argues:

> In the milieu of Algerian society and traditions, women, as such, hardly had a word of their own to say . . . [when] the men had to go underground or flee the country, then they turned over to women tasks that they themselves could no longer carry out. That is to say . . . women were utilized . . . it appears that very few women entered the battle on their own initiative. (p. 162)

Whether these experiences in themselves were liberating for women should also be questioned. False hopes and false dawns might be a more appropriate description of the way in which women were utilized by national movements throughout the region during the era of independence. The making of myths, the women *fedayeen*, resistance fighters, bombers and heroes of the struggle were manipulated by the leadership of Arab progressive national movements to portray their struggles as social revolutions in traditional societies where women were a silent force. Yet, the great national consciousness-raising of women in these societies never occurred either during or after the revolution. Indeed, the leaders of Arab independence hoped to satisfy women with incremental rather than full-scale reform of legislation relating to their status post-independence. As Knauss (1987) highlights in the case of Algeria, post-independence rhetoric was firmly rooted in patriarchal attitudes; as such, 'the imperative needs of the male revolutionaries to restore Arabic as the primary language, Islam as the religion of the state, Algeria as free and fully independent and themselves as sovereigns of the family' communicated a clear position on the role of women in all this (p. xii).

Bourgeois feminism (nationalist and Islamic in character) emerged among the small elite of women in cities such as Cairo, Damascus, Beirut, Algiers and Baghdad. As a result, associated with the nationalist movement for independence in the Arab world, it did achieve some important changes. As Hatem highlights, 'they created a new social climate and a political economic system that accepted women's rights to public space, where they were expected to pursue public activities like education, work, and some forms of political participation, especially suffrage' (Hatem, 1993, pp. 39–40). The achievement of public space for women was a remarkable step forward in itself, as Badran highlights in the example of Egypt: 'Feminist movements . . . in the first half of the century and public policy under Nasser's programme of Arab socialism assisted women in making vast inroads into all aspects of society. Today they are found in virtually every sector of the economy and all levels, although generally not heavily clustered at the top' (1994, p. 209). As we shall see in the following sections, the battle to maintain women's rights to public space throughout the Middle East has been hard fought, with as many defeats as victories. In the present day it has been associated with the current resurgence of religion. In addition, although the street may have belonged to women, other issues affecting their rights would either be slow in coming or would never materialize at all.

As I have already pointed out, the nationalist agenda did not incorporate a clear position on women's rights and steered clear of controversy by declaring that discussion would be postponed until after independence. Bourgeois feminism was too young in its infancy to challenge the whole edifice maintaining the traditional balance of power in Arab patriarchal society. The freedom that these women enjoyed had not been taken by them but had been granted by men within the framework of a modern movement for national liberation and independence. As such, the granting of the right to public space was as much if not more about anti-colonialism and the portrayal of women through the lens of orientalism than it was about truly recognizing the rights of all women irrespective of their class, religion, education or position in society. The issue of women's rights during this era of nationalism, then, can be described as a battle between the colonial and the Arab male for the possession of women, control over their lives and as a rearticulated patriarchal agenda in Arab society with a façade of modern themes regarding the rights of women.

Identity and independence: status issues

The end of colonialism and the birth of national independence for the states of the Middle East should have heralded an era of democracy and freedom. Issues of Arab, Zionist and Iranian identity post-independence, however, would often be forged through a prevailing patriarchal tyranny and tendency to authoritarianism. From the Maghreb to the Gulf, the new Arab order would change in many ways – agrarian, economic and educational – but the traditional patterns of patriarchy would be maintained through the upholding of often religious legislation regarding women's rights and superficial state-led reform in areas of education. One interesting exception to this position is found in the example of post-independence Tunisia, where the liberal position of President Habib Bourguiba in 1956 was reflected in the new Personal Status Code (1957), which removed religious authority from issues directly affecting women such as marriage, divorce and custody, while at the same time it outlawed polygamy (as previously permitted by *shari'a*) (Salem, 1984). The patriarchal attitudes which prevailed in society, however, were rarely challenged and the state – socialist, progressive or conservative – played an enormous part in presenting an idealized vision of women which consolidated chauvinistic values. In Iraq, for example, the Ba'th party slogan of 'unity, socialism and independence' was interpreted for Iraqi women by the male-dominated military dictatorship led since 1979 by Saddam Hussein. Women's visions of independence and freedom were largely ignored and subordinated to the national agenda, post-independence, of state-building and then state-consolidation.

The fate of women in the radical, progressive regimes of the Middle East has improved in some respects, but in others women have found their notions of identity and freedom challenged not just from within but by the very state apparatus which they played their part in establishing. On the issue of women's rights, the progressive state has often turned its back and maintained the traditional relationship based on patriarchal dominance. In addition, state feminisms have promoted a particular vision of women which has more to do with national economic and political agendas than meaningful rights. Instead, such issues have been harnessed by the state and certain women have been promoted as symbols of particular state policies and visions, which have been sold as reflecting a deep-seated concern with what women want. This useful coalescence of approaches has been particularly pertinent as secular state and Islamist forces entered into battle to win public opinion and support throughout the 1980s and 1990s.

One area of progress has been literacy, but even here men have derived greater benefit than women. For example, according to UNICEF in 2004, among Algeria's literate population 79 per cent were male while only 60 per cent were female. In Syria, 88 per cent were male and 59 per cent were female. While these figures do show an increase in female reading skills in progressive regimes, particularly when compared to conservative states like Saudi Arabia, overall illiteracy among women in the Middle East remains widespread. Very often, women are being held back by the fate of motherhood, which remains idealized by the state and lacks meaningful state assistance in any form. The rapid expansion of population in most Middle East countries, coupled with poor support from the state through education, welfare, health, employment or childcare programmes, policy or planning, means that women in the region are continually burdened and compelled to conform to ideal types which the state constructs as part of its efforts at nation-building and consolidation. In Syria, for example, Ba'th party posters present an image of women which emphasizes the multiple roles they have to play in society – as mother, educator, wife, fighter, worker and passive religious being – while the state itself does little to facilitate or support them in these roles.

Women, even post-independence, remain defined by their status as wife, mother or daughter rather than as individuals with a variety of roles to play in society. In reality, women are denied political equality and are barely represented in formal spheres of power associated with the state. Their economic rights are constrained by the marginal role they are compelled to play in the labour force. Employment opportunities outside the home remain limited to say the least, and are governed by a variety of family- and society-imposed restrictions. In Iraq, for example, employment outside the home often only occurred as a result of war and associated labour shortages. Emancipation for women through the Ba'th party, however, was designed to strengthen the Ba'th within the powerful arena of the home and the family. The women merely acted as vehicles for ideology. Formal politics remains the preserve of men; women are only admitted and utilized to reinforce the state or the party. In Libya, Qaddafi's all-woman bodyguard is supposed to symbolize the notion of equality promoted by the *jamahiriyya*; in reality they are no more independent of any man than the women of Saudi Arabia, who are confined to their homes and prohibited from freedom of movement. In Egypt the *coup d'état* led by Gamal Abdel Nasser and the Free Officers in 1952 proved a setback for the nascent feminist movement. The leftist relations enjoyed by these small feminist groups and leaders proved fatal following Nasser's policy of suppression against the left as he consolidated his power in the late 1950s and early 1960s. Nevertheless, Nasser and his government did incorporate some changes into the socialist state which was established following the *coup*. Like other progressive regimes there was some attempt to improve women's opportunities in areas of education, rights to suffrage and health. The similarity, however, did not end here, as Badran notes: 'Women, other than tokens, did not make it to the top echelons of the government bureaucracy or professions, and they were virtually segregated in areas of work deemed more fitting for females . . . Finally, the old personal status laws remained in force, symbolically and practically oppressive to women' (1993, p. 139). In Egypt, as in other post-independence states, the demise of one male leader and the rise of another did little or nothing to improve the position and rights of women within the state. To date there is no evidence of Arab women playing a leading role in any regime in the region, and even within Israel, where there has been a female Prime Minister, and where women serve in the army and certain rights are legally protected, the battle for equality between the sexes is not over (Sharoni, 1995).

In the 1980s and 1990s, as Arab regimes grappled with internal conflicts, dissension and power struggles, the Arab feminist struggle continued. These feminist movements were secular, religious and activist in nature, though they were largely elite-based (Afshar, 1998). Policies predicated on the continued subordination of women are manifest throughout the region and are contributing further to the instability which seems currently to grip the area. The Arab world is caught between two conflicting creeds. The first is the pressure for modernization, westernization, a liberal economy and more democratic governance. But this has brought immense disruption to Arab society and to the second creed, the traditional way of life. Central to this is the belief that society is determined according to patriarchy. The women's movement symbolizes the struggle over the modern and the traditional that is currently taking place in the Middle East.

Modernization is increasingly viewed as empowering women and leaving men vulnerable and emasculated – a message whose import in a patriarchal society cannot be underestimated. In 2002 the UNDP Arab Human Development report highlighted the debilitating effects on the region's development arising from the exclusion of women in terms of education, employment, politics and society. The report highlighted the lack of political opportunities available for women evident in voting rights (or rather the lack of them) to participation in the region's legislatures. The UNDP report highlighted that women occupied only 3.5 per cent of parliamentary seats in Arab states – making this the lowest in the world. Such data is only contrasted negatively by the progress on political rights for women in Gulf states such as Kuwait, Bahrain and Qatar where for the first time ever women are winning rights to the franchise and participation in limited legislative bodies. Thus while democracy advances for women across the region, it is a hard-won and tortuously slow process and remains woefully inadequate when compared to the political rights of women elsewhere across the globe.

Arab men have come to recognize their emasculation in a variety of settings – during the Palestinian Intifada when they were imprisoned and women ran the home; in Kuwait during the Gulf crisis; in Iraq following the sanctions of 1990; in Algeria during the 1991 civil crisis; in Iran following the Revolution of 1979; and in Egypt following the resurgence of Islam and its manifestation as a political force. In all of these situations, women are identified or targeted as the new threat – order and stability, tradition and harmony, men argue, can only be restored when women are returned to their rightful place. As Tetreault and al-Mughni (1995) assert, 'The conceptualization of women as the "intimate enemy" makes their control by men a primary focus of concern, especially for men whose status and power are threatened by modernization' (p. 415).

Women and Islam

The debate about women and Islam reflects, to a great extent, the issues of modernization, tradition, Islamic resurgence, political power and internal conflict which have been discussed in the section above. The debate is centred on the question of whether or not Islam contributes further to the enslavement or liberation of Muslim women living in the Middle East. This question has no clear-cut answer, but it can be said that the resurgence of Islam across the region has had an important impact on women's lives. Islam does embrace certain attitudes towards women and in the contemporary era these attitudes

have been utilized to portray a certain image which has been dominated by the conservative Islamists. Islam has a lot to say about women;
the Koran and the *hadith* both address the rights, role, behaviour and
ideal of women of faith and outside the faith. Women are often
perceived as the most visible sign of the current resurgence of Islam
and questions concerning their dress, behaviour and rights have been
hotly contested across the region (Jawad, 1998). From the West, the
continuing fascination with the oriental woman persists through
cultural stereotypes of two extremes – the belly-dancing siren of the
harems and the veiled, dour fundamentalists of revolutionary Islamic
Iran. Islam is perceived as significant in the lives of women and the
question of women's issues, which is in itself important in understanding the changes wrought in Middle Eastern societies. The contest
has centred on who has the right or legitimate interpretation of
women's role according to Islam, rather than the attention paid to
women in the Koran and the Sunna (Karam, 1998). Should this interpretation be literal or should it reflect the modern era in which we
live? The contest is undertaken by both men and women, secularists
and Islamists, fundamentalists and liberals, activists and reactionar-
ies, feminists and non-feminists. Indeed, whether one believes the
term 'Muslim or Islamist feminist' to be an oxymoron or not, the
debate which women themselves have engaged in provides the most
beneficial insights (Karam, 1998).

A large number of verses (*sura*) in the Koran deal with women and
the issues affecting them. These verses proclaim on marriage, divorce,
inheritance, child-rearing, menstruation, discipline against disobed-
ient women, adultery and relations with men. The Koran empowers
women – giving them rights in divorce, inheritance, as mothers of
children and widows: 'Divorce must be pronounced twice and then
[a woman] must be retained in honour or released in kindness. And it
is not lawful for you that ye take from women aught of that which ye
have given them' (Sura of the Cow, verse 229). On inheritance, the
Koran declares: 'Unto the men [of the family] belongeth a share of that
which parents and near kindred leave, and unto the women a share of
that which parents and near kindred leave, whether it be little or
much – a legal share' (Sura of Women, verse 7). Thus, for many Muslim
women, their religion has acted as an important shelter and protector
of their rights. Islam provides honour, dignity and strength within the
faith, society and the family. In the era of Islamic resurgence, many
nominally Muslim women have returned to active expression and
adherence to their faith as a new means of independence. This return
has been facilitated by the Islamic movement itself, particularly the
conservative and radical elements which have campaigned to bring
women back to the Muslim faith – conservative regimes in the Gulf

have provided the money for Islamic dress for thousands of women in Egypt, facilitated segregated education from primary to tertiary levels and funded the thousands of books, leaflets, magazines and articles written by Islamists for women. For these women, wearing the veil is an act of empowerment which means they can remain in the workplace with respect and move freely in public male-dominated space.

The conservative Islamist view of women is, however, contested, from those within the religion and outside it. From within the faith, authors such as Mahmoud have identified a 'mixed [or] hybrid discourse' which Islamist thinkers such as Tunisian Rashid al-Ghannushi have promoted to contest the issue of gender. This discourse, while going 'beyond the traditional Islamic position . . . does not go far enough to satisfy the legitimate aspirations of women in Muslim societies to see inequality and gender discrimination redressed' (Mahmoud, 1996, p. 262). As Eickelman and Piscatori remind us, 'The regime, established religious authorities, and counter-regime Islamists all claim to be the defender of family integrity and of the role and rights of women in an Islamic society. In so doing, each makes the ideas of family and women pivotal to contemporary Muslim politics' (Eickelman and Piscatori, 1996, p. 99). Thus, the authenticity of the conservatives is challenged. This challenge, however, has been marginal historically and in the present day represents a minority and marginal view within the region. At the turn of the twentieth century Islamic modernists emphasized the need for reform within Islam and a new interpretation of women's rights and roles. The modernists have seen 'reform on women's issues as centrally important to the reform of society as a whole, and . . . [it] includes women's participation in the public sector (politics and work)' (Stowasser, 1993, p. 14). For modernists, the education, welfare and health of women remains central to a positive regeneration of Islam that empowers them in the contemporary era and withstands the scrutiny of the West. As such, the women who wear the veil to work as a means of empowerment represent this limited modernist trend.

Outside the religion, secular Arab critics of Islam have bemoaned its treatment of women. Writers such as Moroccan sociologist Fatima Mernissi (1985) have argued against the image of Islam which the religion promotes. They point to the important role women have played in society and politics and criticize the Islamists' objectification of women as a sexual threat. Such critics argue that Islam is holding women back and that if fundamentalists had their way women would be further enslaved by Islamists and their literal interpretations of seventh-century scriptures. Secular critics also identify the state as a chief culprit in aiding and abetting the Islamists in their task. By failing to take the initiative on family and civil law, the state allows the

Islamists to win the argument and the state-paid clergy play their part in reinforcing the enslavement of women. Few examples exist in the region where the state has taken the initiative and used the law to change women's status for the better. The former People's Democratic Republic of Yemen (PDRY) is a rare exception, where, as Molyneux (1991) claims, 'the transformations in the structures and practices of law which were brought about . . . had far-reaching implications for women . . . the changes that were introduced can be recognized as important without exaggerating their overall impact or their contribution to "women's emancipation"' (p. 266). For the main part, the debate about women and Islam remains unresolved, with neither side able, to date, to claim victory. What will remain important is the path that women themselves choose in relation to Islam rather than the route that men are currently claiming for them. One example of the new paths which women themselves are choosing is cited by Badran (1994) as 'gender activism': in Egypt in the 1990s feminist, pro-feminist and Islamist women, while remaining grounded 'in divergent ideologies which in turn reflect their different configurations of identity and overlapping and yet distinct visions of the good society', found common ground and issues around which a common activism has been developed (p. 222).

Subjugation through wealth and work

The ideal type represented to women in the Middle East through their state, family, society and religion sees the relationship between women, wealth and work as purely domestic in location. For many decades, this idealized notion was generally accepted by researchers and writers associated with the region. It was assumed that the harem, seclusion and the marginal space which women occupied in Middle Eastern society prohibited their role in the creation of wealth, in employment or work outside the home. In other words, women were perceived as invisible in the world of work and income generation as they were in the realm of formal and state politics. It was assumed that predominant religious and cultural values played their part in excluding women and regulating their absence at a formal level. This assumption stemmed from the absence of women's research in the subject, the domination of social science and other disciplines by men and their failure, as a result either of unwillingness or inability, to come into contact with women in the Middle East and experience the impact of work on their lives. Ultimately, it is surprising that for so long the fundamental changes in the socio-economic environment of the region – modernization, rapid economic growth, industrialization, urbanization, decline of agriculture, population growth, migrant labour patterns, the growth of modern capital-led economies and state-led economic liberalization – were deemed insignificant to women and their lives.

While earlier observations of women and work (or lack of it) in countries like Saudi Arabia or Kuwait may be valid, they assume that women's work patterns in the region are both uniform and the same or similar to male work patterns. But they do not take into account the ways in which women in the Middle East generate income and own property, or the role of wealth-creation which they play both inside and outside the home. Many studies produced in the 1970s and 1980s only reinforced existing stereotypes of Arab women as marginal or absent in relation to productive economy. Indeed, it was argued that a woman's productive capacity was located in the family through her 'reproductive' abilities as well as her duties to rear offspring. In conditions where rates of unemployment have been high, this role has been further emphasized, as Mernissi (1985) argues: 'a society having difficulty creating jobs for men tends to fall back on traditional customs that deny women's economic dimension and define them purely as sexual objects – and to write those customs into law' (p. 148). Women in the Middle East are workers, both in the home and, increasingly, outside it. Levels of participation in the workforce in countries like Tunisia, Egypt, Syria, Yemen, Algeria, Morocco, Iraq and Iran have risen during the 1990s. As a result, women have also begun to challenge the political space traditionally inhabited by men. While this phenomenon is class-based, a strong argument can be made that the proliferation of educated Arab and Muslim women in professional occupations in countries like Tunisia, Egypt, Jordan, Lebanon and Iran correlates with the push by the same women for greater representation of women's issues in the political arena.

Work trends within the region have changed, and with them the role of women. Where previously women's work was underestimated, present-day studies are starting to focus on the role women play as key economic figures in family units (extended and nuclear) and the impact this has on the relative wealth of society as a whole. While such analysis reflects the class-based divisions within society, regional and generational differences, marital status, as well as the predominant Muslim cultural norms, it also recognizes that, while the prospects for women's financial independence may be highly restricted, they do enjoy increased levels of financial decision-making and freedom within the family unit. At official levels, particularly where the state draws up legislation bestowing a concept of national identity and duty, the role of women as independent economic actors is prohibited, as the Personal Status Code of Morocco outlines: 'Every human being is responsible for providing for his needs (*nafaqa*) through his own means, with the exception of wives, whose husbands provide for their needs' (in Mernissi, 1985, p. 148). Within the family, however, wives, daughters and sisters do have an important economic role to play.

In many countries throughout the region women are entering the workforce and rates of income-generation within the home are also increasing. As the costs of living rise, the size of families continues to burgeon and one income becomes insufficient, women from the urban and rural lower classes begin to enter the workforce. The sector which a large proportion of these women enter has been referred to as the informal sector, which is described as a 'residual category, embracing all jobs and activities that do not fall into either the public, or the private formal sector' (Richards and Waterbury, 1990, p. 270). The informal sector encourages the majority of women entering the workforce for the first time for a variety of reasons: it is seasonal, requires low if little capital outlay, is flexible and often located either within neighbourhoods or other locations where women in particular may feel free to bring their children with them. In addition, the informal sector attracts women and their children into labour. The impact of this sector on the economy in general is difficult to estimate, but it has been concluded that the urban informal sector (with its high levels of female and child employment) 'employs at least one-third to one-half of the labour force' in many countries in the region (Richards and Waterbury, 1990, p. 270).

While women's patterns of work have changed, particularly through entrance into the informal economic sector, it is still apparent that across the region as a whole there is little evidence to suggest that women are economically independent. In addition, as Hammami (1993) remarks, 'their access to such resources [financial] is overwhelmingly tied to the mechanism of marriage . . . What this means is that women's standard of living seems largely to be determined by either the spouse or the family – they are, in other words, overwhelmingly dependent' (p. 309). The state, through personal status legislation, often reinforces this dependency and inequality. Cultural pressures, meanwhile, are applied by the male clergy of the region against women seeking to carve out an independent role. Yet without women in the workplace, as drivers of the economy, international organizations such as the UNDP argue that the region will find it impossible to achieve economic recovery in the wake of a two-decade slump. Yet, work has not resulted in the political empowerment of women; rather, it has tended to circumscribe further their role within the family structure and prevent their emancipation on an individual level, as Pool argues:

> Where women first enter the paid workforce, the decision to do so should not automatically be celebrated as a sign of emancipation. It is as likely to be a sign of distress – prompted by approaching landlessness

in a peasant economy for example, or increasing impoverishment as a consequence of crisis in an urban economy. (Cammack et al., 1993, p. 242)

Feminism and gender discourses

It remains an unfortunate fact that many introductory textbooks on the subject of the Middle East consistently fail to address the issue of women in the region. A glance through the index and chapters of these books throws up no or little reference to the subject. When women are cited, they are always associated or cross-referenced within a narrow vocabulary: women – and wearing *hijab*, clothing of, equality, or rights. The impression given from these books is that when it comes to telling the story of politics in the Middle East, the state, Islam, democracy and the military are all vital ingredients, while women and the issues affecting them are not even worthy of a single citation in an index. Even a 1990s text, entitled *Middle East Patterns, Places, People and Politics*, which has a variety of citations for minority groups such as the Armenians, fails to mention at all the place, role, contribution or status of women in the 'patterns, places, people and politics' of the region. What the major textbooks lack, new scholarship, mostly by women, seeks to redress in books specifically dealing with this subject which emerged with increasing frequency in the 1990s. Scholarship on this subject, however, has not emerged in some universal form, as Kandiyoti (1996) reminds us: 'advances in feminist scholarship have been incorporated into studies about the Middle East in a partial and selective manner' (p. 18).

Feminist scholarship on the Middle East has traditionally been Eurocentric. Even Arab feminist scholars from within the region have viewed their experiences through a European social science lens. One impact of colonialism, for example, has been a small educated elite of Arab women who have been schooled by Europeans or according to European traditions of teaching and scholarship. A subsequent outcome of this has been a tendency in the past for Arab feminist scholars to base their work on western political science, sociological or anthropological approaches. Kandiyoti believes that since the 1960s contemporary feminist scholarship and Middle East studies have passed through four 'waves' – from writing which has concentrated on the colonial experience and independence movements of the earlier part of the twentieth century, 'feminism and nationalism', through 'the rise of social science paradigms and developments' and 'dialogues within feminism' to the current wave in which feminist theorists debate which path women should take as one millennium ended and another begins (Kandiyoti, 1996, pp. 1–18). Feminist scholarship in the Middle East also encompasses a variety of disciplines, from anthropologists engaged in traditional studies of women's dress, embroidery and jewellery to social scientists studying the lives of urban Egyptian women in Cairo. In sociology, economics, politics, literature, art, agricultural and development studies, international relations and politics, feminist researchers and authors from inside and outside the region are attempting to rewrite women into the landscape of the Middle East.

In 1986, feminist theorist Beverly Thiele (1986) argued that 'it is common knowledge among feminists that social and political theory was, and for the most part still is, written by men, for men and about men' (p. 30). It takes no great leap of imagination to apply this statement to current writing on the Middle East. The literature on contemporary politics in the region, like so many other aspects of life, has reflected a predominantly male-centric agenda and thus 'their subject matter reflects male concerns, deals with male activity and male ambitions and is directed away from issues involving or of concern to women' (Thiele, 1986, p. 30). The arrival of feminist authors who seek to gender the politics of the region stands as a glimmer of hope in this barren landscape. They are putting women back into the study of politics, particularly in the realm of informal politics where they have greater influence and power. These authors are also challenging the current conceptualization of the region, making it clear that 'ostensibly neutral political processes and concepts such as nationalism, citizenship and the state' are not only Eurocentric but 'fundamentally gendered' and therefore biased as well (Waylen, 1996, p. 5). Given the contested nature of these concepts in the Middle East, the additional gender bias must also go some way in reshaping the ideas and lens through which the region can successfully be viewed and understood.

To what extent the above-stated goals will ever be achieved, particularly in the short term, is highly questionable. The women of the Middle East, like their counterparts in the rest of the Third World, will not be transformed overnight by feminist thinking, approaches and activities designed to transform patterns of patriarchal politics which have dominated the region for centuries. What remains important, however, is the process by which feminist approaches have in one form or another encouraged women to rethink their place – politically, culturally, religiously and economically. Through a gradualist approach, women are starting to look at themselves anew. This is not to say that political emancipation or opportunities for greater personal freedoms and rights have an assured future; the gatekeepers to such processes enabling the transformation of women's lives in the region remain male. In addition, the traditional barriers to women's progress need to be removed in a campaign to win support, not create enemies. Islam, at least in theory, can, for many Muslim and Islamist women, provide a degree of freedom and independence which hitherto remained largely unchallenged. Indeed, there is an increasing trend within the region, from Morocco to Iran, of women challenging the so-called authenticity of male-imposed Islamic prohibitions. The challenge mounted by Saudi women against the Wahabi-inspired prohibition of women driving is just one such example. Authors such as Jawad (1998) also highlight Saudi Arabia's treatment of women to 'highlight the great discrepancy between, on the one hand, the genuine Islamic position vis-à-vis women's education, and, on the other, the policy expressed in Saudi Arabia', which is restrictive to say the least (p. 29). Also, outside as well as within the Muslim realm, aspects of womanhood in the region are celebrated and amongst their own company women enjoy a freedom that celebrates a multi-layered identity of woman-and-motherhood. The gendering of the Middle East provides the opportunity for new frontiers to be established and new thinking to emerge which would be of benefit to everyone.

Case study Palestinian women in the West Bank and Gaza Strip

Traditionally, the call for women's rights and equality in Palestinian society was muted by the broader and stronger appeal for national unity in the struggle against Zionism and later Israeli occupation. From the 1920s Palestinian women were either involved in charity work or served as adjuncts to the male-dominated national movement. In the late 1970s and early 1980s a change in the women's movement occurred; women organized politically affiliated committees to address the issues of work, economy and childcare. Women's participation in decision-making at a national level or in the leadership of the PLO was almost non-existent. The committees, although a step forward, were always subordinated to the PLO and the issues they addressed were subordinated under the call for national unity until independence.

The outbreak of the Palestinian Intifada in December 1987 went some way to altering the traditional patriarchal hold over political activism and women's issues that Palestinian men had previously enjoyed (Said, 1989). The Intifada also presented women with new problems, and serious attempts were made by conservative nationalists and Islamists to undermine the position of women in society and the limited freedoms that many were enjoying for the first time. For better or for worse then, the Intifada changed the lives of many Palestinian women.

For the better, women from all backgrounds and classes, particularly in the first two years of the uprising, enjoyed unprecedented freedom to organize politically both in terms of formal and informal activities. Thus, as well as literally taking to the streets to protest against the Israeli occupation, they were also key figures in the network of popular committees which sprang up throughout the West Bank and Gaza Strip (Jad, 1991). The public space which they occupied was shared, temporarily, with men, but the political structure of the Intifada, the United National Leadership of the Uprising (UNLU) which was the local arm of the PLO, remained male-dominated, and women were largely excluded from decision-making about strike days, demonstrations, strategy and tactics designed to maintain national unity and achieve the goal of ending the occupation.

The uprising also presented women with other dilemmas and difficulties, excluding them in a number of ways. The closure of schools and universities prevented them from gaining or finishing their education, and many young women were pressured into marrying early in the absence of opportunities for education and employment. At home, women were left to carry the burden of responsibility while many thousands of men were imprisoned by the Israeli authorities. The rise of traditional Islamic values fostered by the mainstream Hamas movement also led to increasing authority exercised by men over women's lives. The return to traditional values led to campaigns organized by Hamas and tacitly supported by the mainstream nationalist movement to compel women to stay at home, look after the family, raise and educate children, and dress in a modest and Islamic fashion. As Hammami notes, the impact of the *hijab* campaign waged by Hamas in the early 1990s was manifold, yet initially resulted in women feeling frightened and marginalized from the public space. One unforeseen outcome, however, was the resistance mounted by Palestinian women, feminists and activists to this issue: 'If Hamas succeeded to some extent in Islamicizing Palestinian national culture, it simultaneously succeeded in bringing parts of the Palestinian women's movement to a new feminist awareness . . . that ignoring social issues had been extremely short-sighted' (Hammami, 1997, p. 205).

These campaigns communicated a powerful message to Palestinian women, a message with echoes of the Algerian revolution: women must subordinate their claims to equality, their calls for freedom and choice, and these desires must be sacrificed to the greater goal of an end to the Israeli occupation of the West Bank and Gaza Strip and national independence for the Palestinian people. While the majority of Palestinian women bowed down in the face of political demands from the patriarchal leadership of the nationalist movement, a small minority refused to put their demands to one side. As Glavanis-Grantham (1996) notes, 'Palestinian women activists warn of the dangers of subordinating the social struggle to the national struggle to the extent that women may have the gains of the Intifada subverted and return to and be forced to return to the domesticity of former years, as were women activists in post-liberation Algeria' (p. 176). The reality, however, reflects the Algerian situation more closely than many women would desire. First, a feminist agenda is still regarded with suspicion even by progressive and leftist elements of the nationalist political patriarchy. Second, since the signing of the Oslo Accords between Israel and the PLO in September 1993, the era of 'limited autonomy' under the leadership of Yasser Arafat did little to inspire confidence in these matters.

Palestinian self-rule in the West Bank and Gaza Strip has been beset with a variety of problems since the establishment of the Palestinian National Authority (PNA) in 1993. One major issue associated with the interim period of limited autonomy has been the question of how democracy survives the authoritarian tendencies of the PNA and the cadres of the PLO who have returned from Tunis. The promotion and maintenance of democracy is inextricably linked to the debate about equality and women's rights as well as to the feminist agenda which Palestinians embrace. To date, the outlook is not encouraging; the institutions of the PNA, the Legislative Council and the nationalist hierarchy remain male-dominated. Women such as Umm jihad (the wife of assassinated PLO leader Abu jihad) were utilized in a token fashion to provide a veneer of equality to the political leadership. Women's issues are not being given the long-promised attention they deserve and in areas of basic legislation and law women's rights to equality and equal status are not being acknowledged by the new generation of legislators. Indeed, like most nationalist movements which have attained some form of power within the Middle East, the position of the PNA on women's rights is depressingly familiar. As Hammami (1997) noted, the PNA's stance on the role of women in nation-building is tokenistic: 'wives of the elite as representatives of national womanhood; and a preference for modernist appearances . . . avoidance of changing the real underpinnings of women's oppression by addressing legislation or unequal power relations' (p. 206). Even at community level, the battle for equality has fared little better. As Giacaman and Johnson (1994) remark: 'the increase in feminist consciousness, often remarked on, has so far found little resonance in institutional struggles over women's issues, whether at schools and universities, factories or hospitals – three sites where women's presence and gender inequalities might reasonably engender women's demands' (p. 25). The Palestinian women's movement is, however, today diverse in terms of its voices and its discourse but it faces an uphill struggle in bringing the rights and equality debate to the forefront of local political discourse. The election of Hamas to government in 2006 gave further concern in many circles intent on promoting women's rights.

Case study From beyond the veil – Iran since the Revolution

While the issue of nationalism, feminism and revolution has been addressed in previous sections, the example of the Iranian Revolution of 1979 allows us an opportunity to ask the same questions of Islamic nationalism and the theocracy that was established in its name. The women's movement in Iran since 1979 has experienced mixed fortunes and the rise and fall of two distinct approaches to women's rights – the secularized approach which has been all but forced into exile and the emergence of an Islamic feminism which has struggled to maintain its autonomy from the state. Antagonisms remain, yet there is a consensus that the issue of women and their rights was and remains an important platform in legitimating the populist appeal of the Islamic republic as well as resistance to it (Moghissi, 1995; Afshar, 1998).

Under the regime of Mohammed Reza Shah Pahlavi, progress in women's rights and the women's movement was a state-sponsored exercise. Women enjoyed little if no autonomy from the regime to organize themselves. Social progress under the Shah was dictated by the state not in response to popular will or sentiment, but in an attempt to continue the modernization and westernization of Iran. The remit of modernization and westernization, slavishly replicating the values of the West and rejecting indigenous and authentic tradition, was a public exercise where women were concerned. While the Shah's father had outlawed the veiling of women and his son maintained the public façade of progress, in private – in the home – little progress was made. There the rights of men, the husband, brother, father or nephew, prevailed. Women were still left unprotected, legislation did not emerge and women lived a dual existence. In the workplace and in public they wore mini-skirts, make-up and worked in a mixed environment, because the state dictated it. At home, they obeyed the laws of the family, laws determined by religion and their men. As Paidar (1996) astutely remarks, 'The Pahlavi regime opposed women's independence in the family and their independent presence in the public sphere, and this influenced the logic behind state-sponsored women's organizations which made sure that women's lives inside and outside the home remained under the control of male guardians' (p. 56).

It was this controlling environment that encouraged a generation of Iranian women to turn to Islam as a source for the construction of their identity as women and opposition to the state and its image of the modern Iranian woman. The Revolution of 1979 was notable for the wide-scale participation and support of women. Khomeini and the Shi'a clergy promoted a vision of an Islamic utopia where Iranian women believed their rights would finally be recognized. The theocracy went some way, at least initially, in encouraging women in this belief. The new political leadership was as quick to utilize the issue of women as had been their predecessors. In this version of the story, however, women were idealized in a different way. They were the guardians of Islam, their veiling, their segregation, education and role as mothers and daughters would symbolize the strength of the theocracy. If under Reza Shah women were the epitome of modern Iranian society, then under Khomeini they would be depicted as the symbols of the revolution. This view, however, was almost immediately challenged by women themselves, who in March 1979 organized marches to protest enforced veiling. The impact of this political challenge to Khomeini, however, went unsupported, as a variety of political and social organizations struggled to adjust to the new realities. State repression of this form of activism automatically followed, and this first battle by women was lost (Moghissi, 1994). The state image of women, following this early defeat, was further embedded in the Iranian consciousness during the eight-year war with Iraq (1980–8), when millions of Iranian men were at the battlefront while women maintained the economy and their families at home.

Islamicization of Iran following the Revolution of 1979, therefore, impacted on women's lives in a variety of ways. First, however, there was the unexpected privilege of increased political rights for women, including the franchise and the constitutional right to stand for public positions, except as President. Contrary to western and other expectations, the theocracy in Iran did not ape the conservative regime of Saudi Arabia or other parts of the Gulf in prohibiting women from voting or denying them other rights to political participation. As citizens in their own right – another progressive step away from traditional Islamic fundamentalist approaches – Iranian women were afforded the right to vote in the many elections that would take place for the President, Constitution and *Majlis* (national assembly). While women who stood for election in Jordan were condemned by Islamists, who issued fatwas declaring them heretics, in Iran the Shi'ia clergy actually empowered women in this sphere. Once again, the state set the agenda and women's independence and autonomy was severely undermined (Zubaida, 1997). Thus, while it is true that some considerable difficulties were encountered by women in the early stages of the revolution, aspects of their political, employment, legal and other rights were eventually improved and institutionalized by the state. These early setbacks may have had much to do with the overwhelming desire by Khomeini and his followers to impose an idealized Islamic vision of state and society which was subsequently followed by the much-remarked upon progression to pragmatism. Pragmatism, combined with the idealism of the conservative wing of the ruling *ulama*, has, however, resulted in an often contradictory policy emanating from government on issues such as population control, employment rights and education, which affect Iranian women on a daily basis (Hoodfar, 1997).

Once again, many of the changes have been cosmetic and patriarchy has been strengthened through religious sanction from Iran's hard-line clergy. Initial hopes of the realization of a utopia have been reassessed by Iran's feminists, whether they be secular or Islamic. Women once again sit on the margins of society; real political power is consistently denied to them. The parameters of their power lie in the strict confines of the home, but even here the state has managed to reinforce male dominance and legal rights. Yet, as Paidar (1996) reminds us, there have been some notable changes: 'the transformation of Islamist feminism from post-Revolutionary idealism to realism and pragmatism of the late 1980s has been remarkable. This being the case it is no longer inconceivable to envisage strategic alliances between Iranian strands of secular and Islamist feminisms on women's rights issues' (p. 63). The battle for women's rights in Iran is far from over, but it would be wrong to assume that the establishment of the theocracy in 1979 really did so much to change the nature of the issues affecting women's lives. Nor would it be right to assume that the status of women in Iran is any worse by nature of the Islamic republic in which they live. Indeed, the issue is far more complex and problematic than this. Does the woman of Tehran enjoy more or less rights than her sister in Riyadh, Cairo or Algiers? Increasingly, the question can only be answered by talking of degrees of change, not substantive social revolutions that have changed forever the way the women of the Middle East live their lives.

Further reading

A number of general texts on women and the Middle East have been published, including Tucker (1993), an edited text with four parts examining gender discourses, women's work and development, politics and power and gender roles and relations. These themes are also explored in Kandiyoti (1996), which takes a more theoretical perspective in chapters on Iranian studies, women's writing in Egypt and the Israeli–Palestinian accords. Beck and Keddie (1978), Hammami and Reiker (1988), Ahmed (1992), Moghadam (1994a and 1994b) and Lewis (1996) all debate aspects of the gender and Islam phenomenon. Themes of Islam, gender and sexuality are also further explored in Mernissi (1985 and 1991), Sharabi (1988) and L. Ahmed (1992). Relations between contemporary Islamic movements and gender rights are covered in a variety of texts, including chapters in Moghadam (1994a) by Hale on Sudan, Baffoun on the Maghreb, Bouatta and Cherifati-Merabtine on Algeria. Hatem (1994), Badran (1996) and Karam (1998) debate extensively the Islam–state– feminism matrix in a specifically Egyptian context, outlining the sheer breadth of this debate and its historical precedents. The way in which feminist theory has examined these issues is covered in Mernissi (1991) and L. Ahmed (1992), who both go some way to explain the impact of classical orientalist and Eurocentric discourse on women in the Middle East. Kandiyoti (1991) has also edited a text which critically assesses the relationship between the state, Islam and the role and status of women in the Middle East and South Asia. Women from the Middle East are given a platform to express themselves in Fernea and Bezirgan (1997), where more than twenty chapters provide an opportunity for writing about tradition, transition, colonialism and nationalism as well as future directions. Khoury and Moghadam (1995) have written on gender and development in the Arab world, looking at economic and work issues and this is partly supplemented by Moghadam's work of 2003. Introductory overviews of women's rights, legal status and economic standing are found in Graham-Brown (1994) and Khalidi and Tucker (1994), as well as Doumato and Posusney (2003). Debates and analysis of the Palestinian women's movement and the role of Palestinian women in nationalism and as subjects of Islamic politics are covered in Peteet (1991), Young (1992) and Sharoni (1995). Najjar and Warnock (1992), Strum (1992), Augustin (1993), Mayer (1994), and Fleischmann (2003) all make valuable contributions to this subject. A number of articles or chapters dealing with these issues which are worth reading include Jad (1991) and Hammami (1997), as well as Hiltermann (1991) and Rubenberg (2001), who cover issues of women's politics. The role and voices of Iranian women in feminism and the Islamic republic are covered in a variety of texts, including Tabari and Yeganeh (1982), Tohidi (1991), Gerami (1994), Moghissi (1994 and 1995), Hoodfar (1997), Mir-Hosseini (2000) and Afshar (1998). A historical overview on this topic can be found in texts such as the edited text from Beck and Nashat (2004) and Shahidian (2002). Further light on this theme is also found in Najmabadi (2005).

Ethnicity and Minorities

Introduction

ETHNIC issues, concepts of ethnicity and ethnic rights are familiar in one way or another to all of us. The 1990s saw an explosion of ethnic conflict which hitherto had been suppressed under the tyranny of communism and state socialism in many parts of the world. As ideological conflict of the type witnessed during the Cold War appeared to go into decline, new forms of contestation appear to have arisen, as Moynihan (1993) has described: 'Nation-states no longer seem inclined to go to war with one another, but ethnic groups fight all the time. Inevitably, many of these ethnic clashes make their way into the realm of international politics' (p. 5). The horror of ethnic cleansing entered our vocabulary, whether referring to the Kurds, Rwanda or Northern Ireland. The rise of transnational corporations, the telecommunication revolution and the global village also means we experience the ethnic without venturing from our own shores. Through a barrage of ethnic music, food, art, literature and clothing, the ethnic 'other' is represented, and the boundaries of ethnic identity are constructed. Ethnic identity is a variable in politics (domestic, regional or international); it is also malleable, and whether one agrees or not over whether it has either certain primordial or ascribed characteristics, it is also shaped by subjectively interpreted historical experiences, combining, as Barth explains, to give both objective characteristics, such as language, religion, territory, social organization, culture, race and common origin, and subjective characteristics, which are a mix of any of the above or of any other 'markers' by a group to assert its identity (Barth, 1969). Terms of reference that may formerly have incorporated class or other factors have presently been substituted by the ethnic label which thus, it is presumed, becomes an explanation in itself. Ethnicity, ethnic rights and ethnic claims are symptoms of modernity, the new world order and the continuing inability, whatever way things are presented, to solve, at a global level, the myriad of conflicts involving competing ethnic or minority claims (Horowitz, 1985). Our present-day concerns are recent in origin, 'connections among Biafra, Bangladesh, and Burundi, Beirut, Brussels, and Belfast were at first hesitantly made – isn't one "tribal", one "linguistic", another "religious"? – but that is true no longer. Ethnicity has fought and bled and burned its way into public and scholarly consciousness' (Horowitz, 1985, p. xi). It is the inability to resolve what is now referred to as ethnic conflict that concerns policy-makers and opinion-setters when they look to the Middle East. It is not the ethnic communities themselves that present the problem, rather their conflicts, lack of rights and claims to self-determination and independence which lie at the heart of the issue and could threaten stability within the region. Ethnic politics and ethnic conflict have assumed a new importance, as Esman and Rabinovitch (1988) note: 'In other words, ethnic conflict can explain more of politics in the Middle East than is reflected in academic writing' (p. 4). In addition, this overview of the ethnic dimension once again highlights the important linkages in themes such as nationalism and political Islam, which were discussed in earlier chapters. In the Middle East, then, ethnicity has developed a special meaning. The concept is perceived as a relative newcomer to the region, linked to conflicts and tensions within nation-states. Some might argue that the ethnic tensions of the 1990s and the early twenty-first century are the inevitable result of the failure of the colonial powers years ago to take account of such factors when they carved up the region into new nation-states and forced distinct and diverse groups to live alongside each other under one flag and one nation. The issue of ethnicity and minority rights are inextricably linked with the nation-state, nationalism, popular sovereignty and nationality. The rights of many ethnic groups and minorities in the region have been ruthlessly suppressed, irrespective of the governing ideologies of states as diverse as Iraq and Saudi Arabia. As such, the debate about ethnic and minority rights in the region has as much to say about the nature of the nation-state and its legitimacy as it does about demands for self-determination or independence.

This chapter sets out to explore the concept of ethnicity and look at the experiences of minority groups within the region. While not all minority groups are ethnic in origin, the nature of the nation-state in the region has conspired against such groups in the same way as it has against ethnic minorities. Therefore, while the Copts of Egypt may be a religious minority group, their experiences at the hands of the state and the majority population are very similar to those of the Kurds in Iraq or the Shi'a minority in Saudi Arabia. The case studies of the ethnic claims of Kurds and the minority status of Muslim Alawites in Syria are, however, designed to highlight the problems that exist between ethnic and minority groups and their different relations with the nation-state as it is currently constituted in the region.

Defining ethnicity

The debate about ethnicity, ethnic rights and ethnic politics in the Middle East reflects a number of changes in the scholarship of the region. While ethnic group ties and solidarity have always existed within the region, politics was regarded as significantly unaffected by such issues. Analysis of politics was class-based, or centred on the classical orientalist and post-orientalist positions. Ethnic groups were largely confined to the realm of study by anthropologists and to debates about tribe and clan, and removed from the political study of nation and state (Tibi, 1996). It is useful, therefore, at this point to raise some key theoretical perspectives on the importance, definition and concept of ethnicity within the region. The first debate, outlined by Esman and Rabinovich, is defined as one between primordialism and instrumentalism. In brief, primordialists believe that rooted 'given' identities are a major feature of ethnicity and politics in the region. Islam, for example, is commonly cited as one of these rooted 'givens' and presented as unchanging, rigid and monolithic in shaping politics and political outcomes in society. Instrumentalists, however, appreciate a more subjective construction of ethnicity among the peoples of the region, its relationship to the construction of nation and nationalism. In addition, 'to the more extreme instrumentalists', argue Esman and Rabinovich (1988), 'ethnic and confessional solidarities survive only as long as they pay – as long as they provide more security, status and material rewards than do available alternatives' (p. 13).

The extent to which one accepts either argument or definition will also influence any subsequent analysis of ethnic politics or interaction in the many ethnically plural societies of the region. Brown, for example, perceives ethnic 'givens' – primordial loyalties – as an important factor in characterizing the political culture of the region, exhibited by jealous loyalty to a small-group particularism (religious, ethnic, linguistic, tribal) (Brown, 1984, p. 143). Brown refers to and talks about the persistence of traditional Middle Eastern political culture in the modern age. This political culture is based on a backward-looking mosaic of ethnic, tribal and religious groups which, when faced with the modernizing forces of nation, nationalism and institutions of government based on universal rather than specific characteristics, retreats to primordial loyalties and associated behaviour. This 'given' pattern of political culture, for Brown, explains communal resistance to change and the appeal of so-called traditional religious political forces. Thus, as Bromley (1994) argues, for writers such as Brown (1984) and Bill and Springborg (1994), the problem of ethnicity and minorities is then seen primarily as one of the resistance of such primordial groups and identities to wider, potentially universal notions of ideology, rights and community. This notion of resistance to a particular type of political change is also partially reflected by Esman and Rabinovich (1988), who speak of all ethnic communities in the region as having 'mobilized for political combat' as a result of the new state structures and institutions. A riposte to this perception of ethnic politics and primordial identity can be detected in Zubaida (1993), who argues for a more mobilizational reading of ethnicity, reflecting, in turn, Anderson's (1983) concepts of constructed and imagined identities. In this respect, Zubaida also embraces the instrumentalist approach to explaining the 'political field', pointing out that 'in many countries the ultimate triumph of a particular group or current culminated in the monopolization and the suppression of the whole political field' (1993, p. 146). Ethnic identities and ethnic politics in relation to new political units such as the nation-state, therefore, can be conceived, argues Zubaida, in new ways and the contention that primordial loyalties will always 'out' is resisted through the argument that, while 'communalist sentiments enter into the political field . . . the form they take is shaped and sometimes transformed by the forces and conjunctures of that field' (p. 149). In illustrating his argument, Zubaida reflected on the example of Iraq's Shi'a majority while under the rule of Saddam Hussein, pointing out that 'the Iraqi Shi'a, for instance, never constituted a unitary political force, but that Shi'a interests and outlooks contributed significant inputs into various political movements and forces at different points in time' (p. 149). The same might also be argued in the example of the Armenian community of the West Bank and its role in the Palestinian community, articulation of national identity and struggle for self-determination and independence. In addition, this debate engenders a need for both an historical and comparative perspective which recognizes new scholarship on this subject. In the past much of the debate about ethnicity in the Middle East was posited on a comparative historical and often orientalist perspective. The region was always defined as the exception in relation to, first, comparative experiences in the West and, second, historical observations of politics in the region since the collapse of the Ottoman Empire. In this respect, as I have previously argued, analysis and understanding of ethnicity was tied to debates about the meanings of nationalism and political Islam. If one returns to the first point, however, it is not difficult to discern the myopic Eurocentric tendencies inherent in the approach of, say, Kedourie and his notion of ethnicity and nationalism, which he argues is a modern western doctrine which when translated within the region led to an abuse and destruction of this particular vocabulary of European politics (Kedourie, 1988, p. 31). Yet Kedourie's complaints about abuse of vocabulary and outcomes should be reflected back on the European standard-bearer. Connor (1994) has done this, pointing out that, in the case of nation, 'there is no formula', which presumably leads one to question what will be exported (p. 99). Indeed, in place of formula there are myths, lies and notions of ethnic and racial superiority, which will always alter the way in which writers like Kedourie and Lewis view ethnic bases, identity and loyalties in the region.

In the past, then, ethnicity was viewed from a broad base, the region consisted of Arabs and Persians and was largely constructed as Arab. The Arab world, however, hides a multiplicity of ethnic and sectarian difference, which is evident in a variety of Arab states as well as Israel and Persian Iran. Anthony Smith (1991) writes that by ethnic groups we mean 'a type of cultural collectivity, one that emphasises the role of myths of descent and historical memories, and is recognized by one or more cultural differences like religion, customs, language or institutions' (p. 20). From this definition a variety of groups throughout the Middle East may be described as ethnic – Jews, Arabs, Berbers, Persians, Alawites, Tuareg, Armenians, Maronites, Marsh Arabs and so on. In addition, a variety of countries in the region have in the past or are now experiencing degrees of ethnic conflict or tensions within and across their borders. Ethnicity is perceived as an important element of the politics of identity in the region. While some identities and associated ideologies have waxed and waned, others have arisen to fill the vacuum of ideological retreat and crisis. In an earlier chapter I identified Islam as currently playing this role, co-existing and attempting to replace other identities and loyalties, yet, according to Smith's definition, Islam is but one element of ethnic solidarity and alongside this religious marker co-exist or compete other identities, which people also believe in. From this emerges stratified identity, which includes a variety of elements from the religious, to nation and family. This point is discussed at length by Khalidi (1997) in his historical treatment of the emergence of Palestinian identity at the turn of the century.

Ethnic identity, as I have already mentioned, also created, through belief and perception, something Anderson (1983) aptly described as 'imagined communities'. The example of Israel is a case in point. Until the establishment of the Zionist movement in the late 1890s, the Jews were regarded as a religious minority. Herzl's vision of a revived Jewish nation transformed this dispersed community into an ethnic group from which the establishment of a nation-state would emerge. Israel is an ethnic state, predicated on the survival of the Jewish people, not as a religious collective but as a national and ethnic collective, hence the revival of Hebrew as the linguistic identifier of this group. The Jews, according to Anderson's approach, achieved this task through the imagined community, creating, maintaining and sustaining the perception of a revived Hebrew nation in the Holy Land. Thus, in so far as there is an Israeli nation, it is because its members believe in their difference, sustain difference, celebrate it and have consolidated it through the foundation of a nation-state. The ethnic conflict arises out of Israel's denial of Arab ethnic rights or recognition of the Palestinian community as distinct. The gulf of ethnic division between the Palestinians and Israelis has, thus, appeared as so wide it is impossible to breach. Constructed ethnic identities, therefore, are proving highly durable and a lasting issue for the entire region.

Ethnic conflict in the region is not rare; it is an all-too-frequent fact of political life. Although the majority of state systems in the region have vigorously pursued policies designed to repress and hide from the rest of the world their ethnic problems, one way or another their secrets emerge. Obviously there is a danger in ascribing to conflict an ethnic dimension which is artificially construed. In the twenty-first century our preoccupation with what appears to be the global pheno-menon of ethnic politics, identity, conflict and cleansing, means that we have looked at conflict anew in the Middle East. Disputes which were previously described as nationalist, class-based or otherwise are currently being reassessed by the fashionable and pronounced as ethnic after all. The tragedy of sectarian conflict and civil war in Lebanon is no longer the only case cited. While ethnicity may just be one of the identities the people call on, the conclusion in terms of the Middle East is that it currently assumes greater importance. Protracted ethnic/communal conflicts in the Middle East, of which as many as eleven had been identified between 1945 and 1989, are described as having 'caused more misery and loss of human life than has any other type of local, regional, or international conflict . . . and the source of most of the world's refugees' (Gurr and Harff, 1994, p. 7).

As such, there is also an optimistic belief that if the various regimes or state types of the region – one-party, monarchical, etc. – can change and reform their political systems to accommodate the demands of their minority, ethnic and religious communities, that conflict will subside, economies will prosper and people will be happy to reside in plural and democratic states. This correlation will be tested to its fullest extent in post-war Iraq. Since the toppling of Saddam Hussein's regime in 2003, the extent to which Iraq's main ethnic elements – and in particular the Kurds – have been able to reconcile ethnic demands with the maintenance of the state has been limited to say the least. I say democratic because, as we know from the chapter on democratization, it has been argued that without a democratic injection the politics of ethnicity in the Middle East can never be accommodated in a way which actually reflects the plural nature of society and those individuals living in the region. As Richards and Waterbury (1990) assert:

> It is the case that no sectarian or ethnic groups can be analysed or understood within their own terms of reference. In every instance there will be at stake elements of the distribution of scarce resources, of making concessions that might jeopardize national unity, of reacting to minority demands in such a way as to call the regime's legitimacy into question. (p. 346)

The prospects for the translation of pluralism into patterns of politics in the region, however, are not good. There is a belief that pluralism will naturally be associated with instability and the breakdown of stable political orders. The promotion of politics which recognize the rights of minorities to parity of esteem within the region is absent from the largely homogenic and coercive control of one group over others. The desire, for example, by the Wahabi majority in Saudi Arabia to maintain stability of the state structure and perpetuate the rule of the al-Saud family has effectively stifled any hope for pluralism for other religious or ethnic groups living in that state. The situation is exacerbated by the argument which the al-Saud family forwards in defence of this state of affairs. They use their particular Wahabi interpretation of Islam to argue for stratified notions of citizenship and discrimination on sectarian grounds against other sects within Islam as well as other faiths. Indeed, Islam is commonly cited by orientalists as an obstacle to true plurality of politics in the region, as is its history of ethnic discrimination, tension and conflict. As Vatikiotis (1988) has argued, 'If an Islamic order is, as defined by its proponents, a total system, it cannot entertain political pluralism, only political separatism . . . All this suggests that, despite Islamic protestations to the contrary, minorities remain anxious and apprehensive, and sectarian conflict persists' (p. 68). Not everyone, however, would agree with this view, pointing to historical examples but also positing the argument, as Ben-Dor (1988) has, that Islam can maintain pluralism through notions of stratified community: 'Islam has been known to be tolerant, pluralistic and integrative . . . In some of these cases, Islam is the ultimate community . . . But this does not necessarily undermine the possibility of other communities existing on other levels . . . Therefore, Islamic resurgence and ethnic reassertion are not at odds' (p. 88). Could the same arguments be constructed in the case of Israel's legislation on citizenship which, as discussed in chapter 6, prejudices the rights of its Arab citizens in favour of its Jewish citizens as a deliberately constructed ethnic polity? While it is true that state-led forms of ethnic discrimination or mismanagement are rife throughout the region, the reasons for this method of politics or state control are myriad in source and explanation.

Minority status

Many minorities populate the Middle East and thus it is important to highlight that this chapter is reflecting principally on religious, ethnic or linguistic minority groups such as the Coptic Christians in Egypt, Armenians in Lebanon and Syria or the Jews who used to live in Yemen. Any other talk of minorities, from an economic, gender or other perspective, would not only be time-consuming but largely irrelevant. There is, however, an argument to be made for distinguishing the debate about minorities from ethnicity for two very important reasons. First, while the issue of ethnicity and ethnic politics in the Middle East does have some bearing on the minority status of groups within certain states, like the Kurds in Iran, not all ethnic politics or ethnic conflict is necessarily about minority–majority relations. In addition, not all minority–majority conflict can be ascribed with a strictly ethnic characteristic. It would be unhelpful, for example, to describe the communal tensions in Syria between the Alawite minority and Sunni majority as ethnic, when both groups are Arab in ethnic origin but differ in terms of internally driven religious identities. In addition, the conflict between Iraq's majority Arab Shi'a and minority Arab Sunni population is not ethnic in nature, and has more to do with Ba'th politics and the nature of the state in Iraq than other ethnic debates. Nevertheless, the role of minorities in the Middle East has been and remains an important factor in understanding the nature of the state and politics.

Historically, the Middle East has acted as a magnet for minorities, in particular for the religious of the three monotheistic faiths of Judaism, Christianity and Islam. Within each faith the region has hosted the numerous sects and schisms which have emerged over the centuries. Minority status in religious terms has had both its advantages and disadvantages, as the course of history has shaped the majority composition of the area. For seven hundred years before the collapse of the Ottoman Empire during World War I, the religious status of the majority community had been Sunni Islam. As a result, minority religious and linguistic communities in the region were tolerated according to strict rules and guidelines from the Koran. Jews and Christians would never enjoy equal status, Islam was regarded as a superior and final revelation, but the Prophet Mohammed had passed on God's word and ruled on the special respect and treatment that co-existing religious groups could expect to enjoy. The Ottoman caliphs in Istanbul continued this tradition until the defeat of the empire and the fall of the Middle East into colonial hands. The picture outlined in the narrative above is a general one and cannot account for specific ethnic/religious tensions such as those in Lebanon in the nineteenth century between Christian and Druze. Yet it does remain relevant to the issue of communal relations, say between Jew and Arab in Palestine at the turn of the century, before the country fell into British hands.

The colonizers, the imperial powers of France and Britain, treated the existence of a multiplicity of religious groups in the region quite differently. They had used the claim of defence for their co-religionists to gain a foothold in the region in the latter half of the nineteenth century – this was particularly true in the Levant. Once in the region they further used the 'religious card' as a means of pursuing a policy of divide and rule to weaken Arab claims to national unity, independence and self-determination. In Syria and Lebanon the French actively pursued a policy of divide and rule among the Druze and Maronite Christian community, which exacerbated pre-existing tensions that had already erupted in episodes of violence in the 1860s. In Palestine, the British policy of divide and rule among Jew, Muslim and Christian tore the country apart and plunged the region into a conflict from which it has yet to recover. While it would be untrue to argue that religious tension was absent during the centuries of Ottoman rule, one can assert with certainty that the advent of colonial rule over the region corresponded strongly with an upsurge in tension of this nature. In a world where the boundaries of the region were literally redrawn, where new states were created and new leaders appointed to positions of power, there is an argument that religious loyalty, along with tribal and family affiliations, was resurgent. Under these new political conditions there were perceived advantages among minority groups in seeking alliances and, therefore, benefiting from the colonial rulers, even at the expense of fellow citizens. As Firro (1988) reminds us in the example of the Druze in Syria and Lebanon, the French pursued a policy of divide and rule among and between religious communities, encouraging them to 'establish Alawi, Druze and Lebanese states and grant each of them domestic autonomy . . . the French hoped to co-opt the . . . Druze and thereby gain a weapon to do battle against the Syrian nationalist movement' (p. 188). The minority community gained much under this game of politics, but colonial patronage had its price when the region's states gained independence from the colonial masters.

Religious minorities fared less well in the 1950s and 1960s when universal ideologies such as Arab nationalism and pan-Arabism attempted to render divisive the pre-existing primordial loyalties that had encouraged people into religious or linguistic minorities and particularism. With a few notable exceptions, one of which – the Alawites – is discussed below, religious and other minority groups in the region have experienced decades where their status has been regularly undermined by autocratic politically monolithic and anti-plural states. For example, the Shi'a minority of Saudi Arabia and other Gulf states has had its rights consistently undermined by the state and as a result its lack of autonomy, independence and freedom have forced it into radical political acts. The irony of the situation is that, until states are threatened by minority groups, little is done to encourage them to identify with the state. Yet, the rise of minority consciousness is a global phenomenon; religious minorities in a variety of states and in particular in the Third World are demanding, at the least, fair and equal status. In the Middle East there is barely a country that does not experience serious tensions and conflicts between majority and minority populations. The question this poses is to what extent is this tension the product of authoritarian government in the region and thus the problem which many Arab governments experience in terms of legitimacy. No doubt the answer does lie, to a great extent, in anti-democratic forms of rule which exist in the plural societies of the region, and the legitimacy debate reflects the marginal role many minority groups play in these political systems and governments.

The state and identity

The nature of the state in the Middle East has greatly affected the debate about ethnicity and ethnic politics. Predominant state types, be they monarchical, one-party, imam-chief or post-colonial, have all sought to overcome the problems of creating identity in territorial units which are considered new, the creation of external powers and artificial. State-building, under these conditions, whether in post-colonial Algeria or Hashemite Jordan, has always incorporated a strong desire by the ruling elite to create new identity, including new symbols, which in one way or another transcend pre-existing ethnic, religious, linguistic, tribal or clan loyalties. The process of transcending past loyalties has occurred through a variety of methods, mostly associated with strategies of aggressive statist assimilation or, at the other extreme, marginalization and even ethnic cleansing/genocide. Whatever the strategies, the ruling elite of a variety of states in the region have all faced the same problem, creating new identities in territorial units under which a variety of distinct ethnic or other groupings co-exist. Even relatively ethnically homogeneous states like

Israel, which was established on the premise of special ethnic inclusion for Jews and exclusion of all other ethnic groups, particularly the Arabs, have encountered difficulties in creating a sense of national identity which the majority may aspire to and recognize as their own.

The nation-state, the dominant political unit of the twentieth century, demands much and has created a variety of problems in the Middle East in relation to the region's ethnic, religious and linguistic plurality. This should not be surprising given the debates about national identity within the nation-state that are currently under way in the United Kingdom, with proposed devolution for minorities and ethnic groups such as the Scots, Welsh and Northern Irish – in other words, the states of the Middle East are not alone in facing these issues in the post-Cold War global order. Primarily, however, the nation-state, by its very definition, demands the loyalty of a nation; a sense of national consciousness must exist and the state should derive its legitimacy from its citizens. The nation-states of the region have encountered a variety of difficulties in achieving this consensus and state of national consciousness among its citizens. First, many ruling elites have had to set about creating new identities where other loyalties previously existed. Iraq, for example, is a nation-state, a territorial unit created by the British, which has a national identity; it is a 'nation' that pledges its loyalty to the state and it has been achieved through a variety of strategies employed by successive ruling elites. During the mandate the British established monarchical rule through the Hashemite Prince Faisal and the new nation-state of Iraq over which he (nominally) ruled incorporated a diverse ethnic and sectarian population. The British and its monarch failed to unite the country's diverse population and communal conflict became a regular feature on the political landscape. Following Iraq's independence in 1932 a constitutional monarchy was established but the new independent ruling elite still struggled to create national identity that could transcend pre-existing loyalties, particularly ethnic and sectarian ones. Monarchs, nationalists and a Ba'thist regime in Iraq have all failed ultimately to establish a political system of rule, institutions and government which is both plural enough and strong enough to manage successfully the ethnic and sectarian communities which exist within their borders.

While not all states within the region have suffered the same type of difficulties as Iraq in harmonizing the task of state-building and consolidation with strategies for managing the competing claims of diverse ethnic groups, the majority, as Esman suggests, 'do suffer from the malintegration of state and society, and consequently from limited legitimacy among ethnic groups that are excluded from political power or consider themselves the victims of discriminatory treatment' (Esman and Rabinovich, 1988, p. 277). When integration occurs it is not uniform but usually privileges one majority, or even minority, group (the Alawites in Syria, the Takriti in Iraq, the Jews in Israel) over all the others. This malintegration exacerbates ethnic tension and highlights the lack of formal political mechanisms for plurality and the continuing problem that many states in the region have in generating legitimacy among their citizens. This in turn encourages the dominant regime to employ draconian coercive powers to manage ethnic demands from those groups which remain marginal and outside the political system. In Saudi Arabia, for example, the state has regularly persecuted its Shi'ite population living in the eastern oil-rich Hasa province, treating their co-religionists as alien, ethnically different and marginal to the Wahabi-dominated ruling elite. In other countries, such as Lebanon, malintegration has occurred again because the state is weak, but this time also because the state has failed to balance the demands of this intensely plural society through consociational arrangements. The system collapsed, resulting in civil war (1975–90), because formal mechanisms for plurality were still providing advantages to one group (the Maronites) over others such as the Druze, Shi'ites and Sunni Muslims. In addition, in common with other states in the region, in Lebanon communal problems, ethnic tensions and sectarian differences were exacerbated by the interference of external actors – in this case the Israelis, Syrians and the Americans. Thus, very few, if any, state types in the region, no matter how democratic or authoritarian, have truly managed the pluralism of the societies existing within their borders. Nevertheless, the nation-states of the region have survived, maintained stability and a semblance of national unity for the rest of the world to witness. Obviously, in some states the contrivance of 'nation' is more meaningful than others. In Egypt, successive post-colonial rulers have established the semblance of a nation to which many citizens feel an allegiance without denying other loyalties to family, religion or class. In Kuwait, on the other hand, the privilege of citizenship is bestowed sparingly and notions of national identity, even during times of national crisis – such as the Iraqi occupation of 1990–1 – are largely weak, reflecting a passive attachment to the state which has more to do with wealth than legitimacy and a sense of belonging to a nation. Salame, however, is still content to use Kuwait as an example of a plural society, where 'the principal attraction of the democratic system . . . has been that it is the only system in a position to organize peaceful power-sharing . . . where a hegemonic group could not establish an exclusivist or, at least, an openly dominant position' (1994b, p. 86). Whether the last assertion is true or not, as such, the nation-state in a variety of settings within the region remains in constant conflict with its citizens or inhabitants, and remains weakened by this state of affairs.

Modernization

There is some debate about the impact of modernization on the issue of ethnic politics. Two distinct approaches have emerged around this issue. It is clear, however, that whichever way one looks at it the politics, government and institutions of the region have been affected by the process, and that, in this respect, the Middle East is no different from other regions of the Third World which have experienced the rapid modernization associated with colonialism and post-colonial and independent states. Modernization in the Middle East is believed to imply a process of economic and political development leading to a decline of traditional agricultural and rural-based societies in favour of modern industrialized, urban societies with technological and telecommunications support, increased rates of literacy, decline of the infant mortality rate, improved health care and an open pluralist society that is democratic (Pool, 1993, p. 42). As such, the process of modernization should comfortably incorporate ethnic and minority demands which concurrently become less important the more democratic and responsive government is. In addition, it is presumed that the process of modernization goes some way in weakening traditional 'primordial' loyalties to church, mosque, clan, tribe, ethnic group, etc.

This approach, however, is problematic to say the least. First, there is a huge credibility gap between the idealized and utopian vision of modernization as represented above, and the reality as represented in the contemporary Middle East. Second, unlike the plural societies of the West, the plural societies of the Middle East have not benefited in the same ways, if at all, from the process of modernization. Finally, it has been argued that modernization in the region has strengthened not weakened pre-existing loyalties and ties that people feel to their ethnic group, religious community, tribe, clan and family, and as such the national unity project in the nation-states of the region has been extremely difficult to achieve without regular resort by the state to extreme coercive measures. While the official ideologies of many states in the region have incorporated these goals and themes of modernization, they have remained rhetoric rather than reality. Attempts at modernization within the region, whether socialist, Marxist or capital-led, have encountered a variety of problems of which ethnic and minority rights is one.

For ethnic and minority groups, the process of modernization in their societies has resulted in two types of situation, both of which only serve to heighten their ethnic and communal claims. In the first situation, incorporating a perspective that was prevalent in scholarship of the subject in the 1950s and 1960s, it was argued that failure of the modernization development approach in the Middle East was evident in the continuing importance that people attached to their ethnic, religious or linguistic origins. This situation was evident in Iraq where, despite the *coup d'état* led by Abdel Karim al-Qasim in 1958 and the early promise of modernization and democracy, the Kurdish community and nationalists soon clashed. The revolt of 1961–3 reflected the rapid disillusionment that spread throughout the Kurdish community when modernization failed them. While the national government of Qasim promoted modernization and economic development, the Kurds witnessed a rise in unemployment in their communities, peasant indebtedness, evictions by landlords and uncertainties within the community over the issue of land reform (McDowall, 2003, p. 310). Modernization in Iraq was promoting a sense of isolation within the Kurdish community as they became more marginal, both politically and geographically, from the centre of power.

It would not be true, however, to claim that all ethnic minorities emerged from processes of modernization in the same way. In Algeria, following the war of independence in 1962, the ethnic minority Berbers from the areas of Kabiliya and Aures maintained their role in the nationalist movement and benefited equally from the modernization process, particularly of Algeria's natural gas industry. The Berber political elite, whose leaders had played such an important role in the war of independence, continued to perpetuate and assimilate itself into the new structures of the state form, the bureaucracy and technocratic positions. It is notable that during the Boumedienne period, positive policies of development were instituted for Berber areas, all resulting in the gradual drawing-in of Berber groups. Problems arose as a result of the government policy of the 1970s to 'Arabize' Algeria, eliminate French as the official language and promote a new sense of national identity. Berber dissent, based on the argument that the evolution of national culture should be determined by a free policy of social forces mediated by the state, not directed by it, resulted in a number of disturbances throughout the 1970s and 1980s. Berbers are not nationalists but they have resisted the assimilationist tendencies associated with modernization and promoted by the regime. By the late 1990s, following the alleged government assassination of Berber cultural personalities and leaders, the imposition of Arabic-only legislation and the continuing civil chaos, Berber communal sentiments led to the formation of an armed movement, forcing the government of Lamine Zeroual into a grudging climbdown on certain Berber issues (Silverstein, 1998, p. 3).

Currently, however, many scholars believe, as evident in the Berber example above, that modernization exacerbates ethnic conflict and contributes to it (Esman and Rabinovich, 1988, p. 15). From this perspective, communal conflict rises out of the increased sense of competition generated by the political and economic developments associated with modernization. This places an emphasis on communal and ethnic solidarity and the power attributed to group rather than individual dynamics, leading ethnic or sectarian groups into competition and then conflict, as the case of Lebanon well illustrates. The Lebanese example highlights the strength garnered from strong communal links in the face of a weak non-interventionist capital-led state. Without close communal links in Lebanon, individuals would not derive any benefit from the state. The weakness of the state in Lebanon can be linked to the nature of modernization in the country and the power of laissez-faire policies. It can be concluded, therefore, that civil war in Lebanon was a result of the nature of modernization in the country and the need for communal solidarity in opposition to a weak and ineffective government that failed to disburse basic services to its citizens. Modernization, including its failures, has altered forever the nature of a citizen's links to the state and the ties and support to be derived from ethnic, religious or linguistic communities. Such ties challenge the class-based nature of analysis which was so often used to explain the nature of politics in the region.

Ethno-national and religious battles

The demands of the Middle East's ethnic, linguistic and religious minorities and groups range from modest requests for rights of worship, such as the calls of many Christians living in the Gulf states, to the demand for self-determination and independence made by the Polisario in Morocco's western Sahara. The means by which such groups pursue their claims are dependent on a number of factors, including whether a minority group is compact or scattered, the political character of the state they reside in, the leadership of such communities and the ability or willingness of the dominant regime to concede to a particular group's demands. The strategies employed by minority groups to pursue their various claims range from non-violent petitions and sit-ins, to campaigns of civil disobedience and outright wars of secession. The nature of such strategies is again often determined by the nature of the state they live in. For example, Israel's Palestinian Arab minority are granted citizenship, allowed to participate and compete in the country's democratic elections, run their own municipalities and become members of the Knesset. As such, their grievances are not expressed in terms of secessionist claims or calls for self-determination, but instead focus on issues of equality of rights, opportunities and privilege. While Israel, even though democratic, continues to privilege the rights of one community, the Jews, over the rights of another, the Palestinian Arabs, this minority will remain marginal and continue to put pressure on the government for greater concessions. Consciousness-raising might occur for a number of reasons, including calls for greater rights for a subordinate community, independence and self-determination or autonomy.

Political mobilization around these issues may take place in a variety of ways, for example a vanguard approach might be taken with the political elite (intellectuals, professionals, etc.) claiming to act on behalf of the community. On other occasions the same group or minority will mobilize the whole community into mass-based political acts. In addition, it is worth remembering that internal mobilization around demands for greater autonomy, political or cultural rights, or even self-determination, will result in factionalization, a variety of groups and leaders claiming the support of the minority community. Evidence of such behaviour can be found in the Kurdish example, where a plethora of Kurdish nationalist groups from the Turkish-based PKK (Kurdish Workers' Party), PUK (Patriotic Union of Kurdistan) and the Iraqi-based KDP (Kurdish Democratic Party) have, on occasion, ended up in battle with each other rather than with the dominant states in which they are located. Mobilization around minority and ethnic rights has also resulted in tactics which, in turn, have resulted in episodes of political violence. It is argued that when other avenues of mobilization and expression are closed or have been exhausted, then ethno-nationalist movements will resort to violence in an attempt to achieve their goals. As Esman and Rabinovich (1988) remark, 'When political channels of expression, influence and participation are available, these will be employed; when they are not available or are unavailing, ethnic activists will resort to direct action and eventually to acts of violence or civil war' (p. 20).

The Palestinian Arab community of the West Bank and Gaza Strip, which has been occupied since 1967 by the state of Israel, illustrates the point made above. First, as an occupying power, Israel did not grant Palestinians any political rights; there were, therefore, no legitimate or open channels by which they could express their demands. Until 1993 membership of the PLO was proscribed, no national elections were held, Palestinians had no say in any legislation – economic, political, security or otherwise – demonstrations were banned and public gatherings were prohibited. The leaders of the Palestinian community mobilized against this occupation, demanded an end to Israeli rule and pursued the call for self-determination and independence. Cleavages within this community are evident: the PLO is a nationalist umbrella organization for Fatah, the PFLP (Popular Front for the Liberation of Palestine), DFLP (Democratic Front for the Liberation of Palestine) and PPP (Palestine People's Party). In addition, since the 1980s Muslim political sentiment has also been represented by Hamas and the Islamic jihad organizations. The resort to all of the tactics cited by Esman and Rabinovich can be found in the Palestinian–Israeli example. The issue that also needs to be acknowledged, however, is the extent to which either side in this particular ethnic conflict could ever have reconciled itself to a binational solution to their claims – could some form of consociational arrangement have met the demands of both sides?

The fortunes of such movements are dependent on a variety of factors, chief of which is the nature of the demand and the nature of the state to which those demands are made. One might look at the Copts in Egypt to illustrate this point. Christian Copts are Egypt's largest minority group accounting for some 10 per cent of the population. In the past they held important political positions in government, but since the 1950s the community has been subject to episodes of discrimination and persecution. In addition, the resurgence of Islam has given rise to some attacks against the Copts. The Coptic community has mobilized to resist such changes and by the 1980s the state was supporting their calls. Coptic claims were not radical, the state could support them as part of its ongoing anti-Islamist crackdown and tolerance could be promoted as part of Egypt's policy of political and economic liberalization. The majority of ethnic and religious groups, however, have not been so successful and even the Copts have some way to go before they feel secure in Egyptian society. The prevalence of authoritarian and anti-democratic states in the region, as we shall see below, does inhibit even the most modest demands for pluralism and equality. Without pluralism and equality, the demands of ethnic and minority groups will result in those unwanted episodes of violence and terror which seem to grip the region and further slow the pace of reform and change. The rigid nature of most state systems in the region promotes a vicious circle which seems impossible to break. Political violence and acts of terror become instruments of control and counter-control in which both sides engage. The spectre of ethnic cleansing, first made vivid in Bosnia, has since been used to describe Iraq's campaign of chemical warfare against the Kurds, Syria's massacre of the Muslim Brothers in Hama and Israel's part in the Sabra and Shatilla massacres in Lebanon. Acts of terror are, in turn, perpetrated by the politically impotent and voiceless ethnic and religious minorities of the region.

Conflict-management and regulation

In multi-ethnic or minority states, concessions by the government to one group might result in the same demands from other groups, thereby undermining national unity and possibly fragmenting the state for ever. As already noted, so many states in the region find themselves engaged in ethnic or sectarian conflict with their populations. The state has at its disposal a variety of means for 'regulating' such conflicts. By this I mean that the state can employ a variety of strategies to deal with, react to or end the conflicts in which they are engaged. It is useful for us to employ McGarry and O'Leary's (1993) taxonomy of 'macro-methods of ethnic conflict regulation' in this particular overview of the region. While the approach is not entirely comprehensive, it does allow us to examine the variety of strategies that state elites in the region have employed. As such, McGarry and O'Leary outline their taxonomy in the following way: first, they refer to 'methods for eliminating differences', which can include the act of genocide, thereby physically eliminating the subordinate group. Forced mass population transfers, partition and/or secession, creating displaced populations, are also discussed. The final method or approach for eliminating difference is cited as integration and/or assimilation. The second major category evolves around 'methods for managing differences' and embraces themes such as hegemonic control, arbitration (third-party intervention), cantonization and/or federalization, and consociationalism or power-sharing (McGarry and O'Leary, 1993, p. 4).

In the contemporary Middle East, all of these strategies for conflict regulation can be found at one time or another. Sometimes a variety of strategies is pursued at the same time, at other times just one. Nevertheless, the depressing evidence exists for all cases. Acts of genocide, the elimination of a race or ethnic group, have been perpetrated against Iraq's Kurds by the Ba'thist regime led by Saddam Hussein. As the case study below illustrates, the express intention of the Iraqi regime against not only the Kurds, but the majority Shi'a population and Marsh Arabs who inhabit the southern regions of Iraq, has been to engage in acts of ethnic cleansing and elimination through large-scale murder. Iraq has also been guilty of forced mass population transfers of the Kurdish community in particular (McDowall, 2003). Other regional culprits include Israel, which in both 1948 and 1967 played its part in creating a Palestinian refugee population now numbering millions (Morris, 1988). It might well be argued that Kuwait also engaged in forced mass population transfer when it evicted more than 100,000 stateless Palestinians from the country in the wake of the Gulf crisis. The threat of mass population transfer has not declined and remains a real threat to a number of ethnic groups and minority populations. The empirical evidence of partition and/or secession (self-determination) in the Middle East has only occurred once since 1945. The partition of Palestine into two states, one for the Jews and another for the Arabs, did nothing to resolve ethnic and communal conflicts between the two peoples, and has, in fact, only served to heighten the tensions between them. While a variety of secessionist movements have arisen in the region, including the Kurds, Palestinians and the Polisario of the western Sahara, the state system in the region has strongly resisted any attempt to resolve ethnic conflicts by pursuing this strategy. Interestingly, when the option of secession/partition was at its strongest, i.e. in Iraq in February 1991 after the US and Allied forces encouraged Kurdish and Shi'a uprisings, the coercive arm of the state still resisted fragmentation and kept a firm grip on the institutions of government. Further fragmentation of the region, through partition or secession, as a means of regulating or resolving conflict, is unlikely, given the lack of internal and international support for such proposals. The strategy of integration and/or assimilation has also been avoided within the region. Jordan is a rare example, where the Hashemite regime has attempted to integrate its Palestinian population. Controversy has dogged this strategy of state survival and did not eliminate communal conflict, as witnessed by the war between the PLO and Jordan in September 1970. Since the 1970s, however, the integration of Palestinians into the Jordanian state has been pursued in a less than uniform manner, with Palestinians sharing responsibility in government but not necessarily in the higher echelons of the armed forces.

Evidence of hegemonic control as a system of managing difference in the multi-ethnic states of the region is widely available, from Algeria's management of the Berbers to Israel's management of its Palestinian Arab minority. Hegemonic control, as defined by McGarry and O'Leary, is 'coercive and/or co-optive rule which successfully manages to make unworkable an ethnic challenge to the state order' (1993, p. 23). The Arab nationalist regimes of Syria, Iraq, Libya, Algeria, Yemen, Egypt and the Islamic republic of Iran have all pursued ideological agendas designed to transcend ethnic or sectarian loyalties, and all, for the most part, have failed in their task. The death of the pan-Arab nationalist experiments has once again unleashed hitherto suppressed ethnic tensions and conflict. Arbitration, whether internally or externally, in the region has largely failed to resolve ethnic- or sectarian-based clashes. A difficulty in terms of the region has been associated with the identification of arbiters – particularly on the external level, where even the United Nations is regarded with suspicion. The prospects for cantonization within the region as a mechanism for conflict-resolution are low, especially given the associated fear of instability which the further breakdown of states such as Iraq, Syria or Iran might experience as a result of such a policy. The canton option has proved to be an emergency measure, such as the creation of 'safe havens' for the Kurds in northern Iraq in the 1990s, but it had limited formal impact (autonomy arrangements) on the structure of the Iraqi state. While the Kurds may have proclaimed autonomy in their federated state in northern Iraq, its ties to the rest of the state were not easily broken. Consociationalism – power-sharing, grand coalition of government, proportional representation, community autonomy and constitutional vetoes for minorities (Lijphart, 1977) – however, might stand a chance of success if a pattern of democratization emerges within the region. Although the consociational experiment in Lebanon did not prevent the outbreak of civil war in 1975, it has been resurrected in the new era of peace and, with the codicil of democracy, could offer the best chance of maintaining nation-states in the region, while acknowledging pluralism within societies and the rights of all citizens equally and without prejudice. For the present, however, such perspectives are bolstered more by optimism than reality. The consequences for the leadership of many regimes throughout the region in continuing to ignore the ethnic dimension, however, are not hard to predict, and sooner or later the price for such practices will be paid. While the nation-state may remain a permanent feature of the region, the demographic realities of mosaic communities in large numbers require a more plural approach to politics, rights and privileges than is currently evident.

Case study The Kurds' rights denied

The Kurds are one of the largest ethnic groups in the Middle East, following the Arabs and the Persians. For over two thousand years they have retained a distinct ethnic identity. Essentially they are described as a tribal people living in the mountainous areas occupying a large triangular-shaped region currently divided up among four states in the region: Turkey, Iraq, Iran and Syria. They form a minority population in all four states, making up 23 per cent in Turkey, 23 per cent in Iraq, 10 per cent in Iran and 8 per cent in Syria (McDowall, 2003, pp. 3–4). Although they are dispersed over many countries, they inhabit areas that are closely linked; in fact they are often border neighbours. As a tribal people, their loyalties are based on a mix of kinship and territorial situations (Tibi, 1996).

The Kurdish struggle for self-determination and independence had remained, until the late twentieth century, one of the untold stories of state-formation in the region. Like the Palestinians and other minority groups in the region, when the Ottoman Empire dissolved in the early part of the twentieth century the Kurds and their leaders believed they would be granted their rights by the international community and the colonial powers who held sway over the region. Kurdish claims, however, were sacrificed in the 'undignified' colonial scramble for control, their land vital to British claims to Iran and Hashemite Iraq and French claims in Syria (Entessar, 1992). In Turkey Kemal Atatürk's era of Turkish nationalism allowed no room for competing identities, religious, ethnic or otherwise, and in the Soviet Union the spread of communism put an end to any hopes that the ethnic minorities of Kurdistan or Armenia had of national independence.

The Kurdish cause has been beset by a variety of problems. Internal Kurdish conflicts, for example, have been long-standing and Kurdish unity has been an ideal rather than a reality. This lack of unity has exacerbated the physical divisions that exist between these people who inhabit four different states: 'After 1920 the history of Kurdish nationalism is mainly the history of three separate conflicts in which one or more Kurdish political movements have challenged the governments of Turkey, Iran and Iraq' (Gurr and Harff, 1994, p. 37). As such, it might well be argued that the Kurds have sometimes played their own part in the terrible atrocities committed against their own people by the regimes of Iraq and Turkey. Ironically, though, the Kurdish people have largely rejected assimilation into their host states and although some factions have colluded with the state against their fellow Kurds, they have successfully resisted attempts by, for example, Turkey to reshape their identity into 'Mountain Turks' while denying their Kurdish roots. The Kurdish issue, then, has been a long-standing one and while it is easy to identify their main objective, which is a nationalist call for self-determination and independence from central government, they have remained unsuccessful (with the exception of the short-lived Mahabad Republic) in establishing a nation-state for themselves (Vali, 1996).

From the 1920s onwards the Kurdish minorities of Iran, Iraq and Turkey formed themselves into political movements to put pressure on their governments for independence. However, it must be noted that the struggle for independence has not been just political but has embraced the strategy of armed resistance as well. As Van Bruinessen points out, 'it is easy to portray the Kurdish problem as essentially a conflict between a liberation movement and a central government that tries to enforce its rule over them' (1986, p. 4). But the problem also lies in the fact that the Kurdish national movement appears reactionary in its nature, its organization is not highly politically developed and despite internal struggle it is traditional and conservative. There exists a distinct lack of incorporation of the Kurdish minority into any newly emergent state form. They have been excluded and continue to exclude themselves. In Iraq and Turkey the minority population of the Kurds was perceived as a threat to national unity, a group that could agitate and threaten state legitimacy. The 1961 Iraqi Kurdish revolt is but one example of resistance to central authority imposing agrarian reform.

These factors help explain the nature of the Kurdish issue and the strategies adopted by states like Iraq and Turkey for managing the conflict with their minority population. The experiences of Iraq's Kurds during the 1991 Gulf crisis emphasized the nature of this ethnic conflict within Iraq's borders that threatened both the legitimacy and stability of Saddam Hussein's regime. Even before the Kurdish uprising of 1991, Saddam Hussein had conducted a ruthless campaign against the Kurdish population of northern Iraq. In 1988 he had attacked the Kurds using chemical weapons – for the first time in history nerve gas had been used against a defenceless civilian population. At that time, however, the international community did not come to the aid of the Kurds or support their cause. In March 1991 the situation was quite different. The Kurdish population was encouraged by the international community to rise up against Saddam Hussein at the same time that the Shi'a community in the south of the country was also staging a revolt. The revolt was short-lived; Iraqi forces quickly gained control of Kurdish cities and bombing raids resulted in a mass exodus to the borders with Turkey and Iran. The leaders of two main Kurdish resistance groups, the Iraq Kurdistan Front and the Kurdistan Workers' Party, entered into autonomy negotiations with Baghdad. The refugee problem grew, forcing the international community to take action – by May 1991 a safety zone in northern Iraq had been established. The US administration rapidly abandoned the Kurds, one White House analyst summing the situation up: 'It probably sounds callous, but we did the best thing not to get near [the Kurdish revolt]. They're nice people, and they're cute, but they're really just bandits. They spend as much time fighting each other as central authority. They're losers' (Entessar, 1992, p. 155). The message was clear: even the tyranny of central government was better than ceding to the minorities of the region; the stability of the nation-state had to be preserved, no matter how high the price. Of course that price was exacted by the governments of the US and UK in 2003 when it launched a war on Iraq. The fall of the Ba'thist regime signalled feelings of great optimism among Iraq's Kurdish population. The participation of the Kurds of Iraq in the post-war elections for the Iraqi parliament in January 2005 also allayed fears that the Kurds would press ahead with secessionist rather than federal demands. The elections of Kurds to the new Iraqi legislature signalled an intent to maintain autonomy through a federal approach in the post-war Iraq. The decision to make the Kurdish leader Jalal Talabani the President of Iraq in April 2005 was momentous in terms of the campaign by Kurds to assure their future in the modern state of Iraq. Such ambitions have been viewed with interest in Iraq's neighbouring states where so many more of the region's Kurdish population still reside – without rights or recognition for the foreseeable future.

Case study The Alawites of Syria

The territorial state of Syria, governed since 1970 by the Ba'th Party and its President Hafiz al-Assad, is not an ethnically homogeneous state. In fact, since the creation of a new nation-state of Syria in 1920, initially under the French mandate, a mosaic state of minorities has emerged. The minorities include Sunni Muslims, Alawites, Druze, Christians, Turks, Circassians, Armenians, Assyrians, Jews and Maronites. While some 90 per cent of the population is Arab, minority status in terms of religion is an important factor in the Syrian state. The largest religious group consists of Sunni Muslims who live in the urban areas of Damascus, Aleppo and Homs and Hama. The Alawite Muslims, a Shi'a sect from the coastal areas of Syria, constitute 15 per cent of the population and form a distinct religious minority group which has come to dominate the Ba'thist state. Druze and Christian Arabs form the other major religious groups of the country. The Christian Arabs make up some 10 per cent of the population and include among their number Greek Orthodox, Syrian Orthodox, Greek Catholics, Maronites and others.

The Alawites, considered a heretic Muslim sect, traditionally were concentrated in the coastal area of the Mediterranean near Latakia. Despite the rise of nationalism and more specifically Ba'thism, the Alawites and other minorities in Syria have preserved their religious, linguistic and ethnic identities and remain an important factor in Syrian politics. While some minorities, such as the Kurds, have failed or refused to assimilate into the Ba'th state, others, such as the Alawites, have pursued an assimilationist pattern. Traditionally, Alawite dissent has not been based on any alternative nationalism to Ba'thism or Arab nationalism, but rather, since the 1960s, it has worked within the parameters of the existing political system. Thus the Alawites avoided challenging state policies and in many respects have become identified with the state itself.

In considering the formation and structure of the modern Ba'thist state and the role of the Alawites within this, the crucial point is the rise of Alawites in the Syrian armed forces and the Ba'th Party. While the French had pursued a policy of divide and rule among Syria's minorities, the founders of the Ba'th Party encouraged all Arabs in the country to join their struggle. The Ba'thist agenda had a particular appeal to the rural poor of areas like Alawite-dominated Latakia, and this openness facilitated their entrance and rise into the party. The army, however, remained Sunni Muslim-dominated until the military *coup* of Ba'thists, Nasserists and independent officers in 1963. From this period onwards a power struggle within the officer corps of the Syrian army took place between the Sunni and minority background officers. This period of internal struggle had serious consequences, undermining military and national morale, and was only resolved in the late 1960s following the purge first of Sunni officers, then Druze officers, and finally an internal Alawite power struggle in which Hafiz al-Assad defeated his co-religionist and fellow officer Salah Jadid.

In leading the *coup* of 1970, Hafiz al-Assad had weakened both the Ba'th and the Syrian army as a result of the power struggles of the 1960s, and now he faced the task of consolidating power, promoting stability and encouraging confidence in the new political leadership of the state. From this point al-Assad promoted fellow Alawites in the army and the Ba'th, surrounding himself with a cadre of loyal co-religionists. As Tibi (1996) has noted, the Alawites 'constitute major segments of the ruling military and civilian elites in the current Syrian regime' (p. 176). Al-Assad has also faced the delicate task of promoting Alawites, while at the same time avoiding antagonizing the Sunni majority. As Hopwood (1988) remarks, 'The Alawis have attempted to keep a low profile while at the same time relying on intra-Alawi relationships to retain their position . . . [any] increase in Sunni representation was not, however, at the expense of the Alawis but of other minorities' (p. 97). This delicate balancing act has not, however, always been preserved, and sectarian tension, particularly between the Alawites and Sunnis, has been in evidence during times of internal crisis. Nevertheless, these tensions, acts of discrimination or lack of privilege are not part of the public political domain, where the Ba'th Party acts as the standard bearer of unity and socialism for Arabs, irrespective of sectarian background. Under al-Assad, membership of the party has even been opened up to non-Arabs who feel able to subscribe to the general principles of Ba'thism.

Sectarian difference, however, remains a problem for the Syrian regime. The benefits of Alawite assimilation have prejudiced other minorities and, perhaps more importantly, have antagonized communal relations between Syria's minorities (religious, linguistic and ethnic) and the Sunni Muslim majority. More than thirty years of Alawite-dominated rule of the Ba'th Party and the military in Syria has actually hindered the political leadership of unity among Arabs. For their part, the Alawite minority in Syria serves to highlight the degree to which such groups can dominate politics in the inherently non-plural political systems of the region which have developed since independence. The failure to provide a plural basis for politics and representation in minority states like Syria can, however, all too quickly lead to internal crisis and communal conflict and explains in large part the growth of Sunni opposition in the country. To date, however, 'prospects and possibilities for broadening the real power basis of the Alawite-dominated Ba'th regime in Syria are for the time being relatively limited. The vicious circle in which the Syrian regime has repeatedly found itself still persists' (Van Dam, 1996, p. 146). Even the demise of Hafiz al-Assad did little to harm Alawite domination of the Ba'th, for the structure of the party organization and the military that supports it now plays host to a firmly embedded minority group. Only democratization and pluralism will break the stranglehold on Syrian politics which this particular minority enjoys. What remains to be seen is whether the Alawites maintain power or Syria descends into a Lebanon-style sectarian and communal struggle for political power.

Further reading

For general reading and definitions of ethnicity, the readers edited by Hutchinson and Smith (1996) and Guibernau and Rex (1997) are both excellent sources of concise and extracted explanations by authors such as

Gellner, Hobsbawm, Smith, Hylland Eriksen, Barth and Hechter. While no substitute for the original texts, these readers are useful for general introductory purposes. Ethnicity in the post-Cold War era is explained in a dynamic and refreshing fashion in Moynihan (1993). Dimensions of ethno-nationalism and ethnic conflict are covered comprehensively in texts by Horowitz (1985) and Connor (1994). Theory and case studies form the backbone of texts by McGarry and O'Leary (1993) and Gurr and Harff (1994). Gurr and Harff make particular reference throughout their text to the Kurdish issue. A number of interesting edited collections on the issue of ethnicity, ethnic politics and conflict in the Middle East have been published, including Esman and Rabinovich (1988) and Schulze et al. (1996), while Esman (1994), in his general text on ethnic politics, debates specific aspects of the ethnic divide between Israel and the Palestinians. On more specific examples of ethnic groups such as the Kurds, see McDowall's (2003) comprehensive historical and contemporary account and the introductory text by Izady (1992). Van Bruinessen (1991) has authored a social as well as political history of the Kurds which outlines important aspects of tribe and state. Also worth reading is Jawad (1981), Laizer (1991), Entessar (1992) and Vali (1996), which examines the Kurds in Iran, Iraq and Turkey as well as broader issues of the international context of the Kurdish question. Kreyenbroek and Sperl (1992) covers a variety of pertinent debates on the subject, which can, in turn, be augmented by reference to the regular appearance of articles in journals such as *MERIP* on the subject. The text by Anderson (2003) adds a more up-to-date account of events as they impact on the Kurds of Iraq. On Syria and Alawite influence and power over the political system, the accounts in Seale (1989), Hopwood (1988), Van Dam (1996) and the edited text by Kienle (1996) all provide an insight on this subject. Further insights into the dynamics of Alawite, military, Ba'thist and state power are touched on in Kienle (1990), Hinnebusch (1990 and 1993) and Perthes (1991 and 1992).

The United States and the Middle East: *Pax Americana*?

Introduction

I**N** September 2002, one year after the al-Qaeda bombings in America, the Bush administration issued a national security strategy document that outlined its mission in terms of its bid for global leadership in the twenty-first century. US global leadership would deliver a form of *pax Americana* 'in the service of a balance of power that favo[u]rs freedom'. This strategy would be manifest in three priorities: the US would 'lead the world in defending the peace against global terror and against aggressive regimes seeking weapons of mass destruction'. Second was a commitment to peace through diplomacy and, third, America would 'extend the peace by working to extend the benefits of liberty and prosperity as broadly as possible' through free trade mechanisms (US State Department, 2002). Without a doubt such policy aspirations would have an impact on the Middle East region. For since 1945 the USA's relationship with the Middle East has in one way or another focused on the three priorities that the Bush administration outlined in terms of its national security strategy. Moreover, until 1989, this national security strategy was also shaped and tempered by the Cold War and superpower rivalry with the former Soviet Union. Thus while the strategy had elements of 'innovation' in terms of the war on terrorism and American global leadership of the war, other elements of it were immutable in terms of the Middle East and American policies towards it.

Throughout the period of American engagement in the Middle East, commentators and critics have argued either for or against greater American intervention in the region. On the one side many critics decry that American intervention in the Middle East is severely biased and dangerous in terms of longevity of local regimes and exploitative in terms of the region's oil and other resources. Others, however, maintain that, despite an American disdain for American intervention, various US administrations have been compelled to intervene in the region in the name of the protection of values of freedom and independence and in the promotion of democracy and to stop terrorism threatening the security of the global order.

Whatever the merits of the arguments for or against US intervention in the Middle East or whether such intervention is in pursuit of ideological hegemony and in terms of the furtherance of national interest, there is much about the region that has compelled US policymakers and politicians to develop a series of important relationships with states and other actors. Although it is true that the Cold War and America's rivalry with the Soviet Union did have its impact on the region, as we shall see, there is more to American foreign policy than superpower rivalry or, for that matter, the more recent American adventure in Iraq. There is a question, however, in the wake of 9/11 about the extent to which the war on terrorism (which is conceived as an expression of neo-conservative thinking) has altered dimensions of the American foreign policy agenda with respect to the Middle East.

In this chapter then I will outline the objectives behind US policy in the Middle East. I will then chart the major dimensions or spheres of US involvement as a means of accounting for the impact of such policy objectives on the region and its inhabitants. This section will also include an examination of the impact of Cold War competition for influence and power in the region with the former Soviet Union. Towards the end of the chapter I will also explore and explain the growing debate about the cultural influence of the USA and counter-cultures of Arab nationalism and Islamism in particular that have arisen and respond to what they perceive to be American hegemonic ambitions in their region. I shall also examine the ways in which the fallout from 9/11 and alterations in US policy and American public opinion more widely have changed towards the Middle East. Finally, I will assess the extent to which American foreign policy in the Middle East is considered successful or not. The case studies of Israel – which is America's most important ally in the region – and the Islamic kingdom of Saudi Arabia will be examined in respect of American national interest and foreign policy in the region.

Objective national interest

When America was first involved in the Middle East a number of issues – particularly in relation to the furtherance of national interest – emerged as key to establishing a set of policy objectives that remain largely unchanged some seventy years later. Today, as in the past, the majority of citizens of the United States of America trust their government and its policy-makers to serve that which is defined as national interest (Pew Research Center, 2002). In looking at a specific region of the globe, national interest must always be allied to the wider global foreign policy agenda of the United States of America. Elements of what defines American national interest vis-à-vis the Middle East are of course historically dynamic – some interests wax and wane according to circumstance – but there are some essential elements that have remained relatively unchanged. One element that has remained so is the extent to which oil resources in the region have led the USA to establish important relations with certain states as well as furthering a wider ambition of securing unhindered access for US companies to such resources. Oil, however, is not the be all and end all of American national interest in the Middle East. Even in terms of America's penchant for forming 'special relationships' with particular states in the region, such as Iran and Israel, other factors – such as forming a pro-western alliance against the former Soviet Union – came into play.

It is useful to outline US foreign policy objectives and provide a brief history of their development in the last seventy years. It should be apparent from the start that, despite attempts by various administrations in Washington (Democrat and Republican) to pursue an isolationist foreign policy position with respect to these issues, events in the Middle East have often compelled American actors to intervene in order to protect their interests. Foreign policy-makers in Washington have always outlined four major objectives or key goals in the region that promote the basic national interests. These are primarily economic and this largely means maintaining the free flow of oil from states in the region that possess huge reserves. This in turn means that oil prices are not vulnerable to sharp hikes due to issues of supply and demand. Such states include Saudi Arabia, Iraq and, until 1979, Iran. The question here is why is oil from the Middle East so important to America? The main answer lies in the development of America's advanced industrial economy and growing dependence of this economy on oil. While America is able to produce some of its own oil, it has become increasingly dependent on oil produced in the Middle East. Moreover, experts predict that US energy consumption will increase while domestic production is likely to decline, leaving the country increasingly dependent on the free flow of oil from a region where authoritarian regimes have prevailed (Bahgat, 2001). The United States of America, for example, is dependent on Saudi Arabia alone for some 20 per cent of its crude oil imports. In other words, the maintenance and future growth of the American economy owes much to the import of oil from the Middle East. In this way unimpeded access to that resource is vital to national interest. If there were any doubt that this was not the case, the Arab oil embargo during the 1973 Arab–Israeli conflict, although it occurred more than thirty years ago, remains fresh in the collective consciousness of American policy-makers. The impact of the decision by Saudi Arabia and other Arab states on 17 October 1973 to sever oil exports to the United States of America threw the US economy into chaos. The rising price of oil per barrel in the wake of the Iraqi occupation of Kuwait in 1990 was also an extreme reminder to those concerned with the maintenance of unhindered American access to Middle Eastern oil that what happens in the region directly impacts on Middle America. Even soccer moms need their SUVs to get their little ones to the game and without cheap oil imported from the Middle East any incumbent political administration would feel the pinch at the next electoral opportunity.

The economic relationship is also significant in terms of US military and arms exports with states in the region being seen as major consumers in terms of the armaments market. The export of arms produced in the United States of America to a variety of states in the Middle East has been seen in terms of national interest as a means of supporting friendly regimes against threats that emanate against them from elsewhere in the region. American arms sales to Iran, for example, were seen as essential to national interests in that a well-armed Iran was a bulwark in the northern tier states against the Soviet Union during the Cold War as well as a means of maintaining the state from internal threat. Of course the fact that American-supplied arms were also deployed internally against Iran's citizens was simply overlooked at a time when an authoritarian regime sought to control the masses.

The second feature of American national interest in the Middle East is the survival of Israel. For a variety of reasons, successive American governments have adhered to and maintained a commitment to preserve not just the security but the prosperity of Israel. The nature of the 'special relationship' means that the US perceives Israel as a strategic ally and regional policeman (as Iran also was before 1979) in the Middle East. The factors behind this relationship are significant in terms of diplomacy, aid, arms sales and the increasing importance of religion in American politics as well as strategic considerations.

The third arm of American national interest in the region before 1990 was to maintain the American presence as dominant in the region as a whole through curbing Soviet expansionism – even if this meant that a little instability in the region was the result. It is argued that in the wake of first the Cold War and secondly 9/11, elements of the American policy-making elite contend that American national interest in the Middle East is now best served by replacing Islamist expansionism with the promotion of liberal democratization across the region – even if this means direct military intervention to achieve regime change and impose democracy from above. Finally it is in American national interest to support pro-western states in the region and various administrations have expressed their desire to assist their allies through aid programmes to countries such as Egypt or arms supplies and defence contracts to states such as Kuwait and Saudi Arabia.

These national interests that have underlined American policy in the Middle East also determine its basic features.

- First – an interest in eliminating competitors in the region to assure America indisputable supremacy, even over other western countries. This has been the case, not only in more recent years where America has emerged on the global stage as the one and only superpower, but throughout the latter part of the twentieth century.
- Second – the attempt until 1990 to form a massive regional alliance directed against the Soviet Union and its local allies.
- Third and final – the determination to resort to any means, including military, to satisfy these demands. This we saw illustrated during the Gulf Crisis in 1990–1 and the war in Iraq in 2003.

In addition to all this, the political values behind US policy-making should be acknowledged. The commitment to human rights, democracy and free trade are part of a list of American priorities in the region. Also the US is faced with what is often referred to as the dilemma of the Middle East – what is perceived as one of the least progressive areas of the globe, encompassing as it does problems with political stability, education, democracy, economic development and liberalization and terrorism. At various stages US policy towards the region has been affected to a greater or lesser degree by these objectives and some have assumed greater priority than others. Whether Republican or Democratic, however, the Middle East has been a region that has presented American policy-makers with formidable challenges. Prestowitz contends, however, that US power over the region has negative as well as positive consequences and that today it holds a unique position in the region. He warns that as well as 'talking the talk' about freedom, democracy and the capital economy, America must promote policies in the Middle East that result in the expression of American power that 'walks the walk' and leaves America's critics increasingly bereft of the accusation that American values stand for one thing at home and another in the Middle East (Prestowitz, 2003).

It should be noted that during the Cold War the definition of national interest was easier with respect to the Middle East than it has been since 1990. National interest vis-à-vis the Middle East was subject to definition in opposition or reaction to Soviet policy towards the same region. Containment and the promotion of pro-western regimes appeared to be the best route to successfully securing American interests in the region. In the post-Cold War era national interest has been subject to reshaping that is coloured by new ideological debates. Growing Republican and neo-conservative dominance of this debate has led to national interest being defined as a key element of the war on terrorism, increasingly unilateral, and defence-based – including increased military spending or involvement in respect of force and power within the region. Over 250,000 American troops were deployed to the Middle East in 2002–3 and the amassing of large numbers of these troops at American bases in states such as Iraq and Kuwait implies a continuing presence for the foreseeable future.

National interest is also economically driven in terms of promoting and enhancing the domination of American-based companies and corporations engaged in free trade. US policy-makers now also seek to shore up existing alliances as what is referred to as a 'democratic' bulwark against threats that undermine the American belief in 'peace, prosperity and freedom'. Moreover it has become clear that Republicans want to mould the international system in their own image and take to task rogue regimes that undermine this aspiration. Those who seek to re-make the Middle East in their own image, however, have to contend with a historic legacy of US foreign policy in the Middle East that casts a strong shadow over the region in the present day. It is these events that policy-makers should remain cognizant of. In light of these developments, there is an issue around the degree of difference between America's stated interest and its actual interests as evidenced in its policies and policy outcomes in the region.

Relations and rivalries

The policy relationship between the US and the Middle East was established shortly after the First World War when American President Woodrow Wilson enunciated American support for the right to self-determination and independence for the inhabitants of the region. Such aspirations were, however, thwarted by the continuing imperial ambitions of the British and the French. The true rise of American policy within and towards the region emerged in the years of the Second World War and shortly thereafter. It would result in the establishment of a series of 'special relationships' that would benefit American interests in the region.

In many respects the US was regarded as an heir to the British colonial presence that went into such rapid decline during the years 1945–56. The US was motivated to become involved because of its own national interest in securing access to the oil reserves of the region as well as keeping Soviet influence at a minimum. Containment of the Soviet threat would become a major preoccupation.

The US, as I have previously mentioned, developed an early dependency on oil that compelled it to secure a place for itself in the region. By the 1930s and 1940s American oil companies rivalled British interests in oil-rich states such as Saudi Arabia, Kuwait, Bahrain and Iran. In states such as Saudi Arabia, American oil companies became, in tandem with the ruling family, the engine for the economic growth and development of the kingdom. US technical expertise and know-how played an important part in redefining the infrastructure and political allegiances of states in the region. The US quickly became the major western power in the region. Policy would be developed to protect this position and it meant that the US was prepared to forge a variety of relationships with client states in the region. This meant that from the late 1940s US diplomats would forge important footholds in countries such as Iran, Saudi Arabia and Israel. These client states would serve to maintain US interests in the region. The aim here was to build an axis of pro-western regimes that would act as a foil against Soviet ambition in the region and ensure access to oil.

America was aware that it would need to contain the Soviet threat to the region as well as keep an eye on the burgeoning and restive movements for nationalism and independence. The Soviet threat meant that the Middle East was largely regarded by both superpower rivals as a further theatre of the Cold War. The Eisenhower Doctrine of 1957 was part of the American policy of containing Soviet influence in the Middle East and securing American interest there. The willingness to employ American forces at the request of states in the region in the instance of armed aggression from other states became associated with this doctrine. The doctrine was a response to growing Soviet influence in Egypt and Syria in the late 1950s, and betrayed a desire, particularly in the wake of the Suez crisis and the diminishing esteem of western states as a result, to steer the maintenance of stability in the region according to American national interest. The strategic and economic implications of the Middle East going 'red' under the communist grip of the Soviet Union also compelled the Eisenhower administration to extend its involvement in the region. But Polk contends that the doctrine was ultimately unsuccessful, 'largely redundant since all that it gained was public endorsement by those states [in the Middle East] that had already indicated their friendly attitude toward the same policy in a former guise' (Polk, 1991, p. 399). Moreover it did not seem to play a part in deterring a number of events in the region – in Syria, Lebanon and Iraq – in the late 1950s, all of which were construed as harmful to America. The prospect of Arab or Iranian nationalists seizing control of natural assets such as oil and gas was inimical to American interests. Thus throughout the late 1940s and 1950s, American policy-makers were compelled to rise to the challenge inherent in Arab and Iranian movements for nationalism and greater independence.

By the 1950s, both the Soviet Union and the West competed to offer aid to Egypt as its post-revolutionary leader Gamal Abdel Nasser set about building the Aswan Dam on the Nile River. The West stepped back after it was clear that Egypt would look to the communist East for its arms. Tensions rose as Nasser unilaterally announced the nationalization of the Suez Canal, prompting a crisis that led to a British, French and Israeli invasion in 1956. Much to the surprise of the old western powers, the US and the Soviet Union supported a United Nations resolution demanding an immediate ceasefire. Nevertheless it was the USSR that was able to capitalize quickly on the Suez crisis, winning new friends for itself in the Arab world. Indeed, an alliance of the 'radical' Arab states such as Egypt, Iraq, Syria and Yemen supported by the Soviet Union soon emerged in opposition to the pro-western conservative states of Saudi Arabia, Jordan and Morocco.

This environment of superpower rivalry not only led to the establishment of contention with regard to client states in the region but meant that both states were vulnerable to getting caught up in regional conflagrations. This was demonstrated during the 1970s when the superpower détente was seriously threatened by the war-like actions of their client states. In such a context it was increasingly difficult to discern whether the dog was wagging the tail or the tail was wagging the dog! If client states were locked in enmity, the superpowers were often pulled in.

The policy of containment soon emerged alongside increased support for America's pro-western friends in the region. One result of this was an ever-escalating arms race within the Middle East that was conveniently supported and aided by the US and the USSR. Throughout the Cold War both the US and its opponent sought to use arms sales and military aid as a way to gain and maintain a foothold in the region. The US was keen to establish military bases in the region. By the mid-1970s, America had offered more than $65 billion in terms of military assistance to friendly states. By the early 1980s, 50 per cent of total global arms exports went to the Middle East (Gresh and Vidal, 1990, p. 14).

Furthermore, by the mid-1970s American arms sales to Iran and Saudi Arabia were playing a large part in determining their regional weight against other states. Oil revenues were now being used to fuel the arms race and allow the US and other suppliers to preserve their place in the region. Oil for arms and arms for oil established a deep relationship of dependency that in turn created new perceptions and illusions of power and control within the region. In the case of Iran, American backing encouraged the regional ambitions for power that the Shah had harboured. Halliday asserts that, 'throughout this period, [1960s–1980s] Iran's growth as a regional power has gone hand in hand with the growth of its co-operation with the USA . . . The USA has therefore been the key external factor in Iranian foreign policy since the Second World War' (Halliday, 1979, p. 252). Power-seeking at a regional level was translated into the barrel of the guns, missiles, warplanes, military technology and communications that successive administrations offered to their Iranian ally. Iranian expenditure on US-supplied arms ran into the billions. By the late 1970s, however, when the Shah was deposed and the revolution harnessed by the Ayatollah, control of the Iranian arsenal fell into the hands of a theo-cratic regime that would declare the US its number one enemy. Shi'a Iran was now a threat in the region – particularly to Iraq and Saudi Arabia where there were concerns about their own restive Shi'a popu-lations – but also to America where diplomats and policy-makers feared the fundamentalist tide would sweep the region and end unhin-dered access to oil. This fear was largely born out of their own experi-ences in the region in the early 1980s where those they believed to be linked to Iranian fervour kidnapped, held hostage and killed countless Americans in cities like Beirut and Tehran.

This fear played a significant part in a major policy reorientation towards the Gulf region in the early 1980s. This coincides with the end of the Carter administration and the controversy of the Iranian siege of the American Embassy in Tehran and the ascension of Republican Ronald Reagan to the White House. For Reagan it appeared as if the omens were good. As he swore his oath of office in January 1980, the Iranians released the 52 American hostages that they had held for 444 days. He talked tough on the Middle East and looked across the region for new alliances and with a determination to end the Israeli–Arab conflict. It would not be long before the Reagan administration began to pay a high price for its new policy orientation. In Lebanon in 1983, 241 American service people were killed in a bomb attack that even-tually led the administration to withdraw its troops. America had intervened in Lebanon at the height of the civil war there. Their pres-ence was seen by many there as evidence of American complicity in the Israeli invasion and occupation of the country in 1982 and an attempt to influence the Christian militia elements. The Americans were shocked at the attacks on them. The blame for the 1983 marine barracks bombing was laid by the Americans at the door of a Lebanese Islamist Shi'a organization called Hizb Allah (party of God). This new actor on the scene of Lebanon's scarred landscape of civil war also enjoyed close ties with the revolutionary regime led by Shi'a

Ayatollahs in Iran who were keen to export their revolutionary model elsewhere in the Middle East. By 1983, President Reagan ordered a retreat from Lebanon that demonstrated that American policy had been altered by the wrath of militant and violent Islamists. Moreover, by the mid-1980s the Reagan administration was exposed for its double dealing as news of the Iran–Contra arms deals filtered across the globe.

In 1980 the Iranian regime and neighbouring Iraq became embroiled in a war that would engulf both countries for the better part of a decade. Midway during this war Iran's leaders embarked on a secret quest for US arms. Elements within the Reagan administration encouraged the President to accept the request, arguing that it would enhance their position in the region. Despite a US-imposed embargo on arms sales, President Reagan approved the deal with Iran. The revenues would allow him to covertly fund Contras in Nicaragua. The secret deal was exposed by a Lebanese newspaper in 1986 but by that point Iran had already received over a thousand American missiles. The US investigation into the deal revealed that millions of dollars of Iranian funds had been received by the US and then diverted to fund the Contras. While Reagan eventually emerged from the scandal largely untarnished (enjoying high popularity ratings as he left office), the impact of the affair was not lost in the many capitals of the Middle East region.

Successive American administrations from Eisenhower to Carter pursued policies of direct interference and subterfuge in the political and economic arenas of the Middle East. When in 1953 Iranian Prime Minister Mohammed Mossadegh, for example, announced the nationalization of the country's oil industry and an end to foreign assistance, alarm bells rang in Washington. American officials moved to intervene. By the summer of 1953 the US (in cahoots with the British) had engaged the CIA in 'Operation Ajax' in a move to oust Mossadegh from power and restore the authority of Reza Shah Pahlavi. The mission was a great success as the CIA and MI6 stoked unrest which led to the flight of Mossadegh and the restoration of the Iranian throne to a Pahlavi Shah eternally indebted to the US for his position. The United States considered the Shah a key client in the Middle East and sustained his authoritarian and crooked regime with billions of dollars in aid and arms.

During the 1960s and early 1970s, US policy in the region was restructured. As Soviet influence and Arab enmity grew, Washington's traditional reluctance to supply advanced weapons to conservative Arab states and Israel abated. The war of 1967 had transformed the military and political balance of power in the region. As a consequence Israel's relationship with the US became strengthened. This special

relationship was pursued throughout the Nixon era and the furtherance of this relationship was seen in terms of an economic–military
basis.

These acts of intervention established local and regional distrust of
American policy motives in the region. In the case of Iran it was to
prove fatal both to the regime of the Shah and the American position
there. During the revolution of 1979 the Pahlavi regime collapsed and
with it American influence over this state. The regime of the Islamic
Republic led by Ayatollah Khomeini declared the US a major enemy of
the Iranian people and the wider region. Thus from 1979 Iran was lost
to America and its policy within the Gulf region severely strained.
After 1973 and the oil boycott, however, US policy shifted again
towards the conservative Arab regimes of the Gulf. By 1979 arms sales
had become a political fix-it to obstacles in US policy. The Iranian revolution of 1979, however, upset the US applecart, leaving the Gulf bereft
of a US agent. Israel became the only agent in the region and American
policy-makers were compelled to secure a resolution to the Arab–
Israeli conflict while promoting Egypt as a new client of American aid
and support. This was achieved, as we know, through American sponsorship of the Israel–Egypt peace treaty and the significant promise of
aid to be given to Egypt by the USA. There is no doubt that, as well as
formally ending the enmity between Israel and Egypt, the import of
American intervention in this case was the way in which Egypt was
neutralized as a threat to American interests in the region more
widely. The decision by Sadat to enter into the American-brokered
peace treaty with Israel effectively severed the claim to leadership of
the Arab world and radical Arab nationalism that was previously so
strongly identifiable with President Nasser.

As the US was to discover as a result of other encounters in the
region, the desired outcomes of their foreign policy agendas were not
always understood by those states or elements that they were interact-
ing with. This led successive American administrations to increase
their interactions with the region. As a result dependencies have been
established that have often made it difficult for the US to change
course or tack. This was true of the US–Iranian relationship, and is
true of the US–Egyptian relationship, the US–Israel relationship, and
the US–Saudi relationship. Moreover, as a result of these special or
particular relationships, the US conversely chose to disestablish other
actors in the region who were then accused of acting like Soviet sympa-
thizers, enemies of America and rogue states. This meant that in many
states of the region the US was simply no longer welcome.

The policy of the Reagan administration (1980–8) was dominated by
the realization that the attainment of Israeli objectives had, perhaps
for the first time, been inimical to American interests, objectives or

priorities. In light of this perception the US appeared to try and balance its objectives by pursuing a policy more favourable to some Arab states. However, on closer examination it became clear that the policy change only favoured the objectives of the Gulf states and further enhanced the hold of the US in the Middle East. The 1980s were also characterized by the American attempt to stem the tide of Islamic fundamentalism in the Middle East – which it believed had been triggered by the revolution in Iran. This led them to forge many deals in the region and amongst the region's near neighbours in states such as Afghanistan that would later come to haunt them.

The election of Republican successor George Bush to President in 1988 was not perceived as significant in terms of policy orientation towards the region. The predictable patterns of alliance were expected to be maintained with America rather than the region's actors determining the nature of policy at a state-to-state or region-wide level. There were, however, changes which were foisted upon US policymakers. This compelled them to take a reactive stance that would have profound repercussions for American power in the region throughout the whole of the 1990s.

An early indication of this change was discernible in 1988 when, in response to international pressure and sympathy for the Palestinians engaged in the uprising against continued Israeli occupation, the Americans were compelled to take the initiative on the issue of peacemaking. From 1988 onwards, American Secretary of State James Baker was engaged in various rounds of meetings in an attempt to pursue a peace process between Israel and the Arabs. Yet the problem for America lay not with the Arabs but, as Schiff and Ya'ari remark, 'the problem really lay with America's own client Israel, and the question was how to get the Shamir government to agree to a [peace] process involving the PLO' (Schiff and Ya'ari, 1989, p. 74). A number of analysts began to question the nature of the client–patron relationship between Israel and the US as the Americans appeared powerless in the face of Israeli intransigence over a peace process with the Arabs.

Indeed by the mid to late 1980s there were many who judged US policy in the Middle East to be more a case of failure than success. They pointed to the 1979 revolution in Iran, the 1979 Mecca uprising in Saudi Arabia, the Soviet invasion and occupation of Afghanistan in 1980, the 1981 assassination of peacemaking President Sadat in Egypt, the bombing of American marines in Lebanon in 1983 and 1984, the outbreak of the Palestinian uprising against their ally Israel in 1987 and the bombing of Pan AM flight 103 in 1988. Critics opined that the biases inherent in US policy in the region were reaping negative rewards and creating instability among their pro-western allies. There were widespread fears that if Iran could topple so could other oil-rich states in the region – and America would be vulnerable to spiralling oil price rises. It was this last factor that many cite as the key reason why President George Bush was compelled to respond to Saddam Hussein's invasion of Kuwait in August 1990 (see chapter 4). Whether this is the primary rationale for Operation Desert Storm and the ensuing war of 1991 or not, the American intervention in the region of the Gulf at this point was pivotal in shaping many perceptions (both positive and negative) about America's role in the Middle East.

Under the Clinton administration there did appear to be movement with respect to the greatest political bugbear of the region: the Israeli–Palestinian conflict. There was certainly a ripple effect within the Clinton administration with respect to peace and intervention efforts in Europe (Northern Ireland and the Balkans) and the Middle East. The Clinton administration, however, was also criticized for not effectively containing other actors and threats within the region. Moreover his government left office without having brokered a final resolution to the Palestinian–Israeli conflict which by the end of 2000 was once again mired in a vicious cycle of violence that engulfed Israelis as well as Palestinians. Edward Said wrote of the administration that, 'Clinton himself seems as though he does not much care for foreign affairs and has no inclination or gift for articulating and maintaining an American globalism' (Said, 1995b, p. 84). Said was deeply critical of what he perceived as a failure by the American government to use its power in the Middle East in the interests of what he considered to be a fair and just resolution of the Palestinian–Israeli conflict. American brokerage of the Oslo Accords – in Said's opinion – was a real reflection of US national interest. This is because, as Said argues, American 'peace' in the Middle East

> means the normalization of relationships between Israel and the Arab states; that except for Israel no Arab state may possess weapons of mass destruction or pose any challenge either to Israel or to the oil-producing states; the containment and if necessary the punishment of Iran; that the economies of the Arab states should be open to Israeli and US penetration; both conflict *and* dialogue with political Islam; an unrestricted flow of inexpensive Arab oil to the US; and finally, it means the subordination of all regional and local issues to the US. (Said, 1995b, p. 87)

The dimensions of the American role at this stage in the attempt to resolve the Palestinian–Israeli conflict are described in the following way: 'The United States had several different roles in the negotiations, complex and often contradictory: as principal broker of the putative peace deal; as guardian of the peace process; as Israel's strategic ally; and as its cultural and political partner. The ideas it put forward throughout the process bore the imprint of each' (Agha and Malley,

2001). While it may be true that Clinton left office without having secured a peace treaty and two-state solution between Israel and the Palestinians, failure lay as much in the hands of the Palestinians and Israelis as it did with their American mediators. At the time President Yasser Arafat rather than President Clinton or Prime Minister Barak was blamed for the collapse of a process that appeared at once to be so near and yet so far to a final resolution of conflict between Israel and the Palestinians. But as one Clinton-appointed negotiator admits, 'As for the United States, it never fully took control of the situation. Pulled in various and inconsistent directions, it never quite figured out which way to go, too often allowing itself to be used rather than using its authority' (Agha and Malley, 2001).

Burger bars and belly dancers

> Most Americans lump Arabs together and create a composite in their minds made up of unflattering and false images from films, commentators with an agenda, and exaggerated news clips . . . Americans do not see the rich diversity among countries in the Arab world, and certainly not the diversity within countries. (Edward Walker, President Middle East Institute)

The cultural impact of America on the Middle East is in part associated with foreign policy-making decisions but it is also an expression of American national interest that operates outside the confines of government in Washington. This is not to say that culture is not used as an instrument of American foreign policy but that other actors from within American society also lend their spirit and image of themselves abroad to the wider political project as it relates to the Middle East. Indeed, there has been a growing debate about the cultural impact of America in the Middle East. Moreover Arab nationalism and Islamism can also be seen as a facet of the counter-culture that has arisen in response to what is perceived to be American hegemonic (including cultural) ambitions in their region.

The political dimension of the debate about culture assumed a greater importance in the wake of 9/11 when the thesis of Samuel Huntington on the 'clash of civilizations' and the work of Bernard Lewis on Islam was utilized by the Bush administration in justifying the war on terror. Indeed, despite arguments to the contrary, the visual symbol of the war on terror is identified in the popular consciousness of America as the Arab/Muslim from the Middle East. This symbolism has been reinforced in the American media – television, print, film, and so forth. In this sense the enemy has been consciously constructed as emanating from the Middle East. Pre-existing biases about the region's inhabitants – as the quote above describes – reinforce a sense that dominant Arab/Muslim cultures of the Middle East are the antithesis of American culture and the values of freedom and democracy that they are underpinned by.

The work of Huntington and Lewis has been particularly significant in influencing current debates about how the indigenous cultures of the Middle East (Arab and Muslim) represent a threat to American values. Huntington devised a framework of international relations working from the hypothesis of an inevitable confrontation between Islam and the West in an article published in 1993. His thesis focused on a 'clash of civilizations', where cultures rather than national states would engage in conflicts. Although Huntington addresses some eight major civilizations, it is between Islam and the West that he predicts a fault-line and clash will occur. He perceives 'civilizational' conflict taking place, where 'violent conflicts between groups in different civilizations are the most likely and most dangerous source of escalation that could lead to global wars' (Huntington, 1993, p. 34). Huntington emphasizes the historical roots of antipathy between the Judeo-Christian West and the Muslim Middle East and contends that confrontation will increase between these civilizations. His analysis provided an intellectual backdrop to the war on terrorism and appeared to demonstrate the polarization of opinion between America and the Arab/Muslim Middle East as they faced each other in the twenty-first century. It was as if culture explained the Middle East to America and vice versa. Many on both sides of the geo-strategic divide succumbed to Huntington's thesis. Bernard Lewis's work reinforces the cultural antipathy argument by contending that the modern Middle East is dominated by a discourse of Muslim/Arabism that is bent on a violent confrontation with the West. Lewis contends that:

> It should by now be clear that we are facing a mood and movement far transcending the level of issues and policies, and the governments that pursue them. This is no less than a clash of civilizations – the perhaps irrational, but surely historic reaction of an ancient rival against our Judeo-Christian heritage, our secular present, and the worldwide expansion of both. It is crucially important that we on our side should not be provoked into an equally historic, but also irrational reaction against that rival. (Lewis, 1990)

This input from Lewis has shaped the ways in which the Bush administration views the Middle East and the threats emanating from it in the present day. For Lewis and Huntington the cultural dimension of foreign policy towards the Middle East matters greatly if American national interest in the region is to be better secured. Foreign policy post-Cold War is now redefined in respect of the Middle East through the prism of Islam. Islam is then portrayed as a means of cutting off the region from connections with the rest of the globe – and the West in particular. In this sense the Middle East is labelled as exceptional in terms of faith defining politics and as a countervailing force against the rest of the globe. The force of fragmentation here is political Islam which he sees as a menace and disruptive to international society. Huntington and Lewis have succeeded in convincing many in the Bush administration that this axis of interpretation for the region is appropriate. As such, policies towards the region and its Muslim inhabitants are informed from this standpoint of axial distance rather than mutuality of principles or commonality of ideals.

American media outlets, as I highlighted earlier, have played their part in perpetuating this antipathy. The American media reflect norms and values that shape America's political culture and system. In the past the American media have rarely been critical of any US administration – particularly in relation to US 'special relationships' with client states such as Israel or Saudi Arabia. In this respect it is sometimes difficult to ascertain who sets the news and political agenda as it relates to the Middle East. It is apparent, however, that the American-based media reinforce negative stereotypes of the Arab/Muslim population of the Middle East. American news-based corporations like Fox News have come under attack for reinforcing hostile and negative biases against the Middle East when compared to consumers of other forms of media. The unwitting consumption of such stereotypes as displayed in the media reinforces the normative debate vis-à-vis US policy in the Middle East. In this respect it comes as no surprise that when Americans were asked by Gallup to rank their country's greatest enemies the majority of them included states from the Middle East rather than anywhere else in the world. In some respects, particularly after the events of 9/11, it is difficult to see how the American media can represent the Middle East objectively. The media – reflecting popular trends and government sentiment – thus reinforce prevailing opinion rather than try to turn the tide on it. Editorials, news features, op-ed pieces, documentaries and news specials reinforce the perception among most Americans that the inhabitants of the Middle East remain hostile to them. In this way public opinion informs foreign policy towards the Middle East of either containing or eliminating the threats that the region symbolizes for so many.

The point here is that culture – whether American or otherwise – is employed and exploited as a tool of policy-makers to project a 'positive' image of the United States of America throughout the Middle East. Similarly local movements employ or exploit such symbols in negative protest against the United States of America. In 2002 the US Congress identified anti-American propaganda as 'a real threat to the long-term US interests in the region ... It [anti-American propaganda] has created a culture of hatred, a culture of hatred directed against the United States and our Allies' (US Congress, 2002). The image of America has clearly become tainted across the Middle East, its symbols despised and subjected to protest – including consumer boycotts of American burger and other fast food franchises as well as products such as Pepsi and Coca-Cola. In response, the US government has embarked on counter-propaganda campaigns, setting up Arabic radio stations that play a mixture of western and Arabic music and carry news bulletins that are supposed to counter the news slant of popular Arabic satellite stations such as Al-Jazeera and Al-Arabiya. Moreover, Arabic language magazines have also been set up with a target audience of Arab youth to counter Arabic publications in the region that carry articles that are critical of or hostile to America's role in the Middle East. Clearly, in US foreign policy-making circles there is a belief that the cultures of the Arab/Iranian Middle East are incompatible with that of the United States of America and that policy should reflect a response to this clash of cultures in the global age.

Indeed, Robert Fisk opined, even before the events of 9/11:

> From Afghanistan to the Mediterranean, it is now possible to travel through the Middle East and not pass through more than one country that still boasts a U.S. Embassy ... Yet, incredibly, we are asked to admire the United States' political 'success' in the Middle East – and to have faith that the grotesque imbalance built into the Arab–Israeli negotiations represents a just peace. The unspoken truth is that US policies, and the Arab leaders who have endorsed them, are becoming ever more unpopular throughout the region. (Fisk, 1996)

American foreign policy from Ground Zero

George W. Bush entered the White House in January 2001 with very little intention of engaging the efforts of his Republican administration in the politics of the Middle East. Bush had made it clear during the 2000 election campaign that the status quo in terms of American national interest and the Middle East would not be altered if he won the poll for President. He reiterated a commitment to Israel, to maintaining relations with friendly Arab regimes, but noted that the peace process could not be pushed to a timetable of American making. Moreover he highlighted the extent to which Saddam Hussein of Iraq was considered to be a threat in the region. In other words Bush had no radical 'vision' for the region that he hoped to implement once in power, although it has been contended that Iraq and regime change was on the foreign policy agenda early in the administration.

The attacks orchestrated by al-Qaeda against American targets on 11 September 2001 changed all that and they have had a significant impact on American foreign policy orientations in the Middle East. In some respects policy positions have been reinforced and hardened rather than abandoned or ameliorated. The biggest impact was that President George W. Bush was compelled to abandon a non-interventionist position towards the region. The Middle East became a top priority of foreign policy deliberations. Foreign policy started to matter in terms of the American electorate as well. In the past, foreign policy had never tended to dominate American public discourse. Traditionally foreign policy issues never really determined the outcome of a presidential poll. This has changed in the aftermath of 9/11, the war on terrorism and the American invasion of Iraq. In the presidential election of November 2004 that pitted Democratic contender Senator John Kerry against incumbent George W. Bush, exit polls demonstrated that as much as 34 per cent of the poll was explained by the war on terrorism.

In the wake of the attack, President Bush 'vowed to take the fight well beyond Afghanistan, eyeing in particular Iraq, Iran and North Korea' (Kupchan, 2002, p. 31). In the Middle East not only were Iraq and Iran in his target sights but pressure grew to look afresh at the Israeli–Palestinian conflict, Libya, Saudi Arabia, Yemen, Lebanon, Syria, regional security and arms defence issues, Egypt, the absence of democracy in pro-western regimes such as Jordan, as well as economic factors such as oil and global capital development. Studied unilateralism and intervention, however, would remain the signature to the Bush administration's re-engagement with the region. Moreover, the re-engagement was bullish and confrontational in tone.

This tone was a reflection of how deeply felt was the need to recover the myth of US hegemony and invincibility in relation to the region and its peoples. The attacks had revealed a sense of vulnerability on the home front that the Bush administration was keen to compensate for abroad. In this respect it was argued that the events of 9/11 were a 'wake-up call' for the United States of America (Kupchan, 2002, p. 31). In the aftermath of the events of 9/11, every aspect of US governance came under scrutiny. The realm of foreign policy in the Middle East was where some commentators contended that problems had arisen. Foreign policy – particularly as it related to the long history of intervention through covert actions by elements such as the CIA – had, they argued, ultimately undermined American national interests and security. In part it explained why people hated America (Johnson, 2002). Such commentators also argued that American 'imperial over-reach' had bred radical, hostile, anti-American forces in the region that were rooted in the fundamentalist Islamic tradition (Chomsky, 2003).

Other thinkers and commentators, especially on the American right, have argued for a different interpretation and policy with respect to the Middle East. They argued in the wake of 9/11 that the very fabric of American society – democracy and freedom – was under attack from fanatical Muslim terrorists. In this sense their commentary lent credence to the 'clash of civilizations' thesis. As such they argued for strong intervention in the politics of the region to prevent further threats arising against America. Intervention took the form of military action against Afghanistan (with its effects felt in neighbouring Middle Eastern states such as Iran) and Iraq – again with its effects being felt in neighbouring states such as Syria, Jordan, Iran and Saudi Arabia. Islam has been identified by the right wing as the chief impediment to securing American national interest through 'democracy promotion'. As one such commentator remarks:

> The most realistic response to terrorism is for America to embrace its imperial role . . . Occupying Iraq and Afghanistan will hardly end the 'war on terrorism,' but it beats the alternatives. Killing bin Laden is important and necessary; but it is not enough. New bin Ladens could rise up to take his place. We must not only wipe out the vipers but also destroy their nest and do our best to prevent new nests from being built there again. (Boot, 2001)

This thinking takes account of the changes in US policy in the Middle East in the wake of 9/11 and it has also created a legacy of new and more direct US intervention in the name of the war on terrorism and promotion of democracy that successive administrations will have to deal with. The new thinking was reflected in a growing antipathy towards the Middle East that was reflected more widely in American public opinion and popular culture (Sardar and Wyn Davies, 2002). This antipathy was mutually reinforcing as opinion polls of the Middle East revealed that most people polled also mistrusted America and its recent motives in the region. The success of such actions can only be measured in terms of developments over decades rather than years. The ambition, however, is clearly stated: protect oil, protect Israel, protect America through local alliance and bring democracy to the region as a force for good against the perilous grip that Islam currently has over the Middle East. This also explains better how interests remained relatively unchanged but policy more assertive and unilateral.

Case study   **America and Israel**

The relationship between Israel and the United States of America stems – at the level of inter-governmental bilateral relationships – from the historic fall-out of the Holocaust and American repositioning in the wake of the end of the

Second World War and the outbreak of the Cold War. These events have gone some considerable way in shaping a bilateral diplomatic relationship that in turn has had many additional layers added to it. This relationship is, in many respects, unlike any other diplomatic relationship that the United States of America has conducted with a foreign ally. It is a relationship that both sides admit is 'special'. In 1977, as Israel stood on the brink of peace with its Arab neighbour, Egypt, American President Jimmy Carter affirmed his commitment to Israel declaring, 'We have a special relationship with Israel. It's absolutely crucial that no one in our country or around the world ever doubt that our number one commitment in the Middle East is to protect the right of Israel to exist, to exist permanently, and to exist in peace' (Carter, 1977).

Successive administrations of US government have, since 1945, acted as staunch allies of Israel when many other actors in the international community have criticized the state for its illegal actions with respect to its occupation of the Palestinian territories and the Palestinian people. At international forums such as the United Nations where UN resolutions have been passed to remind Israel of its obligations to the Palestinians according to international law, the United States of America has consistently applied its veto power. UN resolutions condemning Israel for its 'policies and practices in the occupied territories', 'expropriation of land in East Jerusalem', 'settlement activity in East Jerusalem' and 'killing by Israeli forces of . . . UN employees' have all been vetoed by the US representative at the United Nations. One way of interpreting this support is to reflect on the extent to which Israel's interests are seen as part of or a reflection of American foreign policy interests in the Middle East.

The US–Israel relationship has been subject to a process of institutionalization and close links that are reflected in more than one area of the American system of governance and more broadly in American society at large where sympathies for Israel and the Zionist cause remain widespread. Institutionally the extent to which Israel and issues associated with it form a crucial element of American foreign policy in the Middle East is reflected in the office of the President, the State Department, the Pentagon, Congress and Senate. This is due in no small measure to the presence and influence of an important pro-Israel lobby in the USA, the mobilization in the past of the Jewish vote in national elections, sympathies in the highly influential Christian Zionist movement and their current impact on neo-conservative discourse in the USA. It is argued in respect of the influence of the pro-Israel lobby that, 'if the pro-Israeli lobby were to sponsor a resolution on Capitol Hill calling for the abolition of the Ten Commandments, both Houses of Congress would adopt it overwhelmingly' (Avinery, 2005). The US Congress has been predisposed to the arguments of the well-organized pro-Israel lobby. The main lobby group is the American Israel Public Affairs Committee (AIPAC) and it targets Congress and other parts of the American political system directly in an attempt to influence legislation and policy in support for Israel. In other words it seeks to ensure that American foreign policy is supportive of Israel – particularly as a 'lone democracy' in the Middle East. AIPAC seeks to put in force Israeli policy in America rather than the other way round. Israel has benefited greatly from US support. It is, for example, the recipient of the largest amount of US aid in the world. It is estimated that, 'since 1973, Israel has cost the United States about $1.6 trillion. If divided by today's population, that is more than $5,700 per person' (Francis, 2002).

Given the depth of the relationship between Israel and the United States of America, many have examined and questioned it in terms of American interests and their policy agenda in terms of the wider Middle East. The natural sympathies that the US shares with Israel are understandable but dependence rather than mutuality is an issue that has featured in critiques of this relationship. America is now understood as an actor in the region in relation to Israel first and other states second. This in turn has shaped Arab attitudes towards the United States of America and their policies in the region. Such actors complain that 'every issue in the region has to go firstly through the door of Israel before it can be discussed with the United States of America and we simply don't feel this way about everything' (Moussawi, 2005).

In sum, a combination of factors, including the ethical debt America feels that it owes Israel, the impact of the pro-Israel lobby as well as material interests in terms of relations between these two states, continue to account for American foreign policy with regard to this tiny state. As President Bush asserted early in his administration, 'Israel is a small country that has lived under threat throughout its existence. At the first meeting of my National Security Council, I told them a top foreign policy priority is the safety and security of Israel. My Administration will be steadfast in supporting Israel against terrorism and violence and in seeking the peace for which all Israelis pray' (Bush, 2001). The second term of the Bush administration elected in November 2004 appeared set to maintain that pledge (Mearsheimet and Walt, 2006).

Case study America and Saudi Arabia: oil on troubled waters

The foreign relations that the policy-makers of the US have sought with the Kingdom of Saudi Arabia is rooted in a 70-year relationship that was and to the present day remains largely motivated by securing access or control over Saudi Arabia's oil reserves. Successive US governments have had to remain cognizant of a diplomatic, political, economic and security relationship with an Arab state that also claims significant Islamic and in particular Wahabi credentials. The cities of Mecca and Medina in Saudi Arabia are considered the most holy to millions of Muslims from across the globe. Saudi Arabia is a monarchical Islamic state that does not reflect the democratic political profile that the US claims for itself. Over the years, the association between the United States and Saudi Arabia has been cultivated more by necessity than natural political affinity. Since 1932 Saudi Arabia has been a monarchy ruled by the al-Saud family. The al-Sauds are adherents of the fundamentalist Islamic doctrine of Wahabism which they have incorporated into the structures of the state they control. The Saudi possession of oil and its strategic location in the Gulf region make it important in terms of defined American national interest. Diplomatic relations with the kingdom were established shortly after independence in the early 1930s and cemented in a historic meeting in 1945 between President Roosevelt and King Abdel Aziz.

This relationship extended to the facilitation, by the US, of a growing number of US owned oil corporations in the economic development of the kingdom. The oil industry would contribute to the rapid development of Saudi Arabia as a modern state governed by a conservative pro-western monarchy. The pivot in this relationship was the extent to which successive US governments could secure American national interest (oil and strategic influence) with a government guided by principles so radically different from their own. This was largely achieved by treating the relationship with Saudi Arabia as primarily economically driven. Oil from Saudi Arabia was increasingly key to US industry and economy; by the 1970s 20 per cent of US crude oil imports were derived from Saudi Arabia. The US, in turn, became Saudi Arabia's most important trading partner. A key element in US enjoyment of access to Saudi oil exports was, of course, security – particularly in a region that has traditionally been viewed as one of the most volatile in the globe.

US administrators understood this issue as early as the 1950s and persuaded the Saudi monarchy to accept a US base in the Saudi town of Dahran as early as 1953. It was increased spending on US-supplied weaponry plus the role of American oil companies in promoting the modernization of infrastructure in Saudi Arabia that contributed to the establishment of a meaningful relationship between the two sides. The depth of meaning to this relationship, however, extended to certain areas of policy such as economic and military issues. By the early 1980s, for example, there were complaints within the Reagan administration of preferential treatment for the Saudis after the President agreed to sell the advanced AWACS system as well as Sidewinder missiles to the kingdom. There were fears – particularly in pro-Israel circles – that American support for the supply of advanced weaponry to Saudi Arabia could upset the advantage that Israel traditionally enjoyed in the regional arms race.

The importance of the military and security relationship between the USA and Saudi Arabia was underscored following the invasion by President Saddam Hussein of Saudi's neighbour Kuwait in August 1990. Iraq's occupation of Kuwait brought a threat direct to Saudi borders and imperilled the American principle of unhindered access to Arab oil. Nearly 500,000 Iraqi troops were now in occupation of Saudi Arabia's neighbour. There was an immediate fear in both Saudi Arabia and the US that an emboldened Saddam Hussein would order his troops into Saudi. Hence, in early August, at the invitation of the Saudi monarchy, President George Bush ordered the deployment of over 200,000 troops. These numbers were boosted by early January 1991 with the arrival of a further 200,000. This deployment established a US troop presence in Saudi Arabia that would not be terminated until 2003. The presence of American troops in Saudi Arabia was a potent indication of the extent to which the kingdom (one of the wealthiest in the world) was reliant on another power for national security. Moreover the presence of US troops in territory considered by Muslims as the most holy in Islam was exploited by figures such as Usama bin Laden. The decision, moreover, to leave Saddam Hussein in Iraq, until he was deposed in April 2003, also left the region, including Saudi Arabia, with a strategic 'threat' that would have to be contained. This ultimately tied Saudi Arabia to the US with the need for US security for the kingdom remaining a linchpin of their relationship.

Containment was the ultimate hallmark of the Clinton administration with respect to the Gulf region. For it was to be the Arab–Israeli conflict that absorbed his energies with respect to policy-making in the region. It was events on 11 September 2001 that tested the limits of the US–Saudi relationship. When it became apparent that so many of the bombers from al-Qaeda had originated from Saudi Arabia and that Usama bin Laden was behind the plot, it was inevitable that American pressure would grow for the kingdom to take action against what many in American circles believed to be the problem of Islamic terrorism that was rooted in Saudi Arabia. Bin Laden had singled out America as an enemy and accused it of occupying Islam's most holy places (Mecca and Medina in Saudi Arabia). He had demanded an immediate withdrawal of American troops from Saudi Arabia. Many criticized Saudi Arabia for playing its part in promoting an Islamic ideology of anti-westernism and intolerance of the West which they claimed was rooted in Wahabi thinking and its activities abroad. A growing critique of Saudi Arabia in America galvanized rulers in Riyadh to join the American-led war on terrorism. Relations between the US and Saudi Arabia are said to have deteriorated but ultimately the mutual dependence between the two states will ensure that the ties that bind them remain.

Further reading

A good starting point in terms of further reading on American foreign policy would be Walter Russell Mead's book (2001) because it provides a strong historical overview of American foreign policies according to a framework of US categorization and also because the book is considered influential in American circles post-9/11 in terms of historical perspective and future policy options. Reading around this area more generally can then be supplemented by Snow and Brown (1997), Bacevich (2002) on US diplomacy, as well as Kupchan (2002) who examines the growing dilemma for US foreign policy-makers with respect to superpower status and a rapidly changing global context. Nye (2002) raises some of the paradoxes that beset the USA as the sole global superpower in the twenty-first century. There are many critiques of American foreign policy as it relates to the Middle East and the Muslim world. It is worth considering Chomsky's contributions (2003 and 1997) for a perspective on American 'imperial' ambition and its consequences for the rest of the international community and the resolution of conflicts in the Middle East in particular. On the issue of the cultural dimension of America's role in the Middle East Sardar and Wyn Davies (2003), Little (2002), and Crockatt (2003) all tackle dimensions of anti-Americanism and Orientalism. For more specific literature on US policy in the Middle East since 9/11 see Prestowitz (2003), Shannon (2000), and Zunes (2002) for a variety of differing perspectives and accounts. On America's special relationship with Israel, recommended reading would include. Chomsky (1999), Quandt (2005) and Aruri (2003), all of whom develop a critical overview of the relationship with respect to the politics of wider regional issues such as the Arab–Israeli conflict. The development of a critique on the relationship between America and Saudi Arabia is relatively recent. Some available sources are Lippman (2004) and AbuKhalil (2004), both of whom detail the more recent tensions in the American-Saudi relationship.

Epilogue: The Middle East and the Twenty-first Century

WHILE the chapters of this book combine to cover more than a century of politics in the Middle East, the issue of the future has remained largely unaddressed. Since the attacks on America by Arab members of the al-Qaeda terror group, many have speculated on the future of the Middle East in the twenty-first century. Much has been made of a number of new threats within the region, but perhaps more tellingly it is the threat to the West in the post-Cold War era which has preoccupied area specialists, commentators and pundits alike. Indeed, much has been made of the fact that the threats from the Middle East to the West have failed to manifest themselves in the manner that so many confidently predicted in the 1980s and the 1990s. This epilogue, therefore, will not engage in the dangerous task of second-guessing the future of the region or its relationship with the rest of the globe, but in assessing, first, dynamic political factors within the region and, second, in discussing the perceived threats to the West and the current international order that the constituent states and non-state actors of the region pose.

All the themes that have been addressed in this book so far will remain, to a greater or lesser extent, relevant to the nature of the politics of the Middle East in the twenty-first century. The major themes which I have examined play a significant part in affecting the politics of the region and comprehensively explain situations which initially appeared inexplicable to the first-time observer. Politics can be a complex matter, a question of learning to account for a variety of factors and the balances which come into play between them. In this respect, understanding the politics of the Middle East is no different from understanding those of Latin America, south-east Asia or Africa. The reward for such endeavours, as we have seen, is an insight into a fascinating world which is dynamic, political in all respects and which interacts culturally with a variety of forces.

The colonial legacy? East–West relations

While the impact of colonialism may not be directly pertinent to the contemporary politics of the region, the character of Middle East–West relations which was established during the colonial era continues to be significant. By and large, while many governments of the region have established and maintained cordial relations with the governments of the West, the legacy of the colonial relationship can be found in the general expressions of hostility to the West found among a considerable minority of states and a majority of the peoples of the region. The manifestation of at least three 'pariah' states and an 'axis of evil' including states from the region, subject to western censure and international sanction, does not bode well for state-to-state relations in this particular part of the East–West matrix. In addition, successive generations residing in the Middle East have absorbed the 'colonial legacy', its myth or reality, into their national psyche and have grown up regarding western intentions with hostility, suspicion and fear. The fear of new colonial relationships has also been incorporated into the national agenda of many countries within the region, among certain political groups and elites who, for one reason or another, seek capital out of this antagonistic relationship. This is particularly pertinent with respect to the American-led occupation of Iraq which has been widely read in the Middle East as evidence of US ambition for dominance in the region as a whole. The roots of this relationship – the colonial experience – are carefully exposed and exploited in an eternal reminder of the past catching up with the future.

In addition, so long as the international order remains dominated by the nation-state system, the legacy of colonialism will be evident in the Middle East. How the political elites of these nation-states continue to deal with the state system which they have inherited from the colonizers and subsequently reinforced will be dependent on a number of other factors, such as political economy, ethnicity or the impact of political Islam on levels of formal and informal politics, which have been directly addressed in this book. The colonial legacy, therefore, has established a pattern or fabric of politics that is not always natural to the region but has become an accretion or acculturation of political discourse. This tension between the western-style state system and more indigenous state systems of government and politics remains unresolved and subject to a variety of largely external pressures.

The stability of the region may also, by and large, be assured in the future. It is important to recognize, however, that current levels of stability have been secured, in one-party states as well as monarchical tribal states, through authoritarianism rather than western-style liberal democracy. The relationship with the West, and America in particular, however, remains pivotal to the politics of the region. One might argue, as many authors on the left have, that new colonial relationships have arisen in the region, reinforced through the politics of the present. Stability may be guaranteed for the foreseeable future by the determination not just of the ruling elite to perpetuate further their stranglehold of power over many of the citizens of the region, but the collusion of the western governments dependent on models of liberal economies which seek to preserve the stability of the region through tyranny. This state of affairs was highlighted in the 1990s by the Gulf crisis following Iraq's invasion of Kuwait, the collapse of the Soviet Union and the global hegemony of America in the unipolar system of international politics which affects the Middle East as much as any other Third World region. In the Middle East, the role of America in the region is not yet fully assured but its commitment in supporting the conservative regimes of the Gulf, shoring up Jordan's peace agreement with Israel, maintaining its significant hold over Egypt's economy, its occupation of Iraq, sanctions against Syria, demands on Iran, as well as the preservation of the special relationship with Israel, go a long way in helping this particular part of the West remain a key player in the politics of the Middle East. The concept of *pax Americana* in the region is far from assured for among the general populace of the region there is deep mistrust of American motives. Other Westerner actors, such as the states of the European Union, are more aware of the special dynamic that operates between them and the Middle East. In this respect they also represent a new influence on the region that seeks democracy promotion and economic development through the insertion of the Middle East into the global economy.

The future Arab nation

Notions of Arabness through the expression of the ideology of nationalism will also continue to assume importance, along with other identities which continue to bind the citizens of the region together in new forms of ethnic politics and ethno-national tension. While the flaws of the ideologies of Arab nationalism and pan-Arabism have been revealed in the latter half of the twentieth century and the first decade of the twenty-first, its strengths, in creating a form of political identity and unity, have also been discovered. In particular, the liberal values which support, at least in theory, ideas of Arabness, Arab nationalism and the Arab people are still significant in supporting this form of political identity. In cities like Cairo and Baghdad, Beirut, Damascus and Algiers, the twenty-first century may well continue to give rise to a fresh generation of Arab intellectuals and thinkers who seek to reassert Arab identity and pride in Arabness. The traditions of Arab literature, through Nobel prize-winning writers such as Neguib Mahfouz, arts and poetry, culture, science and trading, will be maintained in the twenty-first century and will somehow meet the challenge posed by other ideological blueprints for the region, including political Islam.

Arab identity may well become refined or even redefined in relation to other issues such as gender or Islam. These issues will remain important, particularly in continuing to shape Arab national identities, whether Syrian, Kuwaiti, Lebanese or Jordanian. In the Lebanese case, for example, the Arabness of Lebanese identity will continue to be tested against other factors such as Maronite, Shi'ite and Druze claims. The outcome is most likely to be apparent in the multifaceted notion of identity, including Arabness, which so many inhabitants of the region already seem to have developed.

The political economy matrix

The impact of oil wealth and the battle for finite natural resources such as gas and water will also continue to play their part in the patterns of politics which dominate the region in the present day. Whether oil wells run dry or continue to be discovered and exploited, the impression that this commodity will make on the region and economies outside it will remain significant. Internally, the development of economies in the oil-producing states from Iran to Bahrain, Iraq to Saudi Arabia will determine the nature of politics and continue to affect those states within the region which remain migrant-rich but oil-poor. The future of Egypt, for example, cannot be considered without assessing the issue of migrant labour on the balance of the economy and therefore the dependent relationship which the country maintains with many of the Gulf states. The economies and development of Gulf states such as the United Arab Emirates will also remain, by and large, dependent on external, predominantly Arab, assistance; therefore, inter-Arab relations will remain important within the region, with prosperity for all often linked to the economies of particular countries.

The conflict over water may, however, become more intense within the region. The prosperity, stability and political longevity of many states will become increasingly dependent on control of this increasingly scarce resource. The politics of water, negotiations for shared water usage, territorial disputes over areas with significant rivers and reservoirs may well come to dominate the headlines emerging out of the region.

Structural adjustment, the reconstruction of national economies, economies of indebtedness, aid development, capital expansion and the globalization of market forces will continue to remain especially significant to the political economy of the region. The politics of restructuring such diverse economies will continue to have major ramifications both for power-holders within the region and for the increasingly marginalized poor, who will once again pay the price for poorly managed economies. The increasing tendency to rope the economies of the region even more tightly into the global economic network will only serve to emphasize their relative underperformance on world markets and inhibit regionally generated attempts at greater economic cohesion and unity.

Carry on conflict

As such, conflict – over water, between people and across local borders – continues to characterize the region. The hope that outright war on the major scale witnessed during the 1950s, 1960s and 1970s would become increasingly untenable was shattered by the war on Iraq in 2003. The sheer build-up of military hardware, nuclear weaponry and military forces within the region continues to succeed in making war a plausible option.

Other forms of conflict – whether territorial, gender, ethnic, economic or sectarian – have emerged and persist in characterizing many aspects of political discourse or relations within the region. Here, inter-state and intra-state tensions over issues of, for example, ethnic politics, do threaten to undermine authoritarian control and the hegemonic tendencies of many states from Israel to Saudi Arabia. The likelihood of continuing civil conflict in states such as Algeria, Iraq and Lebanon also needs to be addressed, especially given the failure of political leaders in those countries to repair the mechanisms of political control which encouraged or precipitated warfare in the first place. In addition, the coalescence of such tension at a time in the near future where the hold of many of the tyrants of the region seems increasingly untenable may very well usher in a new era of politics in countries like Syria, Saudi Arabia, Oman, Libya, Bahrain and Kuwait.

Although the politics of peacemaking may prove unsatisfactory, the status quo of permanent conflict, for example between the Arabs and Israelis, has been irrevocably altered, making it virtually impossible to go back to the persistent state of hostilities which characterized the region for so many decades. While conflict resolution may be in its infancy, its role within the region has at last become tenable, providing those with the will the opportunity to find new ways of communicating with their neighbours and a retreat from the politics of the past.

Political Islam: the politics of the future

The impact of Islam within the region will always be important in the majority of Muslim countries and will continue to affect non-Muslim states such as Israel. Islam is the most significant religion of the Middle East and despite the force of globalization its impact on people's lives remains significant in the present day. The relationship between Islam and politics, however, is more difficult to predict. The tidal wave of fundamentalism which was supposed to sweep the region in the 1980s and 1990s, resulting in the collapse of governments from Morocco to Saudi Arabia, has yet to materialize in the form of revolution and transition of one form of government to another predominantly Muslim rule. The nominal notion of Muslim rule, where state elites continue to legitimate their continuing claims to power through Islam, will, however, probably remain the rule for the foreseeable future.

It is in the arena of informal politics, involving non-state actors, that the most significant Islamification of politics is likely to continue to take hold. The portals of state power, however, are likely to remain closed to the Islamist activists who bang so loudly at them. Community politics, welfare rights, social rights and economic inequality are likely to be the issues or the arenas where the political voice of Islam will be predominant. In this respect, in this social advocacy role, Islam is really no different from modern-day Christianity or Judaism, where priests and rabbis in poor urban neighbourhoods champion the rights of the poor, oppressed and powerless.

Where Islam continues to be different is through the expression of political violence. The internal war (jihad) conducted by radical extreme fringe elements in countries like Egypt and Algeria against their fellow Muslims appears to be unfathomable but was largely halted by the late 1990s as a result of draconian state policies. The theological argument for such actions against unjust and allegedly infidel rulers and their citizens is rejected in mainstream Islamic thought. The appeal, however, of radical leaders such as Usama bin Laden indicates a serious problem within many states in the region. The response to meeting state violence with non-state violence has, to date, proved a largely ineffective strategy, exacerbating the tensions between the people, the state and the Islamist opposition. Allegations of state involvement in massacres, torture and cruelty are likely to continue to surface, making the task of resolving conflict of this nature through peaceful means decidedly difficult.

The role of the international community has been and will remain important in the debate and strategies employed in dealing with this issue and those related to political Islam. This role, however, is currently circumscribed by the current fear in the West of the 'Green Peril'. This has led to the establishment of a major disconnection at both formal and informal levels between Islam and the West. Acts or threats of violence or terror by Islamist extremists against western targets have dominated the debate about political Islam in the main-stream media. This in turn has led to the portrayal of all Arabs and Muslims as the type of bloodthirsty criminals and terrorists who drove their planes into the Twin Towers in New York and the Pentagon in Washington. It makes the dialogue and the relationship between the West and Islam incredibly difficult and in its turn has encouraged extremist elements in Islam to stereotype the West and westerners in the same negative image.

Decline of democratization

Democratization, despite elections in Iraq in January 2005, regular polls in states such as Lebanon, Jordan, the Palestinian territories and even local municipal elections in Saudi Arabia, is unlikely to transform the politics of the region in the very near future. Few states in the region have embarked on the experiment in full democratization and, in those that have, little benefit for citizens or ruler alike has been derived from the experience to date. The question of the linkage of democratization or liberalization to certain economic agendas has also hindered rather than facilitated the progress of this political force. This linkage has been over-emphasized by the West and western-based international organizations such as the IMF and World Bank in constructing so-called rescue packages for beleaguered Arab regimes or in rebuilding sanction and war shattered economies. According to this model, the democratization process has become a top-down one involving limited political concessions by elites in response to the dictates of external funding, lending and aid-giving powers.

The real calls for increased democracy, pluralism, increased oppor-tunities for political participation and greater individual freedoms in society, which have been expressed by the discontented masses, have largely been ignored by the rulers of such regimes and by the inter-national community. The voice of the masses is only acknowledged when it has coincided with the political and economic agenda of elites and their supporters. This situation was reflected in the failure of the international community to support the Shi'a and Kurdish uprisings in Iraq in 1991. Although the West fought the Iraqi occupation of

Kuwait as both an economic battle and a crusade against tyranny and dictatorship, when it came to the crunch it surrendered its support for democratic rights. The uprisings in Iraq in 1991 had initially been encouraged by the West, yet once Saddam Hussein had been confined and cowed within his own borders the issue of democratic rights and self-determination for the Kurdish and Shi'a populations of the region fell down the international agenda. It was with no sense of irony that the western governments who argued the case for a war against Iraq in 2003 used the same issue of democratization to plead their case with the international community.

The democracy debate remains pertinent and is a long way from being resolved. Deeper issues of cultural and religious symbiosis with this essentially western construct are a long way from being fully aired, formulated and discussed in the political communities of the region. Much of this debate is stifled by the governing regimes of these states which see democracy as a real threat to the perpetuation of their authoritarian mode of rule. While many commentators in the West have already declared the debate a non-starter, citing the inherent incompatibility between such terms as Islam and democracy, within the region there is evidence, particularly in states such as Egypt, of a burgeoning debate among Arab Muslims and liberal intellectuals which has highlighted a greater depth to this debate than many in the West would give it credit for.

The process of democratization within the region, then, will remain a non-starter, limited and stunted in its growth until these wider philosophical issues are fully debated by all sectors of society. While government-run presses, publications, media and news outlets in Iran, Saudi Arabia, Jordan, Syria and Iraq continue to determine the parameters of this particular issue, the truly democratic nature of the discussion about democracy will never find expression within the region. Even in Israel, the parameters of this debate have become increasingly circumscribed by the tension between religious and secular forces in society who disagree over the national vision for the future of the country. Evolution will remain the key to this particular issue and its development in the politics of the Middle East.

Sisters doing it for themselves

The political future for women in the region remains increasingly significant. Many of the other issues which I have discussed in this text are also related to the issue of gender and the role of women in the politics of the contemporary Middle East. Identity, the nation-state system, conflict, economic conditions, democratization – all of these issues are interwoven with those of gender, women's rights, roles and place in the societies and political systems of the region. The twentieth century resulted in significant changes in the political rights of many women in the region. Enfranchisement was offered to women from Morocco to Iran and those states which did not offer them the right to vote have become the minority rather than the majority. This leads one to question the relative merits of female liberation where millions of women in Egypt enjoy the right to vote but women in Saudi Arabia remain disenfranchised according to a strict interpretation of Islam under Wahabi rule.

Formal political rights, however, even in populous states such as Iran, Iraq or Egypt, remain largely meaningless if they are not combined with increased opportunities for women to access the arenas of political power, if employment is denied, if women's literacy rates remain consistently lower than those of men, if their civil and other rights are not protected and enshrined by state law and if their contribution to the national economy remains unrecognized and abused. In these conditions the political gains made by the women of the region have to be put in perspective.

In the twenty-first century, the predominance of patriarchy throughout the Middle East, from Israel to Yemen, remains as potent as ever. Patriarchy in its turn has led to the development of a largely masculine or macho-military political arena, where women remain marginal to the so-called mainstream national political psyche. Women in the region, however, remain and will remain the mistresses of their own fate and further liberation. It is up to them, not other women outside the region, to organize around the issues which they consider pertinent to their political, social and economic well-being.

Ethnic equations

Horowitz (1985) and Connor (1994) both argued that ethnic conflict was the biggest political problem of the 1990s and would likely remain so for future decades. Yet ethnicity was only one element in explaining political conflicts that arose across the globe and in the Middle East in the 1990s. Conflicts apparent in deeply divided societies such as Iraq, Lebanon or between Israel and the Palestinians have been defined in ethnic terms. Yet many of the so-called current ethnic conflicts and tensions which exist in the Middle East can also be explained in terms of a failure by the international community to apply the principle of self-determination fairly and equally in the region. In the Middle East the moral right apparently inherent in the principle of self-determination is exposed as a fallacy or myth to be applied by the international community only where appropriate and convenient. As Allain noted, 'international law [in the Middle East] is understood to be little more than a tool of the powerful, used for coercion and oppression' (Allain, 2004, p. 1). While many may feel that the Palestinians, for example, have demonstrated their territorial and national and ethnic distinctiveness from Israel and its citizens, these conditions have remained insufficient reason for self-determination and statehood in the eyes of the international community.

We can see, similarly, that the failure to codify the term 'self-determination' as a moral right for all peoples – with peoples existing in an abstract non-specific form – has left the Kurdish people stateless, subjected to progressive ethnic cleansing and acts of genocide. The crux of this issue lies in the difficulty in reconciling the inadequacies of the abstract universal right to self-determination in terms of the territorial majoritarian principle which has translated into a state system imposed on the region at the turn of the twentieth century. As such, the regimes of the present are dealing with issues and claims which are not of their own making, but lie in the colonial legacy and the impact it had on the region.

In the same respect the fate of minorities in the region has also been irrevocably altered by the imposition of the nation-state system and the arbitrary drawing of national territorial boundaries. Minorities have always existed in the region, drawn by the special religious locus of the three great monotheistic religions and the central role of the region as a trade crossroads over a number of centuries. Yet, under the modern nation-state system, the political rights of minority populations have not always been protected by the laws of state. In addition, in states like Lebanon or Syria many minorities find themselves in close proximity to each other and compete for political power and control. This has been achieved with varying degrees of success and failure, leading to civil war in some cases and minority hegemony and domination over a subordinate community in others.

Methods for internal accommodation have not, however, always been fully explored. When they have been, it is the more extreme coercive measures that have been adopted. Consociationalism, with the exception of Lebanon, has not been fully explored by any regime in the region, yet there is potential for significant internal accommodation through this mechanism in a variety of states with multi-ethnic or sizeable and competing minority communities. Even in Lebanon the consociational model was doomed, given the inherent bias initially incorporated into the system towards the Maronite community, allowing them to abuse the system to their own advantage.

While the threat of ethnic conflict may wax and wane, the presence of sizeable ethnic or religious minorities will continue to preoccupy the leaders of governments and regimes throughout the region. The ability of these leaders to face the reality of a plural society in majoritarian state systems will depend on a variety of factors, many of which have been discussed in the chapters of this book. The compulsion to rule through domination and coercion will depend, in part, on the demands of the ethnic and religious minority groups themselves and the support which they enjoy in the international community. Once again, the resolution of the Kurdish situation or the Shi'a minority demands in Saudi Arabia may have as much to do with the balance of power in the international order in the twenty-first century as with the will of individual political leaders to address the demands of their minority populations.

American dreams

The Middle East cannot stand in isolation from the international community and nor should its leaders be allowed to do so. The future of the region is inextricably linked to the rest of the global order and it is up to the self-appointed international arbiter – the USA – to play its part in ensuring an equitable western policy towards the Middle East. At present there is little hope among many in the Middle East region that such parity of esteem will materialize. The communication of the American dream – the ideal of liberty, freedom and democracy – has been interpreted and experienced by many peoples in the region with suspicion and hostility. Intent may well be one thing but experience and perception is another. Yet the significant role that the USA plays in the region – whether in economic, military, or diplomatic terms – cannot be simply reduced to an ugly caricature of a modern superpower intent on creating its mirror image over an entire region of the contemporary globe. When American policy-makers seek to maximize their national interests in terms of the region, they contend with complex politics, conflicts and economy. Access to oil remains an imperative in order to fuel America's economic projects, the intractability of the Arab–Israeli conflict, the prevalence of authoritarian regimes, a demographic boom, high unemployment rates in many countries and a sense of cultural dissonance in relating to Islam amounts to a major challenge for America's role in the Middle East in the twenty-first century.

References

Abaza, M. and Strauth, G. 1988: Occidental reason, orientalism, Islamic fundamentalism: a critique. *International Sociology*, vol. 3:4, December, pp. 343–64.

Abboushi, W. F. 1985: *The Unmaking of Palestine*. Wisbech: Middle East and North African Studies Press.

Abdallah, A. 1992: Human rights and elusive democracy. *Middle East Report – MERIP*, no. 174, January–February, pp. 6–8.

Abdel Magid, F. 1994: *Nasser: The Final Years*. Reading, NY: Ithaca Press.

Abdul-Jabar, F. and Dawod, H. (eds) 2003: *Tribes and Power: Nationalism and Ethnicity in the Middle East*. London: Saqi.

Abed-Kotob, S. 1995: Accommodationists speak: goals and strategies of the Muslim Brotherhood in Egypt. *International Journal of Middle Eastern Studies*, vol. 27, pp. 321–39.

Abou El Fadl, 2004: *Islam and the Challenge of Democracy*. Princeton: Princeton University Press.

Abraham, N. 1990: Algeria's façade of democracy: an interview with Mahfoud Bennoune. *Middle East Report – MERIP*, no. 160, March–April, pp. 9–13.

Abrahamian, E. 1989: *Radical Islam, the Iranian Mojahedin*. London: IB Tauris.

Abu Amr, Z. 1994: *Islamic Fundamentalism in the West Bank and Gaza Strip*. Bloomington: Indiana University Press.

AbuKhalil, A. 1992: A new Arab ideology? The rejuvenation of Arab nationalism. *Middle East Journal*, vol. 46:1, pp. 22–36.

—— 1994: The incoherence of Islamic fundamentalism: Arabic Islamic thought at the end of the 20th century. *Middle East Journal*, vol. 48:4, pp. 677–94.

—— 2004: *Battle for Saudi Arabia, The Royalty, Fundamentalism, and Global Power*. New York: Seven Stories Press.

Abu Rabi, I. 1996: *Intellectual Origins of Islamic Resurgence in the Modern Arab World*. Albany: State University of New York Press.

Aburish, S. K. 1994: *The House of Saud: The Rise, Corruption and Coming Fall of the House of Saud*. London: Bloomsbury.

Adams, C. C. 1968: *Islam and Modernism in Egypt: A Study of the Modern Reform Movement Inaugurated by Muhammad Abduh*. New York: Russell and Russell.

Adams, R. 1991: *The Effects of International Remittances on Poverty, Inequality and Development in Rural Egypt*. Washington, DC: International Food Policy Research Institute.

Addi, L. 1992: Algeria's democracy between Islamists and the elite. *Middle East Report – MERIP*, no. 175, March–April, pp. 36–40.

Afshar, H. (ed.) 1985: *Iran: A Revolution in Turmoil*. London: Macmillan.

—— (ed.) 1996: *Women and Politics in the Third World*. London: Routledge.

—— 1998: *Islam and Feminisms: An Iranian Case Study*. Basingstoke: Macmillan.

Ageron, C. R. 1991: *Modern Algeria: A History from 1830 to the Present*. London: Hurst.

Agha, H. and Malley, R. 2001: Camp David: The tragedy of errors. *The New York Review of Books*, vol. 38:13, 9 August.

Ahmed, A. S. 1992: *Postmodernism and Islam: Predicament and Promise*. London: Routledge.

Ahmed, A. S. and Donnan, H. (eds) 1994: *Islam, Globalization and Postmodernity*. London: Routledge.

Ahmed, L. 1992: *Women and Gender in Islam: Historical Roots of a Modern Debate*. New Haven: Yale University Press.

Ajami, F. 1979: The end of pan-Arabism. *Foreign Affairs*, vol. 57, Winter, pp. 355–73.

Ali, T. 2003: *Bush in Babylon: The Recolonization of Iraq*. London: Verso.

Allain, J. 2004: *International Law in the Middle East: Closer to Power than Justice*. Aldershot: Ashgate.

Allan, J. A. 2001: *The Middle East Water Question: Hydro-Politics and the Global Economy*. London: IB Tauris.

Allan, J. A. and Mallat, C. (eds) 1995: *Water in the Middle East: Legal, Political and Commercial Implications*. London: IB Tauris.

Almulhim, M. 1991: *Middle East Oil: A Redistribution of Values Arising from the Oil Industry*. Lanham, MD: University Press of America.

Amawi, A. 1992: Democracy dilemmas in Jordan. *Middle East Report – MERIP*, no. 174, January–February, pp. 26–9.

Amin, S. 1982: *The Arab Economy Today*. London: Zed Books.

Anderson, B. 1983: *Imagined Communities: Reflections on the Origin and Spread of Nationalism*. London: Verso.

Anderson, E. 2003: *Iraqi Kurdistan: Political Development and Emergent Democracy*. London: Routledge Curzon.

Anderson, L. and Stansfield, G. 2004: *The Future of Iraq: Dictatorship, Democracy or Division?* Houndsmills: Palgrave Macmillan.

Ansari, H. 1984: The Islamic militants in Egyptian politics. *International Journal of Middle Eastern Studies*, vol. 16:1, pp. 56–84.

Anthony, J. D. 2002: *The United Arab Emirates: Dynamics of State Formation*. Abu Dhabi: ECSSR.

Antonius, G. 1969: *The Arab Awakening: The Story of the Arab National Movement*. New York: Putnams.

Arian, A. 1989: *Politics in Israel, The Second Generation*. New Jersey: Chatham House.

Arjomand, S. A. 1984: *From Nationalism to Revolutionary Islam*. London: Macmillan.

—— 1988: *The Turban and the Crown: The Islamic Revolution in Iran*. New York: Oxford University Press.

Aruri, N. H. (ed.) 1989: *Occupation: Israel over Palestine*. Belmont, MA: AAAUG.

—— 2003: *Dishonest Broker: The Role of the United States in Palestine and Israel*. New York: South End Press.

Augustin, E. 1993: *Palestinian Women, Identity and Experience*. London: Zed Books.

Avineri, S. 1981: *The Making of Modern Zionism: The Intellectual Origins of the Jewish State*. New York: Basic Books.

Avinery, U. 2005: King George: The USA sinking to new depths of ugliness and brutality. <www.redress.btinternet.co.uk>.

Avishai, B. 1985: *The Tragedy of Zionism: Revolution and Democracy in the Land of Israel*. New York: Farrar, Straus and Giroux.

Ayubi, N. 1991: *Political Islam, Religion and Politics in the Arab World*. London: Routledge.

—— 1995: *Overstating the Arab State: Politics and Society in the Middle East*. London: IB Tauris.

—— 1997: Islam and democracy. In Potter, D. et al. (eds).

Azmeh, al-, A. 1993: *Islams and Modernities*. London: Verso.

—— 1995: Nationalism and the Arabs. *Arab Studies Quarterly*, vol. 17:1–2, Winter–Spring, pp. 1–19.

Bacevich, A. J. 2002: *American Empire: The Realities and Consequences of US Diplomacy*. Harvard: Harvard University Press.

Badran, M. 1993: Independent women: more than a century of feminism in Egypt. In Tucker, J. (ed.).

—— 1994: Gender activism: feminists and Islamists in Egypt. In Moghadam, V. (ed.), 1994b.

—— 1996: *Feminists, Islam and Nation: Gender and the Making of Modern Egypt*. Princeton: Princeton University Press.

Baffoun, A. 1994: Feminism and Muslim fundamentalism: the Tunisian and Algerian cases. In Moghadam, V. (ed.), 1994b.

Bagot-Glubb, J. 1948: *The Story of the Arab Legion*. London: Hodder and Stoughton.

Bahgat, G. 2001: Managing dependence: American–Saudi oil relations. *Arab Studies Quarterly*, vol. 23:1, pp. 1–14.

Bailey, S. D. 1990: *Four Arab–Israeli Wars and the Peace Process*. Basingstoke: Macmillan.

Baker, R. W. 1990: *Sadat and After: The Struggle for Egypt's Political Soul*. London: IB Tauris.

—— 1991: Afraid for Islam: Egypt's Muslim centrists between Pharaohs and Fundamentalists. *Daedalus*, no. 120, pp. 41–68.

Baram, A. 1991: *Culture, History and Ideology in the Formation of Ba'thist Iraq, 1968–1989*. Basingstoke: Macmillan.

Barghouti, I. 1996: Islamist movements in historical Palestine. In Sidahmed, A. S. and Ehteshami, A. (eds).

Barth, F. 1969: *Ethnic Groups and Boundaries: The Social Organisation of Culture Difference*. London: Allen and Unwin.

Batatu, H. 1979: *The Old Social Classes and Revolutionary Movements of Iraq*. Princeton: Princeton University Press.

Beblawi, H. 1990: The rentier state in the Arab world. In Luciani, G. (ed.).

Beck, L. and Keddie, N. (eds) 1978: *Women in the Muslim World*. Cambridge, MA: Harvard University Press.

Beck, L. and Nashat, G. (eds) 2004: *Women in Iran from 1800 to the Islamic Republic*. Urbana: University of Illinois Press.

Beinin, J. and Stork, J. (eds) 1997: *Political Islam: Essays from Middle East Report*. London: IB Tauris.

Ben-Dor, G. 1988: Ethnopolitics and the Middle Eastern state. In Esman, M. J. and Rabinovich, I. (eds).

Bennis, P. and Moushabeck, M. (eds) 1995: *Beyond the Storm: A Gulf Crisis Reader*. Edinburgh: Canongate.

Bennoune, M. 1988: *The Making of Contemporary Algeria*. Cambridge: Cambridge University Press.

Bergen, P. L. 2001: *Holy War Inc: Inside the Secret World of Osama Bin Laden*. London: Weidenfeld & Nicolson.

Bill, J. and Springborg, R. 1994: *Politics in the Middle East*. London: Harper-Collins.

Bin-Talal, H. 1992: Democracy in the Middle East. *British Society for Middle Eastern Studies Proceedings*.

Boot, M. 2001: The case for American empire. *The Weekly Standard*, vol. 7:5, 10 September.

Botman, S. 1987: Women's participation in radical Egyptian politics 1939–52. In Salman, M. et al. (eds).

Bouatta, C. and Cherifati-Merabtine, D. 1994: The social representation of women in Algeria's Islamist movement. In Moghadam, V. (ed.), 1994b.

Boulding, E. (ed.) 1994: *Building Peace in the Middle East: Challenges for States and Civil Society*. Boulder, CO: Lynne Rienner.

Bresheeth, H. and Yuval-Davis, N. (eds) 1991: *The Gulf War and the New World Order*. London: Zed Books.

Breuilly, J. 1993: *Nationalism and the State*. Manchester: Manchester University Press.

Brittain, V. (ed.) 1991: *The Gulf Between Us: The Gulf War and Beyond*. London: Virago.

Bromley, S. 1994: *Rethinking Middle East Politics*. Cambridge: Polity.

—— 1997: Middle East exceptionalism – myth or reality? In Potter, D. et al. (eds).

Brown, D. 1996: *Rethinking Tradition in Modern Islamic Thought*. Cambridge: Cambridge University Press.

Brown, L. C. 1984: *International Politics and the Middle East: Old Rules, Dangerous Game*. London: IB Tauris.

—— 1988: The June 1967 War: A turning point? In Lukacs, Y. and Battah, A. (eds).

Brumberg, D. 1991: Islam, elections and reform in Algeria. *Journal of Democracy*, Winter, pp. 58–71.

Brynen, R., Korany, B. and Noble, P. (eds) 1995: *Political Liberalization and Democratization in the Arab World*. Boulder, CO: Lynne Rienner.

Bulmer, M. 1998: Ethnic democracy, the case of Israel. *Ethnic and Racial Studies*, vol. 21:3, May, pp. 383–407.

Burke, J. 2004: *Al-Qaeda: The True Story of Radical Islam*. London: Penguin Books.

Bush, G. W. 2001: Address to the American Jewish Committee, 3 May.

Bush, G. W. 2003: Address to National Endowment for Democracy, 6 November. <www.whitehouse.gov/news/releases/2003/11/20031106–2.html>.

Butterworth, C. E. 1980: Review of Orientalism. *American Political Science Review*, vol. 74, March, pp. 174–6.

Cammack, P., Pool, D. and Tordoff, W. 1993: *Third World Politics, A Comparative Introduction*. Basingstoke: Macmillan.

Carter, J. 1977: Remarks at the White House. U.S. White House, 12 May 1977.

Cheriet, B. 1992: The resilience of Algerian populism. *Middle East Report – MERIP*, no. 174, January–February, pp. 9–14.

Chomsky, N. 1997: *World Orders Old and New*. London: Pluto Press.

—— 1999: *Fateful Triangle, Updated Edition: The United States, Israel, and the Palestinians*. New York: South End Press.

—— 2003: *Middle East Illusions*. New York: Rowan and Littlefield.

Choueiri, Y. 1988: Neo-orientalism and Islamic fundamentalism. *Review of Middle East Studies*, no. 4, pp. 52–68.

—— 1989: *Arab History and the Nation State: A Study in Modern Arab Historiography 1820–1980.* London: Routledge.

—— 1990: *Islamic Fundamentalism.* London: Pinter Publishers.

—— 2003: *Modern Arab Historiography: Historical Discourse and the Nation State.* London: Routledge Curzon.

—— (ed.) 2005: *A Companion to the History of the Middle East.* Oxford: Blackwell.

Clark, W. K. 2003: *Winning Modern Wars: Iraq, Terrorism and the American Empire.* New York: Public Affairs.

Cleveland, W. 2004: *A History of the Middle East.* Boulder, CO: Westview Press.

Cohen, M. 1987: *Zion and State: Nation, Class and the Shaping of Modern Israel.* New York: Columbia University Press.

Cohen, P. 1983: Ethnicity, class and political alignment in Israel. *Jewish Journal of Sociology*, vol. 25:2, pp. 119–30.

Collett, N. 1994: Kuwait's real enemy – the budget deficit. *Middle East International*, 18 November, pp. 17–18.

Collings, D. (ed.) 1994: *Peace for Lebanon? From War to Reconstruction.* Boulder, CO: Lynne Rienner.

Connor, W. 1994: *Ethnonationalism: The Quest for Understanding.* Princeton: Princeton University Press.

Cook, M. (ed.) 1970: *Studies in the Economic History of the Middle East.* London: Oxford University Press.

Corbin, J. 1994: *Gaza First – The Secret Norway Channel to Peace Between Israel and the PLO.* London: Bloomsbury.

Cordesman, A. H. 1987: *The Iran–Iraq War and Western Security, 1984–1987.* London: Janes.

—— 1988: *The Gulf and the West: Strategic Relations and Military Realities.* Boulder, CO: Westview.

—— 1996: *Perilous Prospects: The Peace Process and the Arab–Israeli Military Balance.* Boulder, CO: Westview.

Coury, R. 1982: Who 'invented' Egyptian Arab nationalism? (parts 1 and 2). *International Journal of Middle Eastern Studies*, vol. 14:2, pp. 249–81, 459–79.

Creighton, J. 1992: *Oil on Troubled Waters: Gulf Wars, 1980–91.* London: Echoes.

Crick, B. 1990: The high price of peace. In Giliomee, H. and Gagiano, J. (eds).

Crockatt, R. 2003: *America Embattled: September 11, Anti-Americanism and the Global Order.* London: Routledge.

Crystal, J. 1990: *Oil and Politics in the Gulf: Rulers and Merchants in Kuwait and Qatar.* Cambridge: Cambridge University Press.

Daniels, N. 1993: *Islam and the West.* Oxford: Oneworld.

Danilo, M. 2005: On globalization, Iraq and the Middle East, Noam Chomsky Interviewed, *Z-Net.* <www.zmag.org>.

Darwin, J. 1981: *Britain, Egypt and the Middle East: Imperial Policy in the Aftermath of War.* London: Macmillan.

Davis, M. Jane (ed.) 1995: *Politics and International Relations in the Middle East.* Aldershot: Edward Elgar.

Dawn, E. C. 1988: The formation of pan-Arab ideology. *International Journal of Middle Eastern Studies*, vol. 20:1, pp. 67–90.

Deeb, M. J. 1994: Islam and the state in Algeria and Morocco: a dialectical model. In Ruedy, J. (ed.).

Deegan, H. 1993: *The Middle East and Problems of Democracy*. Buckingham: Open University Press.

Dekhayel, ad-, A. K. 1990: *The State and Political Legitimacy in an Oil Rentier Economy: Kuwait as a Case Study*. PhD thesis, University of Exeter.

Dessouki, H. 1982: The new Arab political order: implications for the 1980s. In Kerr, M. and Yassin, S. (eds).

—— 1991: *Foreign Policy of the Arab States*. Boulder, CO: Westview.

Devlin, J. 1976: *The Ba'th Party: A History of its Origins to 1966*. Stanford: Hoover Institution.

Diamond, L., Plattner, M. F. and Brumberg, D. (eds) 2003: *Islam and Democracy in the Middle East*. Baltimore: Johns Hopkins University Press.

Dockrill, M. L. and Douglas Goold, J. 1981: *Peace Without Promise, Britain and the Peace Conferences, 1919–23*. London: Batsford Academic and Educational.

Dodge, T. 2003: *Inventing Iraq: The Failure of National Building and a History Denied*. London: Hurst.

Dodge, T. and Higgott, R. (eds) 2002: *Globalization and the Middle East: Islam, Economy, Society and Politics*. London: RIIA.

Doran, M. 2002: The pragmatic fanaticism of al-Qaeda: An anatomy of extremism in Middle Eastern politics, *Political Science Quarterly*, vol. 117:2, pp. 177–90.

Doumato, E. A. and Posusney, M. P. (eds) 2003: *Women and Globalization in the Arab Middle East: Gender, Economy and Society*. Boulder, CO: Lynne Rienner.

Drysdale, A. and Blake, G. 1985: *The Middle East and North Africa: A Political Geography*. London: Oxford University Press.

Efrat, M. and Bercovitch, J. (eds) 1991: *Superpowers and Client States in the Middle East: The Imbalance of Influence*. London: Routledge.

Ehteshami, A. 1995: *After Khomeini: The Iranian Second Republic*. London: Routledge.

Ehteshami, A. and Murphy, E. C. 1996: Transformation of the corporatist state in the Middle East. *Third World Quarterly*, vol. 17:4, pp. 753–72.

Eickelman, D. and Piscatori, J. 1996: *Muslim Politics*. Princeton: Princeton University Press.

Enayat, H. 1982: *Modern Islamic Political Thought*. Austin: University of Texas Press.

Entelis, J. and Arone, L. J. 1992: Algeria in turmoil: Islam, democracy and the state. *Middle East Policy*, vol. 1, no. 2, pp. 23–35.

Entelis, J. and Naylor, P. C. (eds) 1992: *State and Society in Algeria*. Boulder, CO: Westview.

Entessar, N. 1992: *Kurdish Ethnonationalism*. Boulder, CO: Lynne Rienner Publishers.

Esman, M. J. 1994: *Ethnic Politics*. Ithaca: Cornell University Press.

Esman, M. J. and Rabinovich, I. (eds) 1988: *Ethnicity, Pluralism and the State in the Middle East*. Ithaca: Cornell University Press.

Esposito, J. (ed.) 1983: *Voices of Resurgent Islam*. New York: Oxford University Press.

—— 1984: *Islam and Politics*. New York: Syracuse University Press.

—— 1992: *The Islamic Threat: Myth or Reality?* Oxford: Oxford University Press.

—— (ed.) 1997: *Political Islam: Revolution, Radicalism or Reform?* Boulder, CO: Lynne Rienner.

—— 2002: *Unholy War: Terror in the Name of Islam*. Oxford: Oxford University Press.

Esposito, J. and Piscatori, J. 1991: Democratization and Islam. *Middle East Journal*, no. 45, Summer, pp. 427–40.

Evans, M. 1988: *The Gulf Crisis*. London: Franklin Watts.

Faksh, M. A. 1997: *The Future of Islam: Fundamentalism in Egypt, Algeria and Saudi Arabia*. London: Praeger.

Farouk-Sluglett, M. and Sluglett, P. 1990: *Iraq Since 1958*. London: IB Tauris.

Farsoun, S. K. and Zacharia, C. 1995: Class, economic change and political liberalization in the Arab world. In Brynen, R. et al. (eds).

Feldman, N. 2004: *What We Owe Iraq: War and the Ethics of Nation Building*. Princeton: Princeton University Press.

Fernea, E. W. and Bezirgan, B. Q. (eds) 1997: *Middle Eastern Women Speak*. Austin: University of Texas Press.

Feste, K. A. 1991: *Plans for Peace: Negotiation and the Arab–Israeli Conflict*. New York: Praeger.

Fieldhouse, D. K. 2004: *Britain, France and the Fertile Crescent: The Mandates in Iraq, Palestine, Transjordan, Syria and Lebanon 1900–1958*. London: IB Tauris.

Findlay, A. M. 1994: *The Arab World*. London: Routledge.

Finer, S. 1970: *Comparative Government: An Introduction to the Study of Politics*. Harmondsworth: Penguin.

Firro, K. 1988: The Druze in and between Syria, Lebanon and Israel. In Esman, M. J. and Rabinovich, I. (eds).

—— 2003: *Inventing Lebanon: Nationalism and the State under the Mandate*. London: IB Tauris.

Fischer, S., Rodrik, D. and Tuma, E. (eds) 1993: *The Economics of Middle East Peace: Views from the Region*. Cambridge, MA: The MIT Press.

Fisk, R. 1992: *Pity the Nation: Lebanon at War*. Oxford: Oxford University Press.

—— 1996: The myth of Pax Americana. *The Nation Online*, October.

Flamhaft, Z. 1996: *Israel on the Road to Peace: Accepting the Unacceptable*. Boulder, CO: Westview.

Fleischmann, E. 2003: *The Nation and its 'New' Women: The Palestinian Women's Movement, 1920–1948*. Berkeley: University of California Press.

Francis, D. R. 2002: Economist tallies swelling cost of Israel to US. *Christian Science Monitor*, 9 December.

Fraser, T. 1995: *The Arab–Israeli Conflict*. Basingstoke: Macmillan.

Freedman, L. 1993: *The Gulf Conflict, 1990–1991: Diplomacy and War in the New World Order*. London: Faber and Faber.

Freedman, R. O. 1991: *Moscow and the Middle East: Soviet Policy Since the Invasion of Afghanistan*. Cambridge: Cambridge University Press.

Fromkin, D. 1989: *A Peace to End all Peace: The Fall of the Ottoman Empire and the Creation of the Modern Middle East*. New York: Deutsch, Avon Book.

Gellner, E. 1981: *Muslim Society*. Cambridge: Cambridge University Press.

—— 1983: *Nations and Nationalism*. Oxford: Blackwell.

—— 1993: The Mightier Pen? *Times Literary Supplement*, 19 February.

—— 1994: Nationalism and modernisation. In Hutchinson, J. and Smith, A. D. (eds).

Gerami, S. 1994: The role and place of middle-class women in the Islamic republic. In Moghadam, V. (ed.), 1994b.

Gerner, D. 1984: Roles in transition: the evolving position of women in Arab–Islamic countries. In Hussain, F. (ed.).

—— 1994: *One Land, Two Peoples: The Conflict over Palestine*. Boulder, CO: Westview.

Ghanem, A. 1998: Israel, the case of ethnic state and the predicament of its minority. *Ethnic and Racial Studies*, vol. 21:3, pp. 428–37.

Giacaman, R. and Johnson, P. 1994: Searching for strategies: the Palestinian women's movement in a new era. *Middle East Report – MERIP*, no. 186, January–February, pp. 22–5.

Giliomee, H. and Gagiano, J. (eds) 1990: *The Elusive Search for Peace, South Africa, Israel, Northern Ireland*. Oxford: Oxford University Press.

Glavanis-Grantham, K. 1996: The women's movement, feminism and the national struggle in Palestine: unresolved contradictions. In Afshar, H. (ed.).

Global Agenda 2005: *Egypt 2005: A Commitment to Growth*. London: World Link Publications Ltd.

Gordon, J. 1992: *Nasser's Blessed Movement: Egypt's Free Officers and the July Revolution*. New York: Oxford University Press.

Gosaibi, al-, G. A. 1993: *The Gulf Crisis: An Attempt to Understand*. New York: Kegan Paul International.

Gow, J. (ed.) 1993: *Iraq, the Gulf Conflict and the World Community*. London: Brassey's.

Gowan, P. 1991: The Gulf War, Iraq and Western liberalism. *New Left Review*, 187, pp. 39–71.

Graham-Brown, S. 1994: *Women and Politics*. Washington: MERIP.

Gran, P. 1990: Studies of Anglo-American political economy: democracy, orientalism and the left. In Sharabi, H. (ed.).

Gray, J. 2004: *Al-Qaeda and What It Means to be Modern*. London: Faber and Faber.

Gresh, A. and Vidal, D. 1990: *A–Z of the Middle East*. London: Zed Books.

Guazzone, L. (ed.) 1995: *The Islamist Dilemma: The Political Role of Islamist Movements in the Contemporary Arab World*. Reading, NY: Ithaca Press.

Guibernau, M. and Rex, J. (eds) 1997: *The Ethnicity Reader: Nationalism, Multiculturalism and Migration*. Cambridge: Polity.

Gurr, T. R. and Harff, B. 1994: *Ethnic Conflict in World Politics*. Boulder, CO: Westview.

Hafez, M. 2003: *Why Muslims Rebel: Repression and Resistance in the Islamic World*. London: Lynne Rienner.

Haim, S. (ed.) 1969: *Arab Nationalism: An Anthology*. Berkeley: University of California Press.

Hakimian, H. and Moshaver, Z. (eds) 2001: *The State and Global Change: The Political Economy of Transition in the Middle East and North Africa*. London: Routledge Curzon.

Hale, S. 1994: Gender, religious identity and political mobilisation. In Moghadam, V. (ed.), 1994b.

Halliday, F. 1974: *Arabia without Sultans*. Harmondsworth: Penguin.

—— 1979: *Iran: Dictatorship to Development*. Harmondsworth: Penguin.

—— 1993: Orientalism and its critics. *British Journal of Middle Eastern Studies*, vol. 20:2, pp. 145–63.

—— 1996: *Islam and the Myth of Confrontation*. London: IB Tauris.

—— 2005: How to defeat terrorism. *Global Agenda*, <www.globalagendamagazine.com>.

Hammami, R. 1993: Women in Palestinian society. In Heiberg, M. and Ovensen, G. (eds).

—— 1997: From immodesty to collaboration: Hamas, the women's movement and national identity in the Intifada. In Beinin, J. and Stork, J. (eds).

Hammami, R. and Reiker, M. 1988: Feminist orientalism and Orientalist Marxism. *New Left Review*, 170, pp. 93–107.

Hardy, R. 1992: *Arabia after the Storm: Internal Stability of the Gulf Arab States*. London: RIIA.

Harik, I. 1990: The origins of the Arab state system. In Luciani, G. (ed.).

Harik, I. and Cantori, M. (eds) 1984: *Local Politics and Development in the Middle East*. Boulder, CO: Westview.

Hatem, M. 1993: Toward the development of post-Islamist and post-nationalist feminist discourses in the Middle East. In Tucker, J. (ed.).

—— 1994: Egyptian discourses on gender and political liberalisation: do secularist and Islamist views really differ? *Middle East Journal*, vol. 48:4, pp. 661–6.

Haynes, J. 1996: *Third World Politics: A Concise Introduction*. Oxford: Blackwell.

Heiberg, M. and Ovensen, G. (eds) 1993: *Palestinian Society in Gaza, West Bank and Arab Jerusalem: A Survey of Living Conditions*. Oslo: FAFO.

Held, C. C. 1994: *Middle East Patterns, Places, Peoples and Politics*. Boulder, CO: Westview.

Held, D. 1996: *Models of Democracy*. Cambridge: Polity.

Henry, C. M. and Springborg, R. 2001: *Globalization and the Politics of Development in the Middle East*. Cambridge: Cambridge University Press.

Hermida, A. 1992: Fundamentalists sweep to near victory. *Middle East International*, January.

Hersh, S. 2005: The coming wars. *The New Yorker*, 24 January.

Hiltermann, J. 1991: *Behind the Intifada: Labor and Women's Movements in the Occupied Territories*. Princeton: Princeton University Press.

Hindley, A. 1993: Kuwait: trimming the state. *Middle East Economic Digest*, 12 November, p. 6.

Hinnebusch, R. 1985: *Egyptian Politics Under Sadat: The Post-Populist Development of an Authoritarian-Modernizing State*. Cambridge: Cambridge University Press.

—— 1990: *Authoritarian Power and State Formation in Ba'thist Syria. Army, Party and Peasant*. Boulder, CO: Westview.

—— 1993: State and civil society in Syria. *Middle East Journal*, vol. 47, Spring, pp. 243–57.

—— 2003: *The International Politics of the Middle East*. Manchester: Manchester University Press.

Hiro, D. 1993: *Lebanon: Fire and Embers: A History of the Lebanese Civil War*. London: Weidenfeld and Nicolson.

Hobsbawm, E. 1990: *Nations and Nationalisms Since 1780: Programme, Myth, Reality*. Cambridge: Cambridge University Press.

—— 1997: An anti-nationalist account of nationalism since 1989. In Guibernau, J. and Rex, J. (eds).

Hollis, R. and Shehadi, N. (eds) 1996: *Lebanon on Hold: Implications for Middle East Peace*. London: RIIA.

Hoodfar, H. 1997: Devices and desires: population policy and gender roles in the Islamic republic. In Beinin, J. and Stork, J. (eds).

Hopwood, D. 1985: *Egypt Politics and Society 1945–1984*. London: Unwin Hyman.

—— 1988: *Syria Politics and Society 1945–86*. London: Unwin Hyman.

Horowitz, D. 1985: *Ethnic Groups in Conflict*. Berkeley: University of California Press.

Hourani, A. 1991: *A History of the Arab Peoples*. London: Faber and Faber.

Hourani, A., Khoury, P. S. and Wilson, M. C. (eds) 1993: *The Middle East: A Reader*. London: IB Tauris.

Howe, J. 1992: The crisis of Algerian nationalism and the rise of Islamic integralism. *New Left Review*, 196, pp. 85–101.

Hudson, M. 1977: *Arab Politics: The Search for Legitimacy*. New Haven: Yale University Press.

—— 1988: Democratisation and the problem of legitimacy in Middle East politics. *Middle East Studies Association Bulletin*, no. 22, December, pp. 151–71.

—— 1991: After the Gulf War: prospects for democratisation in the Arab world. *Middle East Journal*, vol. 45:3, pp. 407–27.

—— 1995: Arab regimes and democratization: responses to the challenge of political Islam. In Guazzone, L. (ed.).

Huntington, S. 1984: Will more countries become democratic? *Political Science Quarterly*, Summer, pp. 193–218.

—— 1991: *The Third Wave: Democratization in the Late Twentieth Century*. Norman: University of Oklahoma Press.

—— 1993: The Clash of Civilizations? *Foreign Affairs*, Summer, pp. 22–49.

Hussain, A., Olson, R. and Qureshi, J. (eds) 1984: *Orientalism, Islam and Islamists*. Brattlebro: Amana Books.

Hussain, F. (ed.) 1984: *Muslim Women*. London: Croom Helm.

Hutchinson, J. and Smith, A. D. (eds) 1994: *Nationalism*. Oxford: Oxford University Press.

—— (eds) 1996: *Ethnicity*. Oxford: Oxford University Press.

Ibrahim, S. E. 1993: Crises, elites and democratization in the Arab world. *Middle East Journal*, vol. 47, Spring, pp. 292–305.

IDEA. 2000: *Democracy in the Arab World: Challenges, Achievements and Prospects*. Stockholm: International IDEA.

Ingrams, D. 1972: *Palestine Papers, 1917–1922: Seeds of Conflict*. London: J. Murray.

Ismail, S. 1995: Democracy in contemporary Arab intellectual discourse. In Brynen, R. et al. (eds).

Issawi, C. 1982: *An Economic History of the Middle East and North Africa*. New York: Columbia University Press.

Izady, M. R. 1992: *The Kurds: A Concise Handbook*. Washington, DC: Taylor and Francis.

Jaber, H. 1997: *Hezbollah – Born with a Vengeance*. London: Fourth Estate.

Jad, I. 1991: From salons to popular committees: Palestinian women, 1919–1989. In Nassar, J. and Heacock, R. (eds).

Jansen, G. H. 1992: The impact of the FIS success. *Middle East International*, January.

Jawad, H. 1998: *The Rights of Women in Islam: An Authentic Approach*. Basingstoke: Macmillan.

Jawad, S. 1981: *Iraq and the Kurdish Question*. Reading, NY: Ithaca Press.

Joffe, G. (ed.) 1993: *North Africa: Nation, State and Religion*. London: Routledge.

Johnson, C. 2002: *Blowback: The Costs and Consequences of American Empire*. New York: Time Books.

Juergensmeyer, M. 1993: *The New Cold War? Religious Nationalism Confronts the Secular State*. Berkeley: University of California Press.

Kandiyoti, D. (ed.) 1991: *Women, Islam and the State*. Basingstoke: Macmillan.

—— (ed.) 1996: *Gendering the Middle East*. London: IB Tauris.

Kapil, A. 1995: Algeria's crisis intensifies: the search for a civil pact. *Middle East Report*, no. 192, January–February, pp. 2–7.

Karam, A. 1998: *Women, Islamisms and the State, Contemporary Feminisms in Egypt*. Basingstoke: Macmillan.

Karsh, E. 1997: *Fabricating Israeli History: The 'New Historians'*. London: Frank Cass.

Kaufman, E., Shukri, B. A. and Rothstein, R. L. (eds) 1993: *Democracy, Peace and the Israeli–Palestinian Conflict*. Boulder, CO: Lynne Rienner.

Keddie, N. R. and Hooglund, E. (eds) 1986: *The Iranian Revolution and the Islamic Republic*. Syracuse: Syracuse University Press.

Kedourie, E. 1976: *In the Anglo-Arab Labyrinth: The McMahon–Husayn Correspondence and its Interpretations 1914–1939*. Cambridge: Cambridge University Press.

—— 1988: Ethnicity, majority and minority in the Middle East. In Esman, M. J. and Rabinovich, I. (eds).

—— 1992: *Politics in the Middle East*. Oxford: Oxford University Press.

—— 1993: *Nationalism*. Oxford: Blackwell.

—— 1994: *Democracy and Arab Political Culture*. London: Frank Cass.

Kellas, J. 1998: *The Politics of Nationalism and Ethnicity*. Basingstoke: Macmillan.

Kepel, G. 1994: *The Revenge of God*. Cambridge: Polity.

Kerr, M. 1971: *The Arab Cold War: Gamal 'Abd al-Nasir and his Rivals, 1958–1970*. London: Oxford University Press.

—— 1980: Review of Orientalism. *International Journal of Middle Eastern Studies*, no. 12, pp. 544–7.

Kerr, M. and Yassin, S. (eds) 1982: *Rich and Poor States in the Middle East: Egypt and the New Arab Order*. Boulder, CO: Westview.

Khalidi, R. 1997: *Palestinian Identity: The Construction of Modern National Consciousness*. New York: Columbia University Press.

Khalidi, R. and Tucker, J. 1994: *Women's Rights in the Arab World*. Washington, DC: MERIP.

Khalidi, R., Anderson, L., Muslih, M. and Simon, R. S. (eds) 1991: *The Origins of Arab Nationalism*. New York: Columbia University Press.

Khalidi, W. 1991a: *The Middle East Post-war Environment*. Washington, DC: Institute of Palestine Studies.

—— 1991b: Why some Arabs support Saddam Hussein. In Sifry, M. L. and Cerf, C. (eds).

Khalil, S. 1989: *Republic of Fear: Saddam's Iraq*. London: Hutchinson Radius.

Khoury, N. and Moghadam, V. (eds) 1995: *Gender and Development in the Arab World: Women's Economic Participation, Patterns and Policies*. London: Zed Books.

Khoury, P. S. 1983: *Urban Notables and Arab Nationalism: The Politics of Arab Nationalism 1880–1920*. Cambridge: Cambridge University Press.

—— 1987: *Syria and the French Mandate: The Politics of Arab Nationalism 1920–1945*. London: IB Tauris.

Kienle, E. 1990: *Ba'th versus Ba'th: Conflict between Syria and Iraq*. London: IB Tauris.

—— (ed.) 1996: *Contemporary Syria, Liberalisation Between Cold War and Peace*. London: IB Tauris.

King, J. 1994: *Handshake in Washington: The Beginning of Middle East Peace?* London: Garnet.

Knauss, P. 1987: *The Persistence of Patriarchy: Class, Gender and Ideology in 20th-Century Algeria*. Boulder, CO: Westview.

Kohn, H. 1932: *Nationalism and Imperialism in the Hither East*. London: Routledge.

Kramer, G. 1992: Liberalization and democracy in the Arab world. *Middle East Report – MERIP*, no. 174, January–February, pp. 22–5, 35.

—— 1995: Islam and pluralism. In Brynen, R. et al. (eds).

Kramer, M. 1980: *Political Islam*. London: Sage.

— (ed.) 1987: *Shi'ism, Resistance and Revolution*. Boulder, CO: Westview.

— 1993: Islam vs. democracy. *Commentary*, January, pp. 35–42.

— 1996: Fundamentalist Islam: The drive for power. *Middle East Quarterly*, vol. 3, no. 2 (June), pp. 37–49.

Kreyenbroek, P. G. and Sperl, S. (eds) 1992: *The Kurds: A Contemporary Overview*. London: Routledge.

Kupchan, C. A. 2002: *The End of the American Era: US Foreign Policy and the Geopolitics of the Twenty-first Century*. New York: Alfred A. Knopf.

Kuran, T. 2004: *Islam and Mammom: The Economic Predicament of Islamism*. Princeton: Princeton University Press.

Kyle, K. 1991: *Suez*. London: Weidenfeld and Nicolson.

— 2002: *Suez: Britain's End of Empire in the Middle East*. London: IB Tauris.

Laclau, E. (ed.) 1994: *The Making of Political Identities*. London: Verso.

— 1996: *Emancipation(s)*. London: Verso.

Laizer, S. 1991: *Into Kurdistan: Frontiers under Fire*. London: Zed Books.

Larson, A. P. 2003: Testimony before the Senate Foreign Relations Committee. US State Department, Washington, DC: US State Department, 4 June.

Legrain, J. F. 1991a: A defining moment: Palestinian Islamic fundamentalism. In Piscatori, J. P. (ed.).

— 1991b: The Islamic movement and the Intifada. In Nassar, J. and Heacock, R. (eds).

Lerner, D. 1958: *The Passing of Traditional Society*. New York: Free Press.

Lewis, B. 1968: *The Middle East and the West*. London: Weidenfeld and Nicolson.

— (ed.) 1974: *Islam, from the Prophet Muhammad to the Capture of Constantinople*. New York: Harper and Row.

— 1976: The return of Islam. *Commentary*, January.

— 1982: The question of Orientalism. *New York Review of Books*, 24 June.

— 1990: The roots of Muslim rage. *Atlantic Monthly*, vol. 266:3, September, pp. 47–60.

— 1993a: Islam and liberal democracy. *Atlantic Monthly*, vol. 271:2, February, pp. 89–98.

— 1993b: *Islam and the West*. Oxford: Oxford University Press.

Lewis, R. 1996: *Gendering Orientalism: Race, Femininity and Representation*. London: Routledge.

Lijphart, A. 1977: *Democracy in Plural Societies*. Yale: Yale University Press.

Lippman, T. W. 2004: *Inside the Mirage: America's Fragile Partnership with Saudi Arabia* (hardcover). Boulder, CO: Westview Press.

Little, D. 2002: *American Orientalism: The United States and the Middle East Since 1945*. London: IB Tauris.

Lockman, Z. and Beinin, J. (eds) 1989: *Intifada: The Palestinian Uprising Against Israeli Occupation*. Boston: South End Press.

Long, D. and Reich, B. (eds) 1995: *The Government and Politics of the Middle East and North Africa*. Boulder, CO: Westview.

Louis, W. R. and Owen, R. (eds) 1989: *Suez 1956: The Crisis and its Consequences*. Oxford: Clarendon Press.

Luciani, G. (ed.) 1990: *The Arab State*. London: Routledge.

— 1995: Resources, revenues and authoritarianism in the Arab world: beyond the rentier state. In Brynen, R. et al. (eds).

Lukacs, Y. (ed.) 1992: *The Israeli–Palestinian Conflict: A Documentary Record.* Cambridge: Cambridge University Press.

Lukacs, Y. and Battah, A. (eds) 1988: *The Arab–Israeli Conflict: Two Decades of Change.* Boulder, CO: Westview.

Lukas, A. 2000: 'WTO Report Card III: Globalization and Developing Countries' Trade Briefing Paper, no. 10. The Cato Institute, 20 June.

Lustick, I. 1993: *Unsettled States, Disputed Lands: Britain and Ireland, France and Algeria, Israel and the West Bank-Gaza.* Ithaca: Cornell University Press.

Mahdavi, H. 1970: The pattern and problems of economic development in rentier states: the case of Iran. In Cook, M. (ed.).

Mahdi, K. (ed.) 2002: *Iraq's Economic Predicament.* Reading, NY: Ithaca Press.

Mahmoud, M. 1996: Women and Islamism: the case of Rashid al-Ghannushi of Tunisia. In Sidahmed, A. S. and Ehteshami, A. (eds).

Makiya, K. 1993: *Cruelty and Silence, War, Tyranny, Uprising and the Arab World.* London: Cape.

Makovsky, D. 1996: *Making Peace with the PLO: The Rabin Government's Road to the Oslo Accord.* Boulder, CO: Westview.

Malek, M. 1991: *Iran after Khomeini: Perpetual Crisis or Opportunity?* London: Research Institute for Study of Conflict and Terrorism.

Mansfield, P. 1969: *Nasser.* London: Methuen.

—— 1992: *A History of the Middle East.* Harmondsworth: Penguin.

Marlowe, J. 1954: *Anglo-Egyptian Relations, 1800–1953.* London: Cresset Press.

—— 1959: *The Seat of Pilate: An Account of the Palestine Mandate.* London: Cresset Press.

—— 1970: *Cromer in Egypt.* London: Elek.

—— 1971: *Perfidious Albion: The Origin of Anglo-French Rivalry in the Levant.* London: Elek.

Marty, M. E. and Appleby, S. R. 1991: *Fundamentalism Observed.* Chicago: University of Chicago Press.

——1993: *Fundamentalisms and the State.* Chicago: University of Chicago Press.

Mayer, T. (ed.) 1994: *Women and the Israeli Occupation.* London: Routledge.

McDermott, A. 1988: *Egypt from Nasser to Mubarak: A Flawed Revolution.* London: Croom Helm.

McDowall, D. 1989: *Palestine and Israel: The Uprising and Beyond.* London: IB Tauris.

—— 2003: *A Modern History of the Kurds.* London: IB Tauris.

McGarry, J. and O'Leary, B. (eds) 1993: *The Politics of Ethnic Conflict Regulation.* London: Routledge.

McNamara, R. 2003: *Britain, Nasser and the Balance of Power in the Middle East, 1952–1967.* London: Frank Cass.

Mead, W. R. 2001: *Special Providence: American Foreign Policy and How it Changed the World.* New York: Alfred A. Knopf.

Mearsheimer, J. J. and Walt, S. 2006: The Israel Lobby. *London Review of Books*, vol. 28:6, 23 March.

Méouchy, N. and Sluglett, P. (eds) 2004: *British and French Mandates in Comparative Perspective.* Leiden: Brill.

MERI. 1992: The democracy agenda in the Arab world. *Middle East Report – MERIP*, no. 174, January–February, pp. 3–5.

Mernissi, F. 1985: *Beyond the Veil: Male–Female Dynamics in Muslim Society.* London: al-Saqi Books.

—— 1988: Muslim women and fundamentalism. *Middle East Report – MERIP*, no. 153, July–August.

—— 1991: *Women and Islam: An Historical and Theological Enquiry*. Oxford: Blackwell.

Migdal, J. S. 1980: *Palestinian Society and Politics*. Princeton: Princeton University Press.

Miller, J. 1993: The challenge of radical Islam. *Foreign Affairs*, vol. 72:2, Spring, pp. 43–56.

Milton-Edwards, B. 1991: A temporary alliance with the crown: the Islamic response in Jordan. In Piscatori, J. P. (ed.).

—— 1993: Jordan and façade democracy. *British Journal of Middle Eastern Studies*, vol. 20:3, pp. 191–203.

—— 1996a: *Islamic Politics in Palestine*. London: IB Tauris.

—— 1996b: Political Islam in Palestine in an environment of peace? *Third World Quarterly*, no. 17, pp. 199–225.

—— 1996c: Climate of change in Jordan's Islamist movement. In Sidahmed, A. S. and Ehteshami, A. (eds).

—— 1998: Palestinian state-building: police and citizens as test of democracy. *British Journal of Middle Eastern Studies*, vol. 25:1, pp. 95–119.

Minces, J. 1978: Women in Algeria. In Beck, H. and Keddie, N. (eds).

Mir-Hosseini, Z. 2000: *Islam and Gender: The Religious Debate in Contemporary Iran*. London: IB Tauris.

Mitchell, R. P. 1969: *The Society of Muslim Brothers*. Oxford: Oxford University Press.

Mitchell, T. 1988: *Colonising Egypt*. Cambridge: Cambridge University Press.

Moaddel, M. 2005: *Islamic Modernism Nationalism and Fundamentalism: Episode and Discourse*. Chicago: University of Chicago Press.

Moghadam, V. (ed.) 1994a: *Gender and National Identity: Women and Politics in Muslim Societies*. Boulder, CO: Lynne Rienner.

—— (ed.) 1994b: *Identity Politics and Women: Cultural Reassertions and Feminisms in International Perspective*. Boulder, CO: Westview.

—— 2003: *Modernizing Women: Gender and Society Change in the Middle East*. Boulder, CO: Lynne Rienner.

Moghissi, H. 1994: *Populism and Feminism in Iran: Women's Struggle in a Male-Defined Revolutionary Movement*. Basingstoke: Macmillan.

—— 1995: Public life and women's resistance. In Rahnema, S. and Behdad, S. (eds).

Mohanty, C., Talpade, A. R. and Torres, L. (eds) 1991: *Third World Women and the Politics of Feminism*. Bloomington: Indiana University Press.

Molyneux, M. 1991: The law, the state and socialist policies with regard to women: the case of the People's Democratic Republic of Yemen 1967–1990. In Kandiyoti, D. (ed.).

Monroe, E. 1963: *Britain's Moment in the Middle East 1914–1956*. London: Chatto and Windus.

Moore, C. H. 1970: *The Politics of North Africa: Algeria, Morocco and Tunisia*. Boston: Little, Brown.

Morris, B. 1988: *The Birth of the Palestinian Refugee Problem, 1947–1949*. Cambridge: Cambridge University Press.

—— 1998: Refabricating 1948. *Journal of Palestine Studies*, vol. 27:2, Winter, pp. 81–95.

Mortimer, R. 1991: Islam and multiparty politics in Algeria. *Middle East Journal*, no. 45, Autumn, pp. 575–93.

Moussalli, A. 1995: Modern Islamic fundamentalist discourses on civil society, pluralism and democracy. In Norton, A. R. (ed.).

—— 2003: *The Islamic Quest for Democracy; Pluralism and Human Rights*. Gainesville: University of Florida Press.

Moussawi, N. 2005: Interview with author.

Moynihan, D. P. 1993: *Pandemonium: Ethnicity in International Politics*. Oxford: Oxford University Press.

Murphy, E. C. 1996: The initiation of economic liberalisation in Algeria, 1979–1989. In Nonneman, G. (ed.).

Muslih, M. 1993: Palestinian civil society. *Middle East Journal*, vol. 47, Spring, pp. 258–74.

Muslih, M. and Norton, A. R. 1991: The need for Arab democracy. *Foreign Policy*, no. 83, Summer, pp. 3–19.

Najjar, A. O. and Warnock, K. 1992: *Portraits of Palestinian Women*. Salt Lake City: University of Utah Press.

Najmabadi, A. 2005: *Women With Mustaches and Men Without Beards: Gender and Sexual Anxieties of Iranian Modernity*. Berkeley: University of California Press.

Nasr, S. V. 1989: Islamic economics: novel perspectives. *Middle Eastern Studies*, no. 25, pp. 516–30.

—— 1995: Democracy and Islamic revivalism. *Political Science Quarterly*, vol. 110:2, Summer, pp. 261–85.

Nassar, J. and Heacock, R. (eds) 1991: *Intifada: Palestine at the Crossroads*. New York: Praeger.

Nettler, R. 1996: Guidelines for an Islamic community: Sayyid Qutb's political interpretation of the Quran. *Journal of Political Ideologies*, vol. 1:2, pp. 183–96.

Nevakivi, J. 1969: *Britain, France and the Arab Middle East*. London: Athlone Press.

Niblock, T. and Murphy, E. (eds) 1993: *Economic and Political Liberalisation in the Middle East*. London: IB Tauris.

Nonneman, G. (ed.) 1996: *Political and Economic Liberalisation: Dynamics and Linkages in Comparative Perspective*. Boulder, CO: Lynne Rienner.

Norton, Augustus R. 1993: The future of civil society in the Middle East. *Middle East Journal*, vol. 47, Spring, pp. 205–16.

—— (ed.) 1995: *Civil Society in the Middle East, vol. 1*. Leiden: E. J. Brill.

—— (ed.) 1996: *Civil Society in the Middle East, vol. 2*. Leiden: E. J. Brill.

—— 1997: Lebanon: with friends like these . . . *Current History*, January, pp. 6–12.

Nye, J. S. 2002: *The Paradox of American Power. Why the World's Only Superpower Can't Go it Alone*. Oxford: Oxford University Press.

Odell, P. 1981: *Oil and World Power*. Harmondsworth: Penguin.

Ottaway, M., Carothers, T., Hawthorne, A. and Brumberg, D. 2002: *Democratic Mirage in the Middle East*. Washington, DC: Carnegie Endowment for International Peace.

Owen, R. 1969: *Cotton and the Egyptian Economy 1820–1914: A Study in Trade and Development*. Oxford: Clarendon Press.

—— 1981: *The Middle East in the World Economy 1800–1914*. London: Methuen.

—— 1991: Epilogue: making sense of an earthquake. In Brittain, V. (ed.).

—— 1995: *Migrant Workers in the Gulf*. London: Minority Rights Group.

—— 2003: *State, Power and Politics in the Making of the Modern Middle East* (2nd edition). London: Routledge.

Paidar, P. 1996: Feminism and Islam in Iran. In Kandiyoti, D. (ed.).

Pappe, I. 1994: *The Making of the Arab–Israeli Conflict, 1947–51*. London: IB Tauris.

—— 2005: *Modern Middle East*. London: Routledge.

Pateman, C. and Goss, E. (eds) 1986: *Feminist Challenges: Social and Political Theory*. Sydney: Allen and Unwin.

Peck, M. C. 1995: Eastern Arabian states. In Long, D. E. and Reich, B. (eds).

Peretz, D. 1990: *Intifada: The Palestinian Uprising*. Boulder, CO: Westview.

Perlmutter, A. 1992: Islam and democracy simply aren't compatible. *International Herald Tribune*, 21 January.

Perthes, V. 1991: A look at Syria's upper class: the bourgeoisie and the Ba'th. *Middle East Report – MERIP*, no. 170, May–June, pp. 31–7.

—— 1992: Syria's parliamentary elections. Remodelling Asad's political base. *Middle East Report – MERIP*, no. 174, January–February, pp. 15–18.

—— 1995: *Political Economy of Syria Under Asad*. London: IB Tauris.

—— 2004: *Syria Under Basher al-Asad: Modernization and the Limits of Changes*. Oxford: Oxford University Press.

Peteet, J. M. 1991: *Gender in Crisis: Women and the Palestinian Resistance Movement*. New York: Columbia University Press.

Petersen, T. T. 2005: *The Decline of the Anglo-American Middle East, 1961–1969: A Willing Retreat*. Brighton: Sussex Academic Press.

Pew Global Attitudes Project 2004: A year after the war in Iraq, mistrust of America in Europe ever higher, Muslim anger persists. *Pew Global Attitude Survey*, Washington, DC: PRCP&P.

Pew Research Center for the People & the Press Survey Reports, 2002: One year later: New Yorkers more troubled, Washingtonians more on edge. The personal toll persists policy opinions change. 5 September.

Pfeifer, K. 1997: Is there an Islamic economics? In Beinin, J. and Stork, J. (eds).

Picard, E. 1990: Arab military in politics: from revolutionary plot to authoritarian regimes. In Luciani, G. (ed.).

Pipes, D. 1983a: Understanding Islam in politics. *Middle East Review*, no. 162, pp. 3–15.

—— 1983b: *In the Path of God: Islam and Political Power*. New York: Basic Books.

Piscatori, J. P. (ed.) 1983: *Islam in the Political Process*. Cambridge: Cambridge University Press.

—— 1986: *Islam in a World of Nation States*. Cambridge: Cambridge University Press.

—— (ed.) 1991: *Islamic Fundamentalisms and the Gulf Crisis*. Chicago: AAAS.

Polk, W. R. 1991: *The Arab World Today*. Cambridge, MA: Harvard University Press.

Pool, D. 1993: The links between economic and political liberalization. In Niblock, T. and Murphy, E. (eds).

Potter, D., Goldblatt, D., Kiloh, M. and Lewis, P. (eds) 1997: *Democratisation*. Cambridge: Polity/Open University Press.

Prestowitz, C. V. 2003: *Rogue Nation: American Unilateralism and the Failure of Good Intentions*. New York: Basic Books.

Provence, M. 2005: *The Great Syrian Revolt and the Rise of Arab Nationalism*. Austin: University of Texas Press.

Quandt, W. B. 1986: *Camp David, Peacemaking and Politics*. Washington, DC: Brookings Institute.

—— 2005: *Peace Process: American Diplomacy and the Arab–Israeli Conflict since 1967*. Berkeley: University of California Press.

Qutb, S. 1978: *Milestones*. Beirut: Holy Koran Publishing.

—— 1988: *The Religion of Islam*. Kuwait: Holy Koran Publishing.

Rabinovitch, I. 1991: *The Road Not Taken: Early Arab–Israeli Negotiations*. Oxford: Oxford University Press.

Rahnema, S. and Behdad, S. (eds) 1995: *Iran after the Revolution: Crisis of an Islamic State*. London: IB Tauris.

Rejai, M. and Enloe, C. H. 1969: Nation states and state-nations. *International Studies Quarterly*, vol. 13:2, pp. 140–58.

Richard, Y. 1995: *Shi'ite Islam – Polity, Ideology and Creed*. Oxford: Blackwell.

Richards, A. 1982: *Egypt's Agricultural Development, 1800–1980*. Boulder, CO: Westview.

—— 1993: Economic imperatives and political systems. *Middle East Journal*, vol. 47, Spring, pp. 217–26.

Richards, A. and Waterbury, J. 1990: *A Political Economy of the Middle East*. Boulder, CO: Westview.

Roberts, H. 1992: The Algerian state and the challenge of democracy. *Government and Opposition*, Autumn, pp. 433–54.

Rodinson, M. 1977: *Islam and Capitalism*. Harmondsworth: Penguin.

—— 1979: *Marxism and the Muslim World*. London: Zed Books.

Roff, W. R. (ed.) 1987: *Islam and the Political Economy of its Meaning*. London: Croom Helm.

Rothstein, R. L., Ma'oz, M. and Shikaki, K. (eds) 2002: *The Israeli–Palestinian Peace Process: Oslo and the Lessons of its Failure: Perspectives, Predicaments and Prospects*. Brighton: Sussex Academic.

Rouhana, N. 1997: *Palestinian Citizens in an Ethnic Jewish State: Identities in Conflict*. New Haven: Yale University Press.

Roy, O. 1994: *The Failure of Political Islam*. London: IB Tauris.

Rubenberg, C. 2001: *Palestinian Women: Patriarchy and Resistance in the West Bank*. Boulder, CO: Lynne Rienner.

Ruedy, J. 1992: *Modern Algeria*. Indianapolis: Indiana University Press.

—— (ed.) 1994: *Islamism and Secularism in North Africa*. Basingstoke: Macmillan.

Russell, S. S. 1990: Migration and political integration in the Arab world. In Luciani, G. (ed.).

Rustow, D. A. 1971: *Middle Eastern Political Systems*. Englewood Cliffs, NJ: Prentice-Hall.

Sabagh, G. 1990: Immigrants in the Arab gulf countries: 'sojourners' or 'settlers'. In Luciani, G. (ed.).

Sabah, al-, S. M. 1980: *The Oil Economy of Kuwait*. London: Kegan Paul.

Sadowski, Y. 1997a: The new orientalism and the democracy debate. In Beinin, J. and Stork, J. (eds).

—— 1997b: The end of the counterrevolution? The politics of economic adjustment in Kuwait. *Middle East Report – MERIP*, no. 204, July–September, pp. 7–11.

Sahliyeh, E. 1988: *In Search of Leadership: West Bank Politics since 1967*. Washington, DC: Brookings Institute.

—— 1992: Beyond the Cold War: the superpowers and the Arab–Israeli conflict. In Spiegel, S. L. (ed.).

Said, E. 1981: *Covering Islam: How the Media and Experts Determine How We See the Rest of the World*. London: Routledge.

Said, E. 1982: Reply to B. Lewis. *New York Review of Books*, 12 August.

—— 1989: Intifada and independence. In Lockman, Z. and Beinin, J. (eds).

—— 1993a: *Culture and Imperialism*. London: Chatto and Windus.

—— 1993b: 'Culture and Imperialism'. *Times Literary Supplement*, 4 June.

—— 1995a: *The Politics of Dispossession, The Struggle for Palestinian Self-determination*. London: Vintage.

—— 1995b: *Peace and its Discontents: Gaza-Jericho 1993–1995*. London: Vintage.

—— 1995c: *Orientalism* (2nd edn). Harmondsworth: Penguin.

Saikal, A. and Schnabel, A. 2003: *Democratization in the Middle East; Experiences, Struggles, Challenges*. Tokyo: United Nations University Press.

Salame, G. (ed.) 1994a: *Democracy Without Democrats? The Renewal of Democracy in the Muslim World*. London: IB Tauris.

—— 1994b: Small is pluralistic: democracy as an instrument of civil peace. In Salame, G. (ed.).

Salem, E. A. 1995: *Violence and Diplomacy in Lebanon: The Troubled Years 1982–1988*. London: IB Tauris.

Salem, N. 1984: Islam and the status of women in Tunisia. In Hussain, F. (ed.).

Salibi, K. S. 1993: *The Modern History of Jordan*. London: IB Tauris.

Salman, M., Kazi, H., Yuval-Davis, N., al-Hamdani, L., Botman, S. and Lerman, D. (eds) 1987: *Women in the Middle East*. London: Zed Books.

Salvatore, A. 1997: *Islam and the Political Discourse of Modernity*. Reading, NY: Ithaca Press.

Salvatore, A. and Eickelman, D. F. (eds) 2004: *Public Islam and the Common Good*. Leiden: Brill.

Sardar, Z. and Wyn Davies, M. 2003: *Why Do People Hate America?* Cambridge: Icon Books.

Satloff, R. B. 1994: *From Abdullah to Hussein, Jordan in Transition*. New York: Oxford University Press.

Sayyid, B. 1994: Sign O'Times: Kaffirs and infidels fighting the ninth crusade. In Laclau, E. (ed.).

—— 1997: *A Fundamental Fear – Eurocentrism and the Emergence of Islamism*. London: Zed Books.

Sayyid, al-, M. A. 1994: The third wave of democracy. In Tschirgi, D. (ed.).

—— 1995: The concept of civil society and the Arab world. In Brynen, R. et al. (eds).

Sayigh, Y. 1997: *Armed Struggle and the Search for a State: The Palestinian National Movement 1949–1993*. Oxford: Clarendon Press.

Schiff, Z. and Ya'ari, E. 1984: *Israel's Lebanon War*. New York: Simon and Schuster.

—— 1989: *Intifada, the Palestinian Uprising, Israel's Third Front*. New York: Simon and Schuster.

Schulze, K., Stokes, M. and Campbell, C. (eds) 1996: *Nationalisms, Minorities and Diasporas: Identity and Rights in the Middle East*. London: IB Tauris.

Schwedler, J. (ed.) 1995: *Towards Civil Society in the Middle East: A Primer*. Boulder, CO: Lynne Rienner.

Seale, P. 1988: *The Struggle for Syria: A Study of Post-War Arab Politics 1945–58*. London: IB Tauris.

—— 1989: *Asad of Syria: The Struggle for the Middle East*. Berkeley: University of California Press.

Shafir, G. and Peled, Y. 1998: Israel, ethnic democracy. *Ethnic and Racial Studies*, vol. 21:3, May, pp. 408–27.

Shahidian, H. 2002: *Women in Iran: Gender Politics in the Islamic Republic.* Westport, CN: Greenwood Press.

Shannon, V. 2000: *Balancing Act. US Foreign Policy and the Arab–Israeli Conflict.* London: Ashgate.

Sharabi, H. 1966: *Nationalism and Revolution in the Arab World: The Middle East and North Africa.* New York: Van Nostrand.

—— 1988: *Neopatriarchy: A Theory of Distorted Change in Arab Society.* Oxford: Oxford University Press.

—— (ed.) 1990: *Theory, Politics and the Arab World.* London: Routledge.

Sharoni, S. 1995: *Gender and the Israeli–Palestinian Conflict.* Syracuse: Syracuse University Press.

Shehadi, N. (ed.) 1988: *Lebanon: A History of Conflict and Consensus.* London: IB Tauris.

Shlaim, A. 1990: *The Politics of Partition: King Abdullah, the Zionists and Palestine, 1921–1951.* Oxford: Oxford University Press.

Sidahmed, A. S. and Ehteshami, A. (eds) 1996: *Islamic Fundamentalism.* Boulder, CO: Westview.

Sifry, M. L. and Cerf, C. (eds) 1991: *The Gulf War Reader.* New York: Times Books.

Silverstein, P. A. 1998: The rebel is dead. Long live the martyr! Kabyle mobilisation and the assassination of Lounes Matoub. *Middle East Report – MERIP*, no. 208, Fall, pp. 3–4.

Simons, G. L. 2004: *Iraq: From Sumer to post-Saddam.* Basingstoke: Palgrave Macmillan.

SIPRI 2002: *Yearbook 2002, Armaments, Disarmament and International Security.* Stockholm: SIPRI.

Sivan, E. 1985: *Radical Islam: Medieval Theology and Modern Politics.* New Haven: Yale University Press.

Sluglett, P. and Farouk-Sluglett, M. 1993: *The Middle East, the Arab World and its Neighbours.* London: Times Books.

Smith, A. D. 1979: *Nationalism in the Twentieth Century.* Oxford: M. Robertson.

—— 1986: *The Ethnic Origins of Nationalism.* Oxford: Blackwell.

—— 1991: *National Identity.* Harmondsworth: Penguin.

Smith, C. D. 1992: *Palestine and the Arab–Israeli Conflict.* Basingstoke: Macmillan.

—— 2004: *Palestine and the Arab–Israeli Conflict: a History with Documents.* Boston: Bedford/St. Martin's.

Smooha, S. 1990: Minority status in an ethnic democracy: the status of the Arab minority in Israel. *Ethnic and Racial Studies*, vol. 13:3, pp. 389–413.

Snow, D. M. and Brown, E. 1997: *Beyond the Water's Edge: An Introduction to U.S. Foreign Policy.* New York: St Martin's Press.

Solh, R. K. 1989: Pan-Arabism or regionalism, the historical interplay between Arab unionism and regionalism. *Arab Affairs*, vol. 9, Spring–Summer, pp. 17–27.

Spencer, C. 1996: The roots and future of Islamism in Algeria. In Sidahmed, A. S. and Ehteshami, A. (eds).

Spiegel, S. L. (ed.) 1992: *Conflict Management in the Middle East.* Boulder, CO: Westview.

Stephens, R. H. 1971: *Nasser: A Political Biography.* London: Allen Lane.

Stewart, F. 1995: *Adjustment and Poverty, Options and Choices.* London: Routledge.

Stone, M. 1993: *Politics of Algeria.* London: C. Hurst.

Stowasser, B. (ed.) 1987: *The Islamic Impulse*. London: IB Tauris.

— 1993: Women's issues in modern Islamic thought. In Tucker, J. (ed.).

Strum, P. 1992: *The Women are Marching: The Second Sex and the Palestinian Revolution*. Brooklyn, NY: Lawrence Hill.

Suleiman, Y. 2004: *A War of Words: Language and Conflict in the Middle East*. Cambridge: Cambridge University Press.

Tabari, A. and Yeganeh, N. (eds) 1982: *In the Shadow of Islam*. London: Zed Books.

Tahi, M. S. 1995: Algeria's democratisation process: a frustrated hope. *Third World Quarterly*, vol. 16:2, pp. 197–220.

Taraki, L. 1991: The Islamic resistance movement in the Palestinian uprising. In Nassar, J. and Heacock, R. (eds).

Tauber, E. 1993a: *The Emergence of the Arab Movements*. London: Cass.

— 1993b: *The Arab Movements in World War I*. London: Cass.

Taylor, A. R. 1991: *The Superpowers and the Middle East*. Syracuse: Syracuse University Press.

Tessler, M. 1994: *A History of the Israeli–Palestinian Conflict*. Bloomington: Indiana University Press.

Tessler, M., Rogers, J. and Schneider, D. 1978: Women's emancipation in Tunisia. In Beck, L. and Keddie, N. (eds).

Tetreault, M. A. and al-Mughni, H. 1995: Modernization and its discontents: state and gender in Kuwait. *Middle East Journal*, vol. 49:3, pp. 403–17.

Thiele, B. 1986: Vanishing acts in social and political thought: tricks of the trade. In Pateman, C. and Goss, E. (eds).

Thomas, H. 1986: *The Suez Affair*. London: Weidenfeld and Nicolson.

Tibawi, A. L. 1977: *Anglo-Arab Relations and the Question of Palestine*. London: Luzac.

Tibi, B. 1987: Islam and Arab nationalism. In Stowasser, B. (ed.).

— 1992: Major themes in the Arabic political writings of Islamic revivalism. *Islam and Christian–Muslim Relations*, vol. 3:2, pp. 183–210.

— 1994: Redefining the Arab and Arabism in the aftermath of the Gulf Crisis. In Tschirgi, D. (ed.).

— 1996: Old tribes and imposed nation states in the Middle East. In Hutchinson, J. and Smith, A. D. (eds).

— (ed.) 1997: *Arab Nationalism: Between Islam and the Nation State* (3rd edn). London: Macmillan.

Tignor, R. L. 1984: *State, Private Enterprise and Economic Change in Egypt, 1918–1952*. Princeton: Princeton University Press.

Tohidi, N. 1991: Gender and Islamic fundamentalism: feminist politics in Iran. In Mohanty, C. et al. (eds).

Tripp, C. 2002: *A History of Iraq* (2nd edn). Cambridge: Cambridge University Press.

Tripp, C. and Owen, R. (eds) 1989: *Egypt under Mubarak*. London: Routledge.

Tschirgi, D. (ed.) 1994: *The Arab World Today*. Boulder, CO: Lynne Rienner.

Tucker, J. (ed.) 1993: *Arab Women: Old Boundaries, New Frontiers*. Bloomington: Indiana University Press.

Turner, B. 1994: *Orientalism, Postmodernism and Globalism*. London: Routledge.

UNDP 2004: *Arab Human Development Report 2003*, New York: UNDP.

UNDP 2005: *Arab Human Development Report 2004*, New York: UNDP.

US Congress 2002 <http://commdocs.house.gov/committees/intlrel/hfa78802.00/hfa78802_0.html>.

US State Department 2002: National Security Strategy Seeks to Defend Peace and Prosperity. <http://usinfo.state.gov>.

Usher, G. 1995: *Palestine in Crisis*. London: Pluto.

—— 1999: *Dispatches from Palestine: The Rise and Fall of the Oslo Peace Process*. London: Pluto Press.

Vali, A. 1996: *Kurdish Nationalism, Identity, Sovereignty and the Dialectic of Violence in Kurdistan*. London: IB Tauris.

Van Bruinessen, M. 1986: The Kurds between Iran and Iraq. *Middle East Report – MERIP*, July–August.

—— 1991: *Agha, Shaikh, and State: The Social and Political Structures of Kurdistan*. London: Zed Books.

Van Dam, N. 1996: *The Struggle for Power in Syria: Politics and Society under Asad and the Ba'th Party*. London: IB Tauris.

Vatikiotis, P. J. 1987: *Islam and the State*. London: Routledge.

—— 1988: Non-Muslims in Muslim society: a preliminary consideration of the problem on the basis of recently published works by Muslim authors. In Esman, M. J. and Rabinovich, I. (eds).

Vitalis, R. 1994: The democratization industry and the limits of new interventionism. *Middle East Report – MERIP*, March–June, pp. 46–50.

—— 1995: *When Capitalists Collide: Business Conflict and End of Empire in Egypt*. Berkeley: University of California Press.

Walters, F. P. 1952: *A History of the League of Nations*. London: Oxford University Press.

Warburg, G. R. and Kuperferschmidt, U. M. (eds) 1983: *Nationalism and Radicalism in Egypt and the Sudan*. New York: Praeger.

Wasserstein, B. 1978: *The British in Palestine: The Mandatory Government and the Arab–Jewish Conflict*. London: Royal Historical Society.

Waterbury, J. 1983: *The Egypt of Nasser and Sadat: The Political Economy of Two Regimes*. Princeton: Princeton University Press.

—— 1994: Democracy without democrats: the potential for political liberalization in the Middle East. In Salame, G. (ed.).

Waylen, G. 1996: *Gender in Third World Politics*. Buckingham: Open University Press.

Wiktorowicz, Q. 2001: The new global threat: transnational salafis and jihad. *Middle East Policy*, vol. 8:4, December.

Willis, M. 1996: *The Islamist Challenge in Algeria: A Political History*. Reading, NY: Ithaca Press.

Wilson, K. M. (ed.) 1983: *Imperialism and Nationalism in the Middle East: The Anglo-Egyptian Experience 1882–1982*. London: Mansell.

Wilson, R. 1979: *The Economies of the Middle East*. Basingstoke: Macmillan.

—— (ed.) 1991: *Politics and Economy in Jordan*. London: Routledge.

—— 1995: The regional economic impact of the Gulf War. In Davis, M. Jane (ed.).

Woodhouse, C. M. 1959: *Britain and the Middle East*. Geneva: PIUHII.

Yapp, M. E. 1991: *The Near East since the First World War*. London: Longman.

Yariv, A. 1992: The crisis experience in the Middle East: conflict management triumphant. In Spiegel, S. L. (ed.).

Yiftachel, O. 1993: Debate: the concept of ethnic democracy and its application to the case of Israel. *Ethnic and Racial Studies*, vol. 15:1, pp. 125–36.

—— 1999: Democracy or ethnocracy: territory and settler politics in Israel/Palestine. <http://www.merip.org/yift.htm>.

Yildiz, K. 2004: *The Kurds in Iraq: The Past, Present and Future*. London: Pluto Press.

Young, E. G. 1992: *Keepers of the History: Women and the Israeli–Palestinian Conflict*. New York: Teachers' College Press.

Zartman, W. 1994: The challenge of democratic alternatives in the Maghrib. In Ruedy, J. (ed.).

Zubaida, S. 1992: Islam, the state and democracy: contrasting conceptions of society in Egypt. *Middle East Report – MERIP*, no. 179, November–December, pp. 2–11.

——1993: *Islam, the People and the State*. London: IB Tauris.

——1997: Is Iran an Islamic state? In Beinin, J. and Stork, J. (eds).

Zunes, S. 2002: *Tinderbox: US Foreign Policy and the Roots of Terrorism*. London: Zed Books.

Index